The Grand Union

The

ACCIDENTAL ANARCHISTS OF

WENDY PERRON

Grand

DOWNTOWN DANCE, 1970–1976

Union

WESLEYAN UNIVERSITY PRESS

Middletown, Connecticut

Wesleyan University Press
Middletown CT 06459
www.wesleyan.edu/wespress
© 2020 Wendy Perron
All rights reserved
Manufactured in the United States of America
Typeset in Miller and Magma
by Tseng Information Systems, Inc.
Library of Congress Cataloging-in-Publication Data
available upon request
Hardcover ISBN: 978-0-8195-7932-4
Paperback ISBN: 978-0-8195-7966-9
Ebook ISBN: 978-0-8195-7933-1
5 4 3 2 1

Frontispiece: GU at NYC Dance Marathon, 14th Street Y
(Emanuel Midtown YM-YWHA), 1971. From left: Yvonne Rainer,
Trisha Brown, Barbara Dilley, David Gordon. In background:
Becky Arnold. Photo: James Klosty.

This book is dedicated to Sally Banes because we loved the same things, and the Grand Union was one of them.

CONTENTS

The Grand Union

INTRODUCTION

Although Grand Union existed for only six years—a blip in the span of dance and performance history—it made an impact on those who witnessed its collective genius. Word spread, and even now the name of the group is legendary. Grand Union was the bridge between Judson Dance Theater—that explosion of experimentation that changed the face of modern dance—and the illustrious careers of its long-term members, some of whom formed the bedrock of postmodern dance: Yvonne Rainer, Trisha Brown, Steve Paxton, David Gordon, Barbara Dilley, Douglas Dunn, and Nancy Lewis. Grand Union was both a culmination of early experiments and a laboratory for future work.

The confluence of these brilliantly idiosyncratic minds/bodies gave rise to a flow of human interaction that was wayward, minimalist, excessive, ludicrous, annoying, goading, uproarious, or deeply moving. It epitomized the spirit of the sixties: flaunting freedom from the usual (unwritten) rules, solving dilemmas (largely) peacefully, and creating an accidentally leaderless democracy (while coping with a typical array of resentments).

Grand Union's mode was improvisation—the most ephemeral form of an ephemeral form. There is no choreography to look back on and analyze. There was no method, no treatise, no plan. We were watching people deal with whatever came up. They were out there in the wild. This wasn't improvising on a stated theme, the way jazz musicians and theater people do; this was being thrown into an empty space, onto a veritable blank canvas, with nothing to fall back on but their instincts. They made structures as they went along, or rather they built upon the structures that arose organically during performance. It wasn't anarchy as we usually think of it, but as I explain in the "Leaderless? Really?" interlude, the antihierarchical stance of anarchism threads through the arts of that time, particularly the thinking of Rainer and Paxton.

I saw Grand Union only three or four times during its six-year life span. I don't remember many specific sequences, but I remember how I felt while watching the group perform. I felt wide awake and ready to respond to every new decision as each episode unfolded. Seeing shape and intention materialize before my eyes—and realizing the risks the performers took—put me in a state of high alert. I rode the ups and downs with them from my seat, accumulating new insights about each person/dancer/character and their relationships to dance and to each other. I was in awe of their ability to remain resolutely themselves while also fully participating in the group. They could instinctively either reinforce what was going on or sharply counter it. Harmony and absurdity in equal measure. Giddy Dada Zen.

I remember one time, in 1975 at La MaMa Experimental Theatre Club, when Nancy Lewis was standing under a blue blanket for a long time. Various duets and trios were going on, and she suddenly asked out loud, from under the blanket, "Am I doing anything important here?" The audience cracked up laughing, and the laughter burst into applause. But it was more than a joke; she was admitting that she didn't know. Not knowing was a way to start at zero, and stillness was a way to let others take the focus. An acceptance of nothingness as a gateway to somethingness. A possibly "important" foil to a colleague's more defined plan.

I remember watching Barbara Dilley and David Gordon chasing each other with pillows around the perimeter of the Eisner Lubin Auditorium of New York University's (NYU's) Loeb Student Center. Their physical sparring was impulsive, ambiguous, and intimate. They could have been a pair of particularly witty siblings or impetuous lovers—until strains of hostility crept in. I remember wondering: Are they really mad at each other or just playing?

Turns out, they were wondering too. The line between art and life, as John Cage, Anna Halprin, and Allan Kaprow had championed, was blurred. That merging was fascinating to behold but was also destabilizing and probably a factor in the group's demise. But until that collapse, this kind of confusion helped crack open the possibilities of performance.

Knowing that some archival videotapes existed, I started wondering if the tapes would hold up to my memory. In fact, seeing the tapes is what sent me into Grand Union fever. The screen sizzled with—what?—a kind of readiness to engage, to accept any reality and move through it. Even though what came up on the screen was limited by a single camera angle, I could see the moment-to-moment decisions the dancers made to burrow further into their own private exploration, accept the bid of another player, or interrupt another's intention.

After watching a few hours of the tapes, I came away with the thought that Grand Union back then possessed a kind of collective wisdom. The organic flow of the group's movement/interactions/fantasies revealed a natural, grounded-yet-buoyant way of being in the world, all the while not knowing what the next moment would bring. That not-knowingness led to a state of mind rarely exposed in public, and witnessing it was exciting. It escaped the airtight construction of locked-down choreography. It allowed us to see the dancers not only as movers, but also as thinkers, craftspeople, rebels—each with a defined voice. They were (unintentionally) teaching me/us lessons that reflected the slogan of the day, "Go with the flow," in the deepest, most complex ways. They responded to any impulse with bristling readiness and to any overture with a fearless range of options.

Watching the tapes, I got that same sense of awe that I had had more than forty years earlier. I felt I could learn a lot from studying the videos—not only about dance, or performance, or improvisation, but about life. I didn't want to dance with them (anachronistically speaking) or to attain their mastery at improvisation. What I wanted was to be able to navigate through my life the way they were navigating through unforeseen circumstances.

What they had found together was, in Douglas Dunn's words, a "possible ideal world."[1] They could give voice to their innermost selves and at the same time weave an intricate tapestry of the whole group. Barbara Dilley's explanation is that there was a "group mind" at work.[2] In David Gordon's words, Grand Union was "a miracle."[3]

The videos spurred questions: What was happening in the culture to produce such an egalitarian world, however flawed and temporary? How did these dancers ride the ebb and flow so organically? To what extent were they a utopian society, and to what extent did they reveal/conceal antisocial behaviors? How could they be such a strong per-

forming unit while refusing to rehearse together? What other improvisation collectives were around at the time? What made the seventies
audience so ready for GU's brand of anarchy? What pulled the group
apart after six years?

After watching a few hours of this material[4] I started talking to my
husband Jim about it. He was about to go out, but when he saw my
excitement—and that I couldn't *stop* talking about it—he sat down,
still wearing his jacket, to listen. I was raving about how natural the
dancers were, how their bodies erupted with the kind of impulsiveness that children have, yet they also had a disarming sophistication.
After the first wave of my gushing, he said, "I think this is your next
book."

A quick Internet search showed that not much had been written
about Grand Union in the burgeoning "dance studies" field. Fortu-
nately, a dissertation from the eighties had been published in 1991 as
part of a theatrical series. I am indebted to Margaret Hupp Ramsay
for her book *The Grand Union (1970–1976): An Improvisational Performance Group*, which has interviews as well as listings of performance dates and reviews. She supplied good interview material, but
the book is thin on historical and artistic context. I have the advan-
tages of first, knowing the Grand Union members and their work
as individual choreographers; second, having danced with some of
them; and third, having access to archival videos that were not available in the eighties.

Nothing that's been written on Grand Union comes close to Sally
Banes's last chapter at the end of her landmark book *Terpsichore in
Sneakers*. Banes divided this section into two parts: her scholarly
analysis and the dancers' written responses to her questions. Her
loving attention to them was clear. She didn't have to say, as she did in
a later essay, that Grand Union was "one of the most brilliant projects
of the postmodern dance."[5] Sally and I were close friends, sharing
similar tastes and curiosities since the mid-seventies. In the early
eighties we worked together on separate but overlapping projects for
Judson Dance Theater, involving some of the same dance artists who
were in Grand Union.[6] We remained close until her tragic stroke in
2002. I sometimes feel, as I embark on this book, that we're doing this
together, that she is looking over my shoulder, checking in with me.

There are many approaches to dance improvisation today. Melinda

Buckwalter has described twenty-five of them, from Simone Forti to Min Tanaka to Lisa Nelson, in her book *Composing While Dancing: An Improviser's Companion*. The Wesleyan anthology *Taken by Surprise* is another excellent source. And *Contact Quarterly* regularly publishes ideas and reports on many approaches to both improvisation and somatic practices. These publications provide an array of starting points, methods, and discussion topics for those who may have had only conventional dance training. I was one such student in the sixties, when my solid training in ballet and modern dance didn't put a dent in my stomach-churning dread of improvising.[7]

But the book in your hands now is not a manual for learning improvisation; it will not coax anyone into improvising or give advice on how to form a collaborative improvisation group. Perhaps Grand Union was a fluke, never to be repeated. I feel the stars aligned briefly to create something as rare as a total solar eclipse. As Claire Barliant has written about 112 Greene Street (more about that commune-like artists' space in chapter 3), "[T]he reason these projects and venues are so fantastic is precisely that they're not meant to last forever."[8] As my improvising colleague Stephanie Skura pointed out, very often a particularly vital period of creativity has a finite life span.[9] In the case of Grand Union, between six and nine artistically fertile, eccentric, and delightfully subversive dance artists came together to create a potent mix of elements, a union of grandeur. Their process required a kind of psychic nakedness—and once or twice, the other kind too.

I am writing this book as a witness to a slice of dance history that could disappear. In some ways, it's a continuation of my research on Judson Dance Theater[10] and Anna Halprin and Simone Forti.[11] As opposed to Judson Dance Theater, which I did not witness firsthand, I saw and heard Grand Union and never forgot it.

While watching the videos, I found myself transfixed by every entwinement and interaction, not to mention the dancing, so vivid and so unique to each person. I was hungry to speak with all the living GU members and find people who had seen them more often than I had. Three of my dance colleagues confessed to having been "groupies." Grand Union *was* kind of like a rock band but on a smaller economic scale: a leaderless group (not that rock bands don't have their power struggles) with a special synergy that excited fans. Sometimes people would declare their favorites, as in, "Who is your favorite Beatle?" As with the Beatles, each member was essential to the whole. The interactions could be brazen, bristly, odd, unpolished, combative, or unexpectedly tender.

The audience in the downtown milieu was ready for Grand Union. I was ready for it. Many young, post-Judson dance artists were ready for it. As Marcel Duchamp pointed out, a work of art is not complete without the audience. "The onlooker is as important as the artist," he has said. "In spite of what the artist thinks he's doing, something stays on that is completely independent of what he intended, and that something is grabbed by society. . . . [I]t's the onlooker who has the last word."[12] Each new art has to find its audience, and in the case of Grand Union, it was the other artists of SoHo. It was also the audiences in places like Oberlin College in Ohio and the Walker Art Center in Minneapolis, where the group had time to cultivate familiarity.

An extra poignancy comes with this project for me: I joined the Trisha Brown Dance Company in November 1975, just a few weeks before her last appearance with Grand Union in Tokyo. Trisha's desire to start a more full-time company was her second reason for dropping out (the first being her ambivalence from the start). I danced with her until 1978, and we remained friends until her death in 2017. Her departure from Grand Union prompted David and Steve to also call it quits. So in some circuitous, time-machine way, having participated in the group that ferried Trisha away from Grand Union, to the current moment when I am writing about this, I am making a full circle.

Much has been written about Trisha Brown's choreography, but no scholar has discussed her performances in GU as *part of her work*. Watching the tapes is a way for me to fit her improvisational work into her oeuvre as a whole. The same could be said for David, Steve, Barbara, and Douglas: though reams have been written about each of them, very little focuses on their remarkable contributions to Grand Union. I try to remedy this in chapter 22, on GU as a laboratory for their individual work.

I embark on this book, too, as a challenge to what I've come to see as the arbitrariness of dance history. Some of the most astonishing dance artists I saw in the seventies, like William Dunas and Kenneth King, are not part of the canon of dance history. I feel that the work of Grand Union is similarly imperiled.

Although writing this book has been daunting in many ways, I feel comfortable riding in this particular saddle. My path has crossed with almost all the Grand Union members in the last forty-plus years. I danced with Steve when he was a guest artist in Trisha's company. I pulled in Yvonne, Steve, and Trisha to the Bennington College Judson Project in the early eighties; I invited Steve to teach at the Jacob's Pillow-at-Bennington workshop that I directed in the early nineties. In 1980 I hung out with David and Yvonne in France at the Festival de la Sainte Baume, where we were all teaching workshops (I learned *Trio A* from Yvonne there); I've done several curatorial projects with Yvonne since then. I share with Nancy two choreographers we have both danced for, Jack Moore and Twyla Tharp; I have taken a workshop from, and written about, Barbara; and I was part of a fleeting improvisation group with Douglas in the late nineties. In working on this book, I have deepened my knowledge of each of them through scrutinizing the videos and engaging in multiple conversations.

This book looks back at an ecosystem that valued collaboration as well as the individual imagination. In the twenty-first century, it feels like a luxury for me to be spending hours and days with these artists I admire so much ... a luscious immersion ... swimming in the waters of collective creativity. The fact that Grand Union existed at all is due to the spirit of collaboration encouraged in that milieu and to the possibilities of functioning (gloriously) without a leader. Although Grand Union was very much of its time, it refracted the timeless issues of the individual versus the group, freedom versus cooperation, virtuosity versus the everyday, and the relationship between art and life.

NOTE TO READERS

NAMES

The names Barbara Lloyd and Nancy Green were used during Grand Union up until 1974 or 1975. At that point, the two women reverted to their maiden names, Barbara Dilley and Nancy Lewis. I have chosen to honor that decision and use their maiden names throughout. Likewise, Douglas Dunn was known during most of Grand Union as Doug, but he now prefers Douglas. Anna Halprin was known as Ann until the 1970s, but I use Anna consistently as that is the name she goes by now.

The name "Grand Union" was suggested by David Gordon as a tongue-in-cheek reference to the booming supermarket chain at the time. It was initially supposed to be without the "the," but David,

Trisha, Barbara, and Yvonne routinely referred to it as "the Grand Union." Nancy, Douglas, and Steve use the name bare, without the article in front of it. In keeping with that lack of agreement, I use the "the" sometimes but not at other times.

A final point about names is that I start my story by referring to known figures in the standard way, using surnames. In part II, however, I transition into referring to each dance artist by her or his first name, a decision I explain along the way.

INTERLUDES

In order to provide a fuller picture of Grand Union than I can give alone, I've included other voices. Most of the interludes are excerpts of published pieces; one is an edited interview (Dianne McIntyre) and another is an invited reminiscence (Joan Evans), and still another is from an email message (Richard Nonas).

THE "GROUP INTERVIEW"

By July 2017 I had held initial interviews with Yvonne, Douglas, Nancy, and Barbara. When I contacted David to schedule an interview, he requested that we wait till Steve came to town—for the Trisha Brown memorial—so that I could interview them together. We invited Yvonne, and then Douglas, even though I had already interviewed them both, to join us, so it ended up being a group interview in David's loft—but not with the whole group. Barbara and Nancy do not live in New York, and I did not attempt to include them by phone because I felt the disembodied voices would affect the flow of the conversation. (I had already interviewed both of them anyway.) Therefore, when I refer to the "group interview," it is with only four people: David, Steve, Douglas, and Yvonne.

PART I Seedbed

Anna Halprin's deck, ca. late 1950s, Kentfield, CA. Photo: The Estate of Warner Jepson.

CHAPTER 1

ANNA HALPRIN, JOHN CAGE, AND JUDSON DANCE THEATER

In the sixties, the West Coast and East Coast had different styles of rebelling against the conventions of modern dance. Judson Dance Theater, the collective breakthrough of experimentation that ushered in postmodern dance, was a child of both. It was, at least partially, the encounter between Anna Halprin's nature-loving, task-dance approach from California and the rigorous, John Cage–inspired chance methods of New York that ignited the Judson revolution.[1]

Living and working in Marin County, Halprin took dance out of the theater and into natural and urban spaces. She infiltrated streets, airports, plazas, and the side of a mountain. She shed her modern dance training in order to honor the natural, unadorned (and sometimes unclothed) body. She deflated the high drama of modern dance with human-scale task improvisations. She wanted to dance where trees were swaying in the wind and birds were chirping. So in 1955 her husband, landscape architect Lawrence Halprin, along with designer Arch Lauterer,[2] built an expansive outdoor deck as a gift to her. Here she could commune with nature as she developed her own approach to dance. Rather than romanticize the glory of the theater, she romanticized dancing outdoors, harking back to Isadora Duncan.

In her resistance to concert dance, Halprin was reacting to what she had seen at the Bennington School of the Dance, which relocated to Mills College for the summer of 1939. She felt that the officially sanctioned giants of modern dance—Martha Graham, Doris Humphrey, Charles Weidman, and Hanya Holm—were training dancers to be imitative rather than creative. Dance historian Ninotchka Bennahum writes that Halprin became "disenchanted with modernism's codified disciplining of the human body."[3] She recoiled from their highly stylized theatricality, reverting instead to the teachings of Margaret H'Doubler, her mentor at the University of Wisconsin, Madison, in the thirties. Inspired by John Dewey's idea of the mind and body working together, H'Doubler did not demonstrate steps but taught about kinesthetics with the help of a human skeleton. She was all about exploring rotation and flexion to expand range of motion. Continuing in that vein but, as described by dance scholar Janice Ross, "progressing from raw, improvised action into dance with an emotional resonance,"[4] Halprin forsook technique per se and committed herself to wide-ranging exploration. The deck became a place to gather, observe, experiment, and respond to the rustling of nature rather than to prepare choreography for the stage.

Also in the mid-fifties, another gift was bestowed on Halprin: Simone Forti. A budding visual artist with a sensuous movement quality and a poetic imagination, Forti had none of the mannerisms associated with either ballet or modern dance training. She was a sensitive, fearless explorer who, encouraged by her then husband, Robert Morris (later to become a major minimalist sculptor), had been physically active while painting large canvases. Forti's grounded simplicity, her love of nature, and her mercurial sense of play made her the ideal collaborator for Halprin's new approach.[5] Along with Forti and her other dancers, Halprin developed "scores" (written or drawn instructions to be interpreted by the performers) for the interplay of dance and sound, for paying attention to the environment, and for ritualizing the everyday.

The Bay Area was a hub of artistic collaboration in the sixties, and Halprin got caught up in the swirl of the local music scene. According to critic John Rockwell, who performed in some of Halprin's events, "[T]he fluid borders between the avant-garde and San Francisco rock music encouraged constant crossovers."[6] Halprin participated in the trippy Trips festival, provided dancers for the Grateful Dead's light shows, and led the audience in a dance at a Janis Joplin concert.[7] John Cage sent his protégé, La Monte Young, to work with her,[8] knowing she would be fine with whatever ear-abusing noises or cross-genre actions he came up with. Halprin was delighted to be part of this vibrant arts community, occasionally working with Beat poets like Michael McClure and Richard Brautigan.[9] "What was popular art, what was fine art, what was experimental art all got kind of moved together."[10] In addition to the communal, feel-good aspect of these exchanges, Halprin's embrace of collaborations also yielded artistic breakthroughs. In talking about her best-known work, *Parades and Changes* (1965), for which she had collaborated with composer Morton Subotnick (known as "the father of electronic music") and visual artist Charles Ross, she said, "The results are often new forms that not one of us alone would have found."[11]

The New York environment also produced new forms during this era. In his famous course in experimental music composition at The New School for Social Research from 1956 to 1960, John Cage challenged the class to break barriers between genres. He wanted to expand the definition of music to include the sounds of everyday life and to expand the definition of theater to include any art event that spanned time. The course unleashed a band of rule-breakers, including Allan Kaprow, George Brecht, Richard Higgins, Jackson Mac Low, Al Hansen, and Toshi Ichiyanagi, who was married to Yoko Ono at the time.[12] They created happenings, assemblages, and early performance art before these forms had a label. Like Halprin's community events, their performances sometimes required the audience to be active. Life was crashing into art and vice versa.

The group that emerged from Cage's course overlapped with the Fluxus artists. Influenced by Duchamp, Fluxus was a loose group of obstreperous, neo-Dadaist artists that included Nam June Paik, Yoko Ono, and George Maciunas (more about him in the next chapter). Fluxus events, as well as the happenings by Kaprow, Claes Oldenburg, and others, were meant to be temporary, not preserved or sold. Not everyone took Fluxus seriously. Experimental theater director Richard Foreman described its events as "an attempt to believe that everyday things could be art."[13] But the Fluxus performers were capable of activities that were both beautiful and daring. One of the rare documented Fluxus events was Yoko Ono's *Cut Piece* (1964). As seen in the film (accessible on YouTube), Ono sat demurely on the floor with a pair of scissors next to her. One at a time, audience members approached, cut away one piece of clothing, and walked away with the swath of cloth in their hands.[14] As each person wielded the scissors close to her body, the expression on Ono's face maintained a serenity flecked by the tiniest hint of anxiety behind the eyes. This was a typical Fluxus act, fraught with contradiction and not repeatable. According to Ono's longtime associate Jon Hendricks, *Cut Piece* reflected her "desire to free herself from cultural straightjackets."[15]

Halprin, Cage, and Merce Cunningham were also trying to free themselves from various cultural confines. For Cunningham, it had to do with space. During a lecture he gave on Halprin's deck in 1957, he said that what he liked about the wooden platform amid the madrone trees was the freedom it gave the dancer. "There is no necessity to face 'front,' to limit the focus to one side."[16] In his remarks, he included the fluidity of time as well as space: "My feeling about dance continuity came from the view that life is constantly changing and shifting, that we live in a democratic society, and that people and things in nature are mutually independent of, and related to each other."[17]

Cunningham's idea of fluidity in space and time, Cage's idea of creativity through chance procedures, and Halprin's blurring of performers and audience are all part of the larger shift from modernism to postmodernism. All three tried to strip down to essentials, which is a hallmark of modernism. But they went further. While modernism presented a monolithic statement, postmodernism is pluralistic. Dance artist Mary Overlie has characterized that change in a nutshell: "Modernists were looking for the truth, the answer, and they were sure that these were possible to find.... Postmodernism, by adopting a pluralistic Both/And approach, challenges the very basis of Modernism."[18]

One cannot overestimate Cage's influence on the arts. Deborah Jowitt called Cage the "godfather to many works produced during the sixties by composers, choreographers, artists, dancers, playwrights, and directors. His book, *Silence*, came out in 1961, disseminating a wealth of unsettling ideas."[19] One of those ideas was the permeability of art and life, another was that there is no need for the music to "match" the dance, and a third is that choreography can be structured in ways other than the conventional theme-and-variations or A-B-A format.

As a precursor to postmodernism, the Dadaists in Europe, with their cut-ups and collage techniques, had embraced a pluralistic view of reality in the early twentieth century. Viewers could not count on a cohesiveness ready and waiting for them; they had to choose where to focus. Cage's use of chance was another method of disrupting the cogency of modernism. He felt, as the Dadaists did, that methods that tapped into a certain level of randomness were more like life. For him, deploying chance methods like tossing dice or consulting the *I Ching* (The Chinese book of changes) reflected the belief that, quoting philosopher Ananda K. Coomaraswamy, "the responsibility of the artist is to imitate nature in her manner of operation."[20]

Jill Johnston wrote about the gradual, if limited, acceptance of Cage's subversive ideas: "The heresy of Dada and Cage is the abdication of the will. In a culture brought up on the pride of accomplishment in subduing the brute forces of nature, the admission of chaos seemed like madness from the beginning. But the philosophy has persisted and Cage has had an enormous influence on contemporary artists. The madness has become a new kind of order, and the possibilities extend in every conceivable direction."[21]

Although the Cage/Cunningham revolution and the Halprin revolution both fueled the transformation from modern to postmodern dance, their styles differed markedly. Cunningham held the body upright, with limbs extending away from the center (as in ballet). He was a master choreographer, creating brilliant movement sequences while keeping the separation between performer and audience intact. Halprin was less formal and less formalist, more connected to the natural environment, and determined to merge performer and audience. She was more affected by—and part of—the sexual revolution. Nudity was commonplace for her. One could point to a Dionysian aspect of her work, while Cunningham and Cage were primarily Apollonian. Rockwell writes, "Cage remained esthetically distant from the California scene. His and Cunningham's chance procedures were ultimately too controlling for the looser, more improvisatory, more natural and nature-oriented Halprin and her musical cohorts."[22]

Halprin would send students into the surrounding landscape on the side of Mount Tamalpais, asking them, for example, to walk on various textures underfoot: the wood of the deck, the soft earth, dead leaves, prickly plants. They would then convene to share the sensations and movement impulses they had experienced.

Cunningham scattered spatial patterns across the stage and made the dynamics appear random, but he never accepted quotidian movement into his palette. Cage's philosophy that all sounds can be music did not extend, in Cunningham's studio, to all movement being accepted as dance. That particular aspect of Cage's teachings was left to the Judson dancers to realize; they yoked the exploratory wishes of Halprin to Cage's expanding definition of performance. "Cunningham used to say that we were John's children and not his,"[23] Rainer recalled.

The person who stood at the intersection of Halprin and Cage/Cunningham was Simone Forti. A bridge between West and East Coasts, Forti carried the improvisational urge in her body across the country after four years of working with Halprin. It was Forti who persuaded Yvonne Rainer to come study with Halprin in August 1960, and that is where they both met Trisha Brown.[24]

Brown, who was from Washington State, shared with Halprin a love of the outdoors, but for her, too, it was with Forti in New York that Halprin's approach took root. Brown once called Simone "the leader of us all."[25] Forti had a luscious movement quality, which, coupled with her clear intention while improvising, attracted Brown and Rainer as well as Paxton. Forti could seem like an oracle at times, so elemental were her movement desires. She had ideas that were not Ideas, but poetic musings and wonderings (or wanderings off to the zoo to watch the bears). Her connection to nature, nurtured by Halprin, was a strong foundational aesthetic for her. She only needed to find a conceptual framework.

And that happened in Robert Dunn's composition class.

Now we get to the central part of the oft-told creation myth of Judson Dance Theater and postmodern dance.[26] For our purposes, I tell this story slightly differently, emphasizing its bearing on what ultimately became the Grand Union.

In the fall of 1960, John Cage was tired of teaching dance composition in the Merce Cunningham Studio, which was on the top floor of the Living Theatre's building on Sixth Avenue and 14th Street. He asked Robert Dunn, who had taken his course at the New School, to teach the class. Dunn had been an accompanist at several dance studios and had seen, firsthand, how formulaic the composition classes of Louis Horst and Doris Humphrey had become. (Interestingly, he felt that Martha Graham's composition classes were OK — more intuitive, less didactic.)[27] He was determined to teach differently, to give the students multiple avenues into their movement imaginations.

The class started with five students, including Paxton, Forti, and Rainer,[28] the last two of whom were fresh from Halprin's deck. Forti soon persuaded Brown to come to New York and study with Dunn. The class grew to include not only Brown but also Deborah Hay, Lucinda Childs, Elaine Summers, Rudy Perez, Sally Gross, Ruth Emerson, and David Gordon. Visual artists like Robert Rauschenberg and Robert Morris (who, as Forti's then husband, had participated in Halprin's workshops in the late fifties), as well as musicians like Philip Corner and John Herbert McDowell, attended the class less regularly.

Like Cage at the New School, Dunn gave assignments in indeterminacy,[29] which enabled performers to make choices on the spot. He discussed Satie's attention to durational lengths and turned the composer's mathematics into physical problems to solve. Students could create their own scores (structures), using chance methods to generate movement. For instance, one student decided to let the rotation of the moon provide a timeline.[30] Sometimes the assignment was a simple time limit: make a three-minute dance in three minutes. Other assignments involved game structures or the minimalist idea of a unifying "one thing."[31] The students responded unabashedly with an anything-goes fervor—even those students who, like David Gordon[32] and Trisha Brown,[33] considered Dunn more of a catalyst than a prime mover.

Forti, who missed the California landscape, found an artistic home, or laboratory, in Dunn's class: "There was an atmosphere of intense freedom, coupled with a very analytical approach to each person's compositional solutions. It was incredibly stimulating."[34]

Improvisation, however, was not part of Dunn's classes. Nor did Cage condone improvisation as an element in performance. (In fact, he was offended when Leonard Bernstein interpreted his idea of indeterminacy—giving performers certain choices—as improvisation.)[35]

Whatever the stylistic differences between Halprin and Dunn's workshops were, they were both focused on process. The discussions were never about whether a student's piece was good or not. As Brown recalled, Dunn always asked, "How did you make that dance?"[36] Sometimes the dancers were taken aback by his mode of curiosity rather than evaluation. Rainer remembers that one of the students "did a kind of quasi burlesque strip tease which embarrassed me, but Dunn was only interested in how she made it!"[37]

Dunn's class was remarkably productive. After about a year and a half, the students showed some of their works at the Living Theatre, on the first floor in the same building. (James Waring, who was a major pre-Judson influence, had already presented a program of work there by his students, including David Gordon.) They started looking for a larger venue. First stop: the 92nd Street Y, the stronghold of American modern dance, where one could see choreography by Martha Graham, Hanya Holm, Pearl Primus, José Limón, and the young Alvin Ailey.[38] Rainer, Paxton, Gordon, and Ruth Emerson auditioned before a panel of modern dance mavens to be considered for its Young Choreographers series. The jury consisted of Marion Scott, who taught Humphry-Weidman technique;[39] Jack Moore, an Anna Sokolow dancer who had gotten attention for his own choreography;[40] and Lucas Hoving, already a luminary within the Limón circle.[41] This jury watched each of the pieces, one by one, and turned them down. (Considering that the Y presented dance on a proscenium stage, I now think they made the right decision—for the Y and for the future of dance. But their rejection does speak of a certain obliviousness toward the artistic potential of these young dancers.) Undaunted, the students kept looking. Rainer knew that Judson Poets' Theater and Judson Gallery were already thriving at Judson Memorial Church in Greenwich Village. So Rainer, Paxton, and Emerson "auditioned" for senior minister Al Carmines, and he accepted them with open arms (i.e., an offer of rehearsal space as well as performance space). Their first concert, on July 6, 1962, comprised twenty-three dances by fourteen choreographers. The group soon called themselves Judson Dance Theater.

The students worked so well together—no doubt a result of Dunn's avoidance of competitiveness—that when Dunn stopped teaching the course after that first concert, they continued to meet. This came about because Rainer suggested that they create their own leaderless workshop, and Paxton spread the word.[42] After the first month in Rainer's studio, these weekly workshops moved to the basement gymnasium of Judson Church. For each new concert, a three-person committee was organized to make decisions on program order, publicity, and technical needs.[43] The numbered concerts (some of them at venues other than the church) continued up to number 16, in April 1964.

∎

I'd like to take you on a brief detour to the Bauhaus movement. The Bauhaus artists who migrated from Europe to the United States in the thirties and forties provided an underpinning for both the Cage/Cunningham approach and the Halprin approach. In fact, art historian Susan Rosenberg, author of *Trisha Brown: Choreography as Visual Art*, calls both Halprin's and Dunn's workshops "post-Bauhausian interdisciplinary experimental workshops."[44] The Bauhaus center in Dessau, Germany, which had cultivated the mixing of disciplines, was shut down by the Nazis in the thirties, and many of the artists fled to the United States. Lázló Moholy-Nagy landed in Chicago, where he established the School of Design; Walter Gropius led an arts program at Harvard; and Josef and Anni Albers came to Black Mountain College.

Five Bauhaus concepts were instrumental in the development of the new dance on both coasts. First, choose materials that are close at hand. (Anni Albers made necklaces out of paper clips.) Second, pay attention to the uniqueness of the materials. (What does wood do, what does copper do, what does the human body do?) Third, think of art as functional in society, not merely decorative. Fourth, experiment with collage, combining radically different elements. (Robert Rauschenberg, who had been a student at Black Mountain, created *Monogram* [1955–1959], for which he hung a car tire around the middle of a stuffed goat. This was one of his early "combines"—and it made Yvonne Rainer almost fall down laughing when she first saw it.)[45] And last, a corollary of the fourth: cross different disciplines, creating new forms.

Halprin, whose husband Lawrence was pursuing a master's degree in landscape architecture at Harvard in the forties, would tag along to lectures by Bauhaus figures Walter Gropius, Moholy-Nagy, and Marcel Breuer. The Bauhaus ideas of the functionality of art—that art serves society rather than exists merely as a passive object of beauty—as well as the Bauhausian crossing of disciplines, made a lasting impact on both Halprins.[46]

During the same period, John Cage found the teachings of Josef Albers at Black Mountain stimulating. The Bauhaus approach reinforced his idea that the line between art and life should be as permeable as possible. (He had briefly been on the faculty of Moholy-Nagy's School of Design in Chicago in 1941.)[47] It was in the dining hall of Black Mountain in 1952 that he created *Theater Piece No. 1*, which later became known as the first "happening." This storied event was so discombobulating that each of those who were present remembers it differently. David Tudor played the prepared piano[48]—but Katherine Litz remembers Cunningham also at the piano (!). Robert Rauschenberg suspended his white paintings like a canopy above the audience while he cranked up an old gramophone. Cage spoke at a lectern—or maybe a stepladder—delivering a lecture with timed silences. Charles Olson read poetry from another ladder and possibly handed out strips of paper with poetry fragments written on them. Either slides or films were projected. The audience was divided into quadrants; Cunningham danced in X-shaped aisles between them—chased by a dog that was either barking or not barking. Possibly gamelan instruments from composer Lou Harrison's collection were played in a corner. There were two cohesive elements: Cage's "time brackets," meaning periods when the performers could or could not be active, and the fact that an empty cup placed near each audience seat in the beginning was filled with coffee at the end—if it hadn't already been used as an ashtray.[49]

The Merce Cunningham Dance Company, which was formed at Black Mountain College the following year, continued to experiment, at least occasionally, with chance and spontaneity in an interdisciplinary setting. For Cunningham's *Story* (1963), Rauschenberg decided to assemble a different set each time, depending on what materials he found in the neighborhood of the theater where they were appearing. He stuffed two duffel bags full of found clothing for the dancers to change into at will. According to longtime Cunningham dancer Carolyn Brown, Rauschenberg "presented us with an endlessly inventive, deliciously unexpected succession of surprises. To add more spice to the indeterminate mix, we could select anything from the outlandish array of thrift-shop garments and other oddities, including football shoulder pads."[50] The order and choice of the eighteen possible sections were determined by chance and posted backstage a half-hour before curtain. On tour in Tokyo, Rauschenberg placed the clothing bags onstage instead of in the wings. While Cunningham, Brown, and Viola Farber performed a trio, Barbara Dilley changed costume and was momentarily nude upstage, causing a bit of a stir, presaging the chutzpah she brought to Grand Union.[51]

■

Although the dances produced at Judson were usually short, they served as springboards for long-term explorations. It was partly because of this that Rainer has referred to Judson as "the crucible." Paxton describes it this way: "You get this parade of formal explorations that were mind-boggling. Judson was that for me. It was an idea about questioning what the elements of dance were. So in my question, I started removing choreographic ploys. I wanted to work with an element of human beings that was not constructed, technical movement, and I began to look at walking."[52]

If Paxton's long-term interest was walking, then one could also point to Rainer's interest in running, Brown's in falling, and Gordon's in talking while dancing. To give you an idea of how these preoccupations surfaced, I describe one of each of their Judson pieces, noting how these concerns followed them into Grand Union.

One of Paxton's walking pieces was the solo *Flat* (1964). Wearing a suit, he walked in a circle or a straight line; occasionally struck an athletic pose, like being up at bat; and sometimes sat on a chair. He would periodically stop, then strip off one piece of clothing, revealing hooks affixed to his bare skin. He then hung his jacket, shirt, or trousers on one of those hooks. He also sometimes froze mid-dressing, for instance when sitting on a chair while peeling off a sock. You'd hold your breath because it really felt like he was interrupting himself. Paxton experienced an almost unbearable urge to leave the room: "The more I felt that I was exposed, I wanted to get out of there.... I knew I was transgressing that whole aesthetic of pacing and keeping things moving." He called *Flat* "pedestrian and boring.... On the other hand, it delivers this gentle weirdness." Like many Judson dances, *Flat* required a flat delivery, but there was a structural arc in that the cycle happened three times: first when he was fully clothed, then partially clothed, then again fully clothed. By the end, as Paxton later said, "You know something very intimate about someone's body that doesn't show through your clothes, covered up again. It's like a secret has been revealed and concealed."[53] The shunning of theatrical pacing and the "gentle weirdness" of *Flat* were aspects that Paxton brought to Grand Union as well.

Rainer had loved the action of running ever since childhood. For *We Shall Run*, she asked twelve performers—both dancers and non-dancers—simply to run, but in highly complex patterns. A recording of the powerful "Tuba Mirum" section of Berlioz's *Requiem* provided a contrast to the familiarity of running, reflecting Rainer's taste for

Lightfall (1963), by Trisha Brown, Judson Memorial Church.
With Brown and Steve Paxton. Photo: Al Giese © Hottelet (Giese).

Dadaist juxtapositions. This was "everyday" dance with a vengeance. *Village Voice* writer Jill Johnston, who championed Judson Dance Theater from the start, wrote that the dance "finally bloomed absolutely heroic. The heroism of the ordinary. No plots or pretensions. People running. Hooray for people."[54] The idea that the performers are people rather than dancerly figures was a key element of Grand Union.

In Brown's *Lightfall* (1963), she and Paxton took turns perching on each other's backs until the supporting person moved, eventually causing the sitter to fall off. Much of the dance was spent awkwardly sliding off the other person's back or sprawled on the ground. This typified Brown's interest in falling, and since Paxton was her partner, possibly contributed to the development of Contact Improvisation a decade later. According to Banes, *Lightfall* grew out of the improvisations she had been working on with Forti and Dick Levine outside of Dunn's classes. The sound for *Lightfall*, a recording of Forti whistling, was a way to include Forti, who was not involved in Judson. (Forti had acquiesced to the request of her new husband, experimental theater director Robert Whitman, to participate only in his work and not to create her own.)[55]

David Gordon's *Random Breakfast* (1962) consisted of six mostly improvised sections, each with its own characters and costumes. It appeared on Concerts #5 and #7 after premiering in Washington, D.C., at the America on Wheels Skating Rink in May 1963.[56] His compulsion to make himself and his audience uncomfortable was fully aired. In the section called "Prefabricated Dance" he lectured off the cuff about how to make a dance, satirizing the methods of both Louis Horst and Robert Dunn—while Valda Setterfield, his wife and Cunningham company member, danced to Vivaldi's *The Four Seasons*. It was intended as a comment on what he called "the Judson Church Dance Factory Gold Rush in which choreography ran rampant."[57] "I talked about timing, subject matter, content, and how to get the audience in the palm of your hands.... I conceived of it as a scathing dismissal of current values and methods. The audience thought it was very funny."[58] The performance earned Gordon and Setterfield the term "classic wits" in Jill Johnston's review.[59] In another section, Gordon spoofed a Spanish dance while wearing full Carmen Miranda regalia. "I'll be made so uncomfortable by appearing in a strapless dress and a wig and a mantilla I'll do anything!"[60] Gordon's talking while dancing, commitment to embarrassing himself, and penchant for exotic costumes all bloomed into full flower in Grand Union.

■

Although the dance artists could follow their individual interests at Judson, there were also collaborative occasions. As Paxton has said, Judson was "a big barbecue, with all the neighbors dropping in."[61] The evening that most typifies that description was Concert #13, subtitled "A Collaborative Event, November 19–20, 1963" (ending only two days before the assassination of President Kennedy). The sculptor Charles Ross, who had worked with Halprin on the West Coast, proposed an evening wherein all the choreographers on the program would address, confront, or coexist with the environment he created. In the Judson sanctuary, Ross constructed two different edifices. One was a big trapezoid made from metal pipes, a kind of swing set without the swings. The second was a huge wooden platform about ten feet above the floor that served as a kind of diving board for Rainer and the other performers to jump into a pile of tires.[62] Toward the end of the evening, Ross started piling folding chairs on top of that platform, so that Ross in action and the growing mountain of chairs were part of the set. In between the nine pieces were interludes of "free play" that made it hard to distinguish when one choreographer's work ended and another's began. The choreographers included Rainer, Lucinda Childs, Deborah Hay, Alex Hay, and Carla Blank.

Rainer remembers Concert #13 as a highlight. She felt her escapade for that concert, *Room Service* (1963), was her only real collaboration with a visual artist. But the whole collaborative event registered on her even more strongly than her single piece. "I think that was one of the most amazing evenings. Everyone's thinking was so radically changed by these enormous structures. We had to deal with them ... and everyone came up with quite different pieces."[63]

In Concert #13, the "neighbors who dropped in" were not necessarily from the same discipline. But they could all partake of the same meal, as it were. The sharing process at Judson, which began in Robert Dunn's classes and continued through the leaderless workshops held in the basement, reflected a growing interest in a democratic process in the wider art world. Other performing arts groups, like Bread and Puppet Theater in Vermont, San Francisco Mime Troupe, the Living Theatre, The Performance Group (later the Wooster Group), Mabou Mines, Pilobolus, the Negro Ensemble Company, Sonic Arts Union, and Videofreex, were also at least partly collaborative. In the visual arts, artist-run galleries like Hansa, Tanager, and Brata Galleries of the Tenth Street Gallery scene were cooperatively run. Most of these galleries, like SoHo spaces later on, were places where artists could, according to gallery director Lynn Gumpert, "experiment with new art forms in unexpected and blatantly noncommercial venues."[64]

Judson Dance Theater did not produce masterworks, nor was that its goal. The whole idea of a masterpiece had already been thrown into question by happenings and Fluxus. The literary counterpart, *The Floating Bear*, produced poetry, drawings, and art reviews that were about new forms—the Beats, the Black Mountain writers—without regard for existing masterworks. This homemade newsletter was delivered free to subscribers. Like Judson Dance Theater, it was a collaborative effort among artists of different disciplines: poets Diane di Prima and LeRoi Jones (later known as Amiri Baraka) edited, James Waring typed, jazz pianist Cecil Taylor ran the mimeograph machine, and dancer Fred Herko collated. Other writers who contributed were Frank O'Hara, Charles Olson, Denise Levertov, and Allen Ginsberg. This newsletter was inextricably interlaced with Judson Dance Theater. Taylor played for Fred Herko's *Like Most People* in the first Judson dance concert, and *The Floating Bear* carried the only review of that concert, written by di Prima.[65]

INTERLUDE

SIMONE FORTI'S LIFE IN COMMUNES

Simone Forti, who was an active member of the Robert Dunn class, was also part of the art world. In 1960 Claes Oldenburg, who had cofounded Judson Gallery,[1] and Jim Dine, who had visited Cage's class at the New School,[2] invited her to contribute to an evening at the Reuben Gallery. This was a short-lived, unheated space that Kaprow had helped establish as a place for performances and happenings.[3] "At that time there weren't any firm boundaries between different artistic practices," said Forti in an interview, echoing Halprin's sense of the ferment on the West Coast. "We were all more or less concerned with an art of process rather than with producing stable, marketable aesthetic objects."[4]

In the Cage-influenced tradition of happenings by Kaprow and theater pieces by her then husband, Robert Whitman, Forti did not feel the need to classify her pieces. In 1961, when La Monte Young invited her to create an evening at Yoko Ono's studio on Chambers Street, she came up with several events she called "dance constructions." Both Yvonne Rainer and Steve Paxton performed on this evening—Rainer in *See-Saw* (1960)[5] and Paxton in *Huddle, Slant Board*, and *Herding*.[6] In each of these pieces the object and movement are essential to each other. Many years later, in 2015, the dance constructions were acquired by the Museum of Modern Art as part of its recognition of performance as art.

In 1969, after Forti's marriage to Whitman broke up, she attended the Woodstock Festival. When the festival was over, she roamed from one commune to another for about a year. Here she speaks about what one might call the dreamy side of communality:

It was an extraordinary moment in my life. Like everyone else I took a lot of drugs—hash, marijuana, acid, mescaline. But the most important thing had something to do with a way of being together— which was not at all theoretical, on the contrary. There was at one and the same time an incredible freedom and a mutual respect that was unheard of until then. It took me a year to come down. I lived communally—in a situation where the only tacit rule was to value silence. You could develop a practice of listening, of attention: to others, to space, to time, and to action. In this way I never stopped dancing—in a thousand different ways. I remember one morning I got up at dawn and while two friends prepared breakfast I was outside in the landscape, perched on a large rock, another small rock balanced on my head. I was experimenting with the degree of flexibility of my dorsal spine that such an arrangement permitted. You see, these were often very simple experiments and experiences. And there was an intensely pleasurable but unspoken connection and understanding between this activity and that of my friends who were cooking their porridge.[7]

Freedom. Respect. Silence. Listening. Dancing. Experimenting. Connection. Was it absolutely necessary to ingest drugs to attain these states of mind? Forti has speculated that "drugs had a lot to do with it, everybody tripping together so much."[8] Perhaps so. As Richard Foreman recently reminded me, Timothy Leary's advice to "turn on, tune in, drop out" was useful when it came to breaking habits and opening one's eyes to other ways of living.[9]

But qualities like silence and listening are aspects of creativity that both Cage and Halprin valued—with or without substances. And they fed into Forti's improvisational abilities, which she passed on to Rainer, Paxton, and Brown. She listened to her own impulses when she danced; she could stick with something for a long time, and she could just as easily spring away from it. If she was banking in circles, she could get so caught up in the momentum that she would keep it up for a long time. But if another image or thought suddenly occurred to her, she would go for it. There was no conflict between mind and body—like a cat that is tired of scratching the sofa and suddenly pounces on a ball. Forti's close observations of animal behavior contributed to that kind of impulsive break.

Simone Forti in her *Fan Dance* (1975). Photo: Babette Mangolte.
Courtesy of the artist and The Box, LA.

In Forti's world, even objects—or perhaps especially objects, considering her dance constructions—were part of it. As she has written, again about living on a commune, "Objects, though moved by people, seemed to follow their own paths, to be part of the flow."[10] This sense that both living and inanimate things were part of one big process was bedrock to Grand Union.

CHAPTER 2

ONLY IN SOHO

The scattered community of artists in Lower Manhattan continued to experiment into the seventies across disciplines, fervor undimmed. But finding affordable living and working space was an uphill battle. A solution was masterminded by Lithuanian immigrant and madcap visionary George Maciunas. Informed by ideas from Bauhaus and European agriculture collectives, he jumpstarted an artists' colony in SoHo (the area from Houston Street to Canal Street, and from Sixth Avenue to Crosby or Lafayette Street, aka the cast-iron district) by setting up 80 Wooster Street as a cooperative "Fluxhouse."

At the same time, the interdisciplinary hub of 112 Greene Street was fertile soil for SoHo's budding art colony. Pioneering visual artists and performance artists like Gordon Matta-Clark, Vito Acconci, Richard Serra, Laurie Anderson, Alan Saret, and Richard Nonas added to the rich cross-disciplinary ferment, as did composers Philip Glass, Richard Landry, and Ornette Coleman. Venues in SoHo that presented dance and performance included The Kitchen, founded by video artists, and galleries run by Paula Cooper and Holly Solomon. It wasn't much of a stretch for Laurie Anderson to call SoHo of that period the center of the art world.[1]

■

In 1967 the artists who had been involved with Judson started hearing that George Maciunas was buying loft buildings in SoHo and selling them cheap to artists. Small manufacturers of clothing, corrugated boxes, candy, or dolls were fleeing New York, leaving behind a landscape of empty warehouses. Maciunas, later known as the "father of SoHo," had a vision of cooperative loft living for artists. In exchange for taking on the risks of illegal occupancy, artists paid a low price for gobs of space. Maciunas was charging only two dollars a square foot, and word spread like wildfire.[2] According to performer and movement therapist Joseph Schlichter, Trisha Brown's husband at the time, "Everyone in Judson Theater was rumbling about it. There were 150 or 160 people who were interested. We had to roll dice to determine who got in."[3]

Maciunas, who came to these shores in 1948, had studied architecture at Cooper Union and Carnegie Institute of Technology. He had also studied with Richard Maxfield, a student in John Cage's famous course in experimental composition at the New School, instilling in him an interest in artists who were mixing genres. As the leading member of Fluxus, he gave the group its name and organized events in both Europe and New York.

Maciunas fought for what he believed—in eccentric ways. Charles Ross recalled him chasing away a city building inspector with a samurai sword. Maciunas once bought two huge batter mixers from a baker and installed one as his bathtub.[4] He aligned himself with the Soviet ideal of workers sharing in ownership. According to Sally Banes, he even called his cooperatives *kolkhoz*, the Russian word for collective farm.[5] He not only organized housing for artists but also got them work. He hired musicians as plumbers, including Philip Glass, Rhys Chatham, and Yoshi Wada, who used giant plumbing pipes to make new sounds.[6]

The first artist to go in with Maciunas, in 1967, was filmmaker Jonas Mekas, a fellow Lithuanian immigrant. Mekas and Maciunas transformed the ground floor of 80 Wooster Street into Fluxhouse Cooperative II. (Fluxhouse I, on Greene Street, was eventually repurposed.)[7] It became the new home for the roving Filmmaker's Cinematheque, which showed films by avant-garde filmmakers like Stan Brakhage, Michael Snow, and Andy Warhol, as well as Mekas.[8] Others who performed there included poet Allen Ginsberg and video pioneer Nam June Paik.[9] Because Yoko Ono was an active Fluxus artist, sometimes she would drop by with John Lennon.[10] It was there that Philip Glass presented the first concert of his own work in 1968.[11] But because of lack of proper licensing, the Fluxhouse only lasted until July 1968. Budding theater director Richard Foreman, who had helped to build the theater, then produced four of his early plays there.[12]

Trisha Brown and Joseph Schlichter moved into the top floor of

80 Wooster with their two-year-old son, Adam. In the beginning, the building's only bathroom was in the basement. Running water did not reach the seventh floor, so Trisha would bring a bucket to a lower floor and fill it from a spigot every day.[13] Schlichter grew marijuana and tomatoes on the roof and used the water tower as a swimming pool for children—to the dismay of other parents.[14]

Sculptor Charles Ross, the mastermind behind the collaborative Concert #13 at Judson, moved into the fourth floor.[15] Conceptual artist Robert Watts, who was involved in happenings along with Allan Kaprow, moved into the fifth floor.

Brown found the raw space to be fertile ground for her choreographic—and architectural—imagination. In a way, she was collaborating with the space around her rather than with other artists. In workshops, she gave students the instruction to "read the wall." The idea was simply to let one's body respond to the markings on the well-worn wall. In 1967 she drove foot holes into her wall "in order to reach the ceiling but also to move on a vertical plane."[16] This was undoubtedly in preparation for her 1968 equipment piece *Planes*. She started off her 1970 concert "Dances In and Around 80 Wooster Street," with her iconic daredevil work *Man Walking Down the Side of a Building*. A tiny audience clustered below in the courtyard, looking up in awe. The film of this event[17] shows a man at the top of 80 Wooster, facing downward, body horizontal, walking so slowly and deliberately that he could just as well be taking the first steps on the moon. (This was only a year after the Apollo moon landing was seen on television.) SoHo artists Richard Nonas, Jared Bark, and David Bradshaw stood on the roof and let the cord out safely.[18] Then the audience went inside the building to see *Floor of the Forest*, in which Brown and Carmen Beuchat crawled on an eye-level grid of horizontal ropes that were strung with garments. The two slithered into and out of the shirts, pants, and dresses. With this work, Brown brought the domestic mess of family life to the pristine grid of minimalism. At the same time, the piece referred to the uneven terrain of the forest, which Brown had called her "first art lesson."[19] Audience members had to create their own uneven terrain, squatting down or rising up to get a glimpse of the performers.

Last, the audience went outside onto Wooster Street to see Brown's *Leaning Duets I*. This was a partnering task dance related to what she

Man Walking Down the Side of a Building (1970), by Trisha Brown.
Joseph Schlichter, 80 Wooster Street. Photo: Carol Goodden.

had been exposed to on Anna Halprin's deck as well as to Forti's *Slant Board* (1961) and her own *Planes*. Five pairs of people had to keep their feet in contact with their partner's feet while leaning away from each other and trying to take steps without falling. The two would talk to each other ("Give me more of your weight" or "I need to twist to my left") to keep in balance and go forward. This kind of discuss-what-you-are-doing banter became rife in Grand Union.

When Brown moved into SoHo, huge trucks were moving through the streets to deliver rags or other cargo to manufacturers. She picked up the lingo of the driver teams and brought those commands into Grand Union. In the last performance at LoGiudice Gallery,[20] during an ultra-slow, ultra-gentle duet between Gordon and Paxton, she carried on with a gruff, street voice: "Easy now, easy now, easy now. C'mon now. Move it along, move it along. Over we go, now. C'mon, easy does it. Let's go, move it, keep it going. Keep it movin', keep it movin'. Up and over, watch out now. Move it along. [Th]at's it, easy does it."

Brown wasn't dreaming of dancing in a theater. Learning her Bauhaus lessons well, she made her art in the place where she lived. "All of the pieces I performed at 80 Wooster had rambled in my head for a long time. My rule was, if an idea doesn't disappear by natural cause, then it has to be done. I wanted to work with the wall but not by building one. I looked at walls in warehouses and as I moved around the streets ... I chose this exterior wall and then thought—why not use mountain climbing equipment?"[21]

Brown also made short works at other sites in SoHo. Her *Roof Piece* premiered with audiences viewing from 53 Wooster Street in 1971; *Woman Walking Down a Ladder* (1973) took place on the rooftop of 130 Greene Street; *Group Primary Accumulation* premiered at Sonnabend Gallery the same year (later to be performed in Central Park and other outdoor areas); and *Spiral* (1974) was inspired by the columns at 383 West Broadway (later Ivan Karp's OK Harris Gallery), where she also premiered *Pamplona Stones*.[22] When she reprised *Roof Piece* in 1973, retitling it *Roof and Fire Piece*, the number of rooftops stretched to fifteen.[23] The photograph of this piece, taken in 1973 by Babette Mangolte, later came to represent the revolutionary SoHo arts scene to Europe.[24]

■

Roof Piece (1971), by Trisha Brown. Foreground: Sylvia Palacios Whitman; at upper left, Douglas Dunn. Photo: Babette Mangolte, 1973.

Although Maciunas was creating a cooperative artist colony with what he considered a "selfless spirit of collectivism,"[25] he was an autocrat. With an architect's training, he was very sure of what he wanted. As Richard Foreman recalled, "He saw things in his own way and if you didn't accept the way he saw things happening, he would get very mad."[26] Foreman described working with Maciunas as "a kind of a perverse spiritual test."[27]

Maciunas, however, cared about the artists he knew and alerted them if a good deal came up. When he discovered 541 Broadway, with its good proportions (wider than the usual twenty-five feet), no interior columns, and floors made of wood—not just wood over concrete—he knew it would be perfect for dancing. He contacted Trisha Brown, who relocated there in 1974 or 1975, soon to be followed by

David Gordon and Valda Setterfield.[28] Douglas Dunn moved there, from a block away, in 1982.[29] Lucinda Childs of the Judson days also lived in the building, and on the Mercer Street side lived—and still live—hybrid artists Joan Jonas and Jackie Winsor. Simone Forti, along with dance artist Frances Alenikoff, musician Yoshi Wada, and artist Emily Harvey, lived in the next building at 537 Broadway.

Maciunas felt that his artists' colony, which grew to sixteen buildings over ten years, was in line with the ideals of Bauhaus and Black Mountain.[30] In the Cagean and Fluxus spirit of making art out of everyday life, he was creating spaces where artists lived, made work, and gathered. Trisha Brown, with her uncanny ability to nestle the human body into, or use the body to extend, existing architecture, was in line with Maciunas's vision. Brown helped shape the values of SoHo and vice versa. During this period, she was working with Grand Union as well as making her equipment pieces and accumulation pieces.

Like Brown, both Marilyn Wood and Mary Overlie devised ways to embed the moving body into the SoHo landscape. A former Cunningham dancer, Wood devoted herself to site-specific dance, performing internationally with her Celebration Group as well as on the fire escapes on Prince Street. In 1976 and 1977 Overlie, who had performed a speaking role in Rainer's piece at Oberlin in 1972 and had been a guest of Grand Union at 112 Greene Street in 1972, performed with her dancers in the windows of Holly Solomon Gallery, creating a stir of enchantment on West Broadway.[31]

■

Another hotspot in SoHo made possible by low cost was 112 Greene Street. A cluster of artists, including married couple Jeffrey Lew, a self-styled anarchist, and Rachel Wood, a dancer, inhabited the building. They had bought the building—Wood had family money—directly from a rag factory in 1970.[32] The pioneering site artist Gordon Matta-Clark, who briefly lived in the basement, was constantly altering the space with his outrageously deconstructionist actions. In an episode of "guerrilla gardening," he piled soil into a small hill in the basement and planted a cherry tree in it. In order to give the tree space to grow, he cut a big hole in the ground floor of the building, which became his signature mode—literally deconstructing buildings. Though he died in 1978, he is known as one of the great instigators of large-scale, space-altering work, addressing the deterioration of New

Glass Imagination II (1977), by Mary Overlie. Photo: Theo Robinson.

York City buildings with his manic imagination. Matta-Clark, whose godfather was Marcel Duchamp,[33] was a forbear of later huge projects by the likes of site artists James Turrell, Michael Heizer, and Christo.[34]

The glory of the lone artist, however, was losing its luster. In his book *Another Little Piece of My Heart: My Life of Rock and Revolution in the '60s*, cultural critic Richard Goldstein wrote this in reaction to Norman Mailer's novel *Armies of the Night*: "[I]t seemed like a violation of the countercultural ethos that I'd come to share. We kids saw politics as a collective activity, something we did together. Radicals in Mailer's generation had struggled to maintain their individuality, but we fought to maintain community."[35]

During this period, 112 Greene became a hangout for all kinds of artists and dancers, including Barbara Dilley, Douglas Dunn, Nancy Lewis, and Steve Paxton. Rachel Wood was a member of Dilley's group, the Natural History of the American Dancer. This all-woman group also included Carmen Beuchat (who was also dancing with

GU at 112 Greene Street, 1972. From left: Paxton, Lewis, Overlie (as guest), Rainer (face hidden), Scott in chair. Photo: Babette Mangolte.

Brown), Cynthia Hedstrom, Mary Overlie, Suzanne Harris, and Judy Padow.

The works that took up space at 112 Greene broke all existing conventions of art-making etiquette. Louise Sørensen, in the introduction to *112 Greene Street: The Early Years*, wrote that "112 Greene Street was synonymous with a remarkably concentrated period of the New York art world where creativity and idealism went hand in hand—a product, no doubt, of the 1960s counter-culture."[36] It was a non-gallery gallery. As conceptual artist Bill Beckley recalled, it "was a raunchy kind of place where you sometimes couldn't tell the mess from the art or vice versa."[37]

SoHo was a counterculture in both art and leisure. Its artists were decidedly uncommercial, not looking to make money from their art. Beckley felt they were "redefining" art. "It was the cusp of modernism and postmodernism."[38] Some called them "post-minimalist."[39] The social life mingled with the art life. According to Rachel Wood, "[W]e had incredible parties: rock 'n' roll music, dope and alcohol, and dancing like mad for hours."[40]

Padow, who also lived at 112 Greene, described how the group named the Natural History of the American Dancer emerged from those parties: "It's a party but everyone's dancing and improvising. It got formed almost like an outgrowth of the lifestyle at 112 Greene Street. There was not a fine line between having dinner and performing eating dinner. Someone sitting on a sofa would rise up and suddenly you'd notice that someone else has risen. The cues … the picking up of someone else's gestures would happen at a spontaneous level."[41]

Paxton, however, doesn't feel that 112 Greene held a corner on this kind of social life. Asked, via email, if he felt 112 provided the soil for endeavors like Grand Union, he replied: "The *times* were that soil, I believe. The transition of SoHo into artists' spaces rendered it especially fertile; a failing industrial area was transformed into a colony of activist artists, musicians, poets, dancers [having] huge parties, pranks, hijinks, performances and a confluence of a new generation of artists."[42]

Douglas Dunn often went to the dancing parties at the Byrd Hoffman School for Birds on Spring Street, the studio of experimental theater director Robert Wilson. Daily improvisation sessions there also bled into social parties. "These places were so cheap and it was so much fun and so interactive. Grand Union was sort of an extension of this kind of familiarity and intimacy of artists at that time."[43] The sexual revolution was still young, and the calamity of AIDS hadn't hit yet. "There was plenty of erotic energy in the mix and sometimes it ended up being physical connections and sometimes it didn't," Dunn said. "It was one of the driving forces, not just in Grand Union but in SoHo in that era. Sometimes these relationships fed the work and sometimes they distracted from it."[44] A graphic that reflects that randiness, with a certain elusive humor, is the flyer that Paxton designed for the February 1971 performances at Bob Fiore's loft on East 13th Street.

∎

The 112 Greene Street denizens, like many young artists, tended to be skeptical of capitalism and against the war in Vietnam. According to artist Mary Heilmann, "Most of us came to 112 as bohemian outsiders and almost Marxists—against capitalist culture."[45] According to Rachel Wood, Jeffrey Lew was so opposed to art making as

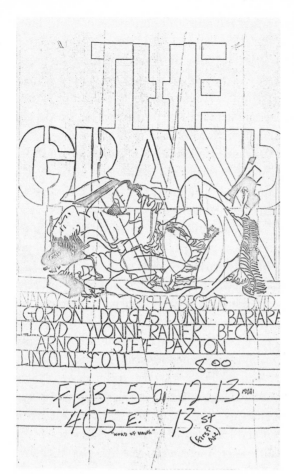

moneymaking that one of his criteria for accepting a work of art at 112
Greene was that it not be intended for sale.[46] It was more honorable
to make work that was embedded in the life they were living. In 1972
Matta-Clark made a piece called *Walls Paper*, for which he photographed walls of decaying buildings, made giant prints of them, and
mounted them up on the walls of 112 as a new kind of wallpaper.[47]
Also in 1972, he made a performance piece in a dumpster on Greene
Street. Beckley's memory: "[Y]ou saw the umbrellas peeking up from
the dumpster, moving around. That was pretty good."[48] As with Trisha
Brown, this was part of the aesthetic of bringing art outside the gallery
or theater and into the streets.

Another urban project of Matta-Clark's brought graffiti writers down from the Bronx. He photographed sides of subway cars, mounted them on long panels, and set them up as an exhibit on a Mercer Street sidewalk. According to Terry O'Reilly, who assisted him, "Originally he set up his camera on subway platforms and photographed the trains when they came to a stop. This did not work well, so he went out to the train yards and broke into the yards just like the kids would do and photographed their work."[49] Matta-Clark's application to exhibit these images at the Washington Square Art Fair was rejected, so he parked his delivery truck and invited his graffiti friends to decorate the truck. At the same time, he displayed some of his train-sized photographs of their work, which he called photoglyphs, right there on the sidewalk and called it the Alternatives to Washington Square Art Fair; he exhibited more photoglyphs at 112 Greene. This celebration of the "ordinary" predates the art world's love affair with graffiti.[50] (But I note that Twyla Tharp had already gotten the idea to have graffiti writers onstage as part of the set design for *Deuce Coupe*, which premiered with the Joffrey Ballet in 1973.)

Matta-Clark's anarchistic streak was reinforced by others at 112 Greene Street. As the casually organized "Anarchitecture" group—which included Matta-Clark, Harris, Nonas, Carol Goodden, Jene Highstein, Tina Girouard, and Laurie Anderson—they would get together and discuss architecture, space, language, and the possibility of subverting existing norms.[51] They held an exhibit of their work in March 1974 at 112 Greene Street. Each artist contributed anonymous photographs that she or he felt represented her or his "idea of anarchitecture, such as liminal or overlooked spaces, and they made the works look anonymous."[52] It was the last show at 112 Greene.

The sense of possibility in SoHo was heady. Highstein (who found mover's work for his cousin Philip Glass in SoHo) called 112 Greene "a free-for-all.... It really was an open forum. It didn't have any structure. It was just a room, a big room where anything could happen."[53] Like Trisha Brown at 80 Wooster Street, the artists were finding ways to fit their actions into the existing architecture. Sculptor Richard Nonas, who helped Brown outfit her performers in harnesses for her gravity-defying equipment dances, said, "There was no separation between the works and the space."[54] And, possibly because there was no profit on the horizon, things were fluid. Multidisciplinary artist Tina Girouard (video, installation, fabric, paintings) recalled that the exhibitions would change continually, becoming more like performance.[55] Suzanne Harris, who had performed with Brown, produced a double installation of *Flying Machine* and *The Wheels* in 1973. For the first, she invited viewers to strap themselves to ropes attached to a specially made ceiling. Next to it was a contraption made of four large wheels that audience members could set in motion.[56] "The base of it stayed stable but the different parts rotated," Beckley recalled. "She went from one rotating thing to another. It was like a bridge from the sculptural aspects of 112 to the dance."[57] Others who presented performances or exhibits at 112 Greene were Vito Acconci, Alice Aycock, Jared Bark, Joseph Beuys, Keith Sonnier, and William Wegman. The Grand Union performed there in February 1972 with Mary Overlie as a guest.

■

Since they didn't want to make a living from their art, this cluster of close-knit friends, having given many dinner and dance parties, figured out how to create a communal business: they opened the restaurant FOOD. In 1971 Carol Goodden, who was living with Matta-Clark and dancing with Trisha Brown, bought a small Puerto Rican food shop on the corner of Prince and Wooster Streets. With the help of other SoHo friends, they transformed it into a center run by and for artists. Philip Glass installed the radiators,[58] and visual artist Jared Bark put up a new ceiling.[59] Goodden was determined to pay artists well for their work and accommodate them with flexible hours.[60] FOOD was the only restaurant in the neighborhood with healthy fare, a welcome warm spot on the otherwise empty streets. It specialized in fresh fish, soups, and salads, and the menu changed daily. Members of the theater group Mabou Mines, musicians from Philip Glass's ensemble, and dancers of the Natural History of the American Dancer cooked, served, and stocked supplies. When it was her turn to cook, Barbara Dilley made food you ate with your hands: "Shells from mussels in broth become scoops for rice pilaf. There were artichokes to dip in melted lemon butter."[61] Nancy Lewis remembers making salads while her future husband, musician Richard Peck, washed dishes.[62] Artist Robert Kushner was dessert chef. Everything about FOOD was cooperative. They took turns cooking, relying on family recipes and artistic flair for presentation. Rauschenberg, Don Judd, and Keith Sonnier all did stints as guest chefs.[63]

In one of his first acts of deconstruction, Matta-Clark tore down the

Woman Walking Down a Ladder (1973), by Trisha Brown, 130 Greene Street.
Photo: Babette Mangolte.

walls separating the kitchen and dining area, putting the cooking in full view of patrons as though it were a performance. In fact, Goodden and Matta-Clark thought of FOOD as a long-term art piece.[64] One example of Matta-Clark's food art is described by Claire Barliant in *Paris Review*: "Gordon did a meal called *Matta-Bones*, where everything he served was on the bone and at the end he drilled holes through the bones to make necklaces."[65]

FOOD thrived as an artist-run restaurant from 1971 to 1974, when it changed hands. (The heyday of 112 Greene Street also ended in 1974; in the eighties it morphed into White Columns in the West Village.) Throwing themselves into the work at the restaurant exemplifies Marcuse's concept of "erotic labor." Richard Goldstein interprets that to mean the kind of work that "enlists your deepest passions.... Lots of people found the pleasures of erotic labor in political organizing. This was about work as an act of love. Marcuse made me see that when work is love it can be liberating."[66]

■

It's often been said that SoHo in the seventies was ideal for artists. But the questions come up: For whom was it ideal, and who got left out? It's no secret that the population in SoHo was largely white, young Americans.

It should be noted, however, that there was a parallel pocket of fervent dance activity for a more diverse group of dance artists about three miles north. Alvin Ailey had helped launch Clark Center for the Performing Arts as a midtown dance space. Affiliated with the Westside YWCA, Clark Center was a crucial hub of dance that was much more racially inclusive than SoHo. Some of the dance artists nurtured in this studio at Eighth Avenue at 50th Street were Rod Rodgers, Eleo Pomare, Donald McKayle, Mariko Sanjo, Brenda Dixon (later Brenda Dixon Gottschild), Dianne McIntyre, William Dunas, Elizabeth Keen, Chuck Davis (founder of DanceAfrica), and Tina Ramirez (founder of Ballet Hispanico).[67] During the 1969–1970 season, I often rehearsed there with Rudy Perez, who had performed at Judson from the start and later became a pillar of postmodern dance in Los Angeles. Performances at Clark Center were more fully produced and more accepted by the modern dance establishment than the anything-goes escapades in downtown studios. The choreographers at Clark Center were clearly preparing for the stage rather than for a loft space or art gallery. Dancer/scholar Danielle Goldman points out that Ailey and his repertoire used "metaphors of uplift" that were aligned with historic modern dance.[68]

Banes has noted: "Postmodern dance was seen by many African American dancers as dry formalism, while African American dance was considered by some white postmodernists as too emotional and overexplicit politically."[69] But a handful of dancers—Gus Solomons jr, Laura Dean, Meredith Monk—shuttled between Clark Center and SoHo. They were accepted socially and aesthetically in both milieus. Solomons explains why most black dancers were not drawn to the aesthetic of Grand Union: "Black audiences and artists typically were interested in messages, be they of rebellion, oppression, or emotion. In general, they didn't see the point in making work that was only about itself and not the human condition as they experienced it."[70] I might quibble with his depiction of downtown dance as not representing the human condition, but his point is well taken.

It wasn't until 1982, when Ishmael Houston-Jones curated a slate of African American dance artists for a series called Parallels at Danspace Project, that many of us recognized that postmodern dance was attracting more black dancers than it had before. Danspace, a center of downtown (heretofore mostly white) dance, had been costarted by Dilley in 1974. When curating Parallels, Houston-Jones included not only Solomons and others who had crossed the black/white divide long before, like Harry Whittaker Sheppard and Blondell Cummings, but also younger dance artists like Ralph Lemon, Bebe Miller, and Jawole Willa Jo Zollar. This series created space for black dancers to feel welcomed in downtown dance houses. They were part of a vibrant postmodern dance as a new art form.

As author Richard Kostelanetz pointed out, SoHo in the seventies was particularly hospitable to new forms of art.[71] While Clark Center nobly upheld the tradition of modern dance, experiments in holography, video art, and book art (and as we have seen, food art) were sprouting up in SoHo or nearby. The Kitchen Center opened in the Broadway Central Hotel in 1971, specifically to nurture the new art form of video.[72] In 1973, when it moved to Broome and Wooster Streets, it welcomed music, soon to be followed by performance art and dance. (When the Grand Union performed there in 1974, Kathy Duncan's review called the troupe a "utopian democracy.")[73] The Kitchen fostered the careers of dancers and other artists who brazenly crossed lines of genre and etiquette, for example Bill T. Jones and Arnie Zane, Philip Glass, Laurie Anderson, Karen Finley, Eric Bogosian, Molissa Fenley, Christian Marclay, Charles Atlas, and Robert Ashley. (My dance company too was presented there.) With a professional staff to generate publicity and raise funds, it was a more polished operation than either 80 Wooster or 112 Greene. The Kitchen could commission new works and could even send an interdisciplinary band of experimental artists to tour Europe.

■

John Cage's ideas pervaded SoHo like a mist. Visual artists like Rauschenberg, Jasper Johns, and Donald Judd were redefining American art, forming all kinds of hybrids and crossovers. Judd presented Philip Glass and his ensemble at his building on Spring Street, the first of a string of gigs for the Glass Ensemble in galleries and museums.[74] Just outside the bounds of SoHo, places like Printed Matter (for artists' books), La MaMa (for experimental theater), The Living Theatre, and The Clocktower (similar to The Kitchen but more site-specific) added to the mix.

The desire to bust out of cultural or genre straitjackets continued into the seventies, and SoHo provided spaces for that to happen. As sculptor Suzanne Harris said, "We didn't need the rest of the world. Rather than attacking a system that was already there, we chose to build a world of our own."[75]

That world was supported by *Avalanche*, a maverick art publication that considered itself a sibling to 112 Greene and FOOD, where it was available to peruse. *Avalanche* advocated new genres like earth art, body art, collaborations, video art, and installation. The cofounders, Liza Béar and Willoughby Sharp, were part of the art scene and presented text and images from the artists' point of view. Grand Union members were often interviewed, and three of *Avalanche*'s thirteen issues, which spanned the same six years as Grand Union, devoted cover stories to Yvonne Rainer, Barbara Dilley, and Steve Paxton. When Grand Union performed in Buffalo in 1973, *Avalanche* coeditor Liza Béar, staff photographer Gwenn Thomas, and production person Linda Lawton drove up to Buffalo to shoot and audiotape the performance. They produced a new response form: photographs with dialog bubbles taken directly from the dancer's improvised conversations.

44

Excerpt of *Avalanche's* comic strip in response
to GU's performance at Buffalo State College,
1973. Design by Willoughby Sharp, photos by
Gwenn Thomas, editing by Liza Béar and Linda
Lawton, lettering by Jean Izzo. Appeared in
Avalanche 8 (Summer/Fall 1973). Courtesy of
Liza Béar and the Estate of Willoughby Sharp.

INTERLUDE

PHILIP GLASS ON JOHN CAGE

Artists of all disciplines were affected by Cage's ideas, either directly or indirectly. I find Glass's interpretation to be less conceptual than most; he focuses on the interdependence of art and audience. The following is an excerpt from his autobiography, Words Without Music: A Memoir.

I had been immersed in Cage's *Silence*, the Wesleyan University Press collection of writings published in 1961. This was a very important book to us in terms of the theory and aesthetic of postmodernism. Cage especially was able to develop a very clear and lucid presentation of the idea that the listener completes the work. It wasn't just his idea: he attributed it to Marcel Duchamp, with whom he was associated. Duchamp was a bit older but he seemed to have been very close to John. They played chess together, they talked about things together, and if you think about it that way, the Dadaism of Europe took root in America through Cage. He was the one who made it understandable for people through a clear exposition of how the creative process works, vis-à-vis the audience.

Take John's famous piece *4'33"*. John, or anyone, sits at the piano for four minute[s] thirty-three seconds and during that time, whatever you hear is the piece. It could be people walking through the corridor, it could be the traffic, it could be the hum of the electricity in the building—it doesn't matter. The idea was that John simply took this space and this prescribed period of time and by framing it, announced, "This is what you're going to pay attention to. What you see and what you hear is the art." When he got up, it ended.

The book *Silence* was in my hands not long after it came out, and I would spend time with John Rouson and Michel [Zeltzman] talking and thinking about it. As it turned out, it became a way that we could look at what Jaspers Johns, Robert Rauschenberg, Richard Serra, or almost anybody from our generation or the generation just before us did, and we could understand it in terms of how the work existed in the world.

The important point is that a work of art has no independent existence. It has a conventional identity and a conventional reality and it comes into being through an interdependence of other events with people. . . .

The accepted idea when I was growing up was that the late Beethoven quartets or *The Art of the Fugue* or any of the great masterpieces had a platonic identity—that they had an actual, independent existence. What Cage was saying is that there is no such thing as an independent existence. The music exists between you—the listener—and the object that you're listening to. The transaction of it coming into being happens through the effort you make in the presence of that work. The cognitive activity is the content of the work. This is the root of postmodernism, really, and John was wonderful at not only articulating it, but demonstrating it in his work and his life.

CHAPTER 3

HOW *CONTINUOUS PROJECT—ALTERED DAILY* BROKE OPEN AND MADE SPACE FOR A GRAND UNION

Ever since Judson, Rainer had been hell-bent on challenging every assumption involved in concert dance. With her emphasis on functional movement and the unadorned body (though she also deployed a wide dance vocabulary), she undermined the bedrock of professional dance: technical mastery. Taking this takedown further, with *Continuous Project—Altered Daily* (CP-AD) she introduced a range of modes that brought the activity of rehearsing into performance. She felt that what went on in rehearsal was as worthy of viewing as a finished piece. Therefore, in addition to performing set choreography, her score (instructions) included the following: marking the choreography (indicating it with a less-than-full-out energy), practicing the choreography, making choices about when an action would occur or whether to join in, and learning new choreography. The last of these plunged the dancers into the state of not knowing, thus robbing them of their physical assuredness. Shorn of set choreography, the performer might as well be shorn of a costume. The dancers were exposed.

For Rainer, the vulnerability of the dancer was part of her plan, part of her aesthetic. With the aid of game structures and absurdist props, she worked toward scraping away any veneer of polish. (She surely agreed with Paxton when he wrote to her in a letter that "finesse is odious.")[1] She wanted the audience to see the labor—the process—of dancing. Toward this goal, she enlisted task, play, pop culture, singular focus, multifocus, dancers bringing in their own material, choosing between options, not knowing what to expect—all of which eventually cracked open the customary director-performer hierarchy.

Rainer was asking questions: How to present two radically different ideas simultaneously? How to let the audience see the process of making? How to give performers creative agency? In addition to the experimental thrust, she valued spontaneity, so she came up with game structures designed to lift the lid on one's natural impulsiveness.

She, along with her small crew of dancers—Becky Arnold, Barbara Dilley, Douglas Dunn, David Gordon, and Steve Paxton—made CP-AD over a period of about nine months, showing it at different stages along the way. It was never meant to be a finished product, since part of the idea was to show the process of making. During this period, the performers were called either Yvonne Rainer and Group or Yvonne Rainer Dance Company.

In 1969, while in residence at American Dance Festival at Connecticut College, Rainer was experimenting with tasks and objects for CP-AD. The atmosphere during the making process was casual and workmanlike, with a ready sense of play.[2] Five dancers (Steve Paxton was not able to join them) were working, lifting, hauling, trying things out. What can a body do with a cardboard box? How can a dancer be lifted the way a box is lifted? What happens if you run with a pillow and use it to cushion another dancer's fall? What happens when all five dancers sit on the floor and try to use the group leverage to all rise together? All this experimentation fostered a sense of trust that was visible in their comfort with touch, mutual support, and difficult maneuvers.

That summer, augmenting her small group with about eighty ADF students, Rainer created a huge performance called "Connecticut Composite" that spread out over several areas of the Connecticut College gymnasium. *Continuous Project—Altered Daily*, a work-in-progress at the time, occupied only one area. In a second area was a studio with twenty-eight students doing *Trio A*, and in a third room one could watch films and hear lectures. Yet another area housed an "audience piece," which was basically Rainer's *Chair Pillow* with an empty seat to be filled by a single spectator. (*Chair Pillow*, which had already been part of Rainer's *Performance Demonstration* at Pratt Institute in March 1969, is a spunky unison piece, setting functional actions like throwing a pillow behind oneself to the beat of Ike and Tina Turner's "River Deep, Mountain High.") Marching through the central area was a twenty-strong "people wall" that advanced and retreated inexorably, scattering audience members as it went. According to Rainer's diagrams, this group changed configuration twenty times.[3]

About CP-AD that summer, dance critic Marcia B. Siegel lauded the "spontaneity, play, and variety" of the activities. She especially noticed the moment when "Rainer took a running leap and swan-dived over two big cardboard cartons into the arms of two men." With all that was going on, including audience members sometimes joining in, she called the performance "rowdy" and said it "had the clangor and conviviality of a Horn & Hardart" (referring to the chain of working-class, cafeteria-style lunch spots in New York and Philadelphia of the thirties through the early sixties).[4]

Don McDonagh wrote that the overall performance, which included Twyla Tharp's commission that summer, brought "a joyous spirit of adventure" back to the festival, which year after year had presented mostly established modern dance companies like those of Martha Graham and José Limón.[5]

Later in 1969, Rainer wrote letters to Paxton and Dilley, who were teaching at the University of Illinois, about the upcoming date at University of Missouri at Kansas City. She sent them her tracings of Isadora Duncan photographs with instructions to make a duet based on them. Her notes of what she expected to happen included this bullet point: "YR randomly monologuing, directing, watching, disappearing."[6] A little foreshadowing, perhaps? Her disappearing act was repeated in various forms during the next three years.[7]

The Kansas City performance, on November 8, 1969, turned out to be a madcap, expansive turning point. Body "adjuncts," created by Deborah Hollingworth, included a pair of feathered wings, a foam insert that turned the wearer into a hunchback, a lion's tail, and a humongous sombrero hat. It also provided the performers a chance to laugh at themselves or each other, deflating the self-importance of the performer.

Dilley, looking back, felt Kansas City was the beginning of the evolution toward Grand Union. Writing in the present tense, she recounted the performance in her book, *This Very Moment*:

Kansas City

Circumstances create unplanned opportunities and, that night, suddenly we make new material in front of the audience. We've never done this before. It is outrageous and fresh. There are moments of exquisite joy and revelation.

I write about it in a letter to Yvonne: *I remember the opening*

yvonne Rainer

bars of the Chambers Brothers "In the Midnight Hour" and doing Trio A *slow, very slow, and Steve [Paxton] joining me and then fast, with and against Steve's tempo. It was sheer delight. I felt sexy moving through material I know that slowly. I remember you ... grinning at the pleasure we had. Oh, and the wings. I remember watching the pillow solo and then during* Trio A *the wings would sometimes flap in my face. The literary images, the dream images, the animal images....*

After the performance we stay up most of the night, sprawled across some hotel bed, talking through what happened over and over. Yvonne calls it "spontaneous behavior." There's no going back. We are about to become the anarchist ensemble the Grand Union, where we make up everything in front of audiences.[8]

Rainer, too, felt a huge release with the discovery of "behavior" as performance. In a loving, admiring letter to her dancers, she told them that because of their performance, she had an epiphany: "I got a glimpse of human behavior that my dreams for a better life are based on—real, complex, constantly in flux, rich, concrete, funny, focused, immediate, specific, intense, serious at times to the point of religiosity, light, diaphonous [*sic*], silly, and many leveled at any particular moment."[9] (I would say that her words mesh with my own experience of watching Grand Union.) When Rainer described the specific actions that excited her, they seem quite ordinary. (By then, with the help of past teachers Halprin and Dunn, she had mastered "ordinary.") That was the point: what is ordinary can be art. The following is from a letter she wrote to her dancers after Kansas City:

Steve's concentration and presence during the lifting lesson; his lying on the floor at the end; his observation of me doing the pillow-head routine. Doug sitting across the room looking at our shenanigans with a baleful eye.... David seriously working on the new stuff by himself; his interrupting me at the microphone to ask for help. As you see, I am talking mostly about behavior rather than execution of movement. It is not because I value one over the other, but because the behavior aspects of this enterprise are so new and startling and miraculous to me.[10]

Rainer was delighted to see good ole human behavior in an art context. It aligned with her larger project of putting life onstage, breaking the barriers between art and life.

Although the UMKC audience, having no context for Rainer's work, could not have perceived the nature of the breakthrough, the student newspaper did report a warm response. "Not knowing what to expect," wrote Tresa Hall, "yet not expecting what they got, the audience reacted in a very pure and delightful way."[11]

After the breakthrough in Missouri, Paxton may have been the only one who saw the possibility of improvisation on the horizon. "While we were in Kansas City having a late-night talk about the performance we had just done, I said, 'It is very obvious that we are heading for improvisation of material,' and thereafter came a long series of responses on how impossible that was."[12]

■

As much as the "behavior" was welcome, the aspect of dance as labor was also central to CP-AD. Rainer was influenced—not for the first time—by the minimalist sculptor Robert Morris, her lover and fellow Judson choreographer. Rainer took the title *Continuous Project— Altered Daily* from an installation he devised at the Castelli Warehouse in Harlem and later performed at the Whitney Museum. For this "installation," Morris went into the gallery every day and changed the arrangement of a myriad of objects.[13] Rainer was impressed that he had created a fluid experience rather than a finished exhibition. (Let's not forget that, back in the late fifties and early sixties, when Morris was married to Forti, he had tagged along to workshops given by Halprin and Robert Dunn.) Art critic Annette Michelson described how Morris's Whitney installation involved various craftspeople and museum staff who "worked at the transport of the huge cement, wood, and steel components, converting the elevator into the giant pulley which hoisted them to the level of the exhibition floor."[14] Morris himself describes the installation as "[n]o product, just the heaving and throwing and shoving and stuffing."[15]

It is this type of labor that Rainer wanted to get at. She wanted to show dancers as workers. I believe she felt this would demystify dance, move toward a more egalitarian attitude toward women, and scrape away the narcissism that she felt comes with the territory of performing.[16]

Continuous Project—Altered Daily (1970), Whitney Museum. With Rainer and Dunn.
Photo: James Klosty.

Rainer's love of work, especially women working together, goes back to her participation during Judson Concert #13, "A Collaborative Event in 1963," mentioned in chapter 1. In her autobiography, she describes the teamwork necessary to accomplish Carla Blank's piece *Turnover*, in which eight or nine women literally turn over Charles Ross's huge trapezoid-like metal frame: "As half the group lifted a lower bar of the contraption from the floor, the other half reached for the top bar on the other side and in the process of bringing it to the ground raised the first four or five performers high in the air. The second group then moved to the other side to lift another part of the structure, thus lowering the dangling ones to the ground. In this fashion the whole configuration rolled crazily around the space. I found it breathtaking to engage in this heavy and slightly dangerous work with a team of women."[17]

The audiences of CP-AD also had to work. In order to make sense of the radical juxtapositions (a term coined by Susan Sontag when describing happenings in 1962),[18] they had to encompass two contradictory ideas at the same time (F. Scott Fitzgerald, anyone?). Rainer was fond of butting two opposite actions or moods up against each other. She wasn't interested in snap judgments, in audiences being able to grasp an idea instantly. She wanted to engage them long enough to provoke serious thought. In a 2001 interview, when she had reentered the dance field after making independent films for twenty-five years, she was discussing the relatively new genre of video installation as performance. "I'm still interested in making things that require a certain amount of time to comprehend," she said. "With the standard video installation, you go in, stand there for two minutes, say 'I get it,' and walk out. I don't think of images in that way."[19] She preferred a complexity of images or actions, not with an obvious center or point. Like Cunningham, who scattered actions all over the stage, she liked to have several tasks going on at once. She wanted the audience to grapple with what they were seeing (the way she grappled with life), rather than to just passively receive it.

Another way that Rainer explored the complexity of images was her insight into the relationship between the body and objects. About the Whitney performance of *Continuous Project* (which was not only the premiere in 1970 but also its last performance before the group mutated into the Grand Union), Rainer wrote:

I love the duality of props, or objects: their usefulness and obstructiveness in relation to the human body. Also, the duality of the body: the body as a moving, thinking, decision- and action-making entity and the body as an inert entity, object-like. Active-passive, despairing-motivated, autonomous-dependent. Analogously, the object can only symbolize these polarities: it cannot be motivated, only activated. Yet oddly, the body can become object-like; the human being can be treated as an object, dealt with as an entity without feeling or desire. The body itself can be handled and manipulated as though lacking in the capacity for self-propulsion.[20]

The idea that a woman could be like an object in performance (not, I hasten to add, a sex object) fit nicely with Rainer's budding feminism. It offered a solution to the "problem" of a woman's body in performance, which was often exploited as an object of sexual pleasure for men. In the ballet world, a woman was either seducer or sylph; in modern dance, she was often either a matriarch or a woman in various states of desire. In *CP-AD*, a woman could either lift a box, be lifted like a box, toss a pillow, or help a mate fall or get up. So could a man. In this way, *CP-AD* was as ungendered as her previous works, like *We Shall Run* and *The Mind Is a Muscle* (1966). Rainer's device of never looking at the audience in *Trio A*, which was initially part of *Muscle*, was an attempt to escape the usual tyranny of what was later called the "male gaze." (Ironically, Rainer has often admitted that she likes being looked at as a performer.) Scholar Peggy Phelan has pointed out that "*Trio A* in particular anticipates" the concept of the male gaze as coined in Laura Mulvey's landmark 1975 essay, "Visual Pleasure and Narrative Cinema."[21]

The active/passive duality she set up was *not* keyed to gender. This concept was foundational to *CP-AD* and continued through Grand Union. It seems to me there were two types of passivity in *CP-AD*: one was for the body to assume an inanimate state, as object or sculpture, and the other was for the body to go soft, almost liquid, like water. The latter was embodied most expertly by Steve Paxton. In one section, with three limbs being pulled by Gordon, Dilley, and Douglas Dunn, he went limp, trusting them as they pulled him in different directions.[22] The necessity of trust became a theme, a challenge, a shared understanding in the Grand Union, and continues to be a cornerstone of Contact Improvisation. (More about Contact Improvisation in Nancy Stark Smith's interlude and in chapter 22.)

■

As part of the Whitney performance of CP-AD (March 30 to April 2, 1970), Rainer arranged for several spoken recitations during the performance. She had always fed her intellectual hunger with an array of serious reading. For the Whitney, she invited prominent people in the arts to read passages she'd found about performing—written by Buster Keaton, Louise Brooks, Barbra Streisand, W. C. Fields—thereby adding another layer of inquiry into the nature of performance. Among the readers were fellow choreographer Lucinda Childs, theater director Richard Foreman, filmmaker Hollis Frampton, and art critic Annette Michelson.[23] The readings at the mic, juxtaposed to the game-like physical actions, left some audience members confused, or merely unmoved. But *New York Times* reviewer Don McDonagh found it stimulating that "an almost contagious joyfulness" could appear side by side with a section that he considered "drained of freshness." He felt it was all part of Rainer's "voracious embrace of all movement full of its own weight and justification."[24]

Because the task-oriented movement did not require highly trained bodies (though most of the dancers were trained professionals), McDonagh wrote, "A curious side effect of the work was the frustration of not being able to participate except vicariously in something that appeared to be fun."[25] This illusion that anyone could do it (which continued as CP-AD morphed into the Grand Union) had its roots in Halprin's explorations in public spaces and her wish to blur the line between performer and audience, making dance more democratic.

In some ways, McDonagh (who had only the year before called Rainer's *Rose Fractions* "leaden" and "stultifying")[26] represented the ideal viewer. First, because he relished the challenge of making sense of radical juxtapositions. Second, because he had enough physical responsiveness to catch the fun of it.

Another critic who enjoyed the range of moods, though she was far from effusive, was Nancy Mason of *Dance Magazine*: "Projecting different sides of their personalities—reserved and methodical, warm and whimsical—they use their bodies in unique ways to ventilate a primitive urge to move and express." Mason also enjoyed Hollingworth's bizarre "adjuncts" that were donned, at random times, by the dancers: "Barb affects an imitation lion's tail, which bobs jauntily around as she buries her head in a pillow on the floor. David looks like a mini-Mexican beneath his giant, colorful sombrero."[27]

Rainer was under no illusion that she was doing something new by allowing process into performance. Rauschenberg had created "live décor" while on tour with Cunningham; in addition to providing an assortment of found items to wear for *Story*, he sometimes loaned himself as part of the scenery. When the company performed *Story* in Devon, England, he and Alex Hay were ironing shirts upstage.[28] Charles Ross had done it in the collaborative event at Judson, when he was amassing his mountain of chairs during the performance, and then again with Anna Halprin in her *Apartment 6* (1965), in which he was making a paper animal—a different one each time—upstage during the performance.[29] Performing process was just one device in Rainer's arsenal in deconstructing the conventions of the theater.

■

Rainer had a history of crossing from private to public that prepared her for the vulnerability in *CP-AD*. How intimate can a work of art be? She'd seen Rauschenberg's *Bed* (1955) mounted on the wall. Was it a painting, a sculpture, a found object, a private corner? Mattresses, pillows—the domestic realm, the woman's realm—were now fair game to include. She had performed in Forti's *See-Saw* in 1960, which suggested a domestic relationship seeking balance. In *Inner Appearances* (1972, a prelude to her first film, *Lives of Performers*), her most private thoughts—erotic, rebellious, political, mundane—were projected onto the back wall while she was vacuuming the floor. Perhaps this short trip from private to public was best expressed in the language she used recently when referring to her decision to expose dancers to process in *CP-AD*: "Let it all hang out—or make new stuff right in the performance."[30]

Although Rainer asked the dancers to contribute ideas, she still considered herself the choreographer. According to Paxton, it was a step-by-step process that led to the transformation of *CP-AD* into Grand Union. He enumerated the progressive invitation to dancers to make decisions, to bring in new material, to experiment with learning in performance. He said that "misunderstandings would continue until we had assumed more and more functions that she had under-

Continuous Project—Altered Daily (1970), Whitney Museum. With Gordon and Rainer.
Photo: James Klosty.

stood were her own."[31] Eventually it became clear that the logical next step in this experiment was for Rainer to relinquish control.

But that was not her intention. She felt she was encouraging her dancers to experiment, not to mutiny. She wanted to give them agency as creative people instead of serving merely as "people-material." She wanted to acknowledge the brilliance of her performers. But in a statement read aloud during the 1969 performance at Pratt Institute, she said, "The weight and ascendancy of my own authority have come to oppress me."[32] The piece at Pratt had some of the elements of CP-AD, like bringing in independent material and teaching material in front of the audience. Rainer was already questioning the director/performer hierarchy.

Even those weighty questions did not put a damper on the performance. One Pratt student, Catherine Kerr, who later became one of the longest running dancers in the Merce Cunningham Dance Company, responded to the group's exuberance: "I thought it was fabulous.... It was athletic, it was casual, it was everyday movement. I remember being totally engaged by the performance and their antics. I thought, Wow, that's a doorway."[33]

In her letters to the dancers, Rainer was exquisitely clear about what she wanted to keep control of and what she was willing to let go of. She was excited by what she was seeing: the outsize imagination and daring of her dancers, the unleashing of absurdity, and the possibility for spontaneous behavior, including rollicking laughter. In the documentary film about her, she describes her frustration: "It was like letting the horses out of the barn, but then sometimes I'd want to get the horses back in and they weren't about to get back in."[34]

Although she joked about it years later, Rainer was tormented by the uncertainties at the time:

> A more serious side of the process necessarily entailed a great deal of soul-searching and agonizing on my part about control and authority. It seemed that once one allowed the spontaneous expression and responses and opinions of performers to affect one's own creative process—in this respect the rehearsals were as crucial as the performances—then the die was cast: there was no turning back to the old hierarchy of director and directed. A moral imperative to form a more democratic social structure loomed as a logical consequence. What happened was both fascinating and painful, and not only for me, as I vacillated between opening up options and closing them down.[35]

Rainer's ultimate decision to pull back from leading the group was not only a moral imperative but also a feminist moment. Feminism is about challenging ingrained hierarchies. As a choreographer, she took charge not because she wanted power but because she wanted to make work. She was a harbinger of the seventies and eighties mode of downtown dance groups wherein the choreographer asked for input from the dancers.[36] She respected her dancers and perceived—accurately—that most of them were on the brink of coming into their own as dance artists. (Paxton, of course, had been her equal from as far back as the Bob Dunn classes.) According to Dilley, who credits Rainer with being the first choreographer to be interested in her as a creative artist rather than only as a performer, Rainer had demonstrated a kind of sisterly solidarity.[37]

If you think of supportive sisterhood as an element of feminism, if you think of equity between genders as another element, then Rainer had introduced the elements of feminism before it caught fire later in the seventies. She was generous enough to facilitate her dancers' growth in many ways. She wanted the group to be a democracy of adults. She presented female dancers onstage as thinking, speaking, assertive women. These were some of the reasons Sally Banes called Rainer a "proto-feminist."[38]

If a man were to step down under those circumstances, I think he would have closed shop completely. It seems to me that when a man has power or authority, he usually does everything he can to hold onto that power. But Rainer wasn't interested in power. She was interested in work—and teamwork.

■

It was only weeks after *CP-AD*'s official premiere at the Whitney that Rainer proposed, amid all her ambivalence, to step down as leader. She talked about it with David Gordon after a performance in Philadelphia. Gordon's rendition of how the name of the newly configured group came about is posted on his Archiveography website. (On this site, which carries a very personal account of his career up until 2017, Gordon talks about himself in the third person.) "Yvonne don't wanna be boss no more—she starts to say to us. No more Yvonne Rainer Dance Company—she says. David says—in Philly—after a Rodin Museum visit together—what about a new no dance company name? Like a rock band—he says. How about Grand Union? Like the super market—David says."[39]

The evolution of Rainer's group into Grand Union was confusing and disorienting. During the fall of 1970, three new people joined the group: Nancy (Green) Lewis, Lincoln Scott (aka Dong), and Trisha Brown. Apparently even the new people participated in the discussions of what the group would be. Lewis remembers those sessions: "We sat around a table in Yvonne's loft on Greene Street discussing what and how to do things ... to rehearse or not to rehearse ... to stay together or not.... The others were breaking loose from *Continuous Project*. They were ready to simply mess around ... with no one in charge. I recall it was kind of hard for Yvonne to relinquish."[40]

Douglas Dunn remembers the decision to keep going: "When Yvonne absented herself [as leader], our focus was lost. We tried to rehearse. People brought in improvisational structures, but resistance was obvious. We were not enjoying ourselves. We had to decide: did we want to perform? Yes. Did we want to rehearse? No. The obvious—if outrageous—answer was staring us in the face: to walk onto the stage with no preparation. No preparation, that is, other than who we were and what we, each of us, harmoniously or not, wanted to do next."[41]

Adding to the confusion was a performance at Rutgers on November 6, when Rainer's big group piece *WAR* (1970) was performed concurrently with Grand Union but in a different room. This arrangement, repeated later in the month at the Smithsonian Museum in Washington, D.C., reflected Rainer's interest in what art scholar Carrie Lambert-Beatty calls her split-screen or multichannel mode. Lambert-Beatty points out that "Rainer's aesthetic of concurrence meant that, no matter what you were watching, you were aware of what you were not seeing—of the thing coincident in time but distant in space."[42] Although confusing at the time, this "aesthetic of concurrence," which had clearly been in operation during "Connecticut Composite," became foundational to Grand Union.

Another incident, just a few weeks later, again blurred the line between Grand Union and Rainer's work. In a review of Grand Union at NYU's Loeb Student Center in December 1970, Anna Kisselgoff wrote in the *New York Times* that the program was performed by Rainer "and six members of her company, a group that calls itself the Grand Union."[43]

Deborah Jowitt reflected the confusion of this period in her review of GU's performance at NYU in January 1971, in which all GU members except Scott were present: "The Grand Union is Yvonne Rainer's gang. Now officially leaderless, Becky Arnold, Douglas Dunn, David Gordon, Nancy Green, Barbara Lloyd, Steve Paxton, Yvonne Rainer, Trisha Brown tear Rainerideas [sic] to tatters, worry them, put them together cockeyed, add their own things. Rainer says, 'It's not *my* company.' Hard to tell from her tone of voice whether she's relieved or regretful."[44]

Later that spring the confusion continued, partly because Rainer was still choreographing. When she created her India-inspired, faux-mythological *Grand Union Dreams*, which premiered in May 1971 at the Emanu-El Midtown YM-YWHA (now the 14th Street Y), she utilized Grand Union dancers in the choreography. By that time Trisha Brown was a member of Grand Union and did not expect to have to follow anyone's orders. According to Pat Catterson, a dancer/choreographer who was cast as a "mortal" while Brown and other GU members were playing "gods," Trisha's hackles were raised, and the room was filled with tension.[45]

About the other attempts to share and rehearse each other's choreography, Dilley recalls: "The outcome of it, in my memory is that nobody wanted to be anybody's dancer. We just didn't want to surrender any more, to anybody. It was out of that kind of irritation and frustration and bad behavior and acting out that we just said, OK next time, there are no rules, we'll just show up and begin."[46]

Gordon's version, as told succinctly to John Rockwell at the *New York Times*, was this: "We were not comfortable performing each other's work, but we were comfortable working together."[47]

In pulling back from being the director, Rainer ended one thing—Yvonne Rainer and Group—but she set something else in motion: the Grand Union.

INTERLUDE

THE PEOPLE'S FLAG SHOW

In the fall of 1970, a political protest was brewing against censorship. In the art world, the spurring incident was the arrest of a gallery owner who had shown the work of artist Steven Radich, which supposedly denigrated the American flag. During the late sixties and early seventies, the flag had come to represent US military aggressions against Vietnam and Cambodia. In solidarity with the gallery owner, a coalition of arts and justice groups held meetings to decide on a public action they could take. Among them were the Art Workers Coalition, New York Art Strike, and the Guerrilla Art Action Group. They formed the Independent Artists Flag Show Committee with an eye to inclusiveness, aiming for "equal representation, women and men, of Blacks, Puerto Ricans and Whites." The committee sent out a call for proposals for works of art that would reimagine the flag. More than 150 artists of all disciplines, including Jasper Johns, Leon Golub, and Kate Millett, responded to the call. The three organizers were Jon Hendricks, Faith Ringgold, and Jean Toche.[1]

Hendricks, who had been director of the Judson Gallery, knew that Reverend Howard Moody was a longtime supporter of the arts within community. When Hendricks approached Judson Church to host The People's Flag Show, Moody was already aware of the issue. He had written a long letter of support to a Long Island woman who had been arrested for hanging a flag upside down as a protest against the Vietnam War.[2] On Sunday, November 8, the day the exhibit opened, he gave a sermon defending the artists. He sent the written version to the *Village Voice*, which printed it. Here is the last paragraph: "The flag is a simple symbol, half a lie and half true; more of a promise than a reality. Its respect must be elicited, not commanded; the love of what it means must be given, never forced. When the flag becomes a fetish, we're on our way to a tyranny that all patriots must resist."[3]

After the Sunday service, the artists began arriving with their offerings. This was not a curated exhibit because the participating groups wanted it to be democratic and inclusive. The show officially opened at 1:00. According to Moody, Mayor John Lindsay sent staff to protect the artists.[4]

At 5:00, Hendricks and Toche, representing the Guerrilla Art Action Group and the Belgian Liberation Front, held a flag-burning ceremony in the Judson courtyard.[5] At 6:30, Rainer and four other dancers performed *Trio A with Flags*, which was followed by Symposium on Repression at 7:00. Participants in the symposium included Kate Millett (representing the Women's Liberation Movement), Leon Golub (Artists and Writers Protest Against the War in Vietnam), Cliff Joseph (Black Emergency Cultural Coalition), Abbie Hoffman, Faith Ringgold, and Michelle Wallace. Other groups included the Gay Liberation Front, Women Artists in Revolution, and the Black Panther Party.

Hendricks had invited Rainer to perform for the opening—the only time-based art of the exhibit—prompting her to come up with *Trio A with Flags*. The dancers, in the nude except for a flag tied around the neck like a long bib, performed *Trio A* (which is less than five minutes long) twice through. For Rainer, "[t]o combine the flag and nudity seemed a double-barreled attack on repression and censorship."[6] The dancers who joined her, flags flowing and flapping against bare skin, were Paxton, Dilley, and Gordon from CP-AD and two of the new Grand Union people: Nancy Lewis (then Green) and Lincoln Scott. This was not a Grand Union event per se, but Rainer relied on the GU dancers, most of whom knew the long, intricate sequence of *Trio A*. Becky Arnold, however, refused to perform on the grounds that she was proud to be an American and "proud of the flag."[7]

Feminist writer/sculptor/activist Kate Millett draped a flag over a toilet bowl (or perhaps stuffed it inside), titling the piece *The American Dream Goes to Pot*. This was the same year that her book *Sexual Politics* took the emerging feminist movement by storm, becoming a best seller.

Other offerings: Chaim Sprei assembled a flag out of soda cans. Sam Wiener made a box with mirrors that reflected rows upon rows of flag-draped coffins from Vietnam.[8] Activist Abbie Hoffman came to the People's Flag Show with the same flag shirt he wore when he was summoned to the US House Committee on Un-American Activities in 1967—for which he was arrested.[9] As he spoke at the symposium, he made a point of wiping his nose on the flaggish sleeve.[10]

The district attorney's office ordered the show to be closed, but the church defied the order and kept the exhibit open till the end of the week. Within two days, an unnamed person made a citizen's arrest of Moody and Al Carmines, but then never showed up for the court dates.

The organizers of the People's Flag Show were arrested by the district attorney's office, charged with flag desecration, and dubbed the Judson Three.[11] They were all old hands at activism. Jon Hendricks was a member of Fluxus; Faith Ringgold had previously protested the Museum of Modern Art's exclusion of black artists; and Jean Toche was active in the Guerrilla Art Action Group, along with Hendricks. They were arraigned and released on Friday, November 13, but the legal case lingered. On February 5, the Judson Three plus Abbie Hoffman and their supporters stood on a flag to protest being shut out of a press conference in the court. On May 14, 1971, the Judson Three were found guilty. Ten days later, they were given a choice of being fined $100 or spending thirty days in jail. They paid the fine and wrote a statement saying, "We have been convicted, but in fact it is this nation and these courts who are guilty." It went on to accuse the United States of "mutilating human beings" both in Southeast Asia and at home.[12] Faith Ringgold's poster for the People's Flag Show, a bold design suggesting a flag on a ruby red background, was included in an exhibit at the Phoenix Art Museum in 1996, causing some controversy, and was acquired by Dartmouth's Hood Museum of Art in 2013. "We felt in protesting a dishonorable war that we were acting as patriots," Millett said. "And also we felt we were defending the First Amendment, which is free speech, and to us that was precious and important."[13]

I have gone into some detail in order to give a sense of the political activism that Rainer and most of the Grand Union dancers felt comfortable with at the time.

■

Trio A with Flags is an elegant version of Rainer's signature work *Trio A*. Though I did not see it in 1970, I have seen it performed (and have produced it twice myself, both times at Judson Church) in various contexts over the years. When the audience is sitting on the same level as the dancers—that is, not on a proscenium stage—the potential titillation of their nudity is mitigated by the even, steady dynamic of the choreography. The ongoingness of the phrasing, the precision of the choreography, and the averted focus serve to make the dancers into a kind of sculpture, or objects, much like parts of *CP-AD*. Both the human body and the flag are drained of symbolism. Gender differences, so obvious in the nude, dimin-

Trio A with Flags,
by Yvonne Rainer.
Foreground: Lewis.
Screen grab from
film of The People's
Flag Show, Judson
Memorial Church,
1970. Courtesy
Special Collections,
New York University.

ish in importance because the women and men are doing the same movement with no gender affect. The dance is so calm and uninflected that the
audience is free to focus either on how the specific movements—loping,
tapping the foot, thrusting hips sideways, somersaulting—affect the flag,
or on what it means for an American flag to grace or graze the body as it
moves through odd coordinations.[14]

Watching the archival film, one can feel that the five dancers are all
swimming in the same stream, even though this was not officially a GU
event. Of course, in later performances they would all be swimming in
different directions—in pairs, groups, or alone. But it is also possible to
glean from this film a kind of loose aesthetic container, an awareness of the
breath and rhythms of their coworkers.

CHAPTER 4

A SHARED SENSIBILITY

All the Grand Union members had their own brand of charisma, each vivid in her or his own way. The downtown audience flocked to see them because we felt we knew them. Even their management agent, Mimi Johnson of Performing Artservices, called the group "personality driven."[1] If the term *personality* can be stretched to include compositional flair, responsiveness to others, and the powers of spontaneous decision making, I suppose that is true. But Grand Union members also had something in common, a shared ethos. So I decided to use this chapter to describe those commonalities and then, starting in the next chapter, branch out to their singularities.

They all had a downtown understatedness, a relaxed "everyday body," to quote Jowitt,[2] accented by a Zen-like readiness to pounce. This demeanor, this sly facade of "ordinary" (aka deadpan, which I get to later) had everything to do with the Cage/Cunningham milieu they were all steeped in. Dilley, Paxton, Douglas Dunn, and Valda Setterfield (Gordon's wife and muse, who guested with Grand Union in the 1976 series at La MaMa) had danced in the Cunningham company, and Lewis, Brown, and Rainer had studied with him.

Cunningham had already pried dance away from narrative, creating a new freedom in movement exploration. What Grand Union members understood was that this freedom didn't mean a free-for-all. It wasn't supposed to be like kids just let out of school. Paxton had observed that whenever Cage directed musicians unfamiliar with his work, the composer would sometimes have to explain that "freedom was to be used with dignity."[3]

Cunningham deployed chance operations specifically to divert possibilities away from personal taste. For instance, while working on

Merce Cunningham and John Cage, Westbeth Studio, 1972. Photo: James Klosty.

Summerspace (1958), he applied a chance procedure—probably tossing coins or throwing dice—to eight elements in each dancer's track, including direction, speed, level, duration, and shape. In doing so, he created physically challenging choreography involving many difficult jumps and turns, sudden falls, and abrupt changes of direction and speed.[4]

But there was a more spontaneous way that Cunningham embraced chance, and I saw it once onstage. I think it was at New York City Center, probably in the seventies. While Cunningham was dancing a solo, a baby in the audience let out a howl. An amused grin flitted across his face. He was "in the moment," easily absorbing the world around him—rather than shutting it out, as some performers do. That kind of chance element is what the Grand Union thrived on: being open enough to respond to an unexpected event.

Another common ability is that they could all dance in silence. They didn't *need* music in order to dance. In fact, much of their own work during that period was done in silence—or to sounds rather than music (although John Cage would not make that distinction). They considered music that "matched' the dance to be old school. Rainer even wrote a screed against music as part of a performance text in which she called herself an "unabashed music hater." Although she invented playful spellings like *muzak* and *moossick* in her hilarious diatribe, her main point was that dance should stand on its own.[5] Paxton made a dance in which he used an industrial vacuum cleaner to pump up a room-sized plastic bag and then emptied the air out, intending to record the noise for use in his nearly nude duet with Rainer, *Word Words* (1963). (The recording never did get used for its intended purpose.) Trisha Brown, too, was happy to make dances in silence in the early days—or sometimes to a tape of Forti making sounds, as in *Trillium* (1962), *Lightfall* (1963), and *Planes* (1968). When I was on tour with Trisha in the seventies and we gave lecture-demonstrations, someone would ask, "Why don't your dances have music?" She would counter with, "Do you need music when you are looking at sculpture in a gallery?"

This attitude toward music was of course influenced by Cage and Cunningham, who famously separated dance and music in the working process. It was left for each individual viewer to make aesthetic sense of their convergence. This is related to the Dadaist idea that the eye/ear/mind will create its own cohesion when faced with radically different elements. The Cage/Cunningham mode influenced Grand Union's method of choosing music, which was . . . haphazard. The dancers would bring in records to put on the record player; on tour, they would shop at a local store, buy a pile of records, and give them to the stage crew.[6] Then they might, during the performance, say to a stagehand, "Let's have music here," or motion to a crew member to put a record on, or, trusting even more to chance, allow the crew to choose which record to play when. Because Paxton, Dilley, and Douglas Dunn had all danced with Cunningham, they were familiar with the state of not knowing the music until the moment of performance.

Cunningham revolutionized choreographic use of space as well as of sound. He decentered the stage in much the same way that Jackson Pollock decentered the canvas, so the center of the space was no longer the most compelling spot. As mentioned in chapter 1, Cunningham had proposed in his 1957 lecture on Halprin's deck that the entire performance space could be activated. The audience had to choose where to focus in this new "allover" space (to use a term often applied to Pollock). Another point Cunningham made in that lecture is that it was not necessary to have a single front.[7] In many Grand Union performances, the audience sat in an arc, a circle, or a square surrounding the dancers. These two issues contributed to the democratization of the space, which could affect the way the audience experienced the performance. Barbara Dilley, while watching the archival tapes of the LoGiudice Gallery performances (in which the audience sat on three sides), noticed, "One person looks right, the person beside her is gazing left. There's no proscenium focus here, but rather a three-ring circus."[8]

From Cunningham, they also learned to have a steadiness in phrasing. None of the dramatic Martha Graham–type dynamics or the noble arcs of Doris Humphrey for them. (Trisha once said to me, "I don't know why Martha Graham shoots her wad on every movement." She was talking about the lack of subtlety, the predictability, and what she perceived as false urgency.) Cunningham's sense of timing had an Eastern tinge to it; his phrasing seemed to be ongoing rather than building toward a climax. That ongoingness could have been influenced by Cage's interest in Zen. But it also reflected Cunningham's locating the choreographic impetus in "the appetite for dancing" rather than the desire to tell stories.[9]

Related to this aesthetic was the deadpan, or what Sally Sommer called the "calm face,"[10] which was natural to all GU members. Give nothing away, dramatize nothing. This relaxed expression goes back to Judson Dance Theater. As Paxton wrote when looking back, "there seemed to be some unspoken performance attitude at Judson which called for a deadpan façade." He felt they were searching for a new performance demeanor to match the new choreographic approach in which performers could make choices, and that the solution was to be absorbed in the process. "So we tended to inhabit movement," he concluded, "but not animate it."[11]

■

The classic deadpan can be construed as being influenced by an African American aesthetic. Dancer/scholar Brenda Dixon Gottschild calls this kind of facial composure "the mask of the cool."[12] In her landmark book, *Digging the Africanist Presence in American Performance,* she enumerates the ways that black culture has affected contemporary dance and performance. She doesn't deny the influences of Dada and Bauhaus from Europe, or Zen and martial arts from Asia, but she contends that the Africanist influence (meaning African American as well as African diasporan) has been overlooked. When she focuses on postmodern dance, she claims that "the Africanist presence in postmodernism is a subliminal but driving force."[13] To be specific, she writes, "The coolness, relaxation, looseness, and laid-back energy; the radical juxtaposition of ostensibly contrary elements; the irony and double entendre of verbal and physical gesture; the dialogic relationship between performer and audience—all are integral elements in Africanist arts and lifestyle that are woven into the fabric of our society."[14] Dixon Gottschild identifies Rainer, Gordon, Brown, Dunn, and Paxton as having absorbed some of these qualities.[15] She points out that Contact Improvisation, which emerged from Grand Union, adopted the lingo of black jazz, using the term *jam* for their sessions. When Dixon Gottschild identifies a "cool, mellow state that can be termed 'flow,'" it sounds like a pretty good description of Grand Union's aesthetic. The word "cool" can be used by many people to express many qualities, but I think the following spontaneous remark, taken broadly, could be said to support Dixon Gottschild's point of view: When I gave a presentation on Grand Union showing archival videos at the Seattle Festival of Dance Improvisation in 2018, one woman in the audience blurted out, "Did they know how cool they were?"

Of course all artists draw from a variety of sources. The attraction of white artists during that period to black culture is nicely described by producer/curator Robyn Brentano: "The white avant-garde's interest in and appreciation of African-American dance, music, visual art, and literary idioms, style, and values was motivated by a complex mixture of genuine respect for and appreciation of African-American artistic achievements, a romanticization of blacks that reinforced certain racial stereotypes, and a sense of a shared antibourgeois stance."[16] I think this stew of responses reflects both conscious and unconscious attitudes.

■

Some of the GU dancers, like many in the Cunningham/Cage milieu, were on the rebound from Martha Graham's dominating aesthetic. No one discredited Graham as the pioneering American artist who brought modernism to dance. But these young dancers wanted to go their own way. As mentioned, Halprin had done battle with the Graham theatricality in the mid-fifties. Not much later, Rainer also came up against the Graham aesthetic. At first she was overwhelmed by this icon's artistic and psychological force but later came to prefer Cunningham's subtler style, or what she called his "implicit humanity."[17] The aversion to Graham's style for those who favored Cunningham at the time was perhaps best expressed by Carolyn Brown. She wrote that the classes at the Graham school "seemed to demand a kind of emotional hype that felt dishonest, extraneous, external, and artificial—unrelated to my understanding of Dance (with a capital 'D')."[18]

Some had also done battle with Louis Horst, Graham's mentor, music director, and one-time lover. He had been determined to give shape to the new twentieth-century dance by teaching musical forms as choreographic forms. Horst tried (some say heroically) to steer modern dance away from the ballet lexicon as well as from the too-vague "interpretive" dance.[19] But Horst himself became quite rigid in his teaching. He insisted on the A-B-A format and other musical structures to preserve theatrical cohesiveness. He treated up-and-comers like Trisha Brown and David Gordon with disdain. In a 1973 feature article in *Dance Magazine*, Robb Baker asked both Gordon and Brown about their experiences with Horst at American Dance Festival, which was hosted by Connecticut College during the fifties and sixties. "He made us work in prescribed forms," Gordon complained. Gordon didn't exactly rebel, but he interpreted the definition of a duet with such wide latitude that Horst never called on him again.[20] Brown said he was "unforgiving" about her process and was clearly dismissive of improvisation.[21] When it came time for Horst and a panel of ADF instructors to decide if her solo *Trillium* (1962) was to be included in the final concert, they voted No. (In fact, the students protested the panel's decision and created quite a stir that summer of 1962.)[22] She felt that Horst relied too heavily on musical forms in his assignments. Bob Dunn's class, on the other hand, embraced a plurality of methods, emphasizing process over product—a very sixties philosophy. His approach was both a relief and a stimulation for Gordon and Brown.

■

Dilley had this to say about the Grand Union performers' familiarity with each other as an ensemble:

> We had some kind of subterranean associations that we all
> shared, either from our past history with one another or the fact
> that we were all living in SoHo at the same time. We shared a

kind of collective unconscious ... a mutual vocabulary—psychic vocabulary, physical vocabulary, performative vocabulary, intellectual vocabulary. We were in and out of one another's worlds for many years—not only in the Grand Union but we were in each other's performances, Cunningham and Cage, and then there was Judson. Some people had stronger roots in Judson than I did. But we shared this atmosphere, this collective environment.... It was, for me, a big part of how I navigated everything.[23]

One of the hallmarks of this shared vocabulary was patience, a restraint that balanced out the moments of wild abandon. In the 1975 Guthrie performance at Walker Art Center, Brown began the evening by treading softly and slowly around the edge of the space. Eventually Gordon joined in, mirroring her exact angles as she shifted her weight, barely traveling. She kept her arms folded above the waist, and his hands were stuffed in his pockets. But the body angles were absolutely parallel. For almost twenty minutes this doubling was the main thing happening. Then Dilley joined Brown and Gordon, also mirroring the slow-change angles, but with her hands clasped behind her. Gradually the three started reaching out and making contact, but before that it was like a walking meditation with a steadily shifting sense of direction. The moment they collided with Paxton laying down a swath of silk, the performance took off. But that encounter wouldn't have had an impact if the long period of restraint hadn't preceded it.

■

A pacifist air pervaded Grand Union's concerts. The nonviolent, antiwar protests set the tone of the day, and the dancers were involved in some of those actions. Dilley joined the rough-hewn, peace-loving Bread and Puppet Theater for one of the protest marches down Fifth Avenue.[24] Rainer, along with Douglas Dunn and Sara Rudner, led a solemn peace march through the streets of SoHo to protest the invasion of Cambodia.[25] An Eastern influence, too, wafted in from yoga, meditation, and martial arts forms like tai chi and aikido. When compared with the current craze for aggressiveness in dance performances, Grand Union seems an oasis of calm. The group had plenty of edginess, but they expressed it without resorting to any kind of physical violence.

GU at 112 Greene Street, 1972. From left: Paxton, Lewis, Rainer, Gordon.
Photo: Babette Mangolte.

■

Downtown dancers were becoming very involved in body awareness.
Performing in lofts and churches, they were focusing on the space
in front of them, not "projecting" to the balconies. Those "everyday
bodies" were consciously relaxed; they could let go of the strenuous-
ness that is built into dance training. The label "somatic practice" came
later, but at the time Elaine Summers, who had been one of the first
interdisciplinary artists at Judson, was developing "kinetic awareness." This technique, also known as the "great ball work," uses different sized rubber balls to release unnecessary tension. Influenced by
pioneering somatic practitioners like Charlotte Selver, Carola Speads,
and Mabel Elsworth Todd, she was able to slow down and become
conscious of muscle usage to avoid pain. Summers attributes some
of the development of kinetic awareness to the Judson aesthetic of
more relaxed everyday movement.[26] It was a mutual exchange: both
Brown and Gordon (and later, Douglas Dunn as well) studied with

Summers. Rainer and Lewis studied briefly with June Ekman, who, after spending years in the late fifties on Halprin's deck, immersed herself in Alexander technique, which repatterns movement habits to promote ease of motion. (Halprin is an acknowledged pioneer of somatic practice, starting in the sixties.) Paxton was a serious student of aikido, a form of Asian martial art that teaches how to soften the body while tumbling or responding to aggression.

Banes points out that the dancers' brand of somatic practice was part of a larger zeitgeist of body consciousness of the period, partly fueled by Zen studies and psychedelic drugs. Body/mind therapies like Gestalt, Rolfing, Reichian therapy, and encounter groups that were popular at Esalen Institute in Big Sur, California (where Halprin had given workshops), infiltrated the mainstream. "[T]he bodies created by the early sixties avant-garde included a conscious body that imbued corporeal experience with metaphysical significance, uniting head and body, mind and gut."[27]

■

Without any lessons in theater improvisation, all Grand Union members instinctively understood the edict of comedy improv to say "Yes, and." Whatever was presented by one's fellow performers, you accept it and take it from there. They each had the physical and emotional flexibility to veer off into a fellow improviser's gambit and leave their own exploration behind. Dilley called it "opening up your receptors."[28] This relates to the communal sense I spoke of earlier, the willingness to swim in the same waters as another dancer. The GU members' sense of community meant unwavering support for each other in performance. They each could be leader or follower, active or passive, foreground or background. As Paxton has written, "[F]ollowing or allowing oneself to lead is each member's continual responsibility."[29]

I mentioned radical juxtaposition earlier as a method of Rainer's while making *Continuous Project—Altered Daily*. This possibility of coexisting opposites was part of the awareness of all the GU dancers. Two people can be involved in a tender, slow-motion duet while a third is yelling like a truck driver. The two modes seem at first to have nothing to do with each other. But maybe they do, or maybe they could. According to the Dadaist concept, each viewer makes sense of the collision in her or his own way.

INTERLUDE

RICHARD NONAS'S MEMORY

Richard Nonas, an internationally known sculptor, was part of 112 Greene Street and also assisted Trisha Brown in both *Man Walking Down the Side of a Building* (1970) and *Walking on the Walls* (1971). When I emailed him about this book, he immediately sent the following message:

> I loved the Grand Union. Loved their wild and only semi-controlled interactions *because* I already knew their own individual work. Loved, I mean, the way they stroked and challenged each other. Loved the constant pushing and pulling and teasing while being themselves both pushed and pulled and teased; and acknowledged. Loved the way they trusted and tested each other. The way they surprised each other. And then laughed. They (and we watching) were puppies tumbling, sliding and sometimes hiding in a pet-store window—but the youngest and most curious puppies I could imagine, investigating our own shared world. What a show it was—and what a world.[1]

PART II The Gifts They Brought

In this section I describe the physical and expressive gifts that each dancer brought to Grand Union. I am not including their abilities as choreographers, though obviously those are huge in almost every case. Rather, I am focusing on who they were as performers/improvisers at the time of Grand Union. Each one had a searing uniqueness that is a challenge to describe. I start each mini-profile with a single paragraph about that person's dancing *as I remember it* in the seventies, a snapshot of the dancer in motion. Then I go on to give a bit of background and describe the dancer's abilities that relate to Grand Union. In order to provide a sense of immediacy—to give you the very present sense that I have while I call the dancers to mind—I have put each initial paragraph in the "literary" present tense. Midway through each mini-profile you may notice that I drop the convention of referring to the artist by surname and start using the more casual first name. This is for two reasons: first, I want you to get to know them each in a more familiar way, and second, in the (white) modern dance tradition (as opposed to ballet), we call even the most respected artists by first names: it's Isadora, Martha, Merce, Paul, and Trisha. In the black tradition, it's Miss Dunham and Mr. Ailey. I don't know why these differences occur, but it's been that way for generations.

CHAPTER 5

BARBARA DILLEY

*With a sweet face and a beautifully unforced quality in her
dancing, Barbara Dilley is a quietly magnetic force. Small in
stature, her presence is contemplative yet captivating. She may
begin an evening with simple walking, stretching, or spinning,
with the faith that a steady motion will grow into something larger.
Though she can stay with a kinetic investigation for so long that
it becomes a meditation, she can just as easily glide into another
person's scenario. Her serene, velvety dancing is rooted in the
downtown aesthetic of modest and minimal, but she readily crosses
into more rambunctious terrain. Grounded yet somehow lofty, she
can embody a range of qualities from task-like to mystical.*

Barbara Dilley (born 1938) grew up in a family that moved around.
Born in Chicago, she also lived in Pittsburgh; Barrington, Illinois;
Darien, Connecticut; and Princeton, New Jersey. It was in this last
city that she started taking ballet lessons with Audrey Estee (who also
taught Douglas Dunn a few years later.) For Dilley, dance was a refuge
from always being the new kid at school.[1] After high school she spent
a summer at Jacob's Pillow, where she studied with Ted Shawn, Myra
Kinch, Margaret Craske, and "ethnic dance" specialists Carola Goya
and Matteo. She went on to Mount Holyoke, where she took Graham
technique with Helen Priest Rogers, who steered her to a summer
at American Dance Festival at Connecticut College. There, in 1960,
she was drawn to Merce Cunningham's work. "I liked silence, liked
Merce's physicality."[2] Decades later she said, "Nothing compares to
his piercing clarity and large moving presence and to his passion for
making stuff up."[3]

Rainforest (1968), by Merce Cunningham. From left: Cunningham, Dilley, Albert Reid. Décor of "Silver Clouds" by Andy Warhol. Photo: Oscar Bailey, courtesy of the Merce Cunningham Trust, all rights reserved.

After arriving in New York City that fall, she danced briefly with the Tamiris-Nagrin Dance Company.[4] She studied with ballet greats Alfredo Corvino and Anatole Vilzak as well as with James Waring and Aileen Passloff.[5] She savored meeting dancers "living on the other side of convention."[6]

In 1961 she married Lew Lloyd, whom she had met five years earlier in New Jersey, when she was cast in a local play that he was stage managing. (Lew went on to become business manager of the Cunningham company.) Soon after giving birth to their son, Benjamin, in 1962, she joined Cunningham's company in 1963 and continued until 1968. The first pieces she performed were *Story* and *Field Dances*, both of which made more use of indeterminacy than was usual in the Cunningham repertoire. Cunningham archivist David Vaughan surmised that this sudden (and fleeting) openness to greater choice for dancers was influenced by the young dancers of Judson Dance Theater.[7]

Dilley had already dipped into improvisational sessions here and there. In a studio with Forti and Brown she experienced some of Halprin's basic structures;[8] in Judson Dance Theater Concert #14, the "improvisation" concert, she danced in Deborah Hay's piece.[9] Her own choreography after leaving the Cunningham company involved improvisation, film, or props like candles.[10] She also made herself available for other performances with a measure of indeterminacy. In one of Claes Oldenburg's *Ray Gun* happenings (ca. 1962), she walked across a wooden plank suspended between two ladders—her pregnant belly covered in bright pink.[11] In Bill Davis's *Field* (1963) at Judson, she and Davis wore belts attached to transistor radios tuned to different stations.[12] For Paxton's *Afternoon (A Forest Concert)* (1963), she danced on moist dirt near a tree trunk wrapped in camouflage and later played in a clearing with another cast member, her two-year-old son, Benjamin Lloyd.[13]

But CP-AD was the first time she felt she had agency while improvising in performance. "It was beginning to seep in, the whole idea of letting each performer be able to make decisions in the performance environment."[14] She found she enjoyed this form of dance making, so she pushed for Rainer to invite more contributions from the dancers. According to Rainer, it was Dilley who kept egging her on to let the dancers have more input.[15]

Over time, Dilley developed an exquisite awareness of the dualities of improvisation: individual versus group, public versus private, consciousness versus subconsciousness. She felt the porousness of those binaries. In a 1975 interview she said, "[I]n improvisation you cross back and forth on that bridge between your consciousness and your unconscious energy."[16]

Dilley wanted dance to be more democratic and less elitist. Part of being democratic, along the lines of the Cage/Dunn definition, was the embrace of the "ordinary." She learned that lesson well and made the ordinary resonate:

> [Y]ou take something that's very ordinary and you distort it
> very slightly. Slightly through time or through absurdity or
> through gesture that doesn't necessarily go with what you're
> saying. And it becomes readable as a much larger thing. It
> starts reverberating.... You learn through experience when
> you are feeling a certain way which generates that possibility.
> That vibration.... It's not planned or intended, but it suddenly
> happens. And you're aware of it and you go with it. And you

support it because its rich. It's not only rich to do but it's rich to be around it."[17]

"To be around it" means to me that Dilley was generous with her attention. She was a good collaborator and supported her colleagues' decisions in intelligent, fertile ways. Gordon has said that Barbara "was extraordinary at picking up on someone's material and reinforcing it by lending her body and her mind to the action, stretching the ideas as well as following them." In fact, her support early on helped Gordon to arrive at a turning point. Said Gordon, "I began to realize my material by watching her participation in it."[18]

One of the gifts that she brought from her work with Cunningham was her sensitivity to space. "Space is this aliveness that vibrates every time the curtain goes up." While contemplating a 1963 photo of the Cunningham company in *Suite for Five*, she writes, "We are alone and together in a deep full way."[19] Clearly, she felt that Grand Union continued this sensibility. She often used the term *tribe* to describe the group.

Barbara was highly attuned to feelings and sensations, which could perhaps be traced to being treated for polio as a child. At the age of five, she was quarantined for a month in an isolated hospital room, which her parents were not allowed to enter. She had to hold back her tears from pain and loneliness.[20] As a dancer/thinker, she was psychologically probing, questioning what she wanted from performance. She wanted to be open to the imagination but didn't want to get addicted to pleasing the audience. "In the Grand Union ... we're sort of throwing open the door to everything. Anything that occurred, I could make myself into a fool or a demon or a floozy or a queen ... you had a lot of possibilities."[21]

One of those possibilities was a kind of "subtlety and wanting to create an atmosphere where that subtlety can go on. And where I can then witness my own failures again."[22] That interiority blossomed into spirituality when she followed her curiosity to Naropa University in Colorado, bringing mind and body together through the teachings of Tibetan Buddhist Chögyam Trungpa Rinpoche. It was at Naropa that she formulated her Contemplative Dance Practice in 1974. But one can see in the LoGiudice tapes that she is already zeroing in on contemplative actions like spinning.

For Barbara, spirituality is bound together with an almost romantic view of improvisation: "You can't court it.... But you are, in a way, courting a lover ... you're trying to meet the unknown as a lover, in a curious way. And you're trying to be ... receptive so that whatever drops into your body at that moment, you can completely surrender to that image.... Art or any creative activity is a descending—that's sort of spiritual perhaps—but a descending of something through you.[23]

Whatever is "descending" is spiritual, perhaps in its very impermanence. It descends into the body, and the body becomes a spiritual vessel. The movement descends "through" you, not to be kept by you. This is one of the unwritten foundational ideas of the Grand Union that was so well intuited by Barbara. While others may have focused on the individual freedom or the challenge to be in the moment, she spoke of GU as "teaching impermanence.... You have to take that feeling and that kind of a performance and that expectation falling to dust."[24]

It was not easy for Barbara to let go of a scenario, particularly when another dancer barged in on her carefully constructed character or image. But she realized that "one must let the ego wall down to let the energy flow out into possibility."[25] Her recognition and eventual mastery of this impermanence is a gift she brought to Grand Union.

Barbara and John Cage shared an interest in Buddhism that went back to the early sixties. During the Cunningham company tours of 1963 and 1964, she had conversations with Cage on long bus rides and car rides: "John was so conversational and engaged, always. Many of his lectures as we toured were philosophical and spiritual in that open hearted, fresh way of his. As I become more immersed in the study and practice of Buddhism, I recognized how much John imparted in his lectures etc., and how it had influenced me. It was an American Dharma that he unfolded and I, too, felt that I wanted to transmit this in classes."[26]

She had a deep appreciation for Cage's philosophy of connecting art and life. When he autographed her copy of *Silence*, he added his definitions of the four aims of Hindu life in Sanskrit: "Artha = Goal, Kama = Pleasure, Dharma = Judgment, Moksha = Liberation."[27] Barbara treasures her connection with him, artistic and spiritual. For her, the concept of dharma art as that which springs from "the appreciation of things as they are"[28] is a close cousin to John Cage and silence.

CHAPTER 6

DOUGLAS DUNN

There is nothing easy or breezy about Douglas Dunn's dancing.
He's pulled up and rigorous, not at all willowy or bendy in the
upper body. His limbs extend boldly into space more than those
of the others of Grand Union, who tend to have the released flow
of the downtown aesthetic. Still connected to the stretched, etched
lines of the Cunningham vocabulary, he challenges himself with
technically difficult movement. He provides a certain muscularity
and determination, never staying within his comfort zone. The
motivating force seems to be curiosity. On his face you can read
intense concentration as though he's steadily plowing through
some issues while dancing. And yet he can also take on a silly or
bawdy character that temporarily blots out his usual introspective
quality.

Douglas Dunn (born 1942) came to CP-AD as a young, inexperienced
dancer. He wasn't fighting the artistic powers that be—Graham,
Humphrey, Horst—simply because he didn't know about them. At
twenty-six, he found an affinity with Rainer's work because of his athletic background. "I walked right in the middle of it. I was dancing in
Grand Union with no background, no axes to grind."[1]

Growing up in the hills outside of Palo Alto, California, he knew
how to keep himself occupied. "I invented games for myself because
I had no playmates. So I was improvising already. The idea of improvising was sort of simple to me: you go and you do what you want."[2]
That faith in translating desire into action, coupled with his ability to
explore on his own, went a long way in Grand Union. Whenever he
was stranded in a situation, he always found something to arouse his

interest. He was present at all moments, not just when he thought he was part of something significant. While others waited for an action to coalesce, he always kept his dancing going. Dancing wasn't just a holding pattern, a way station on the path to the next big moment. It wasn't nothing waiting to become something. It was a constant exploration.

Dunn's inner resource of finding focus on his own was an anchor for Grand Union. One time in the 1975 Walker lobby performance, when isolated solos and duets were scattered around the space, he started extending his leg along the floor and edging his toes under a carpet—a small movement that evolved into a full-blown dance sequence.

In the early seventies, Dunn was at a point in his life where he was happy to find a more physical, less verbal field of activity. He had majored in art history at Princeton and spent three years teaching Spanish at a high school. "[M]y life had been much too thought-oriented up to that time, and I was expanding into this intuitive world of dance. It was so satisfying. I didn't want to talk."[3] One can see evidence of this aversion in his nearly monosyllabic answers to Banes's questions about the Grand Union experience at the end of *Terpsichore in Sneakers*. As he later wrote, "[O]ne of the beauties of dancing is silence."[4] It took awhile before he could utilize his remarkable verbal acuity in Grand Union performances.

Dunn could "play" himself, but he could just as easily play a character. I remember when he dressed as a man of the cloth at NYU, and I've read about when he dressed as a Tin Woodsman at UCLA.[5] One time at LoGiudice, he wore a bonnet that gave him a kooky look, like a homeless man who had donned the only head covering he could find. Or maybe he was the "nervous clown," an epithet he used to describe a character he sometimes fell into (and that character became more prevalent in the older Douglas Dunn of recent years).[6] As a dancer/researcher, he was always implicitly asking: Who am I in this environment?

Having spent a lot of time outdoors as a kid, Dunn could envision bringing nature into the theater. In 1975 he collected bags of leaves from their host's backyard in Minneapolis and spread them around the Walker Art Center lobby.

He was open to the space and the people around him. From his time in GU, he developed a taste for the absurd. He describes a performance in Rome's 1974 Contemporanea Festival in a parking lot, where he found a ball the size of a tennis ball. "I put it in my mouth and did a monologue," he said, demonstrating how muffled and obstructed a foreign language might sound. "I never would have thought of doing that without the context of all these people doing very strange things all the time. So it did stimulate characters in me that I didn't know I had available."[7]

In the realm of character, he could be quite loud, boisterous, and even crude. During the 1975 Guthrie performance Gordon cast him as a contestant in a TV show. As a kind of sophomoric frat guy named "Marvin," he became pushy ("Let's get on with this show") and yelled to Dilley to pump the crowd. In the same performance, he colluded with Gordon in talking about how to pick up women. They did it in a funny, absurdist way, but in that particular scene, he was not the thoughtful Douglas Dunn that most of us know.

Douglas rose to the greatest challenge of Grand Union: to make something out of nothing. "The fun for me was to walk in just blank, just completely blank, and to make oneself available to different degrees with other people about what would happen."[8]

He had to build up his confidence, and his confidence would be tested many times. In one skit at the Walker Art Center, in which Gordon had taken on the role of father to Dunn as the son, the father called his son "awfully rotten" and sang, "I can't stand your guts." This was all in character of course, but there was always a fine line in Grand Union between playing and really meaning it. But Douglas gave it right back to David: "And I don't like your sloppy sentimental singing." All during this sketch Douglas kept revolving around himself on the other side of a freestanding door. There was something reassuring about that physical containment and continuity.

An existential air came through whether Douglas was moving or speaking. His dancing always looked so deliberate, but underneath, as mentioned, questions were percolating. One of the questions for him was how to get to the place where instinct reigns. He felt that the nonverbal aspect of dance would lead to a deeper wellspring of behavior.

As we saw in chapter 2 on SoHo, Douglas could think big in terms of space. For a Grand Union performance at Laura Dean's loft in April 1971, during the period when the group was still in flux, he decided

Douglas Dunn in GU performance, lobby of Walker Art Center, 1975.
Photo: Boyd Hagen, courtesy Walker Art Center.

to build a bridge during the performance. So he and a non-GU friend set about assembling it, hammering and drilling. He knew he was being "obtrusive and noisy," and he noticed that the other dancers "all stopped performing and watched us." When they were done building, he and his friend walked on top of the bridge and smoked a cigarette.[9]

Although he could carry off a grandiose feat like bridge building, his manner was completely unpretentious. In 1990, when he was asked what his idea of a masterpiece was for the publication *Dance Ink*, he replied, "No such thing, only moments when the eye soothes, alters, or renews."[10]

Looking back, Douglas stands by his comment to Sally Banes that Grand Union represented a possible ideal world. His definition of a true democracy is when people are "allowed to try to realize their individuality completely, but in relation to other people, necessarily."[11] His positive outlook was shared with many at that time. "I felt ... a kind of ... political optimism about the direction of the country and what was possible. We actually seemed to have stopped the war [in Vietnam]; I felt part of that in a sense, and that our art—dance—was some kind of relevant material in the culture."[12]

CHAPTER 7

DAVID GORDON

*Forthright in movement, quick-witted in words, David Gordon
is the smart, funny boy next door. Though he moves with fluency
and efficiency, he doesn't look like a highly trained dancer. With
thick black hair, a strong body, and a readiness to address the
audience, he can seem more like an actor than a dancer. He
easily takes up the mic, often controlling the stage action with
his ad hoc, absurdist situation comedies. He is quick to catch
us off guard, spin an outlandish yarn, or change the way we see
a mundane object. He's sly, sassy, sardonic, with a comedian's
sense of timing and a playwright's verbal command. And when a
boyish excitement comes over him, he can whip up a whirlwind of
rollicking energy.*

David Gordon (born 1936) grew up on the Lower East Side, in the
bosom of what he calls a "loving battling—claustrophobic—Jewish
family."[1] He listened to *Bob and Ray* and *Let's Pretend* on the radio
and went to the weekly double feature at the local movie house. When
television came in, he watched comedy shows like *Milton Berle* and
Sid Caesar & Imogene Coca: Your Show of Shows. He also borrowed
about eight books a week from the local library, which surely contributed to his outsized verbal ability. As a teenager he wrote stories
and illustrated them for the school magazine, winning the school art
medal at graduation. At Brooklyn College, he studied with some of
the major artists of the day[2] and developed an interest in photography. His New York/Yiddish accent was so strong that he was sent
to a speech clinic. He followed one girl to the modern dance club and
another to the theater department, where he was instantly cast as the

GU in NYC Dance Marathon, 14th Street Y, 1971. From left: Gordon, Rainer. Visible in the audience are Chilean pianist and artist Fernando Torm, wearing boots, and Richard Nonas, leaning on radiator. Photo: Susan Horwitz, courtesy Douglas Dunn.

lead in a play he did not audition for. The director must have thought he was perfect for the soulful witch boy in *Dark of the Moon*.

While hanging out in Washington Square Park in 1957, he happened to meet the choreographer James Waring. Assuming Gordon was—or should be—a dancer, Waring invited him to a rehearsal. There Gordon met the newly arrived British dancer Valda Setterfield, and the rest is history: the two married the following year and have been working together ever since. Gordon created his first duet with Setterfield, *Mama Goes Where Papa Goes* (1960), and performed it on a program of Waring's students at the Living Theatre. He used a chance method in the process: "[t]earing up pieces of paper and tossing them into a hat."[3]

Through Waring, Gordon gained exposure to a motley assortment of artists: Cocteau, Buñuel, Laurel and Hardy, Fanny Brice, Balanchine, Kurt Schwitters, Morton Feldman, Philip Guston, Robert Rauschenberg, Jasper Johns, Maria Tallchief, Groucho Marx. And, Waring advised, "You must see Yvonne Rainer's *Ordinary Dance*; it is extraordinary."[4]

Also eclectic were Waring's costumes. Gordon described getting outfitted for the first piece of Waring's he was in: "All the dancers wore costumes designed by separate artists. Nobody knew what anybody else was wearing and I didn't know what I was wearing at all until the day of performance when Paul Taylor (who Jimmy called Pete) placed half spheres on my shoulders and back and chest and on my head and painted my crotch green through my tights."[5]

But there was another strong influence when it came to costumes. Gordon's day job was dressing windows for Azuma stores, which sold Japanese lanterns and other furnishings. "I began to travel regularly to Japan w/Sato brother—of Azuma stores—stayed in hotels—'yukatas'—cotton sleeping kimonos provided—took 'em home. Also—looked for Japanese paraphernalia—to sell in Azuma stores as exotica—visited street mkts—found piles—small mtns—of second-hand kimonos—including yukatas—persuaded Azuma to buy n' sell 'em—also bought 'em as gifts for family & friends."[6]

His access to what was considered exotic costumes and the way he moved in them—often slowing down—changed not only his own performance but also sometimes the whole feeling in the room. In one of the 1975 La MaMa performances, while Gordon wore a dark robe that made him appear like a "mournful Bedouin,"[7] at one moment all six dancers formed a linear tableau that transported us to some ancient world. Paxton asked for "my song," which turned out to be a soupy instrumental version of "Go Down Moses." The dancers stood in a row, holding hands, looking like six sorrowful nomads about to traverse the desert. They seemed to take on the weight of history and the mysteriousness of a faraway culture. Then, when the song changed to a sped-up version of "Look Away, Dixie Land," the tableau erupted into crazy energy, with everyone dashing around in circles.

Although Gordon's fantasies had the power to gather others into his world, you always knew that the person inside the getup was David Gordon. He was always himself no matter how outlandish the outfit. He could pretend without pretentiousness. As a young man, "I chewed on theater and television and film and literature and the things that interested me personally, none of which I thought about in relation to anything called 'art.'"[8]

When Waring, then Rainer, then Brown, came into his life, he began to recognize that he was participating in making art. "Jimmy taught me about art and developed my taste, but I didn't begin to understand about making work until later, when I performed with Yvonne Rainer. From her I found out what it is to be an artist—a person who makes choices and stands behind them. Then, from working with Trisha Brown in the Grand Union, I learned how to edit, how to boil a thing down to its essence."[9]

He had already encountered movies by W. C. Fields and the Bob Hope/Bing Crosby team in which they make side comments directly toward the camera. He later saw Mike Nichols and Elaine May, who staged an argument so realistically—including his hitting her—that David gasped to see them smile and bow afterward. He learned that "somehow a performance could be disrupted in a way which allows you to ... have what seems like a drama and then you can undercut the entire drama which turns it into a surreal drama or a comedy."[10] (This kind of deceiving the audience also tied in with David's fondness for trompe l'oeil, which he learned about in a commercial art course in Brooklyn College taught by Ivan Chermayeff.)[11]

His ability to take a nearby object and transform it into something else he attributes to studying art at Brooklyn College: "My training had very little to do with drawing a line from here to there. ... and the courses were much more concerned with looking around you. Instead of seeing material as something used only for self-expression, I become aware of material itself and of how I could manipulate it and change its reality."[12]

Looking around in one's environment led to the use of found objects. The bloody lab coat Gordon wore for *Mannequin Dance* (1962) was given him by an artist friend who taught biology.[13] Another kind of found object served as a source for *Sleep Walking* (1971), which he made when Rainer, on her way to India, asked him to keep a group of her students occupied. He brought to these students what he had been watching: "[I]n the streets of New York at that time are a lot of addicts, and they are nodding out in the street.... In the night because I'm not sleeping very well, I take a walk and there are these junkies nodding out ... and they are so far off balance and they don't fall. So I start practicing to see if I can do what they do. How far off balance can I be with my eyes closed without falling over? And reaching for something that's down there, inevitably some piece of dope that they were after, which they never get."[14]

David's antennae were up when he visited St. Vincent's Hospital, where Steve was recovering from an operation. The frail old man who shared the room with Steve would periodically slip downward. He would moan, "Oh god, I'm slipping" until a nurse came to prop him up in his chair. He would slip, moan, and be rescued again. That memory lingered with David, not only for its human vulnerability but also for its repetition. It found its way into Grand Union performances, providing a breakthrough for David, who up until then was just repeating variations of Rainer's *Trio A* in GU performances.

The most obvious and constant gift he brought to Grand Union was his quick-witted, off-the-cuff narrative making. The litany of questions he posed to Barbara in the beginning of the 1974 Iowa performance was a literary accomplishment in its quick associations, fantasies, and word play. (I provide snippets of this passage in chapter 19.) Another example is the changing fortunes of the bed-wetting orphan, which I refer to in the next interlude.

He also had a gift for physical comedy. In the La MaMa performance in 1976, he had gotten caught between two very agile "leaders," Barbara and Douglas. He lurched and flipped and toppled while trying to imitate Barbara's smooth movements and Douglas's sturdy positions. If you didn't already know that Laurel and Hardy were two of David's heroes, you could guess it by watching this episode. At times like these, the audience couldn't get enough of him.

But it wasn't always smooth sailing for David. Even though he had improvised in his sixties works like *Random Breakfast*, he balked when others in the early, waffling period of Grand Union suggested they all improvise together. He was still feeling the whammo of a negative response to his piece *Walks and Digressions* in 1966. The audience had actually booed, and the *Village Voice* came out with a scathing review. (One choice put-down: "[T]he performer is stranded in his own vacuum of self-indulgence.")[15] After that damning review—from Yvonne's boyfriend, Robert Morris, no less—David decided "not to risk that anymore."[16] He gave up choreography for six years. It wasn't until he came up with the "Oh god, I'm slipping" bit that he summoned the confidence to initiate an action. He soon developed a repertoire of ways to channel his quick imagination into action. The

David Gordon we were getting in Grand Union was a man embarking on a fresh start. He was rediscovering his abilities as a mover, improviser, storyteller, framer, and entertainer.

Although David loved the spotlight, he also honored the group as a whole. In 1973, while telling Robb Baker about the recurring motifs, which he called "collective unconscious references," he said, "Grand Union performances are full of them. It's like everyone adding his breath to one big balloon."[17] And although he often dominated scenes with his easily spun narratives, he was very aware of what the others contributed. "I always hope that my excess is balanced by Steve's sincerity," he told Banes.[18]

There were times when he instinctively knew to give over the spotlight. One of those times was during an informal performance at Oberlin, when it was suggested that Nancy dance the whole of Ravel's *Bolero* by herself. He recalled, "I sat down and I remember thinking, I cannot turn my head away from watching Nancy. I cannot appear to have any opinion about what it is I am doing because the audience will see me see her so I have to just sit still and concentrate on [it.]"[19]

Another gift of David's was the unexpectedly tender quality of his touch. (I say unexpectedly because his usual irreverence does not prepare you for it.) In scenes where he was slowly touching—almost caressing—Paxton, Lewis, Brown, or Dilley, his focus was loving, sensual, and absorbed. He was also completely reliable when a falling person needed to be caught. This kind of dependability, which had been developed during CP-AD, fostered an environment in which people knew they could take risks.

And another gift was sheer spontaneity. Gordon could come up with instant variations in a sparring match; he could burst into song (he has a deep, pleasing singing voice). Spontaneity meant being "in the moment," which was a catchphrase of the time, related to Baba Ram Dass's popular book *Be Here Now*.

Being in the moment means not only following through with one's impulses but also yielding to the wishes of someone else. As David has said,

> "In the moment." I never heard the phrase until I got to the Actors' Studio, and actors talk all the time about being "in the moment." I realized that is what I learned in the Grand Union—

to be in the moment. Not only thinking I wanted to do the thing I wanted to do next, but to watch the thing I wanted to do next get subverted by somebody else's thinking what they wanted to do next, and determine what was the next in-the-moment thing that needed to happen between those things, to make them both coexist, to make one of them go away, or to make one of them become the major piece of material that was happening.[20]

Lastly, David's keen sense of framing has been consistent from college days onward. At Brooklyn College, "[w]orking on photos in the darkroom made a big difference as I learned to edit and refocus the photo I originally took."[21] His understanding of the rectangle served him well later as a window designer, and still later as a collaborator in a performance space. In Grand Union he always had a feel for the larger picture, for the multiplicity of things that could be going on in a single, framed space.

CHAPTER 8

STEVE PAXTON

*With a long neck, sloping shoulders, and a Greek-god-like face,
Steve often initiates movement from the head, with the spine
following in snaky succession. His sculpted shapes could suddenly
go soft, a solid transforming into a liquid before our eyes. When
he's got momentum, he can drop into a crouch and spring back
up in the blink of an eye. But when he decides to go slow, nothing
can rush him. He stays rooted, feet planted on the floor, playing
with weight shifts in different parts of the body. That kind of
play easily extends to other bodies: his readiness to touch or be
touched, lean or be leaned on, is a staple of Grand Union's physical
explorations. He is divinely comfortable in actions that would be
disorienting or awkward for other dancers: tilting way off balance,
hanging upside down, or balancing on his elbows. His solemn
demeanor lends a sense of gravitas, making his occasional sly
quips all the more surprising.*

Steve Paxton (born 1939) grew up in Tucson, Arizona, where he ex-
celled in gymnastics. At about the age of six, he was doing cartwheels.[1]
He toured with a school group, then went off to the University of Arizona, down the street from his house. He found the teachers decidedly
unstimulating, especially for his favorite subjects, English and micro-
biology. About his English teacher, he said, "I felt like he was teaching
Snobbism 101."[2] But he had enjoyed the classes in Martha Graham
technique he had taken in Tucson, so he accepted a scholarship to
the American Dance Festival at Connecticut College the summer of
1958. Although José Limón had provided the financial aid, it was his
encounter with Merce Cunningham's work that intrigued him. That

fall, Paxton came to New York, where he continued studying with both Limón and Cunningham.

When Paxton enrolled in Robert Dunn's composition course at the Cunningham studio in 1960, he met Forti and Rainer. Eventually Trisha Brown and David Gordon joined the class too. Gordon has a clear memory of Paxton in those classes: "Steve Paxton, as he has done most of my ever knowing him, would ask the damnedest questions which turned the world upside down and put everybody on the spot."[3]

In 1961 he took part in Forti's "dance constructions" at Yoko Ono's loft on Chambers Street. These works (*Huddle*, *Slant Board*, and *Herding*) jolted him into a state of mind he characterized as "the primal naked mind." They made him question all his dance training. Forti was not going for a dancerly look but for functional movement that engaged with certain objects. For Paxton, the effort to shed his training "was self-shaking, paradoxical, and enlarging"[4]—a good preparation for improvisation.

Forti's earthiness balanced out Cunningham's highly technical choreography for him. Seeing her crawl on all fours after a Cunningham class (probably around 1960), he felt she was trying out "evolutionary pathways" that led to "a whole way of looking at the person not as a tool, an aesthetic tool, but rather an organic part of the earth."[5]

Paxton performed in works by Rainer and Brown as well as his own, in and around Judson Dance Theater. He was also in performance pieces by Robert Rauschenberg, who was his life partner during those years, including *Spring Training* (1965), *Map Room II* (1965), and *Linoleum* (1966). In *Map Room*, he walked with his feet inside the rims of car tires. In *Linoleum*, he lay, belly down, encased by a narrow tube of chicken coop wire, as he ate fried chicken and looked around at the live chicks behind him.[6] Paxton was affected by Rauschenberg's performances as well as his sense of community. "Rauschenberg proposes a community of artists who, by seeing one another's work, weave a complex web of transmissions and permissions."[7]

But he also experienced Rauschenberg's work—and that of others at Judson—as a challenge: "Rauschenberg's whole raison was to expand possibilities. He was fearlessly and endlessly inventive, and a masterful theater-mind. So between him and Cunningham, I had a lot to avoid copying. Plus avoiding the work of my Judson colleagues."[8]

Steve Paxton in GU performance, Guthrie Theater, Walker Art Center, 1975.
Photo: Boyd Hagen, courtesy Walker Art Center.

His early performances at Judson progressed at such an unhurried pace that viewers were either annoyed, bored, or amazed. His choreographic decisions in some ways reacted to the aesthetic environment of the Merce Cunningham Dance Company, where he danced from 1961 to 1964. He wrote that he was consciously countering the "glamour of Cunningham and the speed and the pacing and the Rauschenberg costumes ... all the sparkle that could be generated." Looking back, he called his early work at Judson "tedious."[9] Rainer, impressed with his spirit of resistance, wrote that Paxton maintained "a seemingly obdurate disregard for audience expectations."[10]

Disregard for the audience might not seem like an ideal attribute for a performer. But that kind of obduracy almost guaranteed that Grand Union would not easily cave to audience expectations. Paxton's stubbornness, his insistence on exploration over entertainment, was grounding for the rest of the group.

He had an insight into the transformative nature of objects, possibly influenced by Forti and Rauschenberg. One example during the Judson days was *Music for Word Words* (1963). What started as an attempt to create sound for his duet with Rainer, *Word Words*, using an industrial vacuum cleaner, ended as an indelible image of a man lost in a room-sized bubble of his own creation. Examples during Grand Union are the gym mat that he used to stir up the crowd, as we will see in chapter 14 on the Oberlin residency, and the cloth tubing in a performance at NYU. On this last occasion, he wriggled into this pink cloth and seemed to get stuck inside it. Douglas and Nancy were showing concern for him, hidden as he was. Eventually he emerged from the tubing, totally fine and totally nude.[11]

The deadpan that came naturally to all the Grand Union performers was an area that Paxton had already investigated in concrete, and at times bizarre, ways. Rainer reports that in *English* (1963), he asked the twelve dancers to "erase" their features using a bar of soap.[12] Another strategy was to displace the dancer to a different environment, thereby putting the facial expression in a different context. In *Afternoon (A Forest Concert)*, also in 1963, he brought dancers to perform in a forest near Murray Hill, New Jersey. "I wanted to see the abstracted face of technical dance in a forest."[13]

The agility Paxton gained from gymnastics and modern dance training, combined with Forti's "evolutionary" influence, created a

GU at Eisner Lubin Auditorium, NYU Loeb Student Center. Performance to benefit
the Black Panther Defense Committee, 1971. From left: Paxton, Dilley, Rainer.
Photo: Fred W. McDarrah/Premium Collection/Getty Images.

highly kinetic movement language. For example, in the video of *Continuous Project—Altered Daily* at the Whitney Museum, he is seen swooping one leg up and over, causing him to dip, holding his body low, and then whipping himself into a high arch. He was working on a specific sensation, probably having to do with his core as the fulcrum while his limbs swerved off balance. He was not thinking of how to make it "interesting." If anything, he wanted it to be ordinary—per Robert Dunn's class. But in the search for the ordinary, he would take extraordinary risks. When his proposal to have forty-two red-headed nude people perform at NYU was deemed "obscene" by the powers that be, he replaced it with *Intravenous Lecture* (1970), in which a medical assistant injects him with a needle while he talks about censorship. In his irreverent way, he was asking: What, really, is obscene?

Stillness was a ploy that came in handy in Grand Union, and Paxton could be still for a very long time. In the last LoGiudice performance, he stretched out on the floor, opposite Trisha, both of them belly down. Although she got up and left, he held this position for six minutes no matter what or who was swirling around him. He could have been a bear rug, or some low-lying sculpture that had to be circumvented.

Paxton's preoccupation with walking lent a pedestrian pacing that anchored Grand Union in the everyday. He walked while telling stories; he walked when he was checking out the lighting instruments or looking for a prop; he walked to offset more theatrical scenes. In a statement that sounds like a Zen koan, he said of his sixties investigations, "My question was walking, and my answer is … walking."[14]

Paxton was wary of hierarchies of all types. His ideal in Grand Union was for everyone to "participate equally, without employing arbitrary social hierarchies in the group."[15] He felt that a leaderless group helped defray the effects of what he called "volunteer slavery." That was his term for the unexamined life of following the leaders in our society (or, in the dance world, following a choreographer). Needless to say, his work in Contact Improvisation aimed to replace this kind of hierarchy with a physical form of equality.

Steve had a wry, at times fanciful, sense of humor. He once took up the mic and wove a fictitious tale of "Trisha the wild child."[16] In the Tokyo performance, he sat close to Barbara and Trisha during their kooky gymnastics and narrated how it looked to him: "The camel sees its reflection," or, "The mother kangaroo and her teenage son." Watching Douglas hanging over a pole, he announced, "The bird falls asleep on a branch." Or he would bring the mic to his own lips but not speak. He rode many avenues toward subterfuge.

His juxtapositions of the ordinary and the absurdist were very Cagean, very Dada Zen.[17] He could take ordinary objects and give them a new context. In *Proxy* (1962) at Judson, he included "an aluminum pan, a bucket, or a dishpan." In that piece he had Yvonne stand in a taped off square and eat a pear. "I ate it as you would eat it at home."[18] The aim, for both Steve and Yvonne, was to do things the way you would if the audience weren't there. That anti-showy functionality came into play during the many times he moved furniture around in Grand Union—chairs, sofas, lamps, electric fans—with a workmanlike demeanor. And yet there was also a drama within that functionality.

Steve's commanding presence was softened by an openness to touch and release. While engaged in shaking a carpet out in the Walker Lobby performance, he softened immediately as Douglas took hold of his waist and spun him around—and then, just as readily, resumed his task with the carpet.

Steve was a quiet renegade, so consistently subversive that Rainer called him "the fly in the ointment."[19] About the sixties at Judson, she told *Artforum*, "I think Steve's work was the most far-out—and kind of arcane—of everything that went on there. His stuff was the most resistant to pleasureful expectations. He was physically so gifted but absolutely refused to exploit these gifts."[20]

By the time of Grand Union, he was willing to deploy those gifts— at just the right moments.

CHAPTER 9

TRISHA BROWN

Trisha has a long, lean, collapsible body—almost gangly. She uses her arms sagittally, swinging them easily rather than extending line the way a ballet dancer would or sculpting space the way a modern dancer would. She can drop her weight all at once, or in segments, or she can suddenly seem to levitate. Her facial expression is plain but alert—no hoopla, no drama. But she sometime looks like she has a secret up her sleeve. She ties herself into pretzelly knots, often with Barbara, while working toward some impossible goal, for instance one dancer sending the other aloft. Her body needs no preparation to launch into something new, whether it's a go-for-broke leap or little Geisha-like steps. She never looks lost; she always radiates a sense of purpose. You might see a glint of mischief in her eye that foretells some deflection or deception. She's a trickster, that one.

Trisha Brown (1936–2017) grew up in the Pacific Northwest in an athletic, competitive family. Her older brother, part of an all-state basketball team, coached her and her sister in basketball in their driveway. He also mounted an ambitious, yearlong training of Trisha in pole-vaulting in her senior year, hoping she would make the Olympics.[1] At the same time, she loved nature and walking in the woods. "The forest was my first art lesson," she said more than once.[2] She studied ballet, tap, acrobatics, and jazz dance in her hometown of Aberdeen, Washington, and later studied African dance with Ruth Beckford, a disciple of Katherine Dunham, in Oakland. After graduating from Mills College, which had a strong dance department, she accepted a teaching job at Reed College. Within a few months, she felt the existing methods of teaching modern dance did not help her students, who were not on a professional track, and started to teach improvisation.

As a child, she was already friends with improvisation. According to Jared Bark, who was her romantic partner in the early SoHo years, she described her ability to come up with a new game fast: "They'd be out playing, running around the streets getting bored like at the end of the day, and another kid would say, 'What are we gonna do now?' And she'd say, 'I know what let's do.' And she told me, 'When I started saying it, I had no idea. I was counting on by the time I got to *do*, I'd have something.' She said that she looks back at that as the root of her improvisation: 'I know what let's do.'"[3]

In the summer of 1960 she took Anna Halprin's workshop, which she described as "wide open improvisations day and night by very talented people."[4] There she met Simone Forti, Yvonne Rainer, and June Ekman. About a year later, Forti persuaded her to come to New York and take Robert Dunn's workshop. Dunn's classes supplied her with ways to frame her improvisations. She could devise a score as vague as "Read the wall" or as intricate as *Rulegame 5* (1964), in which performers had to adjust their height level according to the pacing of others in adjacent aisles. (She attempted versions of those ideas with us in the following decade, when I was with her company, but neither of them panned out.)

Her ability to take time to sink into movement was a gift that I think affected her Grand Union colleagues in two ways: first, in the unrushed tempo, and second, in her willingness to stick to one thing for a long stretch of time. She didn't just drop a gambit if it wasn't working right away; she let it play out.

Brown's verbal wizardry was another gift. With very few words, she could make a point. (I'll never forget when she said to me, "The critics like their geniuses … few.") Her voice was sweet and clear as a bell. She had a certain rhythm of speaking during Grand Union that was a mix of Zen patience and daredevil challenge. She might say one sentence or fragment, wait, listen, then say another. She had a unique way of forming spare, verbal phrases. (Having an English teacher for a mother surely helped.) Even in daily conversation, her words were always worth waiting for.

Brown could see any situation from a different point of view. She could see it slant. If someone was in a rut, she could do something to jostle that person into a new perspective. You might be deciding between Option A or Option B, but she would come up with option Z. She could be wickedly funny—or just goofy—in the service of her long-term project to re-see or re-define. One example was her piece *Ballet* (1968). She straddled two ropes, strung out about eight feet from the floor, awkwardly grappling with them on all fours—so much for the dainty virtuosity of that refined form named in the title.[5]

She had a wide dynamic range, deadpan notwithstanding, from restfulness or near stillness to what she called "the rapture" of improvising. She could appear to burst forth with joy. Her energy was contagious.

Trisha was always conscious of how she was communicating with the audience. In her solo *Yellowbelly* (1969) she demanded that the audience yell out the title word to activate her dancing. The audience eventually shouted the insult to get her to move, and she called that relationship "rough and symbiotic."[6] For *Inside* (1966), she improvised around the perimeter of the room near where the audience was sitting. "I added the problem of looking at the audience, not 'with meaning,' but with eyes open and seeing."[7] In her equipment pieces she changed the audience's view radically. For instance, in *Walking on the Walls* (1971) at the Whitney, she created an illusion that felt like a hallucination for the audience. Watching it was so disorienting that it was hard to believe you weren't looking straight down at a sidewalk. Very trippy.

Trisha had a moment on Halprin's deck in 1960 that crystallized her sense of daring. She was performing the task of sweeping the deck, perhaps working on the idea of momentum, when suddenly the force of thrusting the broom catapulted her body into the air, parallel to the ground, propelling her into a crazy moment of horizontal flight. This was witnessed—and never forgotten—by both Forti[8] and Rainer, who characterized it as "the mundane and spectacular all in one go."[9]

A rare gift: Trisha came up with ideas that activated the entire group. In chapter 20, we'll see how she sparked a delightful, funny, convention-flouting, witty, physical, celebratory sequence with a single suggestion. Even in duet mode, Trisha offered ideas that could be built upon. Whenever she was working with David, he was stimulated by her unpredictability. "She did the unexpected—gloriously," he told me.[10] He felt that whatever bid he tossed her way she could

Trisha Brown in her studio, 1978. Photo: Lois Greenfield.

absorb, and whenever she initiated, "I could pick up on it and something would happen because of it.[11]

For Trisha, Grand Union presented an opportunity to improvise with others, which she never lost sight of. She watched, waited, and reacted. When she teamed up with Barbara, they sometimes looked like Rodin's sculptures of wrestlers—and sounded like wrestlers too, with their grunts and groans. Other times they gave each other quiet suggestions for how to make a particular maneuver work. The trust between Trisha and Barbara probably solidified during the exhilarating—and harrowing—*Falling Duet I* (1968), in which each woman threw herself off balance, not giving a clue as to direction, thus challenging the other to cushion her fall at the last second. (This was one of the most hair-raising duets I've ever seen.)

Trisha's ambivalence about being in Grand Union was no secret. She had wanted her own work—seventeen pieces up to that point—to receive more notice, but that didn't happen until she attached herself to Yvonne Rainer's star. Of course, ambivalence on the part of a single person can throw a wrench in the works of "togetherness." But I would say that her ambivalence contributed to a certain emotional texture that scraped away any hint of an all-one-happy-family veneer.

CHAPTER 10

NANCY LEWIS

With her long, sensual limbs and natural verve, Nancy Lewis is a knockout of a dancer. She has an offhand luminousness that is refreshing in the context of the more interior focus of other Grand Union members. She can start dancing with the merest hint of a shiver and gradually let it take over her body until she gets carried away into a legs-swinging, everything-at-once dance. Her gamin face holds mischief just beneath the skin. Her intuitive, spontaneous wit lends her a campy, femmy, "Who, me?" goofiness. In Grand Union performances, she exerts less of a sense of intention than the others. But she can take your breath away with a quick, unfiltered response—or simply with her dancing. She's a team player, a fresh spirit, and a memorable character.

Nancy Lewis (born 1939), who lived in New Jersey until the age of six and then in California, was always athletic: she joined the diving team in high school; she hiked and skied the nearby mountains. She started dancing in high school and attended American Dance Festival at Connecticut College in the summer of 1958. There she studied with Lucas Hoving, one of ADF's beloved teachers/choreographers. Hoving had created major roles in José Limón's repertoire and had developed his own blend of classical and modern dance technique. His signature work, *Icarus* (1964), has been performed by several companies, including those of Ailey and Limón. Hoving had an eye for talent; around the same time that Nancy was a promising student, he arranged for another teenager to attend Juilliard: Pina Bausch.

In her first year at Juilliard, Lewis remembers that Alfredo Corvino, master Cechetti teacher, said to her, "Why are you so relaxed?"[1]

Nancy Lewis with Steve Paxton. Photo: Robert Alexander, Jerome Robbins Dance Division, The New York Public Library for the Performing Arts.

She didn't know if he was alarmed or admiring, but she clearly did not have the formality that is usually instilled during ballet training. Helen McGehee, one of the most austere of the Martha Graham teachers, also noted her as unique.[2]

Even though she received positive attention at Juilliard, Lewis left after two and a half years to study with Merce Cunningham. She gravitated to his work, and he to her. She was tall, attractive, flexible, and had a languid, louche style that in some ways anticipated that of Karole Armitage. But just when he was about to invite Lewis into the company, she got pregnant. (She had married Dylan Green, an actor, in 1962.) After her first child was born, she worked to get back in shape until Merce was about to ask her again, then had a second child. After the third child, it was over between her and Merce.

In the summer of 1960 at ADF she danced in Jack Moore's new

duet *Songs Remembered*. She portrayed a kind of lost love in a duet that critic P. W. Manchester later called a "heartbreaker."[3] In 1964 in New York, she danced the shimmering Sun in Hoving's *Icarus*. I will never forget her in this role. She commanded the stage in a slow walk, each leg turning inward, then swiveling outward before taking the next step. With just a small pulsating of her hand, palm outward, it seemed that she was sending out rays of light.

In some ways Lewis had the most to lose by joining Grand Union. The group's aesthetic was far from her Juilliard training. While Paxton, Dunn, and Dilley had all danced with Merce Cunningham and absorbed the Cage/Cunningham aesthetic, Lewis had been performing works by choreographers more aligned with "historic" modern dance, like Hoving, Jack Moore, and Anna Sokolow. (She had also danced in Twyla Tharp's *Group Activities* [1969]) and *The One Hundreds* [1970].) In fact, Hoving and Moore had both served on the panel of the 92nd Street Y that had rejected Yvonne Rainer and Steve Paxton for its Young Choreographers series. They were so angry with Lewis for decamping to the downtown aesthetic that neither of them ever came to see her in Grand Union. This was a bit sad for her and shows how much of an aesthetic gap she was bridging.

Whenever Lewis danced, people noticed her. At Juilliard, it was her teachers; at ADF, it was Jack Moore and Lucas Hoving. At the Cunningham studio, Barbara Dilley noticed her. In fact, it was Dilley who recommended Lewis to Rainer when the CP-AD group was opening up to new dancers. And then Rainer remembered seeing Lewis at ADF at Connecticut College in 1959 in a piece by Jack Moore. Almost sixty years later, her memory of that performance was so vivid that she imitated for me Nancy crazily moving her malleable mouth with her hand.[4]

Lewis had no training in improvisation, but she remembers improvising as a child on swings and in small performances. According to her older son, Miles Green, she was known as the entertainer in her family.[5] (One could say her talent as a performer runs in the family; her son Miles is a musician and her niece, Juliette Lewis, is a Hollywood actor.) As a dancer, she felt a natural tendency to improvise but "never found anyone to perform it with" before Grand Union. (It's actually remarkable that she could hold her own against the others, who had either been through *CP-AD* or, like Brown, had been improvising in their own dances for years.)

In performance, Nancy responded quickly and intuitively to any overture. If David said to her, "Don't come in, I'm taking a shower" (as he did in Minneapolis), she immediately conjured a bathroom and played into his fantasy with subtle humor. At La MaMa, while tied to a cross, she improbably caught, in her mouth, a chunk of grapefruit tossed in her general direction.[6] At LoGiudice in 1972, when Paxton put the mic up to her face, she instantly summoned a Loretta Young–type glamour as she gave spontaneously trivial answers. Lewis was a chameleon with star quality.

According to critic Marcia B. Siegel, "Lewis is ... the possessor of the quickest imagination. She can become a sylph or a monster or a Grecian shepherdess just like that, can vocalize like a Moroccan at prayer."[7]

The chameleon ability was also noticed by Deborah Jowitt. In 1973, when Lewis was still using her married surname Green, Jowitt wrote, "Gordon and Green together can be outrageously flamboyant and play with all kinds of theater styles; Green with [Douglas] Dunn becomes more of a sober crazy-legs like him."[8]

Nancy could always be counted on to *dance*. In a performance at Oberlin, she danced to Ravel's sixteen-minute *Bolero* alone. Somehow the other dancers knew that this moment was destined to be a solo, and they backed away. Yvonne remembers that solo as a high point: "That scene is riveted in my mind. I thought her dancing was ravishing.... It was a highlight of that performance. With all the disparate, non-sequitur things going on, there was *this*."[9]

But Lewis looks back on those sixteen minutes with distress. "They turned on *Bolero*, and I was out there, and it was for me to dance to Ravel, and I hate that piece and it's long. I had to bop around the length of that piece, in this huge gym, and it was just the worst time I ever had in a performance."[10]

This dazzling dancer could sometimes just be still for a long time. On occasion, it felt like a retreat, for instance in the 1975 Walker Lobby performance. (A full description follows in chapter 20.) Or a dare that wasn't fulfilled, like the time at LoGiudice when she sat still on the floor, topless, in a loose embrace with Paxton—and no, it didn't go anywhere. But these episodes showed an acceptance of simple presence as part of the dance.

Knowing she was more of a performer than a choreographer, Lewis organized her own repertory concert in 1971 at The Cubiculo, a small midtown theater that presented many modern dancers (including myself) in the seventies. She performed short works by Rainer (*Three Satie Spoons*), Paxton (*Smiling*), Gordon ("Liberty," an excerpt from his *Sleep Walking*), and Moore (*Clown Vice*), and improvised *Prelude-in-Sneaks*, a piece partly based on Remy Charlip's "instructions from Paris."[11] And she improvised to music played live by her life partner, Richard Peck.

That concert earned her a compliment from Trisha Brown, who joined Grand Union around the same time Lewis did. Nancy recalled: "I used to be inhibited by her, because she knew that I wasn't sophisticated about anything, really, and she put me down for it. [I was] a California hick plopping down in the middle of [New York City]. But after my performance ... she came back and gave me a tight hug and said, 'I know what you are doing and it's good.'"[12]

Reviewing Lewis's solo program during the 1975 Walker residency, Linda Shapiro wrote: "She projects a glamor which is both juicy and deadpan, a combination of Carol Burnett and Jill St. John."[13]

CHAPTER 11

YVONNE RAINER

Sturdy and strong with chin-length black hair, Yvonne Rainer cuts a compelling figure. She breaks the mold of the lofty or super-articulate female dancer. With a long torso and low-slung ass, she does not have a particularly flexible body (neither did Martha Graham), but there is a readiness in every pore that gives the viewer confidence. She has mastered the task-like style of movement that has nothing to do with balletic line or sculpted modern dance shapes. She is in the moment. She can be reckless, fierce, languid, explosive, or goofy. She goes about her choices, whether expected or outlandish, in a straightforward, robust way. Even when she moves in isolated parts, as in Trio A, *she is not striving; she is just doing: thrust a hand downward, focus upward, flex the foot. Her originality and sheer presence make the ordinary extraordinary.*

Yvonne Rainer (born 1934) grew up in an immigrant family in San Francisco. Her father was an Italian anarchist and her mother was Jewish. It was not a happy family. Rainer and her older brother spent years in foster care institutions simply because their mother felt overwhelmed by the responsibilities of parenting. As a teenager, Rainer enjoyed going to anarchist meetings and lectures at the leftist Workmen's Circle. She was exposed to European art films and the Bay Area cultural ferment of the fifties. She attended poetry readings by Kenneth Rexroth, Kenneth Patchen, and Lawrence Ferlinghetti; she went to see films by Maya Deren and Kenneth Anger. She attended San Francisco Junior College for a year, UC Berkeley for a week, then dropped out. She became involved with the painter Al Held and re-located with him to New York in 1956.

Living with Held in New York City thrust Rainer into the midst of the art world just as it was pivoting from abstract expressionism to minimalism. She absorbed conversations about space, color, framing, and foreground, to be stored up for later use. She was studying act-ing, but it became clear that she had no aptitude for the then current Stanislavski method, which involved corralling one's "inner motives." By her own admission she was a "total washout" as an actor.[1]

In 1959 she started taking modern dance classes with Edith Stephen, then added ballet with Mia Slavenska, a former star of the Ballet Russe de Monte Carlo. She also studied at the Martha Graham School of Contemporary Dance for a year before switching to Merce Cunningham. In 1959 or '60 she was inspired by Aileen Passloff's solo *Tea at the Palaz of Hoon*, which she called "female, funny, robust, and stylish."[2] She sought out Passloff, who advised her to take class with James Waring, which Rainer did, and eventually danced in his com-pany. She also got together with Nancy Meehan (who later became a lead dancer with Erick Hawkins) and Simone Forti in a studio to im-provise. Forti convinced Rainer to come with her to take Anna Hal-prin's summer intensive in Marin County in 1960. It was on Halprin's deck that Rainer experienced Halprin's concept of scoring and the radical sounds of La Monte Young. Rainer liked the task orientation, particularly the effort of holding or carrying objects while dancing. But, as she said later, "Anna was always a child of nature and I felt I was a child of culture."[3] Rainer was more influenced by Forti when they were in New York than by Halprin in California.

That fall, she enrolled in Robert Dunn's course in dance compo-sition at the Cunningham studio. One of his first assignments was to combine the numerical breakdown of measures in Satie's *Trois Gym-nopédies* with an adaptation of John Cage's score for his *Fontana Mix*. Rainer fulfilled the assignment by producing *Three Satie Spoons* (1961), a wry, idiosyncratic, three-part solo with isolated gestures and random, robot-like vocalizations. She spiked the "ordinary" with her natural gift of eccentricity. With a robust appetite to choreograph as well as to perform, she was, along with Steve Paxton, an instigator in the launching of Judson Dance Theater.

In 1963 Rainer made her first full-length work, *Terrain*, and then

Yvonne Rainer, 1964. Photo: unattributed. Photograph collection, Robert Rauschenberg Foundation Archives, New York.

kept challenging herself to make longer works than was typical at Judson. The "Duet" section of *Terrain* had Rainer and Trisha Brown wearing "Hollywood Vassarette lace push-brassieres" and tights.[4] While Yvonne performed a ballet-class adagio combination, Trisha alternated between romantic poses and pelvic thrusts. This may have been the last time Rainer played with sexual stereotypes in performance. In her next big work, *Parts of Some Sextets* (1965), she distributed tasks with no regard for gender. Whether tugging on a rope, hanging limply off a partner's neck, or diving onto a pile of mattresses, these actions were done by both genders.

Rainer was completely at home with the disjointedness of a chance-driven composition. She said that while making *Trio A*, which was initially a trio for David Gordon, Steve Paxton, and herself as part of *The Mind Is a Muscle* (1966), she learned to choreograph a movement sequence to look *as though* it were made by chance.[5] *Trio A*, with its flat dynamics, odd coordinations, and averted gaze, became an iconic dance that embodied a bevy of cultural denials. The postscript of her essay about *Parts of Some Sextets* (1965), got extracted and then disseminated as the infamous "No Manifesto," enshrining her denials even more.[6] This manifesto was quoted so often that in 1981 she wrote that it was "tiresome to live with." About manifestos in general, she wrote that the purpose was to release "a blast of cold air to shiver our satisfied timbers," but that they must be understood in context.[7]

I would say her first gift was the ability to create that blast of cold air. During the making of *Continuous Project—Altered Daily*, as we saw in chapter 3, she was willing to throw everything into question, including the nature of performance.

Her gift as a performer was to dive into the extremes of emotion and at the same time avoid what she saw as the trap of narrative continuity. She could catapult from being dead serious into a screaming fit—whether it was improvising in Simone Forti's *See-Saw* (1960) or performing the third section of her own *Three Seascapes* (1962), all in the name of disrupting the flow. But she could also create her own, more internal flow. In one episode of Grand Union at LoGiudice Gallery, she discovered that she could keep a coin pinched in her eye by looking upward. When a repetitive Terry Riley tune came on, she started rising, swaying, tilting, and revolving, all with her face toward the ceiling.

Yvonne balanced the emotional with the intellectual. A voracious reader, she has incorporated quotes from Carl Jung, Lenny Bruce, Joel Kovel, Vladimir Nabokov, and Colin Turnbull into various performances. The combination of the verbal, physical, and visual components challenged the audience to use different parts of their brains when watching her work.

Although her palette of movement was wide-ranging, her straightforward way of delivering movement without melodic phrasing matched the aesthetic of the minimalists. Yvonne charted the correspondences between minimalism in visual art and her construction of *Trio A* in a 1966 essay. This landmark analysis established her as an intellectual heavyweight in addition to being a choreographic heavyweight.[8]

Yvonne was a natural leader. She communicated clearly, inspired hard work, and challenged her dancers artistically. She was so fair-minded that she sometimes recoiled from her own urge to lead. After she directed performers remotely via earpieces in *Carriage Discreteness* for "Nine Evenings of Theater and Engineering" (1966), she had sharp regrets about the imperious way she had directed the performers "from on high."[9]

She relied on both hard work and intuition. Having started training late, she had to be very focused and diligent. This carried over into her ability to organize. She wasn't wasting any time. She drew up lists of performance modes, props, concepts, behaviors, and sources that clarified her thinking. With strong artistic and physical instincts, she translated her ideas into choreography quickly. Although she came to think of herself as less than a stellar improviser, she was always a charismatic performer who brought a psychological openness to her Grand Union sessions.

For Yvonne, art was not mystical or otherworldly. She unabashedly confronted audience expectations and assumptions. By incorporating everyday objects—mattresses, chairs, a small staircase—into her choreography, she blurred the line between art and life in a concrete yet sensual way. This may be one reason visual artists appreciated her so much. Over the years she received homages, in one form or another, from Richard Serra, Robert Rauschenberg, Louise Fishman, and Eleanor Antin.[10]

Yvonne was indestructible when it came to critics. Her work often launched an assault on existing conventions, for example the expectation that theater should create illusion, thus incurring the wrath of critics. Charges of "disaster," "aimless repetition," "utter boredom" and "without grace," "excruciatingly boring," "ghastly," "totally undistinguished," and "pitiable" were hurled at her.[11] She stood her ground. "I was very proud of those reviews.... [T]he bad reviews meant, in my eyes, that I was effective."[12]

Last, I would say Yvonne had the gift of making any disjointed sequence of steps flow. She intentionally made *Trio A* without any transitions to link what seemed like randomly chosen movements. And yet when she performed them, as seen in Sally Banes's 1978 film, her body gave the choreography a sense of flow—not a musical flow, but a steady-energy, task-like flow.

CHAPTER 12

LINCOLN SCOTT AND BECKY ARNOLD

Lincoln Scott and Becky Arnold were active in Grand Union only for the first year or so. They both appear in photographs of the 1971 Walker Art Center performance, but only Scott continued to the January 1972 Oberlin residency. By the time of the LoGiudice Gallery series that May, he was no longer part of it. I do not have a vivid memory of either of them, so I am relying on other people's descriptions.

LINCOLN SCOTT

Along with Brown and Lewis, Scott (born 1947) joined the group when it was mutating from CP-AD to Grand Union. He had performed in Brown's *Leaning Duets I* (1970), in works by Deborah Hay, and in *Trio A with Flags* (1970). Deborah Hay remembers, "He always brought a modest, serious, and quiet presence to my dances."[1] Dilley remembers, "He was a gentle, fearless improviser and played along with us. And sometimes just watched."[2] Soon after arriving in New York, Scott chose to be known as "Dong." People who knew him had various reactions to the new nickname.[3]

Theresa Dickinson, who was appearing as a guest artist, remembers dancing with Scott when Grand Union came to the San Francisco Art Institute in the summer of 1971. She described the rooftop of the Art Institute, with a high ledge above a deep drop. "Dong and I spent a very long time working on the problem of approaching each other along that ledge, then passing each other and continuing on."[4]

At Oberlin in January 1972, Scott participated fully during Grand Union's evening in Hall Auditorium. Judging from the video, he performed with commitment, energy, and sensitivity to his fellow dancers. He did not often initiate an action, but he joined in the group sweep of things; he had a shopping cart duet with Barbara, a strutting duet with David, and a howling duet with Yvonne.

Lincoln Scott was born in Louisiana in 1947 and moved to the Bay Area when he was young. He attended Berkeley High School, where he was recruited by dance teacher Betsy Frederick (then Janssen) to perform in the chorus of the musical *The King and I*. Frederick took Scott under her wing, cultivating his talent as a dancer. During his senior year, because of problems in his family, he lived in her garage. Frederick's classes included technique and improvisation, and she brought her students to see Merce Cunningham and other companies when they came through the area.[5]

According to choreographer Wendy Rogers, who was a year behind Scott at Berkeley High, it was a large, progressive school with a pro-arts, pro-civil-rights agenda.[6] Although the student population was racially diverse, in the community there was discriminatory housing and, in schools, academic tracking that favored white students. As happened (and still happens) all over the country, students would self-segregate in social situations. But, said Rogers, there was more mixing in dance and physical education. Further, "In the Bay Area dance world, however segregated and prejudiced we still were, there was a desire to change things and to create opportunities to do things together."[7] Rogers remembers at least one occasion when "the two Ruths"—Ruth Hatfield, teaching in Berkeley, and Ruth Beckford, the Dunham proponent who became a force for dance in the city of Oakland[8]—brought their students together: Hatfield's mostly white students and Beckford's mostly black students. This is all to say that Scott may have been socially comfortable in East Bay dance circles.

As always, dance teachers were happy when a boy expressed interest. Jenny Hunter (Groat), who had worked closely with Anna Halprin, probably offered him a scholarship to her school. She was known as a good teacher of both technique and improvisation. Rogers, who also studied with Hunter, remembers one whole session focused on initiating movement from the spine. Shortly after Scott came to Hunter, she invited him into her company, Dance West. They performed a work called *The Effort* at Fillmore Auditorium in 1966, which was advertised as "a subliminal archetype in theater, different every performance, a happenstance ... you can walk around it."[9] Sounds like it could be Grand Union West!

Frederick found Scott likable and congenial. "He wasn't what you'd call tremendously social, but he was nice to be around."[10] He smoked pot, but then so did many others at Berkeley High. When Scott left for New York, Frederick, who had known Paxton in high school in Arizona, gave him Steve's contact information so he would have someone to stay with when he arrived. Scott did stay with Paxton in his place on the Bowery, then in an empty room on the upper floor of the same building, and again with Steve when he moved to Wooster Street.[11]

Scott formed a fleeting intimacy with Cynthia Hedstrom, who was dancing with Barbara Dilley in her group, the Natural History of the American Dancer. She and Scott were hanging out at 112 Greene and FOOD. She was new in New York and felt he had a kind of street smarts that she could learn from. As sculptor David Bradshaw recalled, Scott fit into the downtown dance scene, where "there was a Buddha quality to the whole crowd."[12] In the film documentary FOOD (1972), when Scott enters he is treated with respect and affection by his fellow artists.[13]

For a while Scott held a job at one of Mickey Ruskin's restaurants or nightclubs, possibly Chinese Chance (also called One U, for One University Place, which was not as famous as Max's Kansas City).[14] As in Berkeley, however, he didn't have his own home, and he would crash at his friends' apartments.[15]

Hedstrom says she never saw any instance of racial discrimination when they were together in New York. But she suspected he may have had hidden insecurities about his place in that milieu. "He always had one foot in the door and one foot out of the door."[16] It couldn't have been easy being one of the few African Americans in the largely white SoHo environment. Douglas Dunn remembers a time, probably when Grand Union had a gig in Cincinnati in 1970, when he and Steve and Lincoln were barred from a restaurant because of Lincoln's presence.[17]

Scott was almost a decade younger than most of the other Grand Union members. Dance writer Sally Sommer, who saw many of the early performances, said, "I remember Dong as a presence and thinking he's a very young, sweet guy. He was in the arena with these *enfants terribles*. For any young performer to come up to their performative level was very difficult."[18]

In the flyer for the Oberlin residency, Scott had included the phrase "craft is apprentice" in his brief bio. It's possible he thought of himself

GU at 112 Greene Street, 1972. On left: Scott with mirror; in cluster: Dunn, Rainer, Paxton, Dilley. Photo: Babette Mangolte.

as apprentice to these master improvisers. He also wrote something quite poetic: "Bamboo player by the wind along California coast." He did play a bamboo flute during the Oberlin performance, including making blowing sounds, as though he were the wind.

Steve, who often designed the posters, recounts an unfortunate situation at Oberlin: "A photo of the group was taken, and in a design choice I opted to print it in brown. The color was to make the color of the boots natural. Lincoln thought I chose it to emphasize his race. I think that was the beginning of him leaving, though it was, as most things were with him, not at all clear he was leaving or what he was doing."[19]

Sometime after Oberlin (January 1972) and before LoGiudice (May 1972), Scott drifted away from Grand Union. David's impression was that "Dong left after a while at his own choosing. To me he never seemed comfortable with the work we were doing but we never discussed it with him."[20]

For long stretches of time, Scott stayed in Vermont, in the commune where Steve, Simone Forti, and Deborah Hay were living. According to Forti, it was like an extension of the SoHo and FOOD community.[21] Scott participated in farm life, operating tractors, helping bale hay, and working in the organic garden.[22] However, Forti said he was "unsure of himself" socially, and this may have had to do with his being "the only black person at the farm and for miles around."[23]

Scott periodically returned to California after his stint with Grand Union. Nita Little, an early proponent of Contact Improvisation, met him in Berkeley in 1973 or 1974. She said he was living on the block on Divisadero Street where Anna Halprin's Dancers' Workshop studio was located. (He had at one point been attending weekly sessions with the Dancers' Workshop.) As his girlfriend for a while, Little felt he was very present in a somatic way, especially his sense of touch. She also appreciated his politics because, as a Contact person, she questioned all hierarchy. ("Up is not necessarily good," as she said, "and down is not necessarily bad.") She felt that her conversations with Scott "forced me to have a perspective. . . . It was through him that I came to recognize how acculturated I was in the white culture. He woke me up to behaviors that were classist." He was not overtly part of the black power movement, she said, but he "saw things in a political way."[24] Perhaps he felt more comfortable expressing his feelings about race and politics in California than in New York.

At some point he was hit by a car, badly hurt his leg, and became addicted to painkillers. From Steve: "He was also drinking a lot, so his life started to spiral downward. His last farm stay, a couple of years, was marked by paranoia and rages. He went to California upon the death of his father and dropped out of touch."[25]

A Spokeo Internet search listed Lincoln Scott as having moved from Vermont to Berkeley in 2000, and there is no mention of him after 2017. After several attempts by his high school classmate Wendy Rogers to find him, there is no definitive update.

BECKY ARNOLD

Becky Arnold (born 1936) was in the cast of *CP-AD* as it developed and mutated into Grand Union. But she left New York in January 1972. Before I was able to locate her, I asked Yvonne to describe her: "Becky Arnold was an angel to work with, contentious, devoted, tireless — an accomplished technical dancer. She had no aspirations to do her own choreography or even contribute to mine as other than a worker bee, so when YR and Group was morphing into GU she made it clear the situation was not for her."[26]

According to Pat Catterson, Arnold was strong and assertive, not as relaxed as the others in Grand Union. "She was ... diligent, disciplined, wanting to get it right, and physically brave."[27]

Arnold started lessons in gymnastics at the age of three in New Castle, Indiana. She would make dances for herself and her cousins to perform in her family's garage. As an adult, she worked with Jack Cole and Michael Kidd in summer stock. Rainer saw her in Cunningham technique classes and asked her to come to a rehearsal. Becky's response was, "I don't think I can do your work." But she eventually became a strong member of Rainer's group. Before CP-AD, she danced in Rainer's *The Mind Is a Muscle* (1966) and *Rose Fractions* (1969) and appeared (nude) with a big white balloon in Rainer's short *Trio Film* (1968). She has vivid memories of *Rose Fractions* (1969): "We had a wall of us walking across the stage ... with bags of kitty litter, and we opened them and strewn the litter as we walked across the stage." Another memory: "There was a pile of books on the stage, and Yvonne said, 'I want you to go and make love to the pile of books.' So I did."[28]

The Pratt performance of 1969 was a precursor to CP-AD in that it was the first time Yvonne included a dancer learning something in the performance. That person was Becky, and that material was *Trio A*. She must've done a good job because Catherine Kerr, the Cunningham-dancer-to-be who was in the audience, came away with a strong impression of Becky as a lively performer.[29]

Becky felt very much part of the making of CP-AD—the testing out of ideas, kicking the pillows around, moving boxes, using leverage to stand up with the group supporting her, choosing when to do "Chair Pillow"—even though she was seven months pregnant when they premiered it at the Whitney. For the group hoist, which had been worked out at ADF the summer before, she had to be replaced by Yvonne. Another concession to her pregnancy was that Deborah Hollingworth, who had designed the "adjuncts" for the University of Missouri at Kansas City performance, made a papier mâché hemisphere to cover her belly at the Whitney.

But when it came time to improvise, Becky was not comfortable.

GU at Walker Art Center, lec-dem, 1971. From left: Dilley, Becky Arnold, Rainer. Photo: Tom Berthiaume, courtesy Walker Art Center.

She had felt safe complying with Yvonne's clear commands, but this was a new, open-ended situation. She found this new phase "really upsetting because I wanted to just be told what to do and to know what I was going to do. All of a sudden, I didn't know what was going to happen."[30] The part she liked about Grand Union was the physicality: "One night Steve came over and plopped his body on top of me, and I responded back."[31]

When her husband got a new job in Andover, Massachusetts, she moved away from the city. Well after she had left Grand Union, in 1977, Arnold produced her own concert at NYU, performing works by Rainer, Catterson, Peter Saul, and Dan Wagoner. Since that time, she has studied tango in Buenos Aires and competed in the ballroom scene. She lives in Phoenix, where she still dances at *milongas* twice a week.

INTERLUDE
PEOPLE IMPROVISATION

In a way, this book is an expansion of the review I wrote about Grand Union at La MaMa in 1976, which appeared in my last book, Through the Eyes of a Dancer: Selected Writings *(Wesleyan University Press, 2013). I titled my review, which originally appeared in* SoHo Weekly News, *May 6, 1976, "People Improvisation." Trisha had left the group a few months earlier, and Steve Paxton was probably busy with Contact Improvisation. In their absence, it was decided that Valda Setterfield would appear as a guest artist. Two caveats about this article: first, I have no idea what category of Japanese swordsmen I was referring to or what I meant by traditional Eastern opera, and second, when it came to describing Barbara Dilley, I realize now that I was seeing only a narrow band of this highly dimensional dance artist.*

Ancient Japanese swordsmen would customarily train for many, many years to attain one simple goal: to be ready to accept, and counter, a blow from any direction at any time. The swordsman's decision was not permitted to rely on any previously successful strategy. Rather, he was to take into account all the forces of the present moment and choose the one action perfect for that unique moment.

The difference between this theory and the theory that the Grand Union goes by is that for the latter, there is more than one appropriate action in a given situation. It is the choice, among the range of possible alternatives, that the performers, and we, are interested in. When X does this, what will Y do? Or, when Z does this, what will Z then do? Each initiated action opens up a new realm of possible reactions. Each reaction opens up . . . etc. Endings are beginnings. The performers create a constantly shifting matrix of joinings and separations, rises and falls, quickenings and trailings off, revelations and suppressions.

The way the Grand Union accomplishes all this is by having near-legendary rapport as a group, and by each member having a strong identity of his/her own. Like the loyal audiences of traditional Eastern opera, we have come to know each character well; they are varying degrees of real/unreal for us; and we each have our favorites. A brief run-down is in order:

Barbara Dilley is small and soft, wears comfortable clothes that let her comfortable body extend and curl and twine. She is patient and well grounded in manner and motion. She usually avoids verbal content and when pressed, responds somewhat too earnestly. ("A leader is someone who has wisdom," she informs David Gordon.)

Douglas Dunn is lean and angular, with a determined look on his face. The black clothes and hat he wore on Sunday night made him look preacher-like, and he played into that by striking stark poses. The intention in his dancing is very evident, and he likes to channel this clarity into weight studies—lifting, catching, yielding to, testing another's weight.

David Gordon has an uncommon gift for monologue. He tops his own brilliant witticisms with more brilliant ones. He banters, puns, weaves tales, plays the prophet, plays the victim.

Nancy Lewis is tall and goofy and, although she has been compared to Carol Burnett, I see more of Holly Woodlawn [one of Andy Warhol's gender-nonconforming "superstars"] in her. It is fun to watch her mercurial changes between chic, sulky, and disarmingly sensual. She is a parody of herself, letting us know by a darting glance or a droop of the shoulders that she doesn't believe in this stuff 100 percent. This creates a contrast to her dancing, which is full and swoopy and emanates from an inner center.

Valda Setterfield, who danced with Merce Cunningham for a long time, is long and sleek; she looks the height of elegance in whatever eccentric outfit she drums up. Her dancing is distinctive for its effortlessly clean lines and the matter-of-fact way she drops into and out of movements.

These dancers are such colorful characters that we are drawn to their performances again and again, as though to a new installment of a soap opera. We follow their triumphs, disappointments, dares, and frustrations almost too keenly to be bearable. We feel the challenge of spontaneity, the chaotic assortment of possibilities as we do in our own lives. *We know that there is no plan.* We witness the trust that allows them to bring their personal doubts into play. On one occasion, Lewis stood at the back of the room with a blanket over her head for a long time and finally, during a pause, asked anyone who would listen, "Am I doing anything important?"

However, the group sometimes relies too heavily on bits, or types of bits, that have gone over well in the past. Each member is, at different times, limited by the very illustriousness that makes him or her magnetic.

But the Grand Union is still the best improvisation group around, and there are still those moments that stun you by being so utterly in the present. On Sunday, Gordon had got himself standing on a chair, slowly revolving as he told a story of himself as a bed-wetting adolescent who joined the circus. The narrative seemed unconnected to anything else going on until he eventually directed it to the moment at hand: "I love having hundreds of people watch me turn around on top of this chair. . . . This is the best moment of my life." But moment gives way to moment, and exhilaration gives way to misery: "How long will you let me go on like this. . . . You're *making* me turn around on this chair. . . . *This is the worst moment of my life!*"

Yvonne Rainer, who was a founder and strong influence on the group, has written that "one must take a chance on the fitness of one's own instincts."[1] (*She'd* make a good Japanese swordsman.)

Part of this means an instinct for play, which might loosely be defined as non-goal-oriented exploration. Most of the Grand Union members have children, and I see evidence of that influence in their ability to play. They even use the word "pretend." Gordon: "We were pretending to be chickens mating and I resent your calling it dancing." ("Let's pretend"—that magical gateway to endless delights for children, but a phrase that has been dropped from the adult vocabulary.) This time they even looked like children—children playing dress-up in the morning with their pajamas still on. They all wore combinations of plain and fancy.

"Instincts" can also mean learned abilities. The instinct that improvising requires includes knowing when to let go of an action and when to forge ahead, when to claim the focus and when to give it up, and what proportion of personal wishes and fears to lay bare.

Needless to say, these are the same issues we face in everyday living. Perhaps that's why I leave a Grand Union performance not with a declaration of good or bad, but with an emotional fullness, similar to the effect of a highly charged event in my own life.

After one of the performances, a woman told Barbara Dilley, "I've seen dance improvisation before, and I've seen theater improvisation before, but this is the first time I've seen people improvisation."

PART III Consolidating the Dare

In May 1971 Grand Union was given a week residency at Walker Art Center in Minneapolis, and in January 1972, three weeks at Oberlin College. The following year, the group produced a two-month festival at the Larry Richardson Dance Gallery in New York. These long stretches of time together helped fortify the group as a real ensemble — an ensemble of risk-takers. How did these opportunities arise? After all, it wasn't an obvious choice for a presenter to book a motley crew of improvisers for a residency. The Grand Union wasn't a dance company focused on a single acknowledged genius like Paul Taylor, Merce Cunningham, or Martha Graham. It wasn't even focused on a single up-and-comer like Twyla Tharp or Dianne McIntyre. The presenters who invited them had to be people of curiosity and vision. Suzanne Weil at Walker Art Center and Brenda Way at Oberlin College were up for that dare.

The self-produced Dance Gallery Festival presented seventeen GU performances plus many others by friends in dance, music, and theater.

All three of these long-term situations helped define Grand Union as an ensemble and allowed its members to develop their own work.

CHAPTER 13

FIRST WALKER ART CENTER RESIDENCY, MAY 1971

Grand Union was so steeped in SoHo culture that it was not always warmly received during out-of-town gigs. Although the group got booked almost immediately at colleges and small venues—often on the strength of Yvonne Rainer's reputation as a must-see avant-gardist—the performers might appear desultory or noncommunicative to audiences elsewhere. Their deadpan expressions, louche clothing, and relaxed pacing sometimes alienated people who expected to see a "show." David recalls that, in city after city, the audiences thinned out during their performances. "We would just watch the audience disappear."[1] But when Grand Union had time to involve the community, it attracted a multitude of fans.

The invitation from Walker Art Center in 1971 gave the group an opportunity to break into the national college and art center circuit. Suzanne Weil, the Walker's young, maverick coordinator for performing arts, had heard about the radical Yvonne Rainer and wanted to invite her for the opening of a new building. Her first contact with Rainer's agent was in January 1970, so it was months before Rainer's group morphed into the Grand Union.[2] Only gradually did Weil realize that Rainer had withdrawn as director and was now just one member of this leaderless group.

Weil was intrigued by the web of interdisciplinary relationships in the SoHo milieu, citing the interface between downtown dancers and visual artists like Rauschenberg and Robert Morris. "They were sparking off of each other," said Weil. "It was a very interesting, yeasty time." She was determined to bring them "because I knew they were breaking all the rules."[3]

While in New York a few months in advance, Weil met with Yvonne and David in Rainer's SoHo loft to discuss the residency and field their requests. Yvonne wanted a hundred red rubber balls; David wanted ten men's raincoats. Becky Arnold wanted six black umbrellas and one bicycle. Other requests included two motorcycles, one raft, twenty kites, six jump ropes, and 150 volunteers.[4]

Dancers and nondancers alike signed up to participate in the on-the-spot pieces made by Grand Union members for the Walker. They rehearsed on May 25 and 26 for the community performances on May 27. Journalist Irene Parsons embedded herself among the seventy or so local volunteers. She described the hippie vibe: "They wore everything from leotards to granny skirts to African burnooses; knee boots to bare feet, bushels of hair on head and chin, jeans in states of extreme disrepair. Some alternately nursed babies or swung them casually from a sling."[5]

During the lecture-demonstration on May 26, the Grand Union dancers drifted around the stage of the Walker auditorium, talking to each other. Somehow they invited the audience—whether by plan or by impulse—onto the stage. Critic Scott Bartell recounted a near confrontation that eventually led to a new understanding among the audience:

> [P]eople had expectations about the dancing that weren't being met—"Why don't you all do something together?" one woman asked; "When are you going to begin?" asked another—and the performers became a little defensive. "This is what we do; we're doing it already!" Yvonne Rainer replied.... Gradually, as they began to talk less and move more, the desires of the audience members and performers came closer together and the distinctions between them melted under the warmth of enjoying what was actually happening. The audience was willing, it seemed, to allow their preconceptions about art to be redefined.[6]

It didn't hurt that David was in an exuberant mood. "If I can show you what a good time I'm having, that seems like a good way of giving you a good time, too."[7]

That strategy certainly worked for two future Trisha Brown dancers in the audience: Elizabeth Garren and Judith Ragir. Both were members of the Twin Cities's premier modern dance troupe, the Nancy

David Gordon, Walker Art Center, lec-dem, 1971.
Photo: Tom Berthiaume, courtesy Walker Art Center.

Hauser Dance Company. Garren later said, "We were so blown away."[8]
For Ragir, it was a "life-changing experience." She remembers that
Grand Union rehearsed in the Hauser company's studio and ended up
having a joint improvisation session with Hauser's dancers. She was
duly impressed with Rainer's ability to hold still for a long time (an
ability cultivated by all GU members). But what really caught her was
their sense of freedom. She remembers the rush of adrenaline when
watching them perform: "Trisha, Barbara, and maybe Yvonne were
holding hands skipping around the room to 'You've Got a Friend,' and
my heart went out of my chest, seeing those three women skipping
around to Carole King."[9]

Inspired by Grand Union, Ragir and Garren, along with Gail Turner
(who later joined Meredith Monk's group), formed an improvisational
group that performed in homes and other site-specific spots. Attuned
to Cage's permeability of art and life, they engaged in everyday tasks
as well as fanciful actions. Writer and choreographer Linda Shapiro,
impressed with the group's "startling chemistry" in their site-specific
House Piece, gave the trio a favorable review in 1974.[10] (And I met
these two luscious dancers when I began dancing with Trisha Brown
in 1975.)

GU in lobby of Walker Art Center, 1971. From left: Scott, Dilley, Lewis reaching toward Dilley, Brown bending over, Dunn also bending, Arnold. Photo: Tom Berthiaume, courtesy Walker Art Center.

The daylong performance schedule on May 27 included a piece by Barbara at dawn, a "motorcycle duet" in Loring Park, David's *Sleep Walking* in the old Walker Auditorium, *Meetings* (possibly by Douglas) in the horseshoe pit, Yvonne's *Numerous Frames* at 4:15, *Kites* in Amory Gardens at 5:00, and a performance in the outer lobby at 8:00. The raincoats were put to use for David's *Sleep Walking*, for which the earlier choreography of people slouching against walls escalated into getting shot à la the St. Valentine's Massacre (as seen in the movie *Some Like It Hot*).[11] After the lobby performance, the day concluded with Becky's late-night romp, back in Loring Park, with bicycles and umbrellas. Becky fondly remembers David commenting to her afterward, "That was very Fellini."[12]

GU in lobby of Walker Art Center, 1971. From left: Dilley, Brown, and Arnold singing to Scott. Photo: Tom Berthiaume, courtesy Walker Art Center.

For the performance in the Walker's outer lobby that night, Grand Union transformed the space. Dancer/scholar Judith Brin Inger, who was then a student at Sarah Lawrence College, said: "I remember them constructing, with hammer and nails and wood, an amazing structure in the entrance to the museum. . . . The performance was them building this and hanging on it, under it, and over it. The audience was on a staircase that came down from the upper level of the Guthrie and entered in the foyer. People were standing all around; they could have turned and walked into the museum or into the theater, but instead they were transfixed, watching."[13]

Big cartons were tossed into the middle of this corral-like space. Becky Arnold draped her body on a beam; Trisha hung upside down. Nancy lay on her back on the highest beam, then dove into the cartons. ("I used to dive for the school team.")[14] Douglas stood atop in a wide stance. Barbara, Trisha, and Becky crouched and sang to Scott, who was sitting calmly on one of the beams.

The next day, the performance in the Walker/Guthrie concourse featured a different kind of edifice that took up center stage: a ceramic hippopotamus that Yvonne had borrowed from Nancy Hauser. Critic

Mike Steele, although not entirely positive in his review, caught the wit and playfulness of their antics: "The dancers chant and sing and laugh, while a hippopotamus sculpture stands serene in the middle of the floor (until it is tipped and a leg breaks off, prompting Miss Rainer to stick it down her front and play with it inside her blouse, which prompts Gordon to feign a German accent and demand to remove the lump surgically, which causes everyone to break up)."[15]

Writer Peter Altman felt the performance transcended conventional definitions of art: "The sense of shared life was rare and delicious, and suggested powerfully that whether what the Union had been doing was 'art' or 'beautiful,' the group had forged relationships here that most dance companies in residencies scarcely imagine."[16]

This was the first weeklong residency, and it set the framework for later residencies. David called it "the blueprint." He also articulated a sense of discomfort, a gap between how communal they were expected to be and how individual they really were at that time. "During that residency we established another pattern ... that of seeming to be in support of each other's work. We attended each other's performances conspicuously at all ungodly hours and en masse. To all outward appearances we seemed to be a happily married group (people asked us if we had sex with each other) when in fact I believe we were continually uncomfortable with the work choices of each other (or some of us were, certainly) and the fact that we all seemed to stand for everything that each of us did."[17]

This disconnect is really no surprise considering that from the start they did not like learning each other's work. It also speaks to the naive expectations of viewers who imagined that the harmony they saw in performance somehow extended to the performers' real lives.

One unusual thing about this residency: after the week of community rehearsals and events, and after two GU performances to top it off, Yvonne and Barbara stayed a week longer to give classes and workshops.

INTERLUDE

TRISHA BROWN ON THE GRAND UNION

I remained friends with Trisha up until her death in March 2017. By the time I decided to write about Grand Union, she had descended into dementia. Now it seems like a lost opportunity that we never talked about it. I had joined her company the month before her last GU performance, which was in Tokyo. At that time, she was totally focused on her new works and on us, her new company. Grand Union was in the past. It's a sad irony for me that Trisha, whom I danced with almost every day for three years, is the person least accessible to me of all the GU regulars. But it makes me treasure my conversations with her former comrades that much more. In lieu of having a fresh interview with her, I include this statement, so typical of Trisha's rollicking sense of irreverence and her love of improvising. I don't think she always felt as enthused about Grand Union as this passage suggests. But as Jared Bark reminded me, she was avid about improvising. What follows is her initial response to Sally Banes's second question for the chapter on Grand Union in Terpsichore in Sneakers: *"How did the Grand Union's process develop and change over the six years of its existence?"*

When we began working together, only three or four members of the group knew how to improvise, the others did not and therefore relied on a dance in the Rainer repertory titled *Continuous Project—Altered Daily*. I did not learn that dance, it was my intention to deliver an unpremeditated performance each time. The blank slate approach. At Rutgers on November 6, 1970, my first performance with the Grand Union, I worked alone, unable and unwilling to participate in "known material." This self-imposed isolation caused extreme discomfort, there were so many of them throwing pillows in unison and so few of me looking awkward. Luckily, Steve stepped into my dilemma and asked, "Would you like to dance?" as he extended his arms in the traditional ballroom position of the male lead and we were off . . . for about five years.

There was no way to do something wrong in the Grand Union, improvisation includes error. In the beginning, we were raw and the form unformed and I never knew what was coming next. Steve Paxton arriving with a burning candle installed on his hat symbolizes that period for me. That and the night we verbally reduced a foam-rubber mattress to a kitchen sponge. I pressed for verbal expression (*Yellowbelly, Skymap*) because I liked the state of mind that that exposure produced. In time, all members became multi-voice and could reach cacaphonic heights at the drop of a hat. If you said "Drop a hat," everyone threw them in the air. Subversion was the norm. Everything was fair game except fair game. We were ribald, they were ribald. Too daring. In Tokyo, Steve and David brought a spotlight down to a pinpoint on my face and then hidden by darkness plied my features to music while using the spotlight to "get this." Hilarity pervaded and pervaded and pervaded. There were time lapses, empty moments, collusion with the audience, massive behavior displays, pop music, outlandish get-ups, eloquence, bone-bare confrontations, lack of concern, the women's dance, taking over, paying deference, exhilaration, poignancy, shooting one's wad, wadding up one's wad, making something out of nothing, melodramarooney, cheap shots, being oneself against all odds and dancing. Dancing and dancing and dancing.

Reprinted from Sally Banes, *Terpsichore in Sneakers: Post-Modern Dance* by permission of Wesleyan University Press, 1987, 225–26.

CHAPTER 14

OBERLIN COLLEGE RESIDENCY, JANUARY 1972

It's a tradition at Oberlin that during the winter term students stay on campus if something special is offered them. Brenda Way, who arrived in the dance department in 1970, was determined to give her students something special. Her own history included training at the School of American Ballet (the school affiliated with New York City Ballet) as well as with modern dance greats Jean Erdman and Erick Hawkins. Having done more or less underground theater in Paris, she was all for blurring the line between art and life.[1] Soon after arriving at Oberlin, she put the winter term to work as an immersive time for dance students. For the first intensive, in January 1971, she invited Twyla Tharp and her small company, thus opening a whole new area of quotidian movement for students.[2] For the second year, her choice was Grand Union.

Kimi Okada, a student who later became a founding codirector of Oberlin Dance Collective, said, "Brenda blew the place wide open in terms of exposure for students."[3] Brenda hired experimental theater director Herbert Blau, adding to the creative fervor. He brought some of his California Institute of the Arts students, including Bill Irwin, and mixed them with Oberlin students, who included Julie Taymor and Eric Bogosian.[4] Okada, who was the first dance/theater major, described their presence on campus:

> They immediately disappeared from view and shut themselves into Warner Gym with a sign that said, "Performance Lab in Progress—Do Not Disturb!" For two years we heard screaming every day coming from the room and [we had] no idea what they were up to.... Bill Irwin was one of the more visible members

of the group—he taught an ad hoc "Carnival Techniques" class, which I took. I learned how to eat fire and have a cinder block broken over my stomach with a sledge hammer.... Bill and I shared a love of popular forms—circus skills, tap dance. Given the atmosphere of experimentation and appetite for *everything*, this was not a conflict with "higher art" concepts. We loved both the highbrow and the lowbrow and it was exciting to see how they could coexist. The New Vaudeville movement that happened in the eighties was so much about this.[5]

Having Blau and Way at Oberlin undoubtedly ratcheted up the potential for risk-taking among students.

■

The Grand Union residency at Oberlin, January 2–22, 1972, was the group's longest and most extensive. They committed to teaching two classes each weekday morning and a two-hour workshop in the afternoon. Douglas and Trisha could not be there, so the group consisted of Yvonne, Steve, David, Lincoln, Barbara, and Nancy. Barbara proposed a 9:00 a.m. "Technique Warmup Ritual" and an afternoon workshop open to students of all levels. The 10:30 class was taught by David or Yvonne or both. Nancy offered a daily class that combined Cunningham technique with basic improvisational explorations.[6] According to the schedule, Lincoln gave one open workshop.

Steve held a daily predawn session called the Soft Class. In it he introduced the Small Dance, which is the standing mind-body meditation that is now foundational for Contact Improvisation. (See the "Interlude" on Nancy Stark Smith.) For his afternoon session, Steve decided to work only with men, and only on wrestling mats. He built the workshop around solo material he'd been playing with that drew on his aikido studies. Explaining the genesis of that workshop at a 2008 Contact Improvisation gathering, he said, "I just wanted to be able to leave the planet and not worry about the re-entry ... to get up into the air in any crazy position and somehow have the skill to come back down without damage." He worked with the students on "disorientation ... on colliding and collapsing into the collision, like a soft collision, falling together, falling, rolling together."[7] He focused on the response of the senses within a spherical space, on feeling like the action is all around you rather than on linear paths.

Steve taught with a collaborative spirit, open to ideas from students. Doug Winter, a junior at the time, made a suggestion about the aikido rolls that helped beginners feel safer.[8] Like Nancy Stark Smith in the predawn class, Winter remembers the Small Dance vividly. He felt encouraged by Steve to find his own way into this very interior process. For Winter, his discovery was "close internal corrections I was constantly making in my relationship to gravity ... tiny little circles." He felt the approach was "tremendously natural."[9]

Magnesium, the kinetically charged piece that came out of the men's workshop, was performed in Warner Gym with no designated front. Winter remembers being surrounded by the audience, most of which had gathered on the running track above that ringed the gym. Watching the video, shot by Steve Christiansen,[10] I would describe the contact as bouncing off each other, sometimes bumping chests or ricocheting off each other's backs. *Magnesium* looks like molecules randomly hitting each other, then going their own way. In 2008, Paxton described the action as "a lot of crashing around on a mat, followed by a lift of a randomly chosen sacrifice, one of the guys was lifted up by all the other guys and put way up in the air."[11] Even seen on the imperfect medium of video, the spontaneity is exhilarating. Shortly after that group lift, the men settled into "the stand," when they concentrated on the Small Dance. To the naked eye, it looks as if they are standing still, but we know from Nancy Stark Smith's interlude that a lot of tiny adjustments are going on inside the body.

The January 21 program comprised works by Barbara, Yvonne, and David for the students. Barbara's piece, titled *Prologue — The Figure*, started the evening off outdoors. She describes it as "a large group exploration in duration and repetition and journey" whose pattern was based on a symbol associated with the Bollingen edition of the *I Ching*. It went on for hours and may have continued while other works were performed inside Hall Auditorium. During the course of it, "[W]e sat by the side of the trail, ate snacks, napped and walked some more with new comrades. We might have carried flashlights."[12] Definitely in keeping with Barbara's vision of performance as part of daily life.

During Rainer's piece, made for more than forty students and titled *In the College*, her interest in film surfaced. She showed snippets of old silent movies — but only the intertitles. She used texts from Russian

Nancy Stark Smith and Steve Paxton in a Contact Improvisation session, 1984.
Photo: Bill Arnold

film director Sergei Eisenstein and G. W. Pabst's scenario for *Pandora's Box* (1928). Yvonne, who hadn't actually seen Pabst's film at that point, was enchanted by the production stills of the glamorous Louise Brooks (aka Lulu)[13]—who, by the way, had toured with Ruth St. Denis and Ted Shawn in the early twenties.

Yvonne used text in this piece, both written and spoken. Dreams written down by students were recited. Some of the quotes by Carl Jung that she had used in *Grand Union Dreams* migrated to *In the College*, including this one: "A man who has not passed through the inferno of his passions has not overcome them."[14] In some way, Rainer may have recognized this as relevant to her own passions that had almost destroyed her. (More about her suicide attempt in chapter 18.)

Linda Shapiro, a dancer and faculty spouse who was in the piece,[15] recalled Yvonne teaching them various tasks with the aim of doing them in as straightforward a manner as possible—no flourishes, no impulses. One such task was to "pick the Kleenex out of the Kleenex box, over and over again. And she would say, 'Nope, you're doing that with an impulse.' That was a revelation to me ... that I, automatically, as a dancer, would do something completely unconsciously."[16]

Shapiro also remembers a section about glamour, no doubt sparked by Rainer's fascination with the Lulu stills. "There were a couple of students who were drop-dead gorgeous in this piece. One had a mop of red hair. Yvonne really used the glamorous girls. On the one hand, there was this straightforwardness, and on the other hand there was something about the glamor that was part of it."

David regarded the residencies as an enforced opportunity to choreograph. "When the Grand Union goes and has residencies, we all have to commit to teaching something. I don't have anything to teach, so I just keep making work or teaching people to do the work I've just made. *Sleep Walking* is in the first residency [the Walker in 1971], and *Sleep Walking* leads to *The Matter*."[17] He started with simple tasks in the Oberlin workshop. Paul Langland, who was visiting that day, remembers, "In an improvised group score, he had us each pick up a folding chair, walk in various spatial patterns with it, put the chair down, sit down, get up, pick up the chair, walk and repeat the action."[18]

The Matter became a group work of great complexity when presented at the Cunningham Studio that April.[19] In this beginning effort for twenty-four students at Oberlin, it included a breakfast scene in pajamas, a bathing beauty section, and a scene in which people change into army outfits at the base of the Statue of Liberty, played by Nancy Lewis getting drowsy.[20] It included a reprisal of *Mannequin* (1962), which was originally a solo in which David rotated slowly while wiggling fingers and singing "Second Hand Rose." He also taught the students *Oh Yes*, which was a piece he'd made in a rented studio when he was doing nothing (more details in the interlude on nothingness after chapter 22) while waiting to be inspired to make art.[21]

In the Grand Union tradition of choosing music by chance, David, on his way to rehearsal, happened to hear a student practicing Schubert on a piano. He liked the sound, so he asked the student, Sue Tepley, if he could audiotape her, "with all hesitations and her repeats intact" to use for *The Matter*.[22]

The Grand Union gave its own performance on January 22 in Hall Auditorium. (The group may have performed in Warner Gym earlier in the residency.) From the video, it looks like a typically ragtag performance with the usual assortment of explosive highs and low-energy lulls.[23] Steve, flush from the performance of his *Magnesium* that afternoon, was full of rambunctious energy. Yvonne, on the other hand, was uncharacteristically subdued. However, the video reveals that much of the group's MO was already in place. They were daring, intuitive, rambling, goofy, interactive, highly physical with each other, and patient. They were blessedly free of confrontation; that came later. The student audience was totally enthralled. Many of them had performed in either David's or Steve's piece that afternoon, or Yvonne's or Barbara's the day before.

For Doug Winter, their performance was "my first personal experience of chaos in a dance context." He had an additional reaction that made the first reaction even more intense: "I found those people very hot, very attractive in a core, fundamental way."[24] (There were plenty of us in New York who felt the same way.)

Certain wardrobe motifs threaded through the evening. Everyone seemed to don a silly or regal hat—even a bowl—at some point. And an underwear theme: Barbara and Lincoln wore white long johns, and at one point Steve stripped to his undershirt and some kind of twisted, skimpy loincloth he'd picked up in India. Yvonne was the only one who did not change her outfit during this evening.

What was perhaps most memorable was a single action that involved the audience more than the dancers. Steve, sounding like an auctioneer exhorting the audience to bid ever higher, coaxed them to fetch a huge gymnastic mat from the back of the theater (where he had previously stashed it) and pass it over their heads until it reached the stage. "C'mon, let's go! Get your hands on the mat! There it goes!" As the crowd got hold of the mat, he incited them even more. "C'mon, you can do it. Hands on the mat! Keep it going!" From the sounds on the video (the camera could not follow the mat into the crowd), I could see why Brenda Way called that scene "a conceptual mosh pit." The communal effort caused a storm of hoots and hollers as the mat traveled through the audience. There was much cheering when the mat finally landed at the foot of the stage, undulating like an ocean wave.

Other moments were less spectacular but still compelling. David writhed on the floor while telling a story as Steve placed the mic near his mouth, his chest, his belly. Nancy, way off to the side, mimicked getting shot, as she had learned in David's *Sleep Walking*, but in the most comically histrionic way. Lincoln threw apples to the audience. Barbara stood draped like the Statue of Liberty—wearing a skull mask. Yvonne stepped out into the audience, singing "Steve is dead."

GU at Oberlin, 1972. Foreground from left: Gordon, Scott. Background from left: Rainer, Paxton, Dilley. Screen grab from video by Steve Christiansen.

There was some nice duet work too. Nancy pushed a shopping cart while Lincoln stood in it, waving his arms like a breeze. Steve danced crazy fast and jittery while holding Barbara's hand as she calmly stretched her other hand up to the light. David and Lincoln strutted around in a circle to "Let the Good Times Roll," David in a drum major outfit (probably procured from Oberlin's costume shop) and Lincoln in his long underwear. After the mat arrived on the stage, Steve sculpted his body into yoga-like positions on the mat—in his India-inflected underwear. Yvonne moved toward and away from him as though he were a bronze statue.

The one solo that led to a full ensemble action was Nancy Lewis's rock-star gambit. She was holding, caressing, tilting, and abusing a standing mic while silently howling and growling. She drifted over from the stage-right corner toward center, where the other five fell into place as hyperactive backup singers. Steve and Lincoln jogged in place, Yvonne was springing up and down, Barbara waved a scarf, and David grabbed his crotch as he pranced (a decade before Michael Jackson, let it be noted). Nancy's act morphed into a dancing tantrum until Barbara enveloped her with a scarf and David hugged and swayed with her. When the music changed to a slow, melancholic tune, the group shifted into calm gestures, then held each other's hands or shoulders. By the time the song ended, the whole group had merged, partly covered by the big silk scarf, into a close huddle, gently swaying for three minutes … a grand and quiet union. Even watching on video, you could feel how all six shared this closeness in an almost animal way. A group hibernation.

The Oberlin video provides an opportunity to see some of the dancers in the early stages of their GU development. David was already following Trisha's edict—"Keep talking no matter what!"—with aplomb. As he sat atop the piano, singing a medley that included "Along Came Bill" from *Showboat*, "My Funny Valentine," and "It Had to Be You"—pretty much at the top of his lungs—Yvonne did what she could to obstruct him. She draped her body over his, wrapped her torso around his head, and stood on his thigh. And still he kept his singing going. (The student pianist, Sue Tepley, kept practicing whatever she was practicing, according to plan.) Later, lying on his back, David was stroking his hair as he spoke to Yvonne about a hair dryer. But he was not yet creating characters for anyone else in these monologues, as he did later in New York performances. Between January and June, he seems to have graduated from weaving a solo fantasy to a more populated fantasy.

Steve was into all kinds of mischief, ranging from being virtually invisible—concealed behind the piano except for his hand holding the mic for David just above the piano's backboard—to being the rabble rouser who whipped the audience into a frenzy of passing the mat. Another moment saw him sending a flashlight into the audience, asking each person to keep the light aimed at the raised hand of the person who owned the flashlight. His interest in involving the audience continued through many of the GU performances. But his party dancing with Barbara at Oberlin had a manic, loose-hipped, polyrhythmic quality that I rarely saw in later videos.

Nancy was the shameless entertainer, totally extroverted, whether posing quaintly as an old-time opera singer or launching into her all-out rock-star imitation. This kind of theatricality was natural for her, but she toned it down in later performances.

Lincoln showed promise as a sensitive, willing improviser. He was clearly committed to the group aesthetic and supported his colleagues

GU at Oberlin, 1972. From left: Scott, Rainer.
Screen grabs from video by Steve Christiansen.

with a poetic presence and whimsical choices. He coiled himself in a shopping cart duet, creating a character that Barbara could play off of. During a silly duet between Yvonne and Nancy, he played his bamboo flute, adding a serene note. He made blowing-wind sounds into the mic (as mentioned previously) while Nancy tipped David over in a chair on one side of the stage and Steve and Barbara danced together on the other side. He hardly ever ventured downstage. As mentioned, it's possible that he felt shy among older dancers, among white dancers, and/or among dancers who were technically more experienced.[25] But it's clear from the video that the other GU members accepted him, both physically and theatrically, as a fellow traveler.

Brenda Way, who later formed Oberlin Dance Collective at the college and moved it to San Francisco in 1976, was surprised by the Grand Union performers' physicality. She thought she had invited them for their conceptual strength, but she ended up feeling that their conscious physicality was more notable. She realized they were intuitive rather than strategic, that they collected information "springing from previous improvisations that they'd done, what they knew about each other, and the moment itself. It felt to me like drawing on the resources that their lives had accumulated rather than formal strategies."[26] She came to the conclusion that it was not the form of improvisation that distinguished Grand Union, but the individuality of the dancers. They had no magic prescription up their sleeves—except to be themselves.

Two Oberlin students—Nancy Stark Smith and Curt Siddall—went on to become long-term proponents of Contact Improvisation. But the GU residency had a lasting impact on all the students: "I think it was radical in terms of form, and the definition of dance and what's acceptable," said Brenda Way. "After they came, in composition class for instance, people would walk up and before they were ready to start, someone would say, 'Well, has it started?' That was a real consciousness shift, which I loved.... And the talking, David's verbal approach and the prods he used with verbal narrative, that was something lots of people picked up to play with."

Interestingly, Way felt that *Magnesium* had as much of an impact on the women students as on the men: "Everybody was affected by *Magnesium*. That was one of those radical shifts in body concept that went on, I would say, in great part among the women because they hadn't been part of that first piece.... In a way, it was kind of a feminist impact, that no matter what size body, you could be part of that expanded flying experience that people had thought of primarily as a skinny ballet thing."

Magnesium was a precursor to Contact Improvisation, which went on to sustain itself as a growing, evolving dance form all over the world. As Steve has said, CI had begun to evolve in GU before *Magnesium*. And further back, Steve was involved as a performer in Simone Forti's Dance Constructions and Trisha Brown's *Lightfall*. As you can see in the interlude "Paxton's Clarifying Thoughts" (chapter 17), he was already talking about the preparation necessary for weight-bearing maneuvers before the Oberlin residency. But *Magnesium* took it further. And then, when Steve taught at Bennington College that spring of 1972, it evolved even further into an all-gender, duet form.[27] By June, when Steve performed at SoHo's John Weber Gallery with students from Oberlin, Bennington, and University of Rochester, the form had been named Contact Improvisation.

INTERLUDE

NANCY STARK SMITH ON THE SMALL DANCE

In our phone conversation, Nancy Stark Smith recalled with vividness the Soft Class that Steve taught at Oberlin before dawn. She was the student who, after seeing men perform *Magnesium*, told Steve, "If you ever work like this with women, I'd love to know about it." The rest is history. Nancy Stark Smith (1952–2020) is a legend in her own right, not only for her mastery of CI and for founding and coediting *Contact Quarterly*, but for the joy she took in dancing. Early on, she realized that engaging in CI put her in "a radically altered and rather blissful state."[1] Here are quotes from three sources: the 2008 book by and about her called *Caught Falling*, our phone conversation: and a 1985 edition of *Contact Quarterly* in which she describes "the stand."

> I'd slip in and out of consciousness in the activity, in the dark, with Steve's low, hypnotic voice guiding our attention to our body's sensation, the light in the room beginning to arrive, until by the end of the hour, the sun was streaming through the windows and class would be over. I was touched by this experience in a way that sometimes made me want to weep though I didn't know why.[2]

> The Small Dance was basically standing still and releasing tension and turning your attention to notice the small reflexive activity that the body makes to keep itself balanced and not fall over. So you're standing and relaxing and noticing what your body's doing. You're not doing it but you're noticing what it's doing. That kind of awareness . . . is sort of the basis for Contact training, of feeling the forces in a larger way, like momentum and falling. There are little falls, little catches,

little supports that are happening within standing that we spent a lot of time paying attention to.[3]

The micromovements that occur to keep me balanced are so tiny and yet so magnified, and arise from such a deep feeling of stillness and space, that I get giddy, tickled by the impossible magnitude of such subtle sensations. The disorientation in the stand comes from the feeling that inside the apparent solidity and stillness of standing, there is nothing but movement and space! Each time, I come to feel as precarious standing on the floor on two legs as I might on one leg on a trampoline.[4]

CHAPTER 15

THE DANCE GALLERY FESTIVAL, SPRING 1973

Perhaps spurred by the success of the Walker and Oberlin residencies, the Grand Union dancers (without Yvonne, who had left the group to make films) decided they wanted to perform more. They applied for a grant from the New York State Council on the Arts, rented the Larry Richardson Dance Gallery on East 14th Street for two months, and performed seventeen times during April and May 1973. (How did they get through that many improvised performances? Steve emailed: "We plowed through.")[1] To fill in the nights they weren't on, they invited more than twenty guests, mostly old friends from the Judson days like Deborah Hay and visual artist Alex Hay, as well as theater group Mabou Mines, dancer Carmen Beuchat, and musician Dickie Landry, to perform one or more times. David Gordon had a solo night. Nancy had a night with musician Richard Peck in which they invited other artists and musicians onstage. Steve's "collaborative ensemble" from Bennington, where he was teaching, gave two performances; so did Barbara's offshoot group, the Natural History of the American Dancer.

This two-month marathon was similar to the Walker and Oberlin residencies, but on the group's home turf. The Grand Union had to supply consistent activity and interact with the community. They relied on the willingness of the SoHo "tribe" to be part of an exchange in which they alternated between performing and spectating.

Deborah Jowitt expressed a wish to see all seventeen GU performances. But she wrote a wonderful review after just one, noting that GU eluded the common pitfalls of improvisation:

> [T]hey don't affect any of that false intimacy that some actors and dancers use. Nor do they jump about from one thing to the

next, trying to introduce contrast or draw audience attention. They take all the time they need to let something evolve naturally, without doing too much on-the-spot editing or juicing up of their activities. There is something very unselfish about them: they find satisfying ways to join something that they themselves might not have chosen to do—perhaps out of love or respect for the person who started it.[2]

Jowitt also enjoyed the fun stuff—"a fantastic human pyramid and a lot of very funny dialogue about a family of circus acrobats (maybe)"— as well as the everyday casualness of what they chose to do. She felt that the dull moments were more than offset by the intimacy they projected: "Certainly they can be boring, strained, or arch. But if you were fond enough of them to see a lot of their performances, you'd accept their limitations or low points the way you accept the inadequacies in a person you love."

Nancy has a memory of a Dance Gallery performance that illustrates how involved the audience was. She remembers Trisha walking atop the ballet barre that lined the room and how, when she came to a space between the barres, "it would be nearly impossible for her to navigate! But someone would come flying across from the other side of the space—Steve or Doug—and the audience heaved a sigh of relief."[3]

On another occasion, Douglas, walking precariously on top of that barre, announced that he was thirsty. Someone from the audience offered a cup with a little bit of water in it. Nancy took it and held it up to him. He drank the water, then tossed the cup down.[4]

Grand Union not only invited others to have their own evening, but also invited guest artists to enter into its performance. The members were still curious about what it would be like to work with colleagues who could potentially mesh well. Two of the mostly likely were Lisa Nelson and Simone Forti, both of them daring and sensitive improvisers. And for both, the experience was a dead end.

Lisa had been working with Daniel Nagrin's Workgroup, which in 1972 had more theater than dance people in it. Nagrin had come to watch GU at LoGiudice Gallery, possibly because Barbara had been in his company before she joined Cunningham. Lisa remembers Nagrin and some of the others in the Workgroup talking about GU, but she

GU in Dance Gallery Festival, 1973. Dunn on barre, Lewis handing a cup of water up to him. Below, from left: Dilley, Gordon, Forti (as guest), Brown. Photo: Tom Brazil.

GU in Dance Gallery Festival, 1973. From left: Dilley on floor; Lewis; Forti, as a guest artist, wearing blindfold; Gordon. Photo: Tom Brazil.

had not yet seen the group. She had met Steve while they were both teaching at Bennington the spring of 1972, and they easily landed in a studio improvising together. She was (and is) a superb improviser with a kind of animal nerve center. But she's not a talker onstage, and when she came to the Dance Gallery, David's verbal attempt to make her feel welcome backfired. She ended up sitting out most of the evening.[5]

Simone had worked closely with Steve and Trisha, both of whom have said they were artistically indebted to her. But while actually performing with GU, she reacted with ambivalence. She perceived the kind of "going toward nonsense" in the spoken material as similar to a strain of the work with Halprin in the late fifties that she had gotten exasperated with. At that time she felt the Halprin verbal engagement had become surreal and not grounded in people's feelings. When she encountered this brand of cleverness in GU, she had an opinion: "I was very stuck up about it," she said later. "I thought this is old stuff that they're doing."[6] But she became unexpectedly emotional. "I was crying onstage in performance because I had walked away from that. I couldn't go back to it. I now wish I had."[7]

Another, more unlikely guest was composer Bob Telson, a musician immersed in classical as well as jazz forms. As a student at Harvard, he had played for dance classes at Radcliffe, including when Dilley was guest teaching. Later, his group of jazz musicians and Barbara's group the Natural History of the American Dancer (at that time consisting of Dilley, Lewis, Cynthia Hedstrom, and Mary Overlie) improvised together once a week in his loft in Tribeca. In that merged group, called the Collected Works, sometimes "a couple of us musicians would get out there and move too.... It was a free-flowing thing that was definitely in the spirit of the times."[8] The Collected Works earned a spot in the festival, but in addition, Telson was invited as a guest in one of GU's own performances.

About Grand Union's experiments with new people, David recalled, "It never worked. We had turned into a closed shop somehow."[9]

Nancy remembers the way one particular evening ended: "One night as we were trying to figure out how to end our performance, I felt bad about something I thought was not very good about my performance. So I went to lie down under a bench that was against the wall. Steve came over and lay down beside me, almost squeezing underneath me. Then Barbara came, and then Trisha and David sat down on the bench. It was a good ending—sweet and compassionate."[10]

That moment was caught in a photograph by Cosmos and put on a little comic strip publicity flyer. Nancy added the words, "What are you doing after the show?" as though David were asking Trisha, sitting on the bench.

The festival also gave GU members a chance to engage in their most radical acts. For his April 30 solo night, Steve continued his interest in censorship. His earlier piece, *Beautiful Lecture*, which juxtaposed a porn film with a film of the Bolshoi's *Swan Lake*, had been forbidden when he first proposed it to The New School. In response, Steve had replaced the porn film with a documentary about people starving in Biafra. As with *Intravenous Lecture* (mentioned in chapter 8), he was asking, What, really, is obscenity? For the Dance Gallery version, titled *Air*, he kept the ballet/porn film pairing, with himself "writhing between them."[11] He also incorporated something very of-the-moment and obscene in its own way: President Nixon's first deceitful Watergate speech ("There can be no whitewash at the White House"), played live, that night, on a TV set.

Graphic from GU in Dance Gallery Festival, 1973. From left: Dilley, Paxton, Lewis, Gordon, Brown. This was the last image in an accordion-type flyer designed in 1973. Photo: Cosmos; graphic by Artservices; words by Nancy Lewis.

A former member of GU reentered the fray during the festival with her own radical act, so to speak. Writing in the *New York Times*, Don McDonagh noted "as an unexpected added attraction, Yvonne Rainer doing a stripper's bump and grind with wit and verve."[12]

The festival didn't really have a name, but the blurb on top of the poster reads: "Grand Union and friends and associates in two months of performing and carrying on!"

And carry on they did. Possibly the best record of their raucousness is this passage from Sally Sommer's notes about the time that David and Steve had come to the theater dressed as "twins":

Nothing was working. No one connected. Nancy was obsessed by the hundreds of square pillows. Trish joined her by lying on a stack of them. Nothing. David dropped some of them on Trish. Nancy threw more. Barbara sat on a stack of them. Nothing. Barbara retired. Trish got up to do a duet with Nancy. Nothing. David launched into a TV game show with Nancy and Steve as a soon-to-be-wed couple. More attempts to connect with each other. (Trish to Steve: "Where am I? What the hell am I doing here?") Old gymnastic tricks with a ballet barre. Something, but not much, except Steve's pants rip wide open at the crotch. David offers his pants but Barbara offers both the matching skirts. Steve: "I'm game." They rush off. Hungarian music. Will anything work? Suddenly David and Steve burst out into a mad, exhilarated, bizarre, distorted, quasi-cossack rough-and-tumble melee. It's funny but just as it might get cutesy drag funny, Steve begins some dangerous flying leaps over the barre and then grabs David into frantic spins … flinging him off the floor into the air, plunging him back down … twirling, twisting, dangling, tangling,… but never stopping the frantic dervish of whirling bodies. Collapse. They finish. It worked. Like a volcanic eruption, it worked.[13]

Although moments like these were wildly appreciated, the series was financially a bust. The modest grant from the New York State Council on the Arts barely covered the costs of presenting such a long, complex season, and very little other money, either earned or unearned, was coming in. The upshot was that the dancers were paid only a fraction of the amount projected.[14] But there was this: although only forty or fifty people came most nights—and they tended to be the same people—on the last night of GU's performance, more than two hundred people crammed into the space, lining the staircase as well as the downstairs level.

DOUGLAS DUNN ON THE

"SELFISH/SELFLESS GAMUT"

The following excerpt is from Dancer Out of Sight:
Collected Writings of Douglas Dunn.

As a post–World War II California kid I attended a progressive grammar school where teachers let us run wild but intervened to identify individual versus collective priorities. Learning to distinguish between my and others' needs and desires turned out to be relevant everywhere: on athletic teams, on boards of directors, in subway cars and in dance companies. Grand Union provided a hot caldron for exploration of the selfish/selfless gamut. Deciding to perform without rehearsing meant more than a lack of preparation—it meant absolute freedom. It meant that "nothing has to happen/ anything can happen" was now bounded only by each individual's range of fantasy and courage. Both had fenced limits within me, some already there, some defined by what I knew or imagined others present would dislike. Dancing with Grand Union extended the terrain inside the fences.

Doing what one wants to do in private is one thing, performing in public another, and performing in public in cahoots with colleagues—people with whom one had, to boot, off-stage relations—yet another. One minute we might choose to develop the most benign kind of movement or verbal relating, using a brand of ironic deadpan we often favored which undercut, sometimes by exaggeration, conventional modes of pandering. The next we might thrust ourselves at one another physically in potentially dangerous forms of partnering, or bring up painful personal information, testing whether the other could stay in character sufficiently to handle the heat.

On a good night I had not a single front brain thought for the hour or two we were out there, went instead from one simple or complicated or outrageous activity to the next as if every word and move had been choreographed, as if instincts of the kind that make animals' actions appear assured were guiding me. Hindsight tells me I was, to keep fear at bay, riding two unconsciously conjured clouds of "confidence": the first, that deep down others were not out to "get" me; the second, that no matter what might happen, I could hold my own.

What evolved and remains is a self-reliance grown sturdier through dealing with consistently unruly circumstances. Also, a belief in the synergistic potential of "performed" interaction . . . that deepened through gradually realizing just how complex and radically surprising was our collaboration. I am forever grateful to each Grand Union dancer for daring to participate in this profoundly life-expanding adventure.

Reprinted with permission from *Dancer Out of Sight: Collected Writings of Douglas Dunn* (drawings by Mimi Gross; designed and produced by Ink, Inc., New York, New York, 2012), 139.

PART IV Narrative Unfoldings

Grand Union gave more than fifty performances during its six years, yet only twelve were videotaped (that I know of). There are two reasons for this: first, though it's hard to picture in today's overexposed world, video was not routinely used back then; most video cameras were large and expensive, and not many dancers owned one. Second, Grand Union dancers were not interested in documenting their work. As Nancy Lewis reminded me, they were "adamant" about avoiding any record of their improvised performances.[1] The idea was to be in the moment and not worry about past or future. However, video recordings do exist from Oberlin, LoGuidice Gallery, Walker Art Center, University of Iowa, La MaMa, Seibu in Tokyo, and the University of Montana at Missoula. (There is also a homemade film of the informal performance in Prospect Park, Brooklyn, and a few seconds of confusing footage from the rooftop of the San Francisco Art Institute, both in 1971.) Some were shot by the presenting organization and others by individuals. Not all have been well maintained and digitized.

Video is a far cry from live dancing. The two-dimensional format flattens the dancing, and the camera's framing doesn't tell the whole story. Therefore, I had decided *not* to attempt to "translate" these artifacts to the page. I was planning to rely on interviews, photographs, and people's memories (my own included). And then ... I received a message from the dead.

Let me explain. I came across a book review of Margaret Hupp Ramsay's *The Grand Union (1970–1976): An Improvisational Performance Group*. This book, mentioned in the introduction, has been helpful to me, especially for its listings of performance dates and articles. The review, written by Marianne Goldberg, appeared in *Dance Research Journal* in 1994. (It happens that both Ramsay and Goldberg earned their PhDs from NYU's Department of Performance Studies. Remarkably, they were both in a course that I cotaught at NYU with, and on, Trisha Brown in 1982.)

In her review, Goldberg, who died in 2015, appreciated Ramsay's efforts but wrote: "What is most absent [in Ramsay's book] is sustained description or analysis of performance material. . . . Ramsay does not tell much about how one improvised moment follows others, or about how the shape of an evening or series of evenings progressed, backtracked, cross-referenced, or stalled. Instead she gives glimpses of moments taken from the six-year period. . . . My response to this absence is longing for knowledge about improvisational content, in as much depth as possible."[2]

I fixated on the word *longing*. I realized that I too had this longing, and that the only way to provide the "improvisational content in as much depth as possible" was indeed to "translate" the archival videos to the page. To me, this meant going past the intriguing or hilarious glimpses that people—both performers and audience—remember, and witnessing the ebb and flow of the collectively created waves of activity.

One could watch Grand Union (either live or on video) through any one of several filters. You could concentrate on the performers' individual movement explorations, on how their dancing drew them into interactions with each other, or on how those interactions escalated into psychological dramas. You could watch how a recurring motif found its way into a different situation, accumulating new shades of meanings. You could watch them create or lose momentum. You could watch them knit together scattered actions and watch those strands come apart. You could watch them join a collective fantasy as it gathers steam. Or, you could shift between all these modes, because that is what Grand Union did.

Considering that they were improvising every minute, the flashes of cohesiveness were quite astonishing. There was no set choreography or even a bare-bones structure. And yet they planted seeds that sprouted later in the program or gave hints of narrative to chew on—a ladder here, a length of cloth there. They seemed to have a sixth sense, a subliminal ability to use their peripheral vision—or perhaps

GU performance at NYC Dance Marathon, 14th Street Y, 1971. From left:
Gordon, Arnold, Lewis, Scott, Rainer. Photo: James Klosty.

something like echolocation that only certain species have—to know
where the others were in space.

They each had moments of uncertainty, of drifting or spacing out.
But it was remarkable how rare those moments were. They were more
often in the zone of "I am doing this now. I am not waiting to find out
if it's any good or if I could've made a better choice. I am not judging
myself. I am just throwing myself into it."

Grand Union dancers never laughed at each other's jokes or showed
surprise in any way. They were inside the world they created together,
ready for anything. There seemed to be no limit to their trust in each
other. Their weaving together of intention and happenstance, as inex-
tricable as warp and woof, often yielded moments that were offhand-
edly, startlingly beautiful.

What I've tried to do in these descriptions that I am calling "narrative unfoldings" is to give a sense of the flow—of how one thing led
to, coexisted with, or interrupted another. Physical and psychological interactions unfolded with the illusion of inevitability. Whether
subliminally engaged in narrative or not, the Grand Union dancers

allowed each other to complete the story or the picture. One could say they each had an animal's instinct for knowing they were part of a larger ecosystem.

I've chosen five of the videos to "translate," to give some sense of the ebb and flow: the first, third, and fourth performances from LoGiudice Gallery in 1972, the one at the University of Iowa in 1974, and the lobby event from Walker Art Center in 1975. Most of the performances were about two hours long, shot by a single camera. Some of the action took place outside the camera's frame, and I've edited out some of the detail that *was* visible (or else this book would be thousands of pages long). This means that I have shaped the unfoldings according to my own sense of cause and effect—or sometimes the logic of non sequiturs. Another person would notice different things and break the sessions up in a different ways. However, I've immersed myself in these videos and have strong memories of each dancer in the group. So, consider these "narrative unfoldings" one person's annotated version.

I have used the present tense in order to bring some immediacy to these renderings. In a way, these actions do exist in the present— digitally.

CHAPTER 16

FIRST LOGIUDICE VIDEO, MAY 1972

In the early days of Grand Union, when Yvonne Rainer was still a member, the performances sometimes took on a highly emotional quality. No longer the leader, Rainer had lost some of the sense of purpose that drove her to make CP-AD. In Grand Union, she allowed herself to become unknowing and vulnerable. At the same time, others were feeling their oats. Trisha found she could exert control over her fellow performers; David found he could use words to tell stories, to entertain, or to reverse the course of a scene; Nancy could organically develop a complete solo, building it with intricacy and force; Barbara was not afraid to tread the line between athletic and sexual; Steve could slow things down, exerting a gravitational pull. Douglas (who was not present in this first video) could explore movement with great intention no matter what the others were doing.

Following is a description of the first reel of the four 1972 performances at LoGiudice Gallery in SoHo (downstairs from The Kitchen), which was videotaped under the direction of Carlota Schoolman at the suggestion of Trisha Brown. For a while the narrative seemed to gather around a toy gun: who had it, who refused it, who pulled the trigger. It reminded me of how, while watching José Limón's The Moor's Pavane, *if you just followed the white handkerchief you could get the whole story that way. However, because the single camera lens could not capture everything, I couldn't completely follow the path of the gun. That approach would have ascribed too much cohesiveness to the proceedings anyway.*

One of the typical dynamics we see here is the choice to react or not to react. This is related to a more specific dynamic: daring to fall and trusting that someone will catch you.

Note that, because all the tapes are labeled May 28, 1972, even though the series extended from May 28 to May 31, I am not 100 percent sure this video was the first performance, or even whether it encompassed one whole performance.

Yvonne, wearing big, billowy Indian pants and a sun visor, is dancing to the calypso beat of Harry Nilsson's song "Put the Lime in the Coconut." She's holding Barbara with one hand and holding Steve, who is twisting and turning on the floor, with the other. Thus connected, she's loosely, even carelessly, bopping to the music. Perhaps she's taking the lyrics of the song literally: "You're such a silly woman." A toy gun falls from her clothing and clatters to the floor.

Steve reaches for it, grabs it, and drags himself on his forearms. David, wearing coveralls and sunglasses, saunters by, hands in pockets.

Yvonne is wheeling her arms in big, sagittal circles. Barbara steers Yvonne from behind as they windmill their arms together. They end the song with gentle hip bumping.

The Nilsson album has moved on to "Let the Good Times Roll." (The *Nilsson Schmilsson* album, which had come out that year, was a favorite.)

Each dancer absorbs the song differently: Trisha, standing, just turns her head from side to side as in "no." Steve and David stroll back and forth, shoulder to shoulder, or back to front, both with a supercool, noirish deadpan. When Steve changes his angle, so does David. Steve repeatedly extends the gun toward David, who turns away each time.

■

Barbara, hands on hips, stops dead in her tracks and looks right at Steve, who is standing still. Nancy and Yvonne also pause. Trisha comes over and puts the gun (which Steve must have let go of at some point) into Steve's hand and walks away. David goes to Steve, who is still still. He places a hand on Steve's right arm, the one holding the gun. No one moves. Steve slowly keels over sideways to the floor in one solid plank. It's hard to see in the video, but David has lowered him to the ground.

The song is now "Jump into the Fire," with the insistent lyrics, "We can make each other happy." Nancy picks up a paper airplane from the floor and sends it sailing toward the audience.

Barbara, with hands still on hips, turns her head away from Steve, toward the camera. (Trisha still has her back to the camera.) When Barbara realizes the cameraperson is focusing on her, she slowly turns her whole body to face our direction. With a half Zen-like, half impish expression, she seems to invite the camera to zoom in, which it does for about thirty seconds. As the camera zooms out, Barbara slips behind Trisha, creating an eclipse of her own face.

David has bent over to look at Steve lying still, as though trying to solve a mystery. He picks the gun up from the floor. Nancy looks at Steve, takes off her long, below-the-knee sweater, and covers him with it. David gives the gun to Yvonne, who tucks it into her trousers.

The song has segued into drumming, no vocals. Nancy, standing over "dead" Steve, begins shaking to the beat. She works herself up to a feverish pitch, like a medicine man exorcising spirits.

A few feet away, Trisha is on the floor, belly down, in solidarity with Steve. David lifts Trisha to standing, all in one plank, similar to the way he lowered Steve. She falls back on him again, and he lifts her again.

Yvonne slowly extends the gun into the vicinity of Nancy's vibrational dance. Nancy, head down, is oblivious of this gesture until it actually intercepts her. She takes the toy gun, casually points it to her left, clicks the trigger, and hands it back to Yvonne. [Laughter.] Nancy resumes her manic solo to the point where her whole body is undulating and she's blowing out of puffed-up cheeks. A virtuoso shaker, convulsive but shimmery, she's in the zone. She's making a one-time-only dance that escalates beautifully and finally subsides to just her wrists twisting in and out around her hips.

The gun click seems to have awakened Steve, who crawls, reptile-like, then gradually rises until he's walking, still shrouded under Nancy's hooded sweater.

■

Trisha crouches on the floor, with David sitting nearby. Three times she touches her head to the floor, as though bowing, then sits back up. She gently pulls David to the floor, belly-up, in front of her. This time, when she puts her head to the floor, his chest is there to cushion her. With her face on his chest-pillow, she looks like a peaceful child.

Now on their hands and knees, Trisha and David playfully pull each other's heads down. They grab each other's supporting arms to make the body buckle. Trisha takes keys from her pocket and throws them down. David puts them in his pocket, then finds a piece of crumpled paper in his other pocket and lays it down. She picks it up and tucks it into her shirt. He puts down the keys. They are goading each other like dogs in a dog run. She points over her shoulder, then runs around and lands on his back, sidesaddle, toppling him. They slide, dive, and pounce, all the while keeping their eyes on each other. In the next playful chase, Trisha grabs a heavy, clanking chain from a small mound of props near a pillar—probably Yvonne's stash of stuff.

Yvonne inserts herself into the space between Trisha and David. She points to Trisha accusingly, then grabs the chain and makes off with it. She reenters their playing field and steps on the crumpled paper that is an object of contention between Trisha and David. Like a cat that needs no preparation, Trisha bounds up onto Yvonne's shoulders. Shocked, Yvonne lets out a long, foghorn-sounding yell as though calling foul.

Back to the dogfight with David, Trisha throws down the wad of paper. David ambushes Trisha, grabbing her by the shoulders and throwing her to the ground. The wind knocked out of her, she gasps. Yvonne gets in the middle again. Trisha leaps over Yvonne to get to David. Yvonne ties the chain around one leg and, thus hampered, tries to jump back into the fray.

Steve saunters by with a casual air, creating a shift in tone. David and Trisha start walking too. Trisha walks casually in a big circle while fixing her sleeve. The aggressions are over. Or are they? Suddenly she grabs David and flings him to the floor, as if he were light as a feather, then resumes walking and adjusting her sleeve as though nothing had happened.

■

David and Steve stand facing each other. Trisha kneels between them. David is panting, hyperventilating in a steady rhythm. The moment Trisha looks up at him, he stops. When she turns away, he pants again. She points prayer hands toward him and he stops again. As she rises, he resumes panting, and when she taps his nose with her finger, he stops again. She holds David's chin in her palm; Steve looks on in bemusement. David's hyperventilating turns into laughing. Trisha and Steve join in the laughter, but she still has full control. The second she closes her mouth, David's mirth disappears. Steve, less susceptible to her control, keeps laughing.

Trisha and David's active/passive game is echoed by Barbara and Nancy a few feet away. As Barbara opens packets of white powder (sugar? salt?) and pours the contents onto Nancy lying on the floor, Nancy writhes exactly in time with David's panting, and she goes limp when he stops.

Trisha coaxes her little circle, which now includes Yvonne, to laugh instead of pant. Soon enough, Yvonne's laughter turns to wailing. Steve, David, and Trisha all laugh and start to bounce like monkeys. Yvonne, wailing even louder, has turned her back. The others work themselves into a cacophonous hysteria.

■

Barbara goes off and starts dancing alone. Yvonne yells, "Barbara, Barbara, this is your line! Say it, say it!" Barbara doesn't know what she's talking about. Yvonne vehemently points to a line on a piece of paper. Trisha sticks the paper to her own forehead.

Yvonne to Barbara: "This is your cue." She points to the paper on Trisha's face. Responding to Yvonne's urgency, Barbara stamps and faces Trisha while silently telling her off.

David butts in and tries to kiss Barbara, who pushes him away. While she returns to silently scolding Trisha, David tackles Barbara again. Her defense now turns to offense. When she pushes him this time, they stay glued together, scampering/galloping in a big circle, crazily linked to each other, getting all worked up. She's hanging on him and jumping off of him, and he's agitated and hyperventilating. Trisha claps and stomps, hootenanny style, adding to the melee.

■

Standing in a ragged line, they all rearrange their clothes, tying shirts, changing headgear. Steve, Nancy, and Trisha, softly linked to each other, take a step forward. Yvonne motions enthusiastically to David to come to her spot in the line. David laughs/pants, hysterically reaching out toward the others. He can't stop himself. Barbara tackles

David again, and then, when he's on the ground, she kisses him on the mouth. The kiss calms him; they are quiet and still. She starts to tickle him, which triggers another bout of panting.

Barbara and David recover and sit up. He has regained his composure and places a hand on her shoulder.

David to Barbara: "I really want to thank you for that. You really helped me. *They* stood there and they didn't help me."

Trisha, from her place in the line: "I was thinking about you, David."

David: "But you didn't help. *She* really helped. That's the thing about Barbara. Everybody else stands around and watches what's going on. . . . Barbara is willing to come out of the line. That's a hard thing to leave: a line. Barbara is willing to come out of a line and help a friend."

Yvonne: "She didn't leave the line. She left *me*!"

David: "You mean, she abandoned you."

Yvonne: "Yes, David."

■

Barbara and Trisha are trying out daredevil variations of a gymnastic flying angel. Barbara is squashed on the floor, face down. Trisha mounts Barbara's upper back like a frog and balances for a second; a few in the audience clap as though it's an acrobatic stunt. She falls back down. Barbara gets up to walk, holding her crotch. [Laughter.] David concentrates on pulling Nancy, who is lying down, through his legs. There are two couples now: Trisha and Barbara, and David and Nancy.

Barbara and Trisha try their trick again.

Barbara: "This is it!" They cave in. "That was almost it."

Trying again. They both understand what the goal is, even if the rest of us don't. When Barbara leans forward, it crunches Trisha's knees so much that Trisha blurts out, "Barbara!" They collapse, then switch positions. (Steve stands by, eating from a Chinese takeout container with chopsticks.) Trisha bends way forward in a low squat. Barbara steps onto her lower back, stands up high, and starts doing demi pliés. [Laughter.]

Trisha: "ok, Barbara, come on back down."

Steve and David watch from either side.

David gradually comes up to sitting and drags himself across the floor sideways. Nancy is holding onto his leg, her left arm wrapped around his shoulder.

GU in Seibu Theatre, Tokyo, 1975. From left: Brown; Dilley; Paxton, who is narrating "The camel sees its reflection." Photo: Courtesy Douglas Dunn.

David: "Nancy you're a real drag." [Laughter at this obvious pun.]
Nancy: "But I love you."

■

Trisha raises one foot to Steve's abdomen while he's eating from the takeout box. Barbara tries to jump over her leg, pushing down on Trisha's head for leverage. Then Trisha plants both feet on Steve's stomach while her arms are on the ground, her body forming an L-shaped handstand. Barbara slides and rolls under the bridge made by Trisha's legs.

A lull. No one feels any compunction to make something happen. Trisha is leaning against a column. Barbara goes over to her, takes Trisha's head in her hands, and gives her a kiss. As she walks away we see a toddler enter the space, watching David and Nancy. Nilsson's lyrics are now "I can't live if living is without you. I can't give any more." Barbara returns to Trisha and nestles between Trisha and the column. Trisha's hands slowly come to rest on Barbara's upper back. Barbara extricates herself and walks away. Trisha leans her head toward the column, and Steve leans against the same column from the other side. A poignant moment. A minimalist nuzzle intercepted by a barrier.

We hear the same Nilsson song that opened the proceedings: "Coconut," with its tantalizing calypso beat. Steve, who has set down his takeout container, is feeling it; he's moving to the music, soft and cool. David is rolling on the floor with Nancy holding his feet. He connects with Trisha's extended leg, forming a linked-up diagonal line of Trisha standing at the column, David and Nancy on the ground. Steve continues dancing as he leaves the camera's frame.

DIANNE MCINTYRE AND SOUNDS IN MOTION

In a parallel world to Grand Union, Dianne McIntyre's Sounds in Motion, a company of dancers and musicians, was thriving in a different part of town. She performed often at Clark Center and The Cubiculo, small midtown venues, and she had a studio in Harlem. Much of her work was improvised, but she chose not to divulge that fact to her audience. She collaborated with many jazz musicians, including Cecil Taylor, known for complex compositions and polyrhythmic improvisations. (As mentioned in chapter 1, Taylor played in the first Judson dance concert.) McIntyre has been recognized as a pioneer who opened the way for other black women in contemporary dance. When I saw In Living Color *(1988), a collaboration between McIntyre and musician Olu Dara, I was moved by the emotional intensity and impressed by how the performers wove together movement, music, and story.*

In a public forum at New York Live Arts in 2014, McIntyre said she never told her audiences that she was improvising because they would think her dancers were "just doodling around on the stage." She also implied that white groups like Grand Union had the privilege of being open about their use of improvisation.[1]

It's true that any mostly white group has many privileges. But white dance artists like Anna Halprin and Trisha Brown have also bemoaned the fact that improvisation is not respected. In any case, I wanted to learn more about Dianne's experience and perceptions, so I asked to interview her. In January 2018, we sat down together and I learned about improvisation from her perspective. We started off with her memory of seeing Grand Union, and then we proceeded to her own work, which has continued to grow and change. The following is adapted from what Dianne said that day.

I saw Grand Union around 1973. I was doing improvisation too. I was taken by the fact that it was improvisational and yet had such innate structure. All the people were choreographers who could structure a piece in a traditional way, so when they all came together that's what it looked like. If you didn't know, you could just walk in and feel it was choreographed by someone. They had a unity of mind and spirit. And the daringness of where they would go. All of that was interesting. Wow, and then to know that that was not going to happen again! I saw them in one performance where some of them were completely nude—or perhaps partially nude. In that time, nudity happened in other types of performances as well—theater, on-site gallery performances, etc. I guess it was a political statement—an expression of freedom from restrictions, as improvisation is that freedom.

In music, in the so-called jazz field, there's a tradition that improvisation is a part of your greatness. (I say "so-called" because a lot of musicians don't like their work put in a box. In the seventies, they just called it "the music.") Improvising on a theme is greatly applauded. In your jazz conservatories, you practiced that. Some music students memorized recordings of improvisations of great musicians in order to learn how to get better as improvisers. Some of the musicians I work with call it "spontaneous compositions"; it gives a little bit more heft to it.

In modern, contemporary, or concert dance, it was not a skill that people trained for. I was very interested in improvisation. I had two teachers, Judith Dunn and Bill Dixon, at The Ohio State University around 1967 or 1968. They were my inspiration. They were there for a three-week workshop and that's how I first became introduced to improvisation. She taught technique classes, which were basically like Cunningham, and they taught composition and improvisation together. There was something about it that caught fire in me. I just loved the improvisational experience.

In composition class, they made us jump out of the box in terms of our creativity. First Judith would give us solo studies; some of the studies were not related to how fabulous your movement was. In the time studies, we had to do a certain amount of movement within thirty seconds or sixty seconds. But we were not given go or stop. We must develop what she called "inner time consciousness," not on a metered time. Then we had a study she called "The Fifties": we had to do fifty movements in thirty seconds. You yourself defined what one movement was. We had to know when thirty seconds were over. The Fifties made you move without thinking, without predetermining your movement. We had, after maybe an hour and a half, built up some kind of understanding of creating our own movement with clarity and freedom and also your relationship with other people in a very high-quality way. It was almost like you were in a conservatory for music or in a ballet class learning how to do a pirouette: you repeat and repeat that until you can be steady. So these studies made us stronger and stronger in creating spontaneously. By the end of the class, after we had built up the muscle for it, we were doing totally free studies with no assignment at all.

I was so taken by their work that I came to their workshop in New York. I remember after one study, Bill said, "Why do you have to do everything in the world in one study?" That was my note. I guess I was just overenthusiastic, but it was a good lesson.

One year I also took a summer workshop with the Nikolais company at the University of South Florida, Tampa. Nikolais worked with elements of movement: shape, levels, time, traveling, dynamics. I liked it, along with the improvisation, because it did not lock me into a particular style. When I came to New York I studied with them and with Viola Farber. I liked Viola for building strong technique, expansive lines, and the mental capacity to remember her combinations on the spot.

With Bill Dixon and Judith Dunn, they had that collaborative connection with dance and music. That's what caught me also, not just the improvisation; it was with the music. Their connection was more Cunninghamesque: they were in the same space, but they were not literally connected. It was a more atmospheric connection, one that we the audience were not privy to. It was stunning and very beautiful.

But I was interested in the dance and the music being part of the same band, the same ensemble, so there is a definite connection. Bill Dixon's music was called "new music" or "free jazz." I became enamored of that genre of music and I felt it had an openness that could connect with dance. When I arrived in New York I was going to different clubs and community centers and lofts to hear the music.

I met some musicians who were rehearsing in a day-care center in Brooklyn; they were called the Master Brotherhood. I asked them if it would be OK if I'd go off into a corner and do movement while they were rehearsing. They were like, Sure, it's OK. I practiced moving like they sounded. When

Dianne McIntyre of Sounds in Motion in *A Free Thing*, Washington Square Church, NYC, 1972. With Dorian Williams (Byrd) upstage. Photo: Personal collection of Dianne McIntyre.

they would take solos, I tried to move like their instrument sounded and tried to do the same runs, say, the sax was playing, or the same lyricism of the piano.

That era, 1970–1971, was a period of protest and revolution in young people and in the arts and music. So this was in their music, even though they didn't have any lyrics that might be called "resistance." Their resistance was in the music, and the history of African influences were in the music, the blues.

After I did a solo called *Melting Song* at Clark Center's New Choreographers Concert in 1971, I told Louise Roberts, longtime director of Clark Center, I was planning to have a concert at The Cubiculo, and she said I could rehearse at Clark Center. Very nice. I got a group of dancers together and invited some musicians from the Master Brotherhood. Part of the audition

Rehearsal of Sounds in Motion, directed by Dianne McIntyre, Studio Museum in Harlem, 1980. Dancers: Cheryl Banks (Smith), Mickey Davidson, Bernadine Jennings, McIntyre. Cecil Taylor Unit: Cecil Taylor (piano), Ramsey Ameen (violin), Jimmy Lyons (saxophone). Photo: Personal collection of Dianne McIntyre.

for my concert was that I had the dancers improvise with a couple of the musicians just cold.

There was a disconnect—perhaps that's too strong a word. There was, and has been, separate dance communities related to cultural background. I had a certain kind of following that had a lot to do with being African American. There were people who didn't see my work because it was like in another world. Over quite a few years I was produced by Clark Center, and those dancers, teachers, and supporters were the first people who were following my work. A lot of them were black dancers, actors, gypsies. I was also doing work in theater. Ntozake Shange was my student, and she met some of the early *Colored Girls* performers in my studio. [The full title of Shange's acclaimed 1976 play is *for colored girls who have considered suicide/ when the rainbow is enuf.*]

One of the first productions I choreographed for the Negro Ensemble Company was *The Great MacDaddy*. I met a number of people like Phylicia Rashad, Barbara Montgomery, Cleavon Little, Al Freeman Jr., and Lynn

Whitfield. I have a connection over the years with people in black theater, and then there's the music people. The audience evolved from those connections. Even though I did performances in main dance venues all over New York, those people would be following me. I didn't have what you call the downtown dance crowd, even though the press always followed my work.

I danced for several years with Gus Solomons. Although he had come from the Cunningham tradition, his choreography had a more organic feeling. Some of my inspiration also came from Gus. I wanted to be experimental. Gus flowed back and forth between the black dance artists and downtown. He was able to go beyond that disconnect.

I rehearsed my company, Sounds in Motion, and conducted dance classes in Harlem beginning in 1974. After I renovated a space and established my own studio in 1978 at 125th and Lenox, I also began producing work of other dance artists—as well as some musicians, poets, playwrights. Jawole was one of my students—and my right-hand assistant. [Jawole Willa Jo Zollar went on to form Urban Bush Women, the award-winning company that weaves storytelling, usually about African American lives, into choreography.] I met her at Florida State University when I was doing a residence there. She came to New York to study with me. I was a mentor to her, though she was already a fine choreographer. My rule for whatever they were doing—and sometimes I was the person who would give feedback—was that the piece had to be daring. And you try, if possible, to use live music. The concerts were open to everybody to be presented, but white people were a little nervous to come to Harlem. Each year in our studio works series, Jawole did little pieces, and eventually she did a whole evening, with women who were our students at the studio. That concert had the feeling of what became Urban Bush Women.

I met Nancy Stark Smith at Bates in 2008. She was surprised that I had been inspired by Judith Dunn and Bill Dixon and that we had a common background. We did a wonderful improvisation session at Bates. Bebe Miller was in it too. That was special because we were all on the same page.

CHAPTER 17

THIRD LOGIUDICE VIDEO, MAY 1972

In some ways, this session, which is the third of the four LoGiudice performances, is about voices. Barbara finds the voice of mock indignation, crystal clear despite being in a made-up language. Yvonne finds a complaining/blaming voice, possibly unleashed because of bending over like a beast of burden. Her shouting voice sparks an argument, and all are rescued by Trisha's and Nancy's resilient sense of humor. David finds that saying nothing can become a chant. This video does not start in the beginning of a performance but the middle. Two oft-used Grand Union "bits" that show up here are the staged argument and the fake audition. They never repeated themselves verbatim, but these were two types of, one could say, situation comedy skits that GU members easily fell into.

Trisha and David are playing, goading each other. She's wearing bell bottoms flared at the knee; he's wearing boots. They bump hips; she butts her head against his chest. He takes a spinning whack at shoulder level, knowing Trisha will duck precisely at the right moment. She's enjoying this fake, harmless aggression.

Meanwhile, Steve is laying down a narrow cloth in a big circle on the floor. It is actually a long, stretchy tube of pink fabric. (I know the color, not from the black-and-white video, but from a review.) Nancy is rolling around on top of it. We hear Barbara's voice, off camera, singing and chirping in a wordless language. As she enters the frame, we see that she is on the floor, scooching forward with her legs inside the cloth, which extends many yards in front of her. The tube cloth ahead of her bisects the playing field of Trisha and David. We see the collision coming.

Trisha and David plant their legs on the tube cloth, determined to block Barbara's path. When Barbara reaches the blockade, she stops and looks up at them. Her face is like a little gnome's, both inquisitive and defiant. She shoves their legs, using her elbows to push them out of her way, still singing in gibberish. Trisha and David do what they can to annoy her: Trisha softly kicks her and David flips her hair up. Barbara, indignant, puts a hand on her hip and gives them what for. Sounds like a mix of Swedish and Chinese. She's hilariously self-righteous, with perfect intonation and gestures to make herself understood without a word of English.

Music with a beat starts up, and Trisha and David jounce slightly while continuing to taunt Barbara. Trisha goes into high-gear mock belligerence, yelling and swearing and pushing and almost hitting. It's quite a brawl now, and David tries to break it up between the two women.

As the fracas subsides, Nancy enters the frame from the other end of the tube cloth and inches toward Barbara. Having created a full circle with the cloth, they are now on the floor facing each other. Have they been planning to converge like this all along?

■

Yvonne has placed her body, prone and facing up, in the laps of audience members, asking to be passed along. After she flips over, it seems more of a struggle for the audience to handle her weight. As Yvonne gets passed to Valda Setterfield, Valda says to her, "I don't understand why you're so heavy, Yvonne; all I ever see in your refrigerator is celery."[1]

David takes Trisha into slow-dancing mode. She is telling him about her dance background, but in a voice that is fraught with despair.

Trisha, sad and tearful: "I did acrobatics, toe, and ballet. I was real good in acrobatics. I got better in tap but I was lousy in ballet." Desperate: "I went to college and I majored in dance." Shouting: "I graduated with honors."

David, in a quiet, calm voice, asks who her teachers were.

Trisha, tearful: "Becky Fuller. Eleanor Lauer. Marion Van Tuyl."[2]

■

Yvonne is bent over, carrying Barbara on her back. As the two approach David and Trisha, Barbara reaches out and gamely taps David on the back. Trisha and David pull slightly apart. In response to

GU at LoGiudice Gallery, 1972. From left: Brown, Gordon. Photo: Gordon Mumma.

Trisha's résumé recitation, David says, "I studied with Jimmy Waring and I studied with Merce Cunningham, and I studied with ..." Now he faces Barbara: "How much more do you want to know before you choose which one of us you want to dance with?"

Steve, holding the microphone, takes a drag of a cigarette and blows out smoke.

Yvonne's complaints, at first inaudible, escalate to yelling: "This is the nastiest concert I've ever been to!"

Barbara: "Wait a minute, Yvonne. You know, you don't have to be here if you don't want to."

David: "Wait a minute, wait a minute, Barbara."

Barbara: "Did you hear what she said?!? She said this is the nastiest concert she'd ever been to!"

David, also outraged: "But you said she doesn't have to be here if she doesn't want to. If it weren't for Yvonne ..."

Barbara: "I don't think she should go around badmouthing what's going on."

Yvonne, still bent over, yelling: "Everybody's been badmouthing everybody all night!"

Barbara: "I haven't been talking bad." To Yvonne: "Has somebody been bad to you?"

Yvonne: "No."

Trisha, setting the record straight: "Right in the beginning, when we first started ..."

Yvonne: "Let's hear it."

Trisha: "The thing that set the tone ..."

Yvonne: "Yes, let's hear it."

Trisha: "was that *thing* that came 'round the room, like this:" Trisha makes a distorted monster face and walks stiffly. [Laughter.]

Barbara: "Who was that who was doing that, Trisha?"

Trisha: "Uh, your partner and my partner."

Barbara: "You mean these two?" She points to Yvonne and David.

David starts singing in a low voice, "your partner and my partner," while swaying forward and back, arm still around Trisha.

Yvonne: "I only did it because they ... made me."

David, suddenly pointing to his left: "Nancy was doing it."

Barbara: "*Nancy* made her do it!"

Yvonne: Yelling/singing, "*You made me do it!*"

David to Nancy: "Are you sure you didn't do it? 'Cause that was the best thing that ever happened."

Steve puts a mic in front of Nancy, who is fixing her hair, ignoring Yvonne's wailing. She turns on the charm and looks straight into the camera: "Are we on camera? Are we on television?"

David: "Did you do it?"

Nancy: "How many are gonna watch?" All innocence, she waves. "Hi Mom."

David: "Did you do it, Nancy?"

Nancy: "Gosh it was a sunny day today and I took the kids to the beach and they looked great. Hi Geoff [the name of her brother and her younger son].... What was the question?"

David: "The question was, Did you do it?"

Nancy, looking lovingly into the camera: "Sure, I do it all the time."

David: "And did you do it today?"

Nancy: "Yeah." Then, whipping her head toward David as though he were being fresh: "Stop asking me those questions!" She blows on the mic and makes big eyes to keep the sexual innuendo going. Steve is still holding the mic. "I didn't want to do it but" ... Now she addresses David more casually: "I just fall into your energy and I can't help myself. I have to do whatever David does."

■

Not visible but audible: Barbara speaks gently to Yvonne, who replies only in a loud, yelling voice.

Barbara: "Are you ready [for me to get off you]?"

Yvonne: "*No*, I don't want you to get off."

Barbara: "On your mark."

Yvonne: "*No*, don't you threaten me!"

Barbara: "Are you ready?"

Yvonne: "*No*."

Barbara: "Get set ... Yvonne?"

■

David and Trisha, still with their arms around each other, are rocking forward and back. Trisha slips away, backs up to prepare, and launches into a single, spectacular, twisted leap, probably related to her pole-vaulting past.

Barbara to Yvonne, on whose back she still comfortably sits. "OK, sing me a song."

GU at LoGiudice Gallery, 1972. Dilley sitting on Rainer's back. Photo: Gordon Mumma.

Yvonne, suddenly calm: "OK, what do you want to hear?"

Barbara: "Anything you wanna sing."

Yvonne, still bent over, starts singing/yodeling. The song seems to be a version of "Hush Little Baby." Barbara hums along, patting her on the back, then softly clapping.

■

We don't see David, but we hear him speaking into the mic in a deep voice: "I really don't have anything to say." The camera zooms in on Steve putting the mic in front of David and pulling it away each time David starts to speak. His eyes are fixed on David as he teases him in this way. David goes for it, holds still, then tries again to catch the mic.

Yvonne and Barbara have finished their song.

Yvonne, quietly: "Wanna get down now?"

Barbara: "Yes."

GU at LoGiudice Gallery, 1972. Yvonne Rainer standing; Lewis and Dilley on floor. Photo: Gordon Mumma.

■

Douglas takes Barbara by the hand and leads her, along with Trisha, Yvonne, and Nancy, to a new place in the room. He quietly explains some kind of plan while Barbara weaves in and out, gently touching them, like a fish swimming through seaweed. Douglas finishes and walks to a new spot for himself. Trisha, Yvonne, and Barbara are standing still. Barbara covers her face with her hands. Trisha and Yvonne close their eyes. Quiet. Stillness. Trisha suddenly collapses to the floor, loosening each part of her body separately. It's a magnificent fall. She stands up, turns around with closed eyes, does it again. Barbara collapses in a more all-in-one, melting way. Nancy and Douglas have fallen to the ground outside the camera's view. Only Yvonne is left standing.

David has finally gotten access to the mic. We hear his voice, soft and whispery but growing more audible, repeat this sentence over and over: "I don't have anything to say. I don't have anything to say."

INTERLUDE

PAXTON'S CLARIFYING THOUGHTS

Steve Paxton wrote an essay about his experience in Grand Union for the September 1972 issue of The Drama Review *(pp. 130–34). Since an academic journal like this has a long lead time, my guess is that he wrote it in late 1971, when Grand Union was still very physical and not as verbal as it later became. In any case, readers familiar with* Contact Quarterly *will recognize the style of his writing: focusing on sensation and a sense of discovery through improvisation. These excerpts offer hints of Paxton's thinking on the path from Grand Union to Contact Improvisation. It also reflects his lifelong resistance to hierarchy of any kind.*

Improvisation seems the form in which all could participate equally, without employing arbitrary social hierarchies in the group.

In a work of this kind [referring to *Falling Duets*, conceived by Trisha, and the falling section in *CP-AD*], the eyes learn to judge more acutely, the skin becomes hypersensitive to qualities of touch, particularly the arms; timing in the arc of the topple becomes a game in which you trust as long as nerves allow, pushing your limits. Understanding where another's focus is becomes easy since it is instinctive. It is also crucial to safety and to communication.

Any two people, even superficially aware of each other, are in communication with each other; but I am talking about reinforced communication, in which both parties are sure that the other is aware of the communication and is actively involved in it, however swift. Overt mind-fucking is to be avoided.

Trust, the developing trust, or the acceptance of a condition of frustrated trust (missed trust) seems to me the basis of mutuality and quickness in the transitions between those naturally arising phrases, the "bits." Acceptance is the beginning of trust, bringing in information about the actual state of the other person, and erasing images of the other person as one would have liked him to be. No expectations, no disappointments, no blame. Just results.

Theatrical improvisation is a model of earliest experiences, like infants' cumulative awareness of increasingly complex references, connotations and forms. The Grand Union process is this, coupled with the adult ability to comment on the experience, and with the all-too-human contradictory effort to re-live earlier visions.

I am balanced on my head on the slightly rough floor, pressing painfully, pivoted by an unseen friend at the other end of my body (lower, upper). . . . After being turned over and over in slow time, I am uncoiled to the floor and squat on one leg. Then we huddle, nine of us, and blend our softness together and feel close warm breath and hugs. We stand for a time.

Then one person thrusts away and runs around the room alone. I join and soon we are all hurling ourselves thru the air at each other, colliding forcefully, rebounding to collapse on the floor, and up again to twine about each other in the air, falling as a unit. The arms and legs grip from digits to armpits; the muscles of two bodies blend into a single falling mass, mutually sensitive to reinforce physical communication thru soft-surface, verification of movements too quick for consideration. Crash. Roll and balance across a hip which turns under, propelling me onto a rising back which takes me into a scheme of poses and standing balances, rigorous rules instantly known and quickly discarded for a continuing group boogie around the room. (Paxton's italics)

Freed of habitual denial, the sense of touch can expand beyond the usual allotment of personal space to the architectural enclosure, becoming larger, softer, easily penetrated, or easily encompassing others' personal space. Contact with the body becomes a matter of degree, already initiated with the first possibility of touching or blending enlarged personal space-fields.

The preparation is opening the senses, judgment, building trust; tuning the body for strength, elasticity, getting it ready for quick changes through the range from relaxed to tense. Body and head must be ready for fast control or instant release of that control, when personal control must yield to that imposed by the situation.

A mark of the dancer used to improvisation is his quickness of response. This quickness is faster than habitual movement/thought and is based on acceptance of the imminent forces, letting the body respond to the reality it senses and trusting it to deal with the situation intuitively. Trust is an organic form of communication.

New material comes into range with the ability to relax into contact and attune movement awareness to the demands of the situation. The body can move more swiftly when it acts out of intuition rather than prejudice. Relationships become possible at high speeds that would be arduous if slowed. It becomes evident that dancers have been only touching the surface.

CHAPTER 18

FOURTH LOGIUDICE VIDEO:
FROM DARKNESS TO LIGHT

In the fall of 1971, about a year into Grand Union, Yvonne was despondent. The sculptor Robert Morris, with whom she was in the midst of a tumultuous, on-and-off relationship, had gone off and married someone else. When she heard the news from a mutual acquaintance (another romantic rival, actually), she sank into a deep, rageful depression. It's possible that this rejection triggered the feelings of abandonment she'd had as a small child when her parents farmed her and her brother out to foster care institutions. In a zone that she describes as "automatic pilot," she ordered sleeping pills from three different doctors. On October 15, she ingested the pills and fell into a coma. She was discovered three days later by her friend Jani Novak, who had a key to the loft.[1] Rainer was taken to St. Vincent's Hospital but did not regain consciousness until six days after taking the pills.

As part of her healing, she worked with her psychotherapist on this question: "How could I not have given a single thought to the hurt I would bring to the people who loved me?"[2] Among those people who loved her—and needed her—were her colleagues in Grand Union. In our group interview in 2017, this dark shadow surfaced when we were talking about the death motifs that cropped up in their performances. David said, "Yvonne, I have no desire to talk about this at any length, but some of the dying stuff began when you did what you did." The conversation continued from there:

> David: "The day that you were gonna do what you did to yourself, I was the last person at rehearsal [in your loft]. I was standing outside your door. You said to me, 'Why do you always say good-bye to me like you're never going to see me again?'"

Yvonne, softly: "Really? ... Omigod."

David: "You said that to me and I said, I'm embarrassed, I don't know. Oh, I must be showing my neediness more than I want to. I left and the next thing I knew I was hearing where you were in the hospital. I lived two blocks from the hospital. A great part of the night I was walking around the hospital saying, 'Please god, don't let her die. Don't let her die.'"

Yvonne: "Yeah, they didn't know."

David: "I was angry at you for years."

Yvonne: "You still are."

David: "And I still am. It was devastating."

Yvonne: "I know."

David: "And the fact that you said that [about saying good-bye], the words ring in my head." [His voice rises to such a high pitch that the word "ring" cracks into two syllables.]

[Later, after more conversation:]

Yvonne: "All I can say, I still love you all. Anger and all. All of it."

■

In addition to Bob Morris's rejection, there was another destabilizing factor: Yvonne's trip to India. The six-week expedition came soon after her dance company broke up and morphed into Grand Union. On her return from India, as recorded in her diary, "I went into a deep funk, was flooded with contemptuous feelings toward my culture and my place therein, entertained fantasies of giving up my profession because I had no longer anything meaningful to say and going back to school to learn something more useful (Nursing, marine biology?)."[3] She had witnessed the deep engagement of audiences of all ages with the narrative traditions of Indian dance and theater. The people's connection to their mythology was revelatory for Rainer, who had spent ten years making dances that rejected narrative. She started reading the psychologist Carl Jung on mythology.

In her next piece, *Grand Union Dreams* (1971), Rainer cast her Grand Union buddies as "gods" in a quasi-mythological structure. Other performers she knew, like Valda Setterfield and Fernando Torm, were "heroes," while still other dancer friends, like Pat Catterson and Cynthia Hedstrom, were "mortals." The piece included readings from Jung and recycled choreographic bits from her past. She said in one post-India interview, "It's as though my own life contains possibilities for a mythology."[4] As followers of Rainer know, she eventually came to feel that she could address narrative—specifically personal relationships and political subject matter—better in film than in dance.[5]

Losing her position as director of her close-knit group was also hard on Yvonne. She felt she was not a good improviser, so she had to get stoned to face the challenge. She once told me that the only scene during her two years with Grand Union that she really remembers was when she directed Trisha and Douglas in an action while she read a ludicrous porno passage that suggested contortionist positions. (The result had the audience howling.) Being in the position of director was where she felt at home. Otherwise, in the context of Grand Union, she sometimes felt lost.

While watching the LoGiudice tapes, I thought I perceived that lost-ness in Yvonne, especially compared to her assured purposefulness in the video of *CP-AD*. But I realize, too, this was the same period when she was beginning to work on her first film, *Lives of Performers*, so what I perceived as vagueness or vulnerability could simply have been that she was in a transitional period of shifting her artistic attention from dance to film.

In any case, I decided to ask each of her fellow dancers separately how they were affected by her suicide attempt.

Douglas had noticed "an unhappiness in her personal life that was creeping in a little bit to the rehearsals." (In that first year, there were still a few rehearsals.) But, he said, she never asked for help. After that fateful day, "I found myself having tremendous difficulty going to her in her recovery and trying to be empathetic. It made me realize how much I was counting on her, how much I wanted to be part of what she was doing. And she was not there for me, so I don't know how much of that was some kind of projection of mother stuff."[6]

David was very upset by the suicide attempt, as we have seen. When I followed up, he called it a "betrayal." Explaining that feeling, he said, "Somebody you are invested in—that you think you know, that you think you have a relationship with—is planning to do something which will deprive you forever of them; you're not being warned."[7]

Steve waxed philosophical: "Yvonne's suicide attempt was scary, though I respect such a decision as a person's right. I was very relieved that it failed, by chance. . . . I just put it behind us and trusted that her promise not to try it again would prove true.... I think she gradually withdrew emotionally from her interests up to that time, as she ... struggled to find what she wanted to do next. Remember, she almost died [from a series of massive intestinal obstructions] in 1965 and had health issues from then on."[8]

Barbara was not in New York at the time. After the Walker engagement of May 1971, she and her young son had driven with Yvonne from Minneapolis across Canada to give workshops in Vancouver. They met up again for the Grand Union performance at the San Francisco Art Institute that summer. Yvonne then returned to New York while Barbara was teaching and choreographing on the West Coast. When Barbara heard the news, she recalled, "It was like a huge shattering of my relationship with Yvonne, and when I went back to New York it was really difficult to reconnect with her.... I didn't know how to talk about it."[9]

David, Steve, and Nancy visited Yvonne in the hospital. "Trisha came and threw herself into my arms as I lay in bed. We both dissolved in tears."[10] Pat Catterson gathered a bunch of Rainer's students to perform *Trio A* on the sidewalk below her hospital window. Nancy, who hardly knew Yvonne at that point, helped change bandages on her bedsores once she got home.[11]

Yvonne's emotional pain was felt but never talked about. In the last LoGiudice performances in May 1972, she unleashed her inner abandoned child. This particular performance ended in a transformation that Jung might have called a resurrection. To my eyes, it played out Rainer's statement that her own life contained a kind of mythology. As with the other narrative unfoldings, this is my own perception of a single-camera shoot, and my own interpretation. Another person would make a different story of it.

■

Barbara, off to the side, is spinning with open arms to the Cat Stevens song, "Where Do the Children Play." She sometimes looks upward, as if in prayer. She seems happy, involved, and peaceful. Most of the audience is not focusing on her but on the center of the space, where David, Douglas, Nancy, and Yvonne look aimless compared to Barbara's meditative spinning. But they have picked up flecks of Barbara's turning energy. Nancy is swirling with a scarf, and Douglas and David are tooling around in circles to the lyrics "higher till there's

NARRATIVE UNFOLDINGS

GU at LoGiudice Gallery, 1972. Barbara Dilley. Photo: Gordon Mumma.

no more room up there....You crack the sky.... Will ya make us laugh, will ya make us cry." Steve is the only one directly interacting with Barbara. He's walking back and forth in a straight line as a foil to her circles, setting up a possible collision with her. As the song changes to "Hard-Headed Woman," he makes contact with Barbara, and she starts revolving around him.

■

Yvonne and Trisha are making large, quasi-balletic shapes. Yvonne, balancing in relevé, stretches out almost in an arabesque penché, then comes up and swings her other leg over Trisha's back. Nancy is swooshing through space, picking up speed and power. She has gone from waifish to Isadora-ish to full abandon. Steve and Barbara are dashing around the perimeter, leaping in and out as though on an obstacle course. David has joined Trisha and Yvonne in their big, extended, now precarious positions. Trisha and Yvonne start speaking in loud voices.

Yvonne: "There's only one way to Paradise."

Trisha: "What do you mean?

Yvonne, rising up on relevé, yelling: "Triumphant, victorious.... [Trisha grabs hold of Yvonne's arabesque leg and plants it down.] Forever.... Fire and will and passion ... torches aflame ... just what our mothers dreamed of. Always onward."

Trisha: "Mama, we're coming."

Yvonne: "Mamas everywhere, we're coming!"

Trisha and Yvonne, yelling together: "Mama!"

Yvonne, both arms up: "Ma? Ma. [Like a baby exploring monosyllables.] Ma. Ma-a. Mama. Mama. *Mama*. Ma-*ah*. Maaaama. Mwa." [Yelling with wide open mouth, hair in her face.]

Trisha, finding Steve, yells, "Daddy!" [Laughter.]

Yvonne is now chirping very close to Steve's face, with syllables that sound like "Buppy puppy boppi," while he is busy tying a long piece of cloth. His eyes stay focused on his task, but his face shows a gentle awareness of her seemingly on-the-verge state of mind. As if to try to get her to speak English, he says, though it's hardly audible, "My name's Steve." He wraps the cloth around her. Yvonne approaches Trisha with her baby talk, her face almost touching her friend's. Trisha, bemused, replies in a low, firm, very audible voice: "My name's Trish." [Laughter.] Yvonne goes to Steve again, then lurches toward the cam-

GU at LoGiudice Gallery, 1972. From left: Dunn, head down, hands holding the arms of Rainer, who is mostly hidden; Lewis, mostly hidden behind her; Gordon with chair; Paxton; Brown; Dilley. Sitting in audience at right in white pants is choreographer and somatic pioneer Nancy Topf, who died in the Nova Scotia plane crash in 1998. David has said, "When I see this picture, Nancy Topf is part of that parade." Photo: Susan Horwitz, Jerome Robbins Dance Division, The New York Public Library for the Performing Arts.

era with her madcap "buppi buppi" but veers off toward Douglas and Nancy, who are standing on two chairs. She steps up to join them and puts her arms around both of them. The song is now Harry Nilsson's "Gotta Get Up" from the *Nilsson Schmilsson* album. Yvonne's mood shifts and she gets Douglas and Nancy jiggling to the peppy beat.

Meanwhile, David is walking around the room, stroking his beard and hair in a grooming gesture. Steve starts following him, Trisha follows Steve, and Barbara brings up the rear. Soon all four mash up, glomming onto each other. The song changes to "Driving Along." During the lyrics "Driving along, you can see all the people," David keeps walking until ... they inevitably intersect with the three bouncing on top of the chairs. With Yvonne's arms still draped around his neck, Douglas steps down from the chairs. Nancy lowers herself to the floor so she can take hold of the legs of Yvonne, who is now stretched out like a hammock between Douglas and Nancy. As though it were

The "parade," rear view. From left: Dunn, mostly hidden; Rainer in white pants; Lewis bending over to carry Rainer's legs; Gordon holding chair; Paxton; Brown; Dilley. Photo: Susan Horwitz, Jerome Robbins Dance Division, The New York Public Library for the Performing Arts.

planned, David picks up the two just-vacated folding chairs, which he carries on either side of him—not eagerly, but as a necessary burden.

It's a parade. A slow, lumbering procession that's a cross between a funeral march and a Chinese dragon. It's doleful but funny, and it's been arrived at organically. David makes up a song while Steve's hands, from behind, gently beat time on David's chest: "I love to sing, hear me sing, I love to dance, watch me dance." Nancy, Trisha, and Barbara are whistling, humming, or whoooing along. Although Yvonne's arms are clasped around Douglas's shoulders, her hands are free to clap along. The faces of the audience light up, and some of them clap too. Douglas, leading the pack, is snapping his fingers. David's song shifts to more of a talking tone: "These are my friends; I dance with my friends. You can see us dancing.... This is what there is. This is it, I'm not kidding." David is getting tired. "This is it. This is really ..." He lets go of one chair, "this is really it," and now the other. David, Yvonne, and her two carriers stagger to the ground. Yvonne rolls into a kneeling position and raises her arms in a momentary "Go, team" salute. [Laughter, applause.]

■

It seemed to me there was a purpose to this parade. It was a healing event. It brought Yvonne from a low to a high. In my perception, each of them felt called to be part of this procession to support Yvonne, to hold her with loving, dancing hands. Interestingly, David remembers being angry at the way things were going and surprised when friends in the audience told him afterward that it was "the best, funniest, greatest Grand Union."[12] To me that's an example of how one member could be feeling one way, but the cumulative power of the group had a different effect.

It wasn't long before Rainer split with Grand Union—and with dance. She was reinventing herself as a filmmaker.

INTERLUDE

BARBARA DILLEY:

"AN IMAGISTIC WORLD EXPLODES"

The following is an excerpt from Barbara's book,
This Very Moment: teaching thinking dancing.

I remember running to Harry Nilsson's "Jump into the Fire" and to George Harrison's "My Sweet Lord." When those loud repetitive beats ignite in the air, I drop whatever I'm doing and run. I feel complete joy. If Merce Cunningham and John Cage are my art fathers, the Grand Union is my art mother. Evolving from Yvonne Rainer's *Continuous Project—Altered Daily*, this ensemble marks my genes and continues to inspire my teaching. Entwining our perceptions in front of audiences, we birth a memorable group persona.

Among these dancing outlaws, I learn to follow intuition. I join in and also go it alone. Each performance we build something then burn it down. From the ashes something new arises.

This is an articulate tribe, often talking spontaneously. One evening, during a month of weekend performances at Bob Fiore's loft, I drink a brew of powdered mushrooms, dried on a glass plate and scraped into a glass of water. My throat center bubbles awake. Everything in me and around me vibrates with this breath-source. Language, both familiar and made-up, spills out. I find my voice; I even sing.

During a performance Steve Paxton puts on a record and as it starts to play I realize I had the same impulse but doubted it. Intuition becomes a survival skill. It takes me forward through the unknown. I find companionship. In this environment an imagistic world explodes. I become part of stories bursting forth like Surrealist images.

For each performance I bring a bag of props with me; objects, costumes, records. There is always a record player plugged into a sound system and anyone can put on a record or take it off. This radical independence within an ensemble is difficult to teach. You have to dare to follow impulses and, at the same time, keep an eye on the big picture. No hesitation. No judgments. No fear of hurting someone's feelings. And if it seems to be a failure, stay with it. . . . Yes, we don't make plans. We show up. We become an organism only found in performance.

Reprinted with permission from *This Very Moment: teaching thinking dancing*, Naropa University Press, 2015, pp. 112–14.

INTERLUDE: BARBARA DILLEY: "AN IMAGISTIC WORLD EXPLODES"

CHAPTER 19

GENDER PLAY AND IOWA CITY, MARCH 1974

The Grand Union challenged gender stereotypes right from the start. Part of a larger rebellion against all conventions of style and structure, gender play was constantly percolating. David often wore exotic robes; Steve once wore a sarong; Douglas lifted Steve. Barbara flexed her biceps when preparing to catch Douglas. Trisha hurled David across the floor. David and Steve had tender moments together. In Minneapolis, David pranced like a showgirl during the bowing scene. In Tokyo, Steve offered to "show his leg" for a mock chorus-line audition.

The standard behavior of men lifting women had already been challenged in the sixties in works by Rainer (*The Mind Is a Muscle*) and Brown (*Lightfall*). In *CP-AD*, as in *Parts of Some Sextets*, Rainer assigned tasks without regard to gender. One of her many refusals was not to take on stereotypical feminine characteristics (unless lampooning them as she did in *Terrain*). That refusal was bound up with her refusal (or inability) to "look like" a dancer. Her "failure" to fulfill these expectations is preserved in her oft-repeated anecdote about studying at the Martha Graham School of Contemporary Dance around 1959: "One day when Martha herself was teaching the class, she came over to me as I was struggling with the floor stretch and said, 'When you accept yourself as a woman, you will have turn-out.' Prophetic words. Neither condition has come to pass."[1]

What did come to pass was a more dimensional presentation of what it means to be a woman. Rainer used her athletic abilities to project a more outward, assertive figure and at the same time was not afraid to be introspective. In her solo *Inner Appearances* (1972), she simply vacuumed the floor while her private thoughts were beamed

David Gordon in *Random Breakfast* (1963), Judson Memorial Church.
Photo: Al Giese © Hottelet (Giese).

on the back wall. Her refusal to exhibit herself in any kind of feminine way has contributed to her reputation as a proto-feminist. She was on her way to becoming a complex, feminist filmmaker.

Around the time Yvonne was confronting her supposed shortfall in the department of womanhood at the Graham studio, David was making his first duet, *Mama Goes Where Papa Goes* (1960). Although he recalls that it was mostly based on sexist tropes, he made one section in which Valda lifted him and carried him off.[2] In 1963 he went full drag with a strapless evening gown for his Spanish dancer takeoff in *Random Breakfast*, mentioned in chapter 1. On neither occasion did he intend to make a feminist statement. David points to the tradition of men impersonating women in vaudeville and Hollywood.[3] For instance, his Spanish regalia in *Random Breakfast* harked back to Milton Berle's parody of Carmen Miranda. Whatever his inspiration, David definitely had an elasticity when it came to gender.

Sometimes stereotypes in Grand Union were not exactly challenged but highlighted in a mocking, ironic, almost fetishistic way. David, a window dresser by profession, described this episode: "I am shopping in those thrift shops every week when I go uptown, and I buy three tulle-and-sequined strapless ball gowns—very cheap—for Barbara, Nancy, and Trisha. It's a mindless, spur-of-the-moment, sexist joke that I am doing. And Trisha puts her gown on in performance and runs up the wall of the Larry Richardson Dance Gallery and loops around, making her skirt move in the air, and shouts, *'I'm a girl, I'm a girl!'*"[4]

On the other hand, Trisha could deploy her strength in ways that defied femininity—or, depending how you look at it, expanded her female powers. David recalls a time when, early in Grand Union, she was testing to see if he could keep talking no matter what. In this episode, while lying on her back, she held David in the grip of her hands and feet. And then: "Somehow or other she got off the floor. She's now standing up and holding me in the air and she's slamming my feet into one of the columns and saying 'Keep talking. Keep talking.' And I do what Trisha says for a very long time."[5]

Barbara and Nancy had no problem being girly on occasion, and Nancy could be hyper-femmy. To my eyes she anticipated a kind of campy femminess that surfaced with Debbie Harry of the band Blondie a decade later. But Nancy was not hemmed in by her brand of girliness; she could extend her luscious dancing into space at any moment. She also felt the freedom to match the guys. At one of the Lo-Giudice performances, when Steve took off his shirt, baring his chest, she did the same. Thus exposed, she engaged in a fearless duet with him—leaning, lifting, rolling, arching way over each other and lingering there. It ended with them sitting by a pillar (as mentioned in chapter 10) in a loose embrace, skin to skin, for a long time.

Ballet had always been highly gendered, with women being portrayed as impossibly ethereal or cunningly seductive. Either way, the

GU in "rehearsal" in Trisha Brown's loft, 1975. At left: Dunn, Paxton, Gordon. At right: Lewis, Dilley, Brown. Contact sheet. Photo: Robert Alexander, Jerome Robbins Dance Division, The New York Public Library for the Performing Arts.

men had to lift them. In modern dance, Martha Graham, Paul Taylor, José Limón, and Alvin Ailey all assigned the men to be strong and the women to be delicate, emotional, or sassy. Merce Cunningham was less gender-bound, but he did rely on traditional roles in partnering. As Solomons says about Cunningham's work in a recent documentary, "For years, men never touched men. No lifting was done other than of women by men. How conventional is that?"[6]

■

The Grand Union was part of a wave of gender experimentation in American dance. In Twyla Tharp's *The Fugue* (1970) three women stomped out precise phrases in boots, projecting a don't-mess-with-me fierceness. (She later created an all-male cast.) Meredith Monk donned a mustache for her haunting duet *Paris* (1972) with Ping Chong. Diane Torr, who gave drag king workshops for women ("King for a Day") and performed at venues like The Kitchen, La MaMa, and the wow Café, "reveled in unruly female bodies."[7] The Wallflower Order Dance Collective (now the Dance Brigade), which sprouted up in Eugene, Oregon, in 1975 as the first feminist dance collective, did not shy away from lesbian issues. Since 1974, Les Ballets Trockadero de Monte Carlo, aka The Trocks, has shown that audiences all over the world like to see men dancing on pointe—not only as a comic gimmick but also to claim part of that domain of celestial aesthetics for men too. In the eighties, romantic same-sex duets appeared in choreography by Ishmael Houston-Jones, Mark Morris, Bill T. Jones, and Arnie

Zane. (I remember the lovely shock of seeing two male dancers kissing onstage in Jones's *Social Intercourse* when it premiered at American Dance Festival in 1981.) In Elizabeth Streb's world, each person bounds into the air, dives down to earth, or crashes into a wall with no assistance from another person—though sometimes with help from a giant contraption invented by her. Streb once said, "Whenever I see a pas de deux, I want to yell, 'Put her down! She doesn't need your help.'"[8]

Jane Comfort, a choreographer who took Diane Torr's drag king workshops, reversed the roles of a couple in *S/He* (1995), in which Comfort expertly performed as a male, and Andre Shoals (a professional drag queen) performed as a woman. Then they unperformed their roles, shedding the garb of one gender and taking on the clothing and accoutrements of their biological gender, illustrating exactly what Judith Butler had theorized: that we each perform our gender.

When dancers paired up in Grand Union performances, they were just as likely to form same-sex duets as hetero ones. There was a comfort level with touching any fellow dancer. It was taken as a given that one could be attracted to someone of the same sex. (Remember, the Stonewall Rebellion had happened in 1969, just before Grand Union came into being.) David, Steve, and Douglas were all veering away from what Douglas called "standard American maleness."[9] Nothing could express that veering better than the pop song "Lola" by the British band the Kinks. The lyrics tell of a man who dances with "Lola" at a bar and gradually realizes she's a man but falls in love with her/him/them anyway. I remember one Grand Union performance at New York University's Loeb Student Center when the group played "Lola" over and over—so often that the words about a trans person really sank in: "She walks like a woman but she talks like a man.... Girls will be boys and boys will be girls, it's a mixed up, muddled up, shook up world except for Lola." The song has a great sound, a great beat, and makes you wanna dance. At that time it was kinky, but it was a harbinger of today's embrace of transgender people in the arts.

Meanwhile, in their offstage lives, Nancy, Barbara, and Trisha were struggling with being mothers who were also touring dancers. Trisha once ended a performance by saying she had to get home to her children, at which point David corrected her to say "child."[10] It was all in

GU at Annenberg Center, University of Pennsylvania, 1974. From left: Lewis, Brown, Dilley. Photo: Robert Alexander Papers, Special Collections, New York University.

fun, but I am sure she was dead serious about wanting to be home with her son Adam. At the end of one of the LoGiudice performances, Trisha sat in an audience chair with Adam in her lap and did not budge while the audience applauded. I discovered a memo in Art-services's archives about a possible 1974 engagement in Bordeaux with a note that Douglas, Barbara, Nancy, Steve, and David said Yes or OK, but the response regarding Trisha was "Yes, but Trisha wants to bring Adam." Barbara's son Benjamin was living with his father, Lew Lloyd, from whom she had been separated. In an email to me she called that arrangement "the tender spot," implying that she didn't want to talk about it.[11] Nancy had three children, and though she showed up for all the performances, it was difficult for her. She told me she wept every night during the three weeks of the Oberlin residency. Talking on the phone decades later, she sighed, "They were really little then."[12]

The most sustained commentary on gender in a videotaped Grand Union performance came about at the University of Iowa on March 8, 1974. I include the narrative unfolding here because it is rich in many ways.

At our group interview, Steve and Douglas agreed that the Iowa performance was one of Grand Union's best. But Steve remembered the space as a choir rehearsal room, while Douglas called it a chemistry lab. Watching the video, I thought it was a bit of both. The space was a wide, oval-shaped room ringed with shallow steps leading down into a sunken area. There was a white, portable, door-sized plaster board with a large hole in it (where a microscope once was?). Scattered around the room were dozens of square tiles with reflecting surfaces that could have been used for science experiments.

This session (at which Trisha was absent) contained not only gender politics but also other hallmarks of Grand Union events: self-commentary that bordered on identity crises, doctor games (in this case possibly a gynecologist), porousness with the audience (especially with two different children), witty wordplay, an ordinary task (like plugging in an electric fan) becoming comedic, the collective fantasy (here, a frothy surfer scene), and the almost nothing transforming to an unforgettable something. This last is how I would describe one transcendent moment when Douglas found himself on high, like some kind of deity restoring peace to the land.

Like all GU episodes, this one interwove many subplots within the long, meandering narrative. But I felt that it kept coming back to Barbara and her (character's) struggle with making decisions and seeking a "way out" of what was going on around her.

As we "watch" the archival video together, note that I've edited the descriptions to allow a sense of flow. If it seems heavy on verbal dialogue, that's because this particular episode was almost like playwriting in action. From the ridiculous to the sublime, from the ironic to the bleak, the language was worthy of Ionesco or Beckett. Lisa Nelson, who has had a long-term performing collaboration with Steve, videotaped this session. She may have also transcribed the improvised verbiage, which helped me piece these scenes together.[13]

■

The evening starts with Barbara projecting a film on the free-standing white plaster board. She's calmly telling the audience the film is going backward and there's too much light in the room to see it clearly. David, sitting on the floor at the other end of the room, close to the screen, launches into a series of questions: "Do you need a musical score? ... Do you need a makeup man? ... Do you need a choreographer?" Because of the distance between David and Barbara, the audience has to turn to the right to watch Barbara and to the left to see David, who continues pelting her with questions: "Do you need a barber? Do you need a dogcatcher?" Trying to focus on the film, Barbara refers to the lieder (empty footage) in her film. David picks up on this and turns it into wordplay: "Do you need a leader? Do you need a ladder? Need a loader?"

Steve and Nancy have joined Barbara to form a little trio going back and forth on parallel tracks, while David continues his litany: "Do you need a conductor, carpenter, an electrician, a friend?" This leads to an absurd line of questioning of what Barbara might want from a hired "friend," and how David would like to be paid in "luxury items."

Barbara starts to answer but abruptly interrupts herself with a flash of defiance: "Actually, David, that's not fair. I am taking someone else's idea about what my luxury item is.... I'm so gullible I'll just take anybody's suggestion. In this work, you get so used to taking anybody's idea for anything."

A small child has crawled into David's lap. So, when Barbara asks David what *he* wants, she gets this: "I want to be able to stand up. I want to be able to take off my shirt. I want some space for dancing and I want some music to dance to. I want this pretty child to go back to its father and mother. I want to have a good dinner after the performance is over. I want to fly home safely and not get killed in the air. I want the simple things."

Nancy has been walking toward David in super slow motion. She gently lifts the little girl into her arms and returns the child to her family.

■

A recording of the propulsive Balinese Monkey Chants sends the three men into different modes of fast movement: David whips the mic wire around himself; Steve takes the multilayered chants into an interior medley of the ribs, hips, head, and arms moving polyrhythmically; Douglas picks up momentum, eventually bounding on the different levels of the staircase. When the recording ends, he does a handstand that sparks a series of partnered maneuvers with Steve: gliding, falling, balancing, and twisting.

David thrusts a mic in front of Steve's face, and Steve just breathes into it. Meanwhile, Douglas is still bounding from one stair to another, like a frog on a lily pond. David replaces Steve's mic with another mic. Steve says, "The date: March 21, 1968. The place: Skull Valley, Utah. The inhabitants: a farmer and five thousand sheep." Parts of this cryptic utterance return several times during the evening. David changes the mic again, repeats Steve's syllables but mangles them into new words: "scull" becomes "scald"; "sheep" become "ships." Steve walks away, making an arc to the other side of the space. David follows him, continuing to mess with Steve's story: "A farmer and his son" become "a framer and his sin." Steve says something about "nerve gas," then gives up trying to complete the story. The two, side by side, are now swaying in unison, both holding mics. Steve: "Pulling the wool over the eyes." David: "Hiding the whales over the seas." Steve: "Army . . . dead nerves." David: "Hors d'oeuvres, Mommy." Their rocking back and forth becomes hypnotic, and Steve slips into something about "what my father taught me." They continue swaying in unison.

■

Robert Johnson's classic "Cross Road Blues" is playing. Nancy, who has been sitting in a chair, gets up. She puts on a long, white, Appalachian-style skirt and head scarf and starts vamping as a sexy farmer's wife. She launches into a skit that is apparently a rerun from a previous session, and David plays along. Nancy is fake yelling and sobbing: "You can't do that to me, David, you just can't! We've got to plow the fields. We got to get it done before the rain comes or they might start ruining the crops. If you don't get out there, we're going to drown, and we'll have no harvest in August."

David, casually: "Isn't this the part where the song comes in?"

Nancy: "Yeah. When I say 'August,' then the music comes in."

They continue in this vein of switching between rehearsing and fake acting.

■

Barbara and Douglas have been engaged in a slow duet that has now drifted over to stage right. Without changing their mesmerizing pacing, they've climbed onto a group of bar stools. Thus elevated, they curve and stretch, making beautiful intersecting lines. On the floor near them is a bucket of water.

Nancy: "Steve is supposed to be the thunder. Steve?"

Steve: "I'm ready."

GU at LoGiudice Gallery, 1972. From left: Gordon, Lewis. Photo: Gordon Mumma.

Nancy: "And the wind."

David to Steve: "You're the elements."

Steve rattles a can with a stick: "Not very good thunder, is it?"

Nancy: "You're gonna plug in the wind, and lightning."

Steve goes to get the cord. "It's coming." Steve is setting up the "elements"—a swath of silk, a flashlight, and a chair.

Nancy, in sing-song voice: "The thunder . . . the rain is coming dooooowwwwn."

David coaches her while still lying on his back: "I think you should try for a little more poignancy. Try to get a tear in your voice." He demonstrates: "The thunder starts clapping." They say "clapping" together with dramatically shaking voices. (Steve has turned on the electric fan, making a rumble.) Nancy tries her line again.

David: "With a little more vibrato."

She tries again.

David, gesticulating upward toward her: "Deeper, stronger. Give it the feeling of a classic. You're the woman of all time, plowing the field, saving her men. Bearing the children. Planting the radishes. You're that woman. Give it that feeling."

In a rhythmic counterpart to David's instruction, Nancy, still sitting, strikes a different position with each new command: hand on hip, slump, straighten up, both hands on hips, planting in the earth.

Steve's wind is going strong now. He's flapping the silk in front of the electric fan and holding the mic up to the fan so it sounds like a fierce wind.

Nancy tries her monologue again, this time with woeful fervor. She shakes David: "You've gotta help me. Help me get the harvest, what am I gonna do? I can't do it without you ... cause the *flood*." At the word "flood," David flips over, lifting both arms up and slapping them to the floor. Nancy drags him toward the place where Douglas is now standing still, on top of the stools. Nancy continues her lament, way out of tune: "And the rain came athundering down, down on all the crops and ruined the town, and everybody drowns in the town." She drops her head down toward the bucket and stays drooped over.

Quiet prevails. Barbara and Steve are rippling the swath of silk near the ground. Douglas, who has been standing still during this whole episode, slowly, slowly lifts his arms out to the sides as though blessing all the land. Barbara looks up, sees Douglas's beatitude, and guides the rippling silk toward him. She and Steve lift the silk to Douglas's waist. Suddenly the picture does look like the elements: sun, wind, land, and water. As Barbara and Steve raise the fabric like a banner, it passes over Nancy and David. When it reveals Nancy, she is washing her face in the bucket. We hear the trickle of water.

David, lying on his stomach, not seeing what is happening above him: "I know how to turn this into an up moment. Could we have the Beach Boys, please?" [The song "Surfin' USA" comes on.] "See, now the farm is gone. Forget the farm. Forget the failing crops. Forget the drought. Forget the floods. Forget the old woman and the radishes. Think of young, healthy surfers. Think of sand and sea."

Barbara and Steve wrap the silk around Douglas and give him the corners to hold while Barbara goes to get a book.

Douglas: "When the music comes on ... I'd like to dive into the water."

David drags the electric fan over to the tableau, accidentally pulling the plug out of its socket.

Nancy points: "There's a plug over there."

Douglas points in a different direction: "A plug over there."

Steve points in yet another direction: "There's a plug over there." David staggers around between the different pointings.

As David pulls the fan closer to Douglas, Barbara reads from *The Labyrinth of Solitude: And the Other Mexico* by Octavio Paz: "And what is the game of the gods? They play with time, and their game is the creation and destruction of the world. . . . Each of their pirouettes is a world that is born or annihilated. . . . In their games—which are wars or dances—the gods create, destroy and sometimes destroy themselves."

Steve stretches out on the stool seat, belly-down, torso and legs extended, hands clasped behind his back. Douglas steps onto Steve's back. David brings the blowing silk nearer to Steve and lights it with the flashlight. As the Beach Boys blare "Surfin' USA," the waving silk is the surf and sea, Douglas is a slow-motion surfer, and Steve is the surfboard. Barbara stops reading and joins the party. Nancy and Barbara are now surfer girls undulating in a corny but lovely Hawaiian dance on either side of this American dream. Hips swaying and arms waving, they are fluid, gorgeous, and celebratory. Douglas slow-mo dives toward the bucket of water, with an assist from David and Nancy. [Applause.] Steve, released from Douglas's standing weight, sits up. Nancy and Barbara are still dancing to the song. Douglas's head is still underwater.

Steve to David: "I thought you said you would turn it into an up moment."

David: "Well I didn't know he'd *drown* for Crissakes." With mock concern: "Doug, Doug, Doug!"

Douglas lifts his head out of the bucket and spits out water: "Let's call this piece the resurrection of the surfer."

David: "Let's call this the resurrection of the [inaudible]."

Nancy: "The what?"

Douglas: "Let's call this intermission."

Nancy: "No, no. We're just getting into a place where . . . we have come together."

As the other dancers leave for intermission, Steve speaks directly to the audience: "If you come up and sit on the stage it might be nice."

■

After intermission, Steve runs back and forth, energizing the group and widening their tracks until all five are zigzagging to a Dylan song—dashing down the stairs into the sunken stage and back up the stairs on the opposite side. The Stevie Wonder song "He's Misstra Know It All" from the 1973 *Innervisions* album comes on, and they are leaping, skittering, lurching, galloping through space. Their pleasure in dancing fills the room. It's the kind of music that would get anyone dancing, but the only person in the audience bopping to the music is one small boy in the front row.

The song changes to an upbeat instrumental, and Nancy lifts her arms and flings herself into David's arms. He carries her, cradle-style, tilting her back and forth. Whoopee! Barbara is nearby, also whooping it up. David sets Nancy down and gestures for the music to be cut off.

David: "This is a liberated company." To demonstrate gender equity, he lifts himself into Nancy's arms, also cradle-style. She starts rocking him, same as he did with her. Barbara helps support his upper body, but they can't quite manage David's weight, and the attempt to tilt him devolves into dragging him back and forth on the ground in time with the music. David gets up, looking like he just acquired a few extra aches and pains. As if to prove a point, he takes hold of both women on either side and tilts them back and forth, again to the beat of the music. He sets them down. Exhausted, he settles on one of the shallow steps.

David: "I don't want to say anything but today, when the platforms had to be moved, I noticed three *men* were moving the platform."

Barbara, contrite: "I noticed it too."

David: "The women were talking about *knitting* or *babies* or something like that."

Barbara: "I was having an emotional crisis in my life."

David, getting worked up: "That's the difference, you see. I was having an emotional crisis but I had to move the fucking *platform*!"

The two women take this as a challenge. They try to lift him by his legs and make a mess of it. Steve, off to the side, is really enjoying this. Moving to Stevie Wonder, he does some of the springiest dancing of the evening. Finally, Nancy and Barbara hoist David waist-high and start to swing him. Steve stops the music in order to give a critique: "David, they're good at their part, but you don't look right. You don't look relaxed, you don't look ... glamorous. You don't look supported." David picks up Nancy. She waves her arms and legs to show how easy and fun it is to be lifted. Nancy and Barbara hoist David again. He flails his arms in imitation of Nancy's whoopee act. They set him down.

Steve to David: "You look perfectly liberated and totally immobile."

David: "I don't feel the least bit liberated. They've got my thighs clutched."

They all work together to achieve a raggedy circus pyramid in which the two women lift David, and then Douglas and Steve lift each woman up. Scattered applause and whistling, but the whole thing crumbles quickly.

Barbara: "I just don't have the strength. I don't have the huge muscles and the brawny, tough look to do it."

David steps in front of Barbara and faces her: "You've got that brawny, tough look."

■

Douglas, on all fours, says he wants Barbara to stand on his back as he crawls across the floor. As she carefully balances on his back, the question comes up whether she is supported up there by "somebody else."

David: "Barbara, you *believe* that somebody else is up there too. That's what you're always talking about, somebody else [waving his arms above his head] ... up there."

Barbara: "Don't you mock me in public."

Douglas, suddenly, "Barbara!" Apparently, her foot has dug into him.

Barbara: "Sorry, your coccyx was rubbing against my heel bone. Are you alright?"

Douglas: "I'm fine, just doing the same movement while passing through incredibly different atmospheres in the room: At first it was precarious, then it was humorous, then it was dull, then it was humorous [laughter], then it was humorous [laughter], then it was humorous.

David, singing: "They're on their wayyyy to the promised land."

David: "Then David started singing."

David continues with the song. "They're on their way, Yo ho ho. They're on their way, they'll be there soon. They're on their way ..." He hesitates.

Douglas, filling in for him: "They'll be there soon."

David: "They'll be there soon. I can see them now. They're on their way ... oh ... wow."

GU at Trisha Brown Studio, June 1975. Brown, Dilley, Dunn, Gordon, Lewis, and Paxton gathered for a "rehearsal." This photo session was probably arranged by Artservices for publicity purposes. Photos: Robert Alexander, Jerome Robbins Dance Division, The New York Public Library for the Performing Arts.

Douglas: "David, who writes your lyrics?"

David: "Don't mock me in public."

Douglas, still crawling: "Speaking of insults: When I was first aspiring to be a, shall we say, straight-legged dancer, someone insulted me by saying that I had knobby knees and I'd never make it.... This is gonna cure that." [Laughter.]

Barbara, going back to what irked her: "David, you're right: I'm a spiritual sentimentalist."

■

Barbara is lying down. David comes over. He angles one of the square mirrors at the lower half of her body.

David, in his most sincere voice: "When did the pains begin?" [Laughter.]

Barbara: "Last night."

David: "How long have you felt this way?"

Barbara: "A little bit for a long time. More, recently."

David: "Can you bear going through what's ahead?"

Barbara: "If I don't have to do it alone."

Steve and Douglas are also placing reflectors at different angles above her, creating a play of light all over her body.

David: "Who recommended us?"

Barbara: "I came here by chance."

David: "Had you told anybody where you are?"

Barbara: "I left a note on the kitchen table."

David: "Would you like to call?"

Barbara: "If you think it's a good idea."

David: "I just don't want you to have any guilt."

Barbara: "Guilt!?!" Suddenly it seems an abortion is what the doctor has in mind.

David: "What do you expect us to do for you?"

Barbara: "Show me the way out."

David turns to Nancy, who is sitting on a chair a few yards away: "Miss Hopkins, will you show her the way out?"

Nancy: "I'll be happy to."

David to Barbara: "Just go with Miss Hopkins. She'll show you the way out." Barbara gets up, puts her arms around David. "Thank you, doctor. You've saved my life."

Barbara backs away from him until she reaches Nancy. "I'm ready, Miss Hopkins."

Nancy doesn't say a word; she just points to the exit. Barbara walks toward it, but just before she gets there ...

David: "Wait! Are you sure you want to go?"

Barbara, now unsure, looks toward the exit.

Douglas: "It may be the last time."

Barbara: "You're giving me the runaround again. That's the same old runaround that I get every single time. Why can't you just let me go? What are you worried about—that I might sue you or come back and want my money back, or ...?"

Douglas: "It's a test Barbara, it's a test."

Barbara: "I've read about those.... It's up to me ultimately. The final decision is up to me to make it."

Douglas: "Every one of these tests is a roaring shock" (pun on Rorschach test, a psychological tool, aka the ink blot test).

David yells and drops to the ground, as though to demonstrate the danger.

Douglas: "Does that change your feeling about the way out? Stillness need not represent indecision."

Barbara: "I think I'm going to wait a minute if you don't mind. I'd like to rest. It doesn't seem so important any more to make a decision."

Steve walks past her and exits, stage left.

Barbara: "He just went out! He just went right through that door, didn't he?"

David: "He's a man who knows his own mind."

Barbara: "You men, you're all the same. You all 'know your own mind.'"

Steve comes barreling into the space as though shot from a cannon, landing sprawled out on the floor.

Douglas: "Notice the lack of indecision."

Barbara, who is closest to the just-landed Steve, looks over at him: "He's still breathing. Has he done this before?"

Steve: "I go out there all the time."

Barbara starts walking toward David.

Douglas: "What are you thinking, Barbara?"

She stops and reflects. "This is just like the inside of my head."

David: "Hold it, Barbara. Once you go back you can never go back."

Barbara: "It's the end of the performance, isn't it?"

David starts humming.

Barbara: "I think I've made my decision."

Nancy sings: "I'll build the stairway to paradise."

Douglas watches Barbara exit out the other door, stage right.

David: "Barbara! It's a twenty-foot drop!"

Douglas: "It's still a way out."

[Audience applauds.]

Douglas: "Is there anybody present who would like to audition for the part of the female member?"

David: "The one who throws herself out the window at the end of the performance?"

Douglas: "We'd like to start with someone of similar sensibility, physical proportions, background."

No one steps forward.

Douglas: "Well how about a man, then. That would certainly unbalance our group, to have four men …"

David: "Not if we got him a little black dress."

Barbara reappears.

Douglas, not missing a beat: "This young lady, would you like to audition for the part?"

Barbara, having regained her poise. "Hi."

Douglas extends his hand to her: "Step right up. You're a dead ringer ... for Barbara."

A mock-serious discussion of the silliest possible audition items ensues, including dribbling the lips and blowing a raspberry.

■

Barbara is lying down again. David takes a mirror and angles it near her: "How long have you been feeling like this?"

Barbara: "David, I'm not gonna let you get away with this." She sits up and faces him. Some kind of shift has happened within her. "You guys are making me so happy." She turns back to stare at David. David edges closer to her. He moves in to kiss her. They roll around slowly on the floor.

Barbara: "I ain't been this happy before."

Douglas: "Typical screen test." He watches them roll around more. "She's taking the upper hand."

David, still making out: "God, it's incredible to think I just met you."

Barbara: "I know, but when you know it's going to be good, there's no time like it."

David: "I feel, I feel like we've known each other always, you know what I mean? I've never been with anybody who just felt like I felt."

Barbara: "I know. There's no unexpected moves. We're just alike, you and I."

David: "The thing that's really far out is your colors ..."

Barbara: "My colors?"

They roll by Nancy, pulling her into their twosome.

David, continuing: "Although we're so different, our colors blend."

Nancy separates from them and finds that Douglas is standing nearby. He's signaling with his arm like a traffic cop. She pulls down on one arm, then the other.

Douglas narrates in a stentorian voice as he is being thus accosted by Nancy: "My friends, beware. The sexual revolution is at hand. Increasing of the double standard, formal relaxation, the end of art, the beginning of pantheistic participation."

Nancy to Douglas: Have you met ... my brother?

David now rolls around with Nancy. "Isn't it really amazing that we hardly know each other ...?" [Laughter.]

GU at La MaMa, 1975. From left: Gordon, Lewis, Brown, Dunn aloft, Paxton, Dilley. Photo: Babette Mangolte.

Douglas, who is now the only person standing: "The Oedipus complex complicated beyond academic belief."

Nancy and David kiss a few times then sit up. Everyone holds still for about fifteen seconds.

Douglas: "But this wave of sensuality will no doubt give way to a resurgence of blatant rationality. And those of us lucky enough to live ..."

David comes over and pulls Douglas to the ground to roll around with him.

David to Douglas: "Oh god, you wouldn't believe that we never met before." [Laughter.]

Barbara and Nancy respond by creating their own same-sex makeout scene—but standing up. They hug and slow-dance.

Barbara, confiding in Nancy: "I know the way out, more and more it's becoming clear to me that ..."

Nancy: "Could you tell me the way out?"

Barbara: "I found one way. It was alright. I had a choice when I got out, whether I wanted to stay out or come back. There was nobody out there telling me anything except me. . . . Wanna try it? What do you think?"

Nancy: "I'm not thinking."

Barbara: "I know; it's nice not to think. It's the nicest of all." The two women are still embracing and swaying.

■

Douglas and David, having pulled apart, are lying on the ground.

Douglas: "Liebestod." [He's referring to the love and death scene in Wagner's *Tristan and Isolde*, which music had been played during David's solo for Nancy nodding out as the Statue of Liberty in his *Sleep Walking*.] "Indeed, leave us tote our own road." Douglas starts crawling. "And so, they went their way, collecting bad puns, waiting for the next levitation, the next ecstasy, the next rational exploration of an undiscovered dance problem, another contact, however brief and incomplete, with an audience, most of whom never to be seen again."

The others have collected in an upstage corner.

Barbara: "Countdown: Douglas! You only have ten seconds, come on."

David: "Doug, if you don't come in here soon you're not gonna get any supper tonight."

Douglas, still crawling: "Completion, the incomplete feeling of the motel room . . ."

David: "I call that boy and he never comes when I call him. Douglas! Come back here."

Douglas: "The prospect, tomorrow, a separation from those with whom one has shared as much as one can share [laughter], a psychologic pursuit, a never-ending ending, the contact with the lowest animal desire and the highest intellectual ideal. And at the airport . . ."

Meanwhile others have carried the big white screen with a hole in it toward Douglas, who is still crawling and pontificating. David is crouching on the other side of the plank, waiting for Douglas, who crawls through the hole, lands on top of David, never stopping his monologue. The white plank hides the dancers as they walk to the exit, but Douglas keeps talking from behind the plank: "And occasionally a triumphant exit, leaving everyone with a high sadness and a prospect of a never-ending ending." When the white plank, with all the dancers behind it, reaches the wall, the audience applauds.

INTERLUDE

THE JUDITH DUNN/BILL DIXON
IMPROVISATION GROUP

Another post-Judson improvisation group that left a deep impression on me was Judith Dunn and Bill Dixon's company. I saw them once at the Cunningham studio, around 1972, and they wove a dance-and-music tapestry that was mesmerizing.

Judith Dunn, Cunningham dancer and wife of Robert Dunn, had assisted her husband in the composition classes after the first few months. In fact, David Gordon, who had known of Judith Dunn (née Goldsmith) as a "fabled dancer in the modern dance club at Brooklyn College,"[1] called the workshops the "Dunn, Dunn classes" because he felt that the married couple taught the class together.[2] Judith and Robert had collaborated in performance, too. For two of her dances at Judson, Robert "accompanied" her by setting up simultaneous performances of sound and action based on chance operations.[3]

Then, in 1965, Judith met black trumpeter Bill Dixon. I believe she was immediately drawn to him as a musician, collaborator, and lover. While her work with Cunningham and Judson Dance Theater expanded her range of choreographic methods, the collaboration with Bill Dixon pushed her to grapple with improvisation as the primary mode of performance. About this new phase, she wrote, "I had to come to terms with all my definitions of order and structure. I had to expand my ideas of what dance movement was and could be. What provided me with encouragement and material for study was the example of the improvisational tradition of Black Music, particularly in its most contemporary aspects as demonstrated by Bill Dixon and others."[4]

The pair came to Bennington College (probably right after Ohio State University; see interlude by Dianne McIntyre after chapter 16) in the fall of 1968, which was the beginning of my senior year there. Together they

Day 1 (1971), by Judith Dunn and Bill Dixon, Merce Cunningham Studio. From left: Erika Bro, Judith Dunn, Megan Bierman, Cheryl (Niederman) Lilienstein, Barbara Ensley. Photo: Personal collection of Cheryl Lilienstein.

taught a three-hour improvisation class on Friday mornings that I was too intimidated to attend. But they developed a strong following among the students. "They were both so brilliant, charismatic and politically engaged." said Penny Campbell, a fellow dance major. "I decided, 'This is it. This is liberation.'"[5]

Susan Sgorbati, another Bennington student who was influenced by them, wrote, "Their performance of improvisation was a radical idea at the time. Not that improvisation was radical—it was always a part of dancing. But their idea to take it seriously as a form for performance—that there were skills involved, that it could be practiced, and that musicians and dancers were working as equals—was something very radical for the contemporary dance scene then."[6]

The performance of the Judith Dunn/ Bill Dixon Company that knocked me out was titled *Day 1*. The five dancers (Judith, Cheryl Niederman Lilienstein, Barbara Ensley, Megan Bierman, and Erika Bro), intermingling in a constantly changing cluster, took an hour to cross from one end of the space to the other end. They moved in their own individual ways, related to

Day 1 (1971), by Judith Dunn and Bill Dixon. From left: Lilienstein, Bierman, Judith Dunn, Stephen Horenstein (mostly hidden); Ensley in foreground, Dixon on trumpet (in alcove), Enrico Rava, trumpet on the right. Photo: Personal collection of Cheryl Lilienstein.

but not exactly like Judith's continuous yet intricate, contained style. Each one would extricate from the group to do a solo and be absorbed back into the slowly advancing cluster. As an audience member, you felt the inexorable pull of the dancers toward the musicians, who were playing on the raised platform at the far end.

Barbara Ensley, who was also teaching technique classes at the Cunningham studio, described the basic relationship between the movement and music: "It was the same idea that Merce had about working with the music and also with other artists. We coexisted. They did what they did and we did what we did and it happened for the same period of time and that was it."[7]

Bill Dixon's music did not govern the dancing or relate to it in any obvious way. He and his musicians were laying down a blanket of textures, from rumbles to soaring arias to squeaks. The performance created a sensuous, sound-and-sight experience contained in a Zen-like steadiness. It was like watching a fountain in which you can see tiny water droplets at the same time as you see the thrust of the entire fountain.

According to dancer/scholar Danielle Goldman, Dixon was immersed in "training that developed technique to better realize musical desires as they arose" rather than learning to play notes. An improviser should be "readying oneself to immediately seize musical ideas."[8] Dixon had written that "joint listenings to music" were part of his process with Judith.[9] He felt that movement should be "evocative of the first time one does something; with that kind of purity. That kind of innocence; that kind of electricity and that kind of awareness/and lack of awareness/of how the time/pertaining to rhythm/passes."[10]

Ensley again: "Her idea was that the improviser had to make all the same decisions that a choreographer makes. It was improvisation as composition. It required a heightened presence of mind and awareness of time and space, and of how you and the other dancers were moving."[11]

Megan Bierman wrote in an email that Judith chose specific devices "to organize our minds and of course each of us interpreted these ideas in our own ways. The music was never an organizing principle for the dance. It was brilliant the way Bill was able to create a landscape of sound without smashing the dancers with rhythms that demanded a response. Thus, we could organize ourselves independently of the music, rhythmically and spatially."[12]

Cheryl Lilienstein remembered the process of collectively making *Day 1* in detail:

> *Day 1* was an hour-long piece, and we had rehearsed for one hour several times a week for a year. What we learned together was knowing how long an improvised hour lasted, and how to focus individually and broadly and stay fascinated throughout the hour of dance creation. We would come in to warm up, becoming blank, receptive, and raw, committing to creating new movement each rehearsal, tuning our minds to what we were adding to emerging structures and supporting, amplifying, destroying, contrasting or shadowing them, retaining memory of them for reference, while continuously digging out new material in every rehearsal, and treating

everyone's contribution with weight and sensitivity. Each rehearsal was a unique dance. *Nothing* was carried over from the last rehearsal.

Sometimes musicians were playing in the room but we didn't hear the music as a whole piece until just a few rehearsals prior to the performance. Sometime during the year of work, Judy added five choreographed short unison phrases. They organically "arrived." In performance, I recall knowing a specific unison phrase was going to emerge long before it arrived. I could feel it impending, and it became a focal point or a consolidating force or a landing site for whatever else continued to happen or had ceased.

A unison phrase (if it happened at all) could be done only once and required at least three people in a particular place in space. It could be joined by others, or not. This provided, as I recall, some anticipation and sensitivity training for the rest of the piece. The "rest of the piece" was thrillingly unpredictable and very spacious, because (like the Cunningham Studio), the space of this piece was grand like the freedom of heaven, and the tentacles of feeling and hearing what everyone was doing while creating new experiences was unlike anything I've ever felt since. Embedded in the piece was urgency to continue to create unpredictably and responsively no matter what was emerging. And Bill's music was the four-dimensional landscape we lived and breathed: focused, enveloping, eternally moving, energized, sustained, harsh, sensitive, both mind-bendingly structured and free.

I remember there being some philosophical tension in the air between the *idea* of the Grand Union and what we were doing. I never saw the Grand Union, but I think the tension was about this question: Should people who are talented simply gather and perform and call it improvisation? Or is that offensively presumptuous? I think Bill and Judy had difficulty with the idea of the GU because Bill and Judy were "serious artists" and had a strong work ethic. The GU took the opposite approach, and I think that while Bill and Judy respected the individuals in the Grand Union, they saw the Grand Union as perhaps more frivolous than artistic, and possibly they felt GU's presence in the dance realm undermined their effort to have improvisation accepted as a serious artistic endeavor. After all, we had worked long hours over a long time to produce something original, unique, unreproducible, yet repeatedly performable.[13]

■

Clearly the dancers with the Dunn/Dixon group had a different, more labor-intensive experience of improvisation than those involved in Grand Union. The perception that the latter didn't work hard was not entirely unfounded. After all, they didn't spend hours rehearsing. But the GU performers, like the Dunn/Dixon dancers, were channeling all their composing instincts as they were improvising. They were, as Dixon said about his training of musicians, readying themselves to seize on the ideas presented. There was terrific skill in GU's decisions of the moment that were based on their experience as dancers and their knowledge of each other. Plus, here was the added possibility of occasional, unfettered joy. Given the makeup of the GU crew, I don't think they could have accomplished what they did if they *had* rehearsed. As Barbara Dilley pointed out, the vitality of GU existed only in performance.

There is no one correct way to improvise, and I, as audience, enjoyed both groups' approaches.

■

Tragically, Judith started having medical problems in the mid-seventies and was diagnosed with brain cancer in 1977. The dance division of Bennington College conducted a search to replace her while she was on "medical leave." I was chosen for the position and served on the faculty from 1978 to 1984. One of the classes I taught was improvisation, on Friday mornings. By that time, it didn't scare me as much.

Judith Dunn passed away in 1983. Sgorbati succeeded me on the Bennington dance faculty, essentially stepping into the position passed down by Judith. Sgorbati (who is also director of the Center for the Advancement of Public Action at the College) has been teaching a course called Improvisation Ensemble for Dancers and Musicians for many years, carrying on her own evolution of the work of Dunn and Dixon. From 1985 to 2013, Penny Campbell taught improvisation at Middlebury College. Her students now teach in colleges like University of Iowa, Franklin & Marshall, the Five-College Dance Department, Columbia College Chicago, and Colby College. And that's just one lineage.

CHAPTER 20

SECOND WALKER ART CENTER RESIDENCY, OCTOBER 1975

The 1975 residency, October 5–10, drew on the popularity of Grand Union's 1971 residency. The group held fewer site-specific events but offered more workshops. The performance series included a show in the Guthrie Theater at the beginning of the week, one in the Walker lobby at the end of the week, and solo shows by Nancy and Barbara in between. Audiences were not invited to join the performers, as they had been in the 1971 lec-dem; instead, people could take workshops with Steve, Barbara, David, and Douglas. Steve's three-day video workshop at Minneapolis College of Art and Design generated video material to be used in the final performance in the lobby—a different form of community involvement.[1]

Both the Guthrie and lobby performances were videotaped, so I was able to see some of the consistent features of Grand Union's work together: how the dancers' restraint as performers tested the audience's patience (as in the performance I described earlier that began with Trisha and David slowly inching around the perimeter); how they sustained parallel narratives (at times three couples engaged in three completely different tasks or fantasies); their brilliant use of props (sofa, suitcase, lamp, carpet, portable door, parasol, sticks, dollies, fabrics); and the confusing, sometimes disturbingly porous, line between private and public (the animosity between Gordon's "character" and Dunn's "character" could well have been rooted in real-life tensions). But most of all, I was able to absorb how the legibility of their actions allowed the audience to follow them wholeheartedly.

The scene that really took off, in which a single idea sparked a plethora of variations, inventiveness piled on top of inventiveness, with all players contributing equally, was the bowing sequence at the

Guthrie. It all happened in one continuous flow of steadily building energy. Trisha started it. At a point when it was unclear whether the performance was over or not, she spoke into the standing microphone. In her clear-as-a-bell voice, she suggested, "Why don't we take a bow and then start from there?" This ignited an eight-minute sequence of rollicking exuberance that seemed to emanate from a single choreographic mind. The audience response of clapping and cheering on cue helped make that little miracle possible.[2]

From watching two different camera angles (I'm grateful for the Walker's archival diligence), this is what I saw: when Trisha proposes bowing, David happens to be standing behind her with his arm encircling her waist; as she bows, that makes a doubling of the action. The doubling idea ripples through the group. Steve gestures to Douglas, who comes from behind him as he bows. When Nancy walks forward to curtsy prettily, Barbara gloms onto her from behind. Trisha suggests "prancing into it and out of it." David bounces gently in place, asking, "Like this?" To show what she means, Trisha backs up, then bursts forth, flinging her arms wide, galloping downstage toward the audience. Steve asks for "bow music" and immediately a sound track of an insistent tape loop is heard. It's Steve Reich's *It's Gonna Rain* (1965), and it creates a crazed kind of momentum. Douglas initiates the run-and-slide bow. David shimmies his shoulders in a showgirl bow.

The concept of bowing shifts into any action advancing downstage and retreating upstage. The game has changed, and everyone onstage and in the house catches on. Steve pushes the sofa forward, with Trisha and David joining him. The three pull the sofa back upstage, just in time for Douglas to leap over it and dash downstage for a pirouette. Trisha slides forward on a sofa cushion as if sledding; Steve kneels on a cushion in mock triumph. They run back upstage; they tip the sofa over and—surprise—Nancy rolls out of it toward downstage. Barbara climbs on the sofa, prompting the others to form a shifting sculpture for her to walk on toward the audience. She steps on upper backs and shoulders. David rushes to pull over a portable door and other props to support her descent. Completing her mountainous trek downstage, Barbara somehow ends up upside down, very close to the audience. Wild applause and cheering for a mission accomplished.

They could have ended it right there, on a high—and the critics, no doubt, would have been happier. Instead, they slipped into a narrative of an unsettling argument between "father" and "son," as played out by David and Douglas. It was one of those knotty times when they both seemed to be airing long-held hostilities. But the whole group took it in stride and ended up on the sofa in a relaxed moment of togetherness. The small suitcase that had been used earlier—Douglas and Steve had pulled a bolt of silk out of it, and Barbara had somehow gotten stuffed into it—was on the sofa, and Trisha tossed it out onto the floor. As the lights faded, David asked Trisha, "Why did you throw the suitcase over there?" Trisha: "I wanted to be able to get out fast."

Trisha did want to get out, and she performed with GU only once more after the Walker.

■

The following narrative unfolding is taken from the Walker Art Center's archival video of the lobby performance on October 10. Without Trisha, who had to leave after the Guthrie performance, the group lacked a certain cohesiveness, and there was no moment when all the dancers fell in together as in the bowing sequence. At least one reviewer complained that it had too many endings.[3] But this performance was full of transporting moments. A Mexican rug, a cowboy hat, and a swath of silk suggested faraway places and characters. Hanging from the ceiling in the center of the room was a tent-like canvas bag with two drooping sides. On the walls Douglas had pinned bags of leaves he had collected from Suzanne Weil's lawn.

■

Barbara stands upstage between a small Mexican carpet and a video monitor, lifting and tilting her head. Little white clips are attached to the outside of her knees. The audience trails in, chatting and greeting one another; foam cushions are handed out. Douglas, holding a cowboy hat, saunters toward Barbara. He stops; they lock eyes from several yards away, each slowly lifting one arm. Lithe and sensual, Nancy swirls a stretch of silk to the jazz music of Herbie Hancock's *Man-Child* album and soon spirals her own body without the silk. Her swirling and spiraling through the space contrast with the meditative, rooted quality of Barbara and Douglas's duet. Soon opposite qualities merge, and the dancers are engaged in a loose trio. Douglas gets restless, his long torso tipping and careening, hat still in hand. His limbs reach way out as though being pulled in several directions at once.

David appears in a long, cinch-belted yukata (the Japanese paja-

GU in lobby of Walker Art Center, 1975. From left: Paxton, Dunn, Gordon, and Lewis. Gordon is about to bend down and move the stick.
Photo: Boyd Hagen, courtesy Walker Art Center.

mas he brought home from his shopping trips to Japan). He's inching along the floor, looking down at his feet, which are pushing something. He eventually arrives in the center and stands directly under the big hanging bag. The music has stopped. Nancy, using a stick as a cane, walks toward David, who has now wrapped that bag around his head. David to Nancy: "Don't come in, I'm taking a shower." [Laughter.]

■

Douglas covers Barbara, now prone, with the patterned Mexican carpet; he gets under it with her, cowboy hat now firmly on his head. Barbara is making quiet, wind-blowing sounds.

■

Nancy offers her stick to David: "You want my crutch?" He takes the stick. They turn and walk slowly downstage. He places the stick on the floor, points to it, and asks her, "Wanna step over the stick?" They step over it together, ceremonially. He picks up the stick and lays it down again a few inches in front of them. They step over it again. He picks it up and sets it down again. It's a very plain task yet a touching way of marking time going by. The familiar graduation theme (*Pomp and Circumstance*, March No. 1 in D Major, by Edward Elgar), is suddenly heard; the music swells, lending their slow, stately trek a certain grandiosity. After several repetitions, David indicates that Nancy should go out on her own. She hesitates, then bravely steps over the stick alone. As she walks away, he shouts out a send-off and gives her a salute: "Bye Nancy. So long Nancy. Take care of yourself."

■

Barbara enters and dances alone quietly, facing the audience. The lights dim so we can see that the white clips on her legs are light sensors. Steve joins her; in the dimness the light sensors seem to float. Another pair of floating glow-clips appears a few feet yonder. Nancy is wearing censors on her elbows as she windmills her arms. Still dim. We see the path of light sensors but not much else. Twilight. Barbara starts whistling. Douglas is jauntily swinging a bag of leaves. He slows down and pours the leaves out of the bag, center stage. With his foot, he pushes the leaves into a neat circle.

    David: "That's almost irresistible."

    Douglas: "What's the almost?"

    Steve: "Is somebody in that bag?"

    Douglas: "I didn't look."

    Douglas (perhaps): "Its rigged." [A play on words, since the canvas bag is rigged from the ceiling.]

    Steve: "I want to kick them." [Meaning the leaves.]

    Douglas: "It's almost irresistible.... It'll be interesting to see if anybody kicks them before the evening's over."

    David: "*How* interesting?"

    Douglas: "More than almost interesting."

■

Barbara is softly hooting. Steve starts talking about an ice cave caused by five hundred acres of lava, near a volcano that could erupt any time.

    David, while assuming one position after another: "This isn't the story that ends with you running over your best friend, is it?" [Laughter.]

    Steve launches into a different, much longer story, as he walks around the perimeter, indicating it's a field. This story, about baling hay, is rich in detail—all the stages of cutting, rolling, conditioning, fluffing, and packing the hay onto a wagon—but delivered in a monotone. The upshot is that the hay is packed so tight that a snake, stuck halfway out of one bale, cannot wriggle all the way out. During the storytelling, Douglas slithers bonelessly.

David: "Sounds like a good story for a ballet."

Steve: "If you would care to do a ballet to my story, David …"

David, pointing to Douglas and his snaky movement: "It's been done."

Intermission.

■

Steve and Nancy lounge on the sofa, watching a television monitor. [I believe the video loop, which includes someone tying shoelaces, is a product of the video workshops that Steve taught.]

■

Under the parasol, Barbara and Douglas inch forward on their knees.

Barbara: "Hark, that must be the sound of a babbling brook. It must be water."

Douglas suddenly rises and brandishes the stick. "No water, I think it's the enemy. We must prepare."

Barbara: "I'm afraid. What do I do now?"

Douglas: "First consider that we know they are within earshot." He strikes the parasol with the stick.

Barbara: "I think I better put down my red umbrella." As she slowly lowers the parasol: "Will you … hide me … from the enemy?"

She takes the umbrella, now collapsed into a cone, and lies down on the sofa, which has just been vacated by Steve and Nancy.

■

Douglas whirls a big platform the size of a double bed around so forcefully that it knocks loudly against the floor. Barbara is raking the leaves into one long line that bisects the performance area. Nancy sits absolutely still on the dolly, holding a long twig upright. A bandana covers her face.

■

Steve: "Tell me a story, David."

David: "A hand for your heart. This is the heart."

Steve: "Where'd you get those shoes?"

David: "I want to talk about something poignant like my hand on your heart and you want to talk about high fashion." [Laughter.] "I want to bring a little emotional content to this concert. Could you please put your heart in my hand." He reaches his palm outward, just a few inches from Steve's heart.

Steve: "Sure." He steps closer to David but pushes his hand to the side. Not what David had intended. [Laughter.] Barbara brings over a mic and puts it up to David's mouth. He breathes heavily into it. "Thank you, that's all." Barbara walks away.

David brings his palm up to face Steve again. "If you will not fall toward my hand, will you fall away from my hand?" He softly slaps Steve's cheek.

Steve falls away from the slap, and David catches him with his other hand and sets him upright. David raises his palm above his forehead. Steve jumps up as though to place his heart on that hand, which is of course too high. After a couple more moves wherein they fake each other out, David lies down in an open position, vulnerable. Steve gets down on the floor next to him, belly down.

David softly: "Steve, I can hear the beating of your heart."

Steve sits up: "I turned it on for you. Want me to turn it up a little bit?" He goes back to floor and exaggerates a vigorous, repeated chest bump.

■

Douglas scoots Nancy's dolly close to the central hanging bag. He places an electric fan near her. Nancy drops her stick—the first movement she's done in about fifteen minutes. Douglas lifts the fan and puts leaves in front of it to blow them toward Nancy. A flurry to awaken her from hibernation. But she doesn't move.

■

Steve is sitting on the floor. Barbara walks toward him from behind. Without looking up, he lifts his arms to hold her hands, and they start dancing softly together.

INTERLUDE

JOAN EVANS AND CENTRAL NOTION CO.

BY JOAN EVANS

*In Grand Union's heyday, its members were invited to teach in
New York University's dance department. Joan Evans, who was
a student at that time, was so inspired by the group's lessons that
she cofounded a collective performance group in their image,
Central Notion Co. A former dancer/choreographer, Evans is now
an award-winning director of physical theater. She is also head
of movement at Stella Adler Studio of Acting in New York City
as well as artistic director of its Harold Clurman Center for New
Works in Movement and Dance Theater (aka MAD). Knowing
how much she was influenced by Grand Union, and wanting to
include some sort of nonprescriptive information on educational
methods, I asked Evans to write about her experience with them.*

In 1972, when I was a graduate student at NYU School of the Arts, the acting
director of the dance program was Helen Goodwin, who had been influenced by Anna Halprin. She had the brainstorm to arrange for us to work
with the artists in Grand Union. The classes met at 112 Greene Street in
SoHo, in a large raw space on the ground floor. Barbara Dilley and David
Gordon were our primary teachers. While their teaching styles and artistic
interests were different, the one lesson they both focused on was how to
perform. Barbara talked about "being in the moment" or "just being," by
which she meant open and aware, until something or someone moved you
to join the improvised dance. David instructed us to be more "workmanlike." He taught us short, horizontal walking patterns with frequent changes
of direction and focus. When doing this, we had to put all our attention on
the work.

Trisha Brown introduced her ideas about interruption. An interruption

Central Notion Co. at NYU dance department, 111 Second Avenue, 1972. Sitting from left: Gordon, Joan Evans. Standing from left: Fran Page, Donna Persons. Louise Udaykee is bending over. Photo: GregoryX (Gregory Schmidt).

refocused or completely changed the movement or moment by providing conflict or contrast, a rhythmic shift, and dynamic change. Interruptions helped prevent the material from becoming stagnant.

We had one peculiar class with Steve Paxton. We heard Steve would be teaching and we looked forward to the opportunity to do Contact Improvisation. However, we were all quite sick with colds that day, so Steve brought us upstairs to Jeff Lew's loft and taught us how to clear our sinuses using a saline solution. It proved quite effective.

Yvonne Rainer taught us pedestrian movement sequences at the loft and then engaged us in a game of stick ball between the parked trucks on Greene Street.

Nancy Lewis (then Green) didn't teach us, but she invited me into her home when I needed one to keep working. As a performer, she was an extraordinary inspiration. The fluidity with which she moved her upper torso encouraged me to develop more suppleness in my own spine, and later incorporate that work into my teaching.

The NYU dance students performed, alongside many other people, in David's piece, *The Matter*, in the spring of 1972 at the Cunningham Studio.

We learned about tableau and gesture. At the conclusion of the NYU spring term and the run of *The Matter*, five of us from that class formed Central Notion Co: Fran Page, Donna Persons, Louise Udaykee, Fern Zand, and me.

We attended many Grand Union performances in New York. The performers would arrive at different times and warm up or set up while talking to each other. They stretched the boundaries of dance by simultaneously engaging in witty dialogue, creating designs with whatever was in the space, and dancing together in a gloriously free structure. Sometimes everything happened at once, and sometimes a climactic scene emerged, which seemed to bring all the separate elements into agreement in an almost operatic way. On several occasions, Harry Nilsson's passionate song "Without You" was played in the background.

Central Notion Co. modeled itself after Grand Union. We improvised dances and dialogues, and experimented with objects, set pieces, and costumes. Sometimes, multiple things happened at once, and other times we collaborated on a single motif.

In addition to being colleagues and collaborators, we were also close friends. Our lives and love lives were all intertwined with the work. We hurt each other's feelings and had constant feuds, but making up, which often happened onstage, made for good drama, and an overall intensity, on which we thrived.

We thought that we would benefit from some more guidance, so we asked David and Barbara if they would continue to mentor us after the NYU course ended. We rehearsed and sometimes performed at NYU at 111 Second Avenue in the East Village. David worked with us once a week for a full year, and Barbara met with us once a week for about six months and then whenever she was not traveling. David served as an outside eye, whereas Barbara provided leadership within the improvisation itself.

Barbara had a gentle manner, and we rehearsed more quietly on the days when she was there. Whenever she saw elements that were missing or uninteresting in our improvisations she set up structures to help us. She taught us that space could be an important element in our collaborations. How we saw the space would determine how we related to each other and the type of movement we would do. In one of my favorite sessions, she designated the space as a series of corridors. We each had to stay within our individual lanes and pick up signals from one another, peripherally. We learned to listen not only with our ears and eyes, but with our whole bodies.

Barbara also taught us lessons that extended outside the work. She was

Barbara Dilley with Central Notion Co. at NYU dance department, 1972.
Photo: GregoryX (G. Schmidt). Jerome Robbins Dance Division,
The New York Public Library for the Performing Arts.

accepting of us and wanted us to accept ourselves as well. She encouraged us to trust our instincts and each other. Barbara seemed enlightened about life and was very calm. We all wanted to be around her and saw her as a strong female role model.

We met with David every Tuesday evening. He watched us carefully and then critiqued our sessions in detail. He was truthful and tough, and his comments sometimes stung. He had no tolerance for coyness and would tell us when we were boring. When he liked something, he pointed it out. David demanded we be honest; he reprimanded us when we were false or lost our concentration. Many years later, I realized that David was not just teaching us how to improvise and how to perform, but intended or not, he was helping us develop taste.

David knew how to spontaneously create a scene, and also when to let go of an idea. He challenged us to do the same. He wanted us to develop a sense of how long was enough and what was too long, and to learn to build a scene to a climax. When we were just spinning our wheels, David would sometimes enter the playing area and do something dramatic like start a dance or add objects to the space. Mats and other objects were readily available since we rehearsed in the theater space, where clown and combat classes took place. (All programs in the NYU School of the Arts operated under one roof in the early seventies. In 1982, when it was named Tisch School of the Arts, most of the other arts programs moved from Second Avenue to 721 Broadway.)

One night, David arrived with vintage khaki raincoats and hats that sparked our creativity. We used them to improvise a noir-like scene that we incorporated into our upcoming performance. David liked what we did.

David was very generous. He talked to us about performances he had seen or artists he knew and told us funny stories. He introduced us to his family. At holiday time, he gave us all beautiful long wool scarves. David and Barbara also arranged for Central Notion Co. to perform at a two-month festival that Grand Union members had organized at the Larry Richardson Dance Gallery. [See chapter 15.]

During that time, Central Notion also performed on the Staten Island Ferry, at The Performing Garage on Wooster Street, and at the Hudson River Museum. Fran left the company soon after and settled in Colorado, where she founded the Aspen Dance Connection. Fern left the following year to dance with Rudy Perez, one of the Judson dance artists.

Our all-female company changed further when Bill Gordh, storyteller and musician, joined the company, along with Gregory Schmidt, who played piano and saxophone. We toured to The Theater Project in Baltimore and Wilma Project in Philadelphia.

The summer after Barbara Dilley moved to Boulder to develop the dance program at Naropa, she invited Central Notion Co. to perform there. I recall that Douglas Dunn was out there then, and he attended a performance.

Helen Goodwin stayed in touch with us when she returned to Vancouver, and in the summer of 1974 she arranged a tour for us to British Columbia. Donna, Louise, Bill, our manager Tom Jenkins, and I set out west in a Greyhound bus. We had four performances in three venues but they were spread out over a month. We ran out of money at the end of the tour, so we divided up into pairs and hitchhiked back across Canada to New York City.

In 1975, I created my first set piece, a solo called *Dinner and the News*, and stopped performing with the company. The following year, Louise and

I made a duet called *Two Women Perform a Romance for the New Depression*. I choreographed theatrical dance solos for nineteen years, and I often improvised for months before setting the movement or engaging a director. I began creating and directing ensemble physical theater work in 1996.

In 2012, David asked me to choose four of the Muybridge poses from *The Matter* and have myself photographed doing them. That fall he used my photos and those of other performers from earlier versions of *The Matter* in a new live performance as part of the Danspace Project's series commemorating the fiftieth anniversary of Judson Dance Theater. Forty years after I appeared in the 1972 version, David once again invited NYU students to perform in the piece. Coming full circle, one of those 2012 performers—Madeline Mahoney—happened to be a student of mine at NYU Tisch Theater.

Barbara and David's teaching influenced mine. When I coach actors, I encourage spontaneity and impulsiveness. My students must learn to be spatially aware and listen intently. I instruct them to focus on their partners and on the action, rather than on their feelings. I teach them to engage their physical imagination and explore a moment through improvisation. I developed my own technique to teach these fundamentals. While the language that dancers use may be different than the language of actors, the core values that I learned as a dance student are also applicable in actor training. An honest, imaginative, and responsive performer is a good performer in any medium.

Actors need to transform to play characters. I teach my students to begin by being aware, open, and fully present, what I call "neutral"—and that's pure Barbara Dilley! A neutral starting place facilitates the magical union of belief, imagination, and self, which gives birth to the character. Otherwise the characterization is contaminated by the actor's own habits and limitations.

When we were working on *The Matter*, we had to hold still mid-stride. Back then, we just tried to keep our balance and not get tense. Now I teach my students about "active stillness." While still, the character is a thinking, breathing person whose needs and intentions are ongoing in stillness. We probably would have found performing in *The Matter* easier had we known about active stillness in 1972.

Starting out as an improvisational performer made the transition to choreographing a natural one. Now, when I devise ensemble pieces, I generally start with an image and then develop the material with the actors, who improvise. I give more direction, and then we repeat that process several times. I choose what I like, develop the material further, and become extremely specific in my direction. Above all, I remind my actors to stay present, for that is the most important lesson I learned from studying with Barbara and David and watching the Grand Union perform.

PART V Issues and Endings

CHAPTER 21

PUBLIC/PRIVATE, REAL/NOT REAL

How much of the Grand Union members' personal lives spilled over into performance? Did they always remain "themselves," or did they take on other "personae"? Is there a "real self" that is separate from the performing self?

It's slippery to talk about the "real selves" of Grand Union's performers, as some critics have. This was not a group that laid down ground rules about how to proceed or identify what was off limits. However, they did share certain unspoken understandings. Most of them had made dances at Judson, most (though a different most) had lived in SoHo, and most (yet a different most) had worked with Yvonne on CP-AD. These were all long-term, burnishing experiences.

One of the shared understandings was to make the process visible to the audience. As Sally Banes has written, "Part of its risk-taking was to lay both the process of improvisation and the process of group dynamics open at all times to public scrutiny in performance."[1] If they needed a sofa to complete a scene, they dragged one across the stage. If they disagreed about when to take an intermission, they bickered onstage. These were real tasks and real discussions that allowed the audience to see them navigate their needs and desires. The magic of illusion was not part of it. (The magic existed elsewhere.)

Illusion, that keystone of theatricality, was hard to let go of for some critics. In 1963, *Dance Magazine* reviewer Marcia Marks had written about a James Waring concert: "When David Gordon and Yvonne Rainer began calling each other by name, the last illusion that this might be a public performance was shattered. The evening slipped solidly into focus as a staging of private jokes, private psychoses."[2]

Marks was not the only critic who felt uninvited, uninitiated, or offended by the personal nature of downtown performances. When Grand Union came to Minneapolis, critic Allen Robertson accused the performers of ego-tripping (while parenthetically wondering, "Maybe all improvs are ego-trips?").[3] *Dance Scope* editor Richard Lorber was annoyed by what he felt was a contradiction: "They disdain the 'exploitation of personality,' or the 'star system,' yet they focus audience attention completely on the naked spontaneity of individuals. We come away with a heightened sense of their personal exhibitionism."[4]

The Nation's Nancy Goldner, one of the many American critics devoted to Balanchine's work, believed that "Grand Union banks on the cult of personality."[5] Well, yes, the GU dancers wore their own clothes and danced from their own impulses. Their personalities were not attached to (or recently detached from) a genius choreographer. This autonomy may have offended ballet critics who were accustomed to seeing dancers wearing identical costumes while performing a master's choreography.

As downtown denizens, we soaked up the independence of the GU dancers and the breakdown of illusion. We liked watching them be more or less the same people we knew through taking their workshops or seeing them around the neighborhood. We watched with curiosity, wondering what absurdist yarn David would spin, how Barbara would assert herself (in those prefeminist days), exactly how Steve would deflate a dramatic situation, how Nancy would go along with something but add an unexpected flourish, what outlandish feat Douglas would attempt, or what brilliant idea Trisha would come up with. And how they would fall in with—or resist—each other.

All their actions were based on a continuum of "real self" and "performed self." Words like "character" and "identity" were often used by critics trying to decipher the relationship between the person and the performer. To give an example of two opposing perceptions, the artist and sometime critic Robert Morris wrote that Grand Union was "a collection of individuals who never lose their identity,"[6] while dance scholar Susan Foster claimed that "each performer acquired a variety of personae. . . . None of these characters could be equated with the true identity of the performer."[7]

I think dance critic Marcia B. Siegel put it more poetically. After seeing the 1975 La MaMa show, she wrote, "Six people have agreed to come together and live a part of their lives in public."[8] I don't think this description is entirely accurate either, because these improvisers consciously shaped what they did as performance. But Siegel's statement comes closer to the spirit of Grand Union. The dancers were willing to enter a performance the way they would participate in their own lives: doing tasks, making alliances, taking a chance, engaging in play, taking a break. Valuing the art in the everyday, the everyday in art.

This Cagean meshing of art and everyday life, which was so key to the tenor of the sixties, could be misconstrued as narcissistic. Jack Anderson, looking back on this period years later, points out a paradox in how this alleged narcissism developed: "[I]n contemporary abstract dances performers often appear to be declaring, 'We are ourselves and we're here to dance.' This insistence ... has sometimes been branded as narcissistic. Yet it arose to counter what was regarded as the egotistical pretension of an earlier era."[9]

The pretension he refers to is exactly what Rainer railed against in her "rage at the narcissism of traditional dancing," mentioned in chapter 3 (note 16). She chipped away at that narcissism by giving dancers tasks that made them vulnerable, for example having to learn a new sequence in public. This kind of self-exposure was carried into Grand Union exponentially. No one ever knew what was going to happen. And, as Trisha had said at a gathering of critics and Grand Union dancers, "The tiredness shows, and the confusion."[10]

But what also shows is their caring for each other. At one of the 1975 La MaMa performances, after Trisha dismounted from a ladder that had been supported for a long time by Steve lying on his back, she massaged his legs. As we saw in the Iowa video, Barbara apologized for inadvertently digging her heel into Douglas's lower back when he was crawling underneath her standing weight. At Oberlin, when Nancy was thrashing around as a crazed rock-star-turned-crazed-dancer, David wrapped her in silk and hugged her. Many years later, Nancy cherished that moment: "David put his arms around me and held me tight. He silenced me and calmed me, which I needed. It was beautiful."[11]

■

For critics to say that Grand Union dancers were either always themselves or never themselves is misleading. Each person was different in this regard. David, with his fondness for radio and television, easily

GU in Trisha Brown's loft, in "rehearsal," June 1975. From left: Dunn, Brown, Paxton, Gordon's hand, Lewis's foot. Photo: Robert Alexander Papers, Special Collections, New York University.

slipped into different characters; he found willing accomplices in Nancy and Barbara. Nancy could interrupt her own whirlwind dancing to serve in any far-fetched plot of David's. In fact, she would sometimes initiate a reprise, for instance the farmer's wife desperately yelling to save the crops, as she did in Iowa. She would do so with obvious "bad acting" so no one would ever accuse her of "inhabiting" a role. Her usual goofy/elegant self remained firmly in place. David could pass through being a water detector, a surgeon, and a circus barker in a single performance. But it was his actions, not his acting, that brought him there. For instance, when he held his hands up as though wearing sterilized gloves for an operation, he didn't do method acting to convince you he was a surgeon. (More about this episode later.) It was the gesture itself that suggested the character. Douglas could put on a cowboy hat and make you imagine he was sleeping under the stars. But again, it was just an indication, not a theatrical transformation—or maybe it was just enough of a transformation to allow the audience to use its own imagination.

Steve and Trisha were more stalwart in being dance-based rather than character-based. When Steve donned a sarong for one of the La MaMa performances, he didn't adjust his actions to be more feminine or more Asian. Trisha could imitate a monster for five seconds, but it was mostly to make a point. Yvonne could delve into emotional extremes, but not in a character sense. When at LoGiudice Gallery she escalated the volume and intensity of her calls to "Ma. Ma-a. Mama," she might have been recalling a moment from childhood or releasing an adult cry for help rather than acting out a character.

When the issue came up in our group interview, Steve railed against the implication, from theorists like Foster, that a "real self" or "true identity" exists separately from a performing self. Yvonne, on the other hand, sees a difference between performing a mundane task at home and doing the same task in public: "When you have eyes upon you, something does happen to you.... You're not aware of yourself when you're washing the dishes [at home]; you're only aware of the task. If you're washing the dishes with people looking at you, you are aware of both: being looked at and the task. So there is a difference."[12]

But even for Yvonne, it's a difference of awareness, rather than a difference of one mode being more "real" than the other. For performers, who spend much of their professional lives in front of an audience, it's not particularly constructive to call one behavior real and the other not real. Many dancers feel most "themselves" when they are performing.

The question comes up about David and all his getups. Was he trying to erase himself and become a different person? Sally Sommer, who saw many GU performances, feels that his escapades were more about play, not about inhabiting a character the way an actor would.[13] Yet he admits he felt buoyed by the possibility of escaping himself— even without a costume as disguise: "One of the things I could do at the Grand Union is I could become not me.... I didn't have to change costume, I didn't have to do anything. All I had to do was announce I wasn't me and now I was somebody else and now we would play with whoever it was."[14] (Notice the verb "play.") Yet like Steve, David said he had no interest in teasing out the difference between an alleged "real self" and his play selves.[15]

■

Here's an example of a private mishap that grew into a public narrative. Just before one of the La MaMa performances, David had a back spasm so bad that he couldn't stand up. He had sought help from Elaine Summers, who lived in the building next door, to work on him with her ball work and other healing methods. When he arrived at La MaMa, he appealed to his fellow dancers to be gentle with him, and they presumably agreed.[16] But midway through, in response to a kind of scratch-fest between David, Barbara, and Trisha, Barbara jumped onto David's back. Instead of squawking, David at first played along, reversing his real sensation: "Hey, oh hey. This is more like it." Then, getting his bearings: "We made an agreement and now the agreement is broken." Realizing what she had done, Barbara confessed softly: "I broke the agreement." After Douglas lifted her off David's back, she sighed, "Oh David." David joked, "You couldn't keep off my lower back. You gotta get your hands on it!" He then proposed that, in order to rebalance his body, Barbara should now jump on his *front*. (David was a master at devising opposites.) Barbara expressed nervousness, and Douglas and Steve got involved in what became a beautifully co-ordinated attempt at forgiveness.

To a certain extent, the dancers always played themselves. Douglas was the youngest in the group (after Lincoln Scott left) and often behaved that way. He took physical risks that typically the young take (balancing on a high beam, diving into a bucket of water). In life he tends to be a loner, and with Grand Union as well, he was happy to delve into solo investigations.

Likewise, Steve tends to be philosophical in life as well as in performance. But he also had a deep interest in exploring physical relationships through weight bearing: "I like it when bodies are free and when the emotional state is open and accepting and sensitive. When the psychology isn't hassled or political or tied in knots. I like it when people can do things that surprise themselves. Where it comes from is just human play, human exchange—animal play. It's like horseplay or kitten play or child's play, as well."[17]

Trisha had a way of speaking and pausing in real-life conversation, and this halting rhythm sometimes provided an uncanny suspense in Grand Union.

These are examples of how each person followed her or his own interests or tendencies while also remaining an essential part of the ensemble. No separation between private and public. Kathy Duncan, the dancer/writer who called the group "a collective genius" and "a utopian democracy," said that "much of their success is due to the fact that they're extremely interesting people and have learned to be themselves in the arena."[18]

For some, these interesting people took on the patina of glamour. Experimental theater director Richard Foreman felt they possessed the charisma of Hollywood movie stars like Marlene Dietrich.[19] Art critic Grace Glueck overheard an audience member calling Barbara Dilley and Steve Paxton "the Lee Remick and Paul Newman of the avant-garde."[20] Dance critic Nancy Dalva was quoted as saying about the Judson dancers, "One thing that people don't really talk about is that ... they were so *hot!*"[21] This downtown allure was seen in a negative light by Goldner, who wrote, "Their appeal is similar to that of the Beatles; it's possible to like them without giving a hoot for what they do."[22]

But of course we did care what they did (just as we cared what the Beatles did). We wanted to see them over and over again. I don't think Grand Union members cultivated their "personalities" any more than a visual artist or musician does. How they walked, how they moved, how they made connections—this is who they were as people. And, as Steve pointed out, they were their own material. Rather than utilizing technique or choreographic imagery as material, this was a refreshing way to be oneself in performance. After all, plenty of triple pirouettes and well-rehearsed musicality were on display elsewhere in the dance world.

Their access to their "play selves" was an essential component in Grand Union. For David, it had to do with the ability to weave stories. On his Archiveography site, he says that while in Grand Union, he discovered that "making up stories is improvising—and improvising is related to lying. David makes up stories or improvises. Or lies and invents the truth he needs—or wants—instead of the truth he has."[23]

Douglas too is very clear about the plurality of options. On a lighter note than before, he cites both fantasy and reality as sources: "We all just made up stuff and we all became verbal.... It was fun and very rich because it was full of fantasy and reality. You could say something about what happened with Barbara yesterday and it could be really personal stuff and you had to stay in character and make it a story and

GU at LoGiudice Gallery, 1972. From left: Dilley, Paxton. Photo: Gordon Mumma.

not worry that there's some truth that's gonna have personal import to you. You're just gonna follow it and use as much as you want of what's real and what's not real. It was fantastic."[24]

This shifting back and forth between fantasy and reality contributed, as Barbara has said, "to letting [the unconscious] have a priority, and letting out the kook or the demon or the queen or the whore or the dumb bunny or the smart cookie."[25] She gives credit to David for this fertile strand of improvisation: "There was a lot of projection on one another.... We would build it up and then dissolve it on the spot. ... We took on personas with each other, and David was a very rich teacher in that way for me. He would somehow generate a little situation in which he communicated what persona I [would have] and then I made the agreement to [get] into that persona."[26]

For Barbara, what she calls "character work" was a stretch at first, but she became skilled at it. It was only possible, she felt, if she let the unconscious have free rein. And this was only possible because Grand Union had learned a central concept of theater improv: that play is how you get to the unconscious.[27]

But this unruly play had its dangers. It was never clear whether there was any separation between the "play self" or "other selves" and the person. Again, from Barbara:

> We were spending a lot of time together in this kind of wild, unpredictable universe and our other selves were showing up. I was not always sure whether we were performing or not.... David ... had this ability ... to create a scene. He was offering me a character and I would assume the character work, and then we would play together and sometimes we would get angry with each other. In this [one] particular scene, he was teaching me to sing opera; he was coaching me in an operatic event of some kind. I was going along with it. I was wailing away, singing opera and he was criticizing me, saying, "Do it differently." And at some point, I turned to him in my operatic majesty and sang, "I hate youuuuuu [singing]." Afterwards ... David came up to me and said, "I think you meant that." I looked at him and I didn't know what to say. I mean, I didn't know whether I meant it or not. At the moment I meant it, but I didn't mean it now. It was a very turbulent environment ... when those personal situations

were happening—what was really being revealed and how much could we tolerate it. I felt like I was totally inhabiting the persona.... David and I were not ourselves, but were we, or were we not? It got a little murky sometimes.[28]

For some of us in the audience, that murky area was intriguing. As Robb Baker wrote after seeing a string of Grand Union performances in 1974, "That very no man's land between public and private, between performance and life, is exactly the area explored most fascinatingly in this grand union."[29]

INTERLUDE

LEADERLESS? REALLY?

What kind of organization survives without a leader? We often expect such a group to descend into chaos. But it is possible to operate collectively, more or less—for six years anyway.

Even though the counterculture was rife with communes, it was rare for an arts group to be completely communal or democratic. The long-running participatory arts groups have had leaders: Bread & Puppet Theater has Peter Schumann, the Living Theatre had Judith Malina and Julian Beck, the San Francisco Mime Troupe had R. G. Davis. Loose collectives like Fluxus, which was transatlantic with the crazy George Maciunas as head of it, and Arte Povera in Italy, were short lived. The same was true of Judson Dance Theater and artist-run galleries like Hansa and 112 Greene Street.

But Grand Union was a tight-knit group compared to those loose collectives. The members didn't just share space; they were cocreating as equals in every performance. In a way, it was the culmination of the egalitarian impulse, the ultimate democracy's body, to borrow Sally Banes's term. They physically committed themselves to group process, to listening to each other with their bodies. They were focused on a creative exchange rather than excelling in the eyes of a director.

Even offstage, Grand Union was a democracy. The performers shared administrative duties like corresponding with presenters and applying for grants. In 1972, Artservices International, the main European booking agent for the American avant-garde, branched out to New York. (Artservices, led by Benedicte Pesle in France, handled Merce Cunningham, John Cage, Robert Wilson, and others. The list grew to include Trisha Brown Dance Company and Douglas Dunn and Dancers as well as the Cage-influenced Sonic Arts Union.) The young American Mimi Johnson, whose arts savvy was cultivated by Pesle in Paris, was sent to New York to start Artservices

New York. Two of her first clients were John Cage and Grand Union. (Cage had befriended Johnson in Paris and personally invited her to New York.)[1] The improvisers would designate one among them to deal with Artservices.[2] Technical matters like lights and sound, which were minimal in the early years, were often handled by Steve and David. Then, in 1974, Bruce Hoover was hired as technical director, which made it more feasible for the group to play proscenium theaters.

Leadership during performances shifted continually. To quote Steve again, "Following or allowing oneself to lead is each member's continual responsibility."[3] While watching Grand Union, audience members often imagined a leader or, in their minds, assigned a leader. About the February 1971 loft series, Pat Catterson (who kindly typed up her notes from seeing those early performances) wrote that she felt Barbara Dilley was emerging as a leader. Elizabeth Kendall, too, felt that Barbara "set the tone" and "presided over" the four performances she saw at La MaMa in 1976.[4] Critic Marcia B. Siegel felt that Steve Paxton was "like the conscience of the group, and also a subliminal prime mover."[5] Mary Overlie would agree: "I always thought that Steve brought in the artistic vision. He was the person to set the intellectual tone of the evening."[6] Juliette Crump, who invited the group to the University of Montana at Missoula for its final performance, felt that David "was kind of the head of the company because he was the one who was talking the most."[7] Judy Padow, who had performed with Rainer and watched GU grow out of CP-AD, said, Rainer "was the major think tank behind the Grand Union. She was the one who was really experimenting with giving up choreographic control in favor of the kind of creativity that could be otherwise unleashed."[8] Carol Goodden, who was dancing with Trisha at the time, naturally felt that Trisha was "the star."[9] Perhaps the most even-handed observer was Mimi Johnson from Artservices. She said simply that Grand Union "was led by the people who were willing to actively lead."[10]

Theresa Dickinson, the dancer who guested with Grand Union at the San Francisco Art Institute, saw the ensemble as truly leaderless, similar to the rock bands she later worked with. In the early seventies, she was a freelance camera assistant at San Francisco's KQED television station, filming rock groups like Jefferson Airplane, Grateful Dead, and Quicksilver Messenger Service. Dickinson, who as a Tharp dancer had lived in the same dorm with Rainer's group in the summer of 1969 at Connecticut College, found an affinity between these bands and Grand Union: "I watched with amazement as the band members listened to each other and reacted in real time, producing unexpected turns and passages that were only of that moment. Before then, improvisation didn't interest me. When I saw it as a way of making a work together, new every time because of shifting circumstances, it became exciting, even paramount. That message came to me from the Grand Union and the rock bands, all sharing the fervor of new growth in a searching, idealistic moment."[11]

Grand Union members were not exempt from rock-star fantasies. Yvonne even said she sometimes felt that on tour, they were like a rock band.[12] David had suggested that their publicity shots for Oberlin should look like those of a rock band.

But in a more grounded way, Dickinson's observation rings true. In a band, each musician plays a different instrument, contributing a tone that helps complete the band's unique sound. What I saw in Grand Union performances back then, as well as in the archival videos, was that each dancer was strikingly different, vividly herself or himself and essential to the whole. Each dancer contributed a different range of tones and textures to the group "sound." In performance, the dancers allowed each other to evolve even further into their own selfhood. This brings to mind Douglas's idea of the ideal world, where everyone was "trying to realize their individuality completely but in relation to other people, necessarily."[13] (Of course this is partly a theatrical illusion. I do know, through my many conversations with them, that there were times when some of the Grand Union dancers felt held back.)

The issue of leadership was merrily lampooned in Grand Union. In the 1976 La MaMa performance, Barbara, Nancy, and David are bouncing around like jumping beans at different paces. David slows down and stops while Barbara keeps going.

David to Barbara: "I can't keep up with you.

Barbara: "You shouldn't be tired."

David: "I thought you were the leader,"

Nancy: "I thought *I* was the leader."

David, pointing to Barbara. "She was the leader. I made her my leader, and I couldn't keep up with my leader." He bows down to her on the floor and covers his head.

Barbara, pointing to David: "What does a leader do with . . . ?"

David: "With the fallen people." He starts crawling toward the still prancing Barbara. Barbara sits on the floor near David.

David sits up: "You know what makes a leader? A follower."

Barbara: "I disagree. You know what makes a leader? Wisdom."

David: "You're my leader." He crouches down and covers his head again.

Barbara: "Get up, follower. Follow me."

She sways side to side, arms out. David gets behind her but doesn't follow her arms. He ducks down to be her size, at which point Barbara tells him he has to stand tall.

Losing interest in this, David stands up and goes to join Valda, who has been studiously untangling a knot of string: "I'd like to be your follower."

The concept of leaderlessness leads us to the concept of anarchism. The popularized notion of anarchy as sheer mayhem obscures the underlying humanity of this philosophy. The anarchists of France and Russia believed that cooperation is possible without government, that there is no conflict between individual desires and social instincts, and that government exists only to protect property and to control people by violence and suppression. Emma Goldman, the most charismatic anarchist of the early twentieth century, embraced the idea of an organized society not as coercion but "as the result of natural blending of common interests, brought about through voluntary adhesion."[14]

It is perhaps not by chance that Yvonne started reading Goldman at age sixteen.[15] The philosophy was part of her family background—she attended gatherings of Italian anarchists—but also she was interested in anything that gave off a whiff of rebellion. Anarchism had a meaning that dovetailed with the artistic ferment of the sixties. Yvonne called West Coast poets like Kenneth Rexroth and Kenneth Patchen "nominally anarchists."[16] Banes called John Cage, Jackson Mac Low, and Judith Malina and Julian Beck "anarchist-pacifists."[17] (Cage and the Beat poets were routinely labeled anarchists.) As we saw in chapter 2, Gordon Matta-Clark and some of the 112 Greene Street artists called themselves anarchitects. Artists tend to revere irreverence, so anarchism means something different, something more honorable, in the art world than it does in the usual American parlance.

Early on (probably in late 1971), when Grand Union hadn't yet committed to total improvisation, the members wrote an explanation of their shifting position: "Currently we are thinking about organizing many of the ideas and images that emerged this winter into a new structure—partially set and partially improvised. The pendulum swing between anarchy and

GU at Annenberg Center, University of Pennsylvania, 1974. From left: Brown, Dunn, Gordon, with Paxton on floor. Photo: Robert Alexander Papers, Special Collections, New York University.

thru 'modified democracy' to oligarchy and back again, is being carefully observed by all of us."[18] To me, this means that they were aware of the larger implications of their decision making.

Democracy is one ideal, but it retains a hierarchical order. The anti-authoritarian sentiment of anarchism envisions no one having power over anyone. Jill Johnston wrote of the Judson dance artists, "The new choreographers are outrageously invalidating the very nature of authority. The thinking behind the work goes beyond democracy into anarchy. No member outstanding. No body necessarily more beautiful than any other body. No movement necessarily more important or more beautiful than any other movement. It is, at last, seeing beyond our subjective tastes and conditioning . . . to a phenomenological understanding of the world."[19]

Johnston watched Judson closely, almost keeping vigil over its discoveries. By the time Grand Union started, she was no longer writing about performance. It was her successor, Deborah Jowitt, who kept a similar vigil over Grand Union (though it was one of many interests for her). Each time she reviewed the group, new thoughts emerged. She was not a detached observer but was emotionally involved. In a 1975 review she wrote, "I spend two evenings at La MaMa . . . and come away absurdly comforted—thinking that if I stuck my head out the window and yelled to the street below, 'catch me,' maybe, just maybe, someone would."[20] She gives us a whiff of the anarchy—the good kind—that inspires a crazy level of trust.

Just as Yvonne was influenced by Goldman, Steve was influenced by anarchist philosopher Peter Kropotkin's idea of mutual aid. In a response paper in 2014, he referred to Kropotkin's research on animal societies that suggested the societies with the most mutual aid are also the most open to progress.[21] The idea of mutuality, as we saw earlier, was foundational to Steve's development of Contact Improvisation.

The formation of Grand Union in the fall of 1970 inspired Paxton to jot this down:

A dancer is both medium and artist.
It is time again to attempt anarchy. For one, anarchy is simple.
Anarchy for a group requires conditions of communication.
The Grand Union is a blend of artists. A group. This is a basic
theatrical form: a social group exploring the image and the cultural
appurtenances. The social structure we are produces results, exerts

control beyond our individual devinings [*sic*]. The point, of course, is theater, not anarchy. Occasionally it is good to work alone. Occasionally it is good to work together.

See, see how it comes apart.

See how it goes together.

The Union suits.

Steve Paxton

29 december 1970[22]

CHAPTER 22

GETTING INTO THE ACT:
ARTISTS, CHILDREN, DOGS,
CRITICS, AND HECKLERS

Who came to see Grand Union, and what was their experience? How did the makeup of the audience change over time and over geography? Did audience members ever participate—or was that out of bounds?

As I described in chapter 2 on SoHo, Grand Union sprang up in an environment of border-crashing artists. Being involved in their friends' projects and seeing each other's work were affirmations that there were new ways to do things. According to sculptor Richard Nonas, "[T]he only audience that any of us had for our work was the rest of us. So the dancers were the audience of the painters and sculptors, and the painters and sculptors were the audience of the dancers and the musicians.... Everybody was connected."[1] Some of the other artists in that milieu who came to see Grand Union were sculptor Richard Serra, composers Philip Glass and Gordon Mumma, actors/directors Ruth Maleczech and Joanne Akalaitis from Mabou Mines, Chilean pianist and artist Fernando Torm, and poet Ann Waldman.

The early performances sprawled through lofts and galleries with no theatrical lighting to separate watchers from doers. Knowing the dancers were improvising bestowed on us, the audience, a kind of alertness, a sense of high anticipation. Mary Overlie, who saw the group often, said a GU performance "was almost like a sporting event, some kind of heightened excitement that was kind of gladiator-like, just like hungry and excited out of your mind to watch what was going on there."[2] On the other hand, the GU style could be easily mockable—with affection. Terry O'Reilly, then and now a member of Mabou Mines, had the following memory of the theater group's reaction after one GU performance: "We were rehearsing at Paula Cooper Gallery kind of goofing off, and Ruth [Maleczech] and Joanne [Akalaitis] did a send-up of the Grand Union. It was hilarious. Ruth was pushing a potted plant across the floor of the gallery in some kind of yoga slash dance squat locomotion. Joanne was doing a talking bit, and kind of skipping. Pretty good too."[3]

■

As mentioned, the SoHo denizens were not a racially diverse group. The people who came to see Grand Union in one loft or another were mostly young, white, and in the arts. But they were soaking up something different than audiences at other modern dance attractions. They didn't come to see the latest work of a favorite choreographer like Paul Taylor or José Limón. The Grand Union audiences were more interested in how potential sparks would fly among the six or seven dancers. As Jared Bark said, "They would walk in wearing their street clothes, and you knew that within fifteen minutes something spectacular was going to happen."[4] As John Rockwell wrote in the *New York Times*, "People came back night after night, expecting and getting something new each time and following the permutations of the performers as if they were characters in an ongoing play."[5]

■

In the beginning, when Grand Union was still trying to incorporate the members' choreography, it was pretty fluid as to who was dancing and who was watching. Seven-year-old Sarah Soffer, a neighbor of Yvonne's, gamely joined a group formation at NYU's Loeb Student Center.[6] In January 1971, also at NYU, Jowitt reports that three small boys got into the act at the end; they belonged to Trisha (Adam), David (Ain), and Nancy (Miles).[7]

The following month, while Rainer was traveling in India, the group gave several loft performances that were casual, sparsely attended, and loose with respect to the performer/audience boundary. The Grand Union dancers were performing simultaneously with students who had learned David's *Sleep Walkers*. In this version, called *Wall Sleepers*, Catterson recalls being given the option to leave the wall and join Grand Union proper. At another juncture, Steve asked for volunteers from the audience for an ad hoc piece. Catterson jotted down this description: "Stillness, little jumps, exits, interesting variations, herd closing in a huddle and then opening out with flailing arms and zooming across the space to really great music."[8] Trisha extended her hand to audience member Carmen Beuchat, the Chilean dancer she was working with, and off they went on a "walking and body-weight movement" duet. Catterson remembers one instance when a woman who was *not* invited behaved so strangely that she was worried for the woman's sanity. On a happier occasion, a dog entered the space and Trisha, who loved dogs, danced a duet with it.

By 1972, people crowded into informal spaces like LoGiudice Gallery, paying a two-dollar admission fee (free if it was your second time). For most of the audience, it was understood by then that Grand Union was no longer asking for volunteers. Most of us wouldn't step out of the audience to join them any sooner than we would walk onstage to play with Philip Glass's ensemble. But occasionally a spectator interpreted their spontaneity as an invitation. Choreographer Risa Jaroslow recalled a time during this period when a woman from the audience sat in a chair in the performance area until Trisha whispered to her, then gently nudged her out of her seat.[9]

Trisha had her wits about her on another occasion, too. At The Kitchen in 1974, a dancer named Laleen Jayamanne had entered the fray the night before and was looking to repeat that opportunity. Baker wrote: "Trisha looked at Laleen coolly and said, 'Maybe you could get a group of your own together and call it the A & P.' The audience laughed loud, breaking the ice, and Laleen went back to her seat."[10]

Then there was the time the Grand Union dancers capitulated to a group of charming interlopers. Robb Baker described it in *Dance Magazine:*

> At Pratt, five little black kids decided they wanted in on the fun. Trisha put on a wig and hat and tried to scare them back into non-participation. It didn't work. David Gordon, the most theatrical Union member, seemed the most disturbed by the outside threat. Doug Dunn and Steve Paxton more or less ignored the heckling, but Nancy Lewis and Barbara Dilley kept giving the kids sly little smiles as if they almost welcomed the intrusion.
>
> At the end, the kids took over, rolling oranges, exhibiting their yoyo expertise, funky-chickening it up to the record-player soul of "bright, bright sunshiney [sic] day." The Union members sat on the sides and watched, having changed places with their

challengers. The reversal happened so quietly and naturally that it seemed almost a part of the show.[11]

These examples of audience participation by chance are not related to the Happenings of Allan Kaprow or the community events of Anna Halprin. For both Kaprow and Halprin, the bridging of the performer/audience divide was intentional. With Grand Union, that dividing line just happened to dissolve at times. The dancers' intent was to give a performance for an audience, engaging their attention but not their dancing. As theater theorist Michael Kirby noted, however, the context made people feel they had been invited. He says that "they, the spectators, tend[ed] to project themselves," thinking they could do it too, as no obvious technique was needed.[12] As early as spring of 1971, Grand Union announced that the audience was not to take part.[13]

■

The SoHo crowd was already part of the "tribe," to use Barbara's word—the tribe that kept coming back. But in other cities, it took some work for Grand Union to earn the audience's trust. Minneapolis critic Allen Robertson seemed to understand the intensity of that trust: "The union isn't just between the performers on stage; it's also a bond with the audience. Without our willingness to go along with them, to take some of the same chances that the dancers on stage are taking, this particular Union would be little more than ... meaningless, unorganized antics. We must dare to trust them and take the chance that our trust may go unrewarded."[14]

In venues where there was less preperformance contact, the audience was less involved. (This tends to be the case with any dance company on tour.) Sometimes audience members were clueless about what they had signed up for. According to Grand Union's tech director Bruce Hoover, the people who got dressed up in suits and ties to see "a dance concert" were so appalled by GU's antics that they would sometimes get up and leave.[15]

Then there were times when the audience *had* to stay until the end. For the GU performance at the University of Montana at Missoula, it was compulsory for both the dance students and drama students to attend, and the drama students were not happy about this.[16] Toward the end of a long, slow-moving concert in which Grand Unioners took turns filming with a video camera, Barbara was standing among the audience, aiming the camera toward the stage. As she was explaining something, a loud male voice from the audience behind her yelled "Bullshit!"

Apparently that one heckler was not done complaining. In the video, during the final applause, boos from the audience are also audible. Bruce Hoover's description of the same performance was this: "[T]here was shouting from the audience. Somebody was really angry, and he came backstage after the performance. I think he was a little drunk. He sought out Steve and just started railing at him. 'How dare you all do this? How dare you do this kind of thing? This is just disgraceful that you are doing this on the stage.' Steve really handled it brilliantly. His calm and his peace [were] able to deflect that kind of energy."[17]

Nancy remembers that Steve was eating a grapefruit right after the performance (Douglas had been peeling a grapefruit during the performance) when some of the audience came up onstage, and one young man, said, "You get *paid* for this!?" (Maybe if Steve had told him how little they got paid, the guy would've calmed down.) He may have offered the man a piece of grapefruit, which could be what Hoover described as deflecting the aggressive energy.[18]

■

Critics agreed that being in the audience of Grand Union was a different experience than being at other dance concerts. Robb Baker said that the nature of the work was so private that he felt he was "eavesdropping" in the same fashion one does while watching a soap opera.[19] Elizabeth Kendall felt the audience served as a witness, "an innocent bystander.... What was happening was so much 'inside' that group of people." But audiences had different reactions to that insider feeling. Whereas Baker enjoyed the intimacy of it, Kendall felt vaguely taken advantage of, as though the group hadn't worked hard enough to produce a real performance.[20]

The term "self-indulgent" was flung at Grand Union many times. Jowitt has deconstructed the term, calling it "a critic-ese expression usually meaning that the performers explored an event for longer than you wanted to watch them explore it."[21]

My own feeling is that it's simply a matter of trust—an almost visceral sense on the part of the critic about whether a given artist is

GU at La MaMa, 1975. From left: Dilley, Lewis, Brown, Dunn, Paxton (hidden), Gordon with mic. Photo: Gerald Gersh, personal collection of Douglas Dunn.

believable. And if critics don't feel an immediate sense of trust, or connection, they try to locate their distaste in some artistic error. For instance, Nancy Goldner, in a long review in the *Nation*, described Grand Union's ability to improvise with great eloquence but then called much of the group's dialogue "unbearably fey."[22]

And critics who liked Grand Union sometimes expressed a wish to see the performers in a less theatrical setting. Arthur Sainer, a *Village Voice* theater critic, said he'd rather see them in a workshop situation where they would be under less pressure to make something happen, and where the audience would be more participatory and less adoring.[23]

During a meeting of Grand Union and invited critics (a gripe session, really, which I referred to briefly in chapter 14), critics differed on the challenges of reviewing the group. Robb Baker of *Dance Magazine* offered, "Sometimes I feel a new art form deserves a new writing form. One might write about improvisational dancing with improvisational writing, but I don't know what improvisational writing is." Art critic John Howell, on the same occasion, described the openness as a chore: "Since there is no formal framework, no manifesto, no method, other than the fact that you are going to appear in the space together, the writer has an enormous burden. I tried straight description, once—ridiculous. It could have been a book by itself and it didn't say that much.... [The audience has] to deal with the openness of the situation."[24]

Maybe it's only other artists, people who know what it's like to face the blank canvas, who can appreciate the skill it takes to grapple with a whole evening of improvisation. The dancer/choreographer/writer Deborah Jowitt wrote this about the 1976 La MaMa performance: "[W]hat I appreciate most about the improvised evenings is being able to see the processes that either instigate change or block it. I'm not sure how to make this sound interesting to anyone else, but it means a great deal to me to watch performers *making up their minds*. Grand Union members occasionally embark on crazily risky projects, but I think they risk the most in being willing to show themselves at a loss. Between peaks. High and dry."[25]

∎

Barbara Dilley saw how subjective every audience perceiver was and also how the vibes between performer and audience helped create a community.

> [P]eople witness us through their own eyes and through their own experience. And they interpret it. But it's not necessarily our reality. It is what we're projecting. And it works as theater because it's broad enough to be witnessed in a lot of different ways. But man, I hear that feedback coming in and everybody's seeing it a little differently. The vistas are just broad enough … that if you are honest and genuine with one very simple thing, it can be mythic to anybody. I mean, you can become everyone sort of, a little bit. That's the most ancient aspect of performance. You really surrender yourself to that. Because the audience, when they begin to feel that happening, they're giving you the roles to play.... And in the Grand Union performances where this occurs—it doesn't happen in all of them—there's the distinct feeling that we are making choices to represent certain energies or certain personalities or certain characters because the audience is responding . So you yield to that energy.... [T]he

implications are coming to us through the vibrations of the people watching.[26]

The people who were affected by Grand Union were affected deeply. We felt we were learning life lessons, lessons in how to be oneself while also swimming in the same waters with others. We were learning about flow from a collective guru, with no single person in the lead, and that itself was a kind of utopia.

Jowitt articulated why some of us felt so connected, so involved. She followed "the shifts of equilibrium, the spurts of directed tension, the changes of focus that we're all constantly engaged in—alone or in groups." She identified with "the way they all help each other out of difficulties or lend their weight to accomplish some group purpose. ... [T]hey make us feel that we're all locked into this (this what?) together; we have as much at stake as they do in the turn of events."[27]

This is the kind of connection that Barbara felt from the other side, the performing side. In 1973 she said, "Some people learn a lot about behavior by seeing Grand Union more than once. They empathize with our dilemma, identify with our choices. We become both personal and archetypal figures to them."[28]

INTERLUDE

MUSINGS ON NOTHINGNESS

When we go to see a performance, we don't want to see nothing. We want to see something. But we sometimes forget that something comes out of nothing.

Critics often attacked Grand Union as boring, self-indulgent, nothing happening. They came to see a finished product. It didn't make a difference to some of them that they were watching people create on the spot. Even Minneapolis critic Allen Robertson, who knew that watching improvisation requires patience, seemed offended by being exposed to the process of working things out. After seeing both performances during the 1975 residency at Walker Art Center, he wrote a long, insightful, seemingly understanding review. He was upfront about preferring to see Grand Union dance rather than talk. And then, after describing a lovely trio by Dilley, Dunn, and Lewis, he said, "Less than five minutes later, the evening has become a meaningless, unfocused shambles of nothings."[1]

Each viewer sees things differently, of course. To my eyes, watching that performance on video, the "lovely trio" had been a mere holding pattern, and what came later yielded some amazing work between David and Nancy, a riddle-like duet between David and Steve, and vigorous experimentation between Steve and Douglas. Not to mention some beautiful night-time elegies involving Barbara. (See chapter 20.)

In any case, Grand Union members were used to being on the receiving end of this kind of diatribe. Back in 1966, when Yvonne Rainer premiered *The Mind Is a Muscle, Part I*, which was performed by Rainer, Paxton, and Gordon and later renamed *Trio A*, Clive Barnes wrote this in the *New York Times*:

Total disaster struck Judson Church in Washington Square last night. Correction: Total nothingness struck the Judson Church in Washington Square last night, struck it with the squelchy ignominy of a tomato against a pointless target. . . .

The most interesting event of the evening was when someone, through the long extent of a blissfully boring dance number, threw from the top of the church a succession of wooden laths. Plomp, plomp went the laths and for a time, as these in rigid succession floated earthwards, one had a visual sense of something happening.[2]

Nothingness, of course, is in the eye of the beholder. If you are looking for a particular something and you don't find it, you see only nothing. If you are looking for "meaning" and you don't find it, what you see registers as meaningless. The "blissfully boring dance number" was Rainer's *Trio A*, which is now considered an iconic work of postmodern dance. It is filled with difficult coordinations and a disjointedness that challenges the dancers to make a continuity. The phrasing is not musical, and the actions are uninflected, so it is basically antidynamic. Built into the choreography is an avoidance of meeting the eyes of the audience, so it is anticommunal. If you are looking for dynamics or if you are looking for a lovely performer/audience connection, you won't find it here. You will find "nothing." There is actually a lot of something in *Trio A* that brings up interesting questions: What is performance if the performer and audience do not "connect"? Is the performer an art object? What is phrasing if it's not musical? What is the overall structure if the phrases are not repeated? Can we redefine organic?

What follows are random thoughts on nothing and nothingness, from my cullings and mullings.

■

In 1957, Paul Taylor stood still while Toby Glanternik sat still for the entire four minutes during Taylor's piece *Duet*. The music was a score of silence by John Cage. Taylor described this dance as "nothingness taken to its ultimate."[3] It was part of his concert of seven dances, several others also being minimal, at the 92nd Street Y. Louis Horst's review in the *Dance Observer* contained no words; it was, famously, a blank space of about four inches by four inches. But Doris Hering saw something more than an empty space in this show. Writing in *Dance Magazine*, she called the concert "an effort to find the 'still point' in his approach to movement." And for her, it brought up the question, "Does nothing lead to something?"[4]

■

In Grand Union, nothing often led to something. Granted, there were times when "nothing" just stayed steady at a low plateau. One critic of Grand Union cited low energy, saying that the dancers didn't even try to connect. Could that critic have interpreted patience as low energy? I think it's fascinating to see how things play out when the dancers don't force it but just allow things to happen.

■

Mary Overlie: "Here is how, based on my observations, to begin building an awareness of the performer's more expanded self, eventually leading to a greater command of presence. First, have the performer sit in front of a class, with nothing to perform, and collect data about themselves as they consciously allow themselves to be watched."[5]

■

Robert Dunn, describing his approach to teaching the composition classes that led to Judson Dance Theater, wrote: "From Heidegger, Sartre, Far Eastern Buddhism, and Taoism, in some personal amalgam, I had the notion in teaching of making a 'clearing,' a sort of 'space of nothing,' in which things could appear and grow in their own nature. Before each class, I made the attempt to attain this state of mind."[6]

■

Charles Mingus: "You can't improvise on nothing, man."[7]

■

Could what appears to be nothingness be instead a case of incubation? This is from Oliver Sacks: "Creativity involves not only years of conscious preparation and training but unconscious preparation as well. This incubation period is essential to allow the subconscious assimilation and incorporation of one's influences and sources, to reorganize and synthesize them into something of one's own. . . . The essential element in these realms of retaining and appropriating versus assimilating and incorporating is one of depth, of meaning, of active and personal involvement."[8]

I once heard Oliver Sacks speak about creativity at a conference of the Association of Performing Arts Professionals. While he was emphasizing the importance of a latent period away from the desk or away from the studio, he was speaking in a start-stop rhythm. He would say a couple sentences, then be silent for a few seconds and wait. Or think. Or incubate. Or nothing. His speech pattern was a stutter in slow motion. (He was known to be a stutterer, but it was striking to me how much his rhythm illustrated his point.)

Improvisation is similar but on a different schedule. It falls into lulls, in which dancers may not be connecting on a conscious plane. It may look or feel like nothing is happening, but that doesn't mean the brain or body is blank. Maybe people who come to see improvisation in performance should adjust their expectations. Maybe they should be willing to sit through nothing before being swept away by something. And maybe what looks like nothing to him looks like something to her.

■

"In one Dunn workshop experiment, Paulus Berensohn (one of the first five students in Dunn's class) punctuated a solo with long periods of stillness, claiming that the dance's 'climax' was the longest period in which nothing at all happened."[9]

■

David Gordon, on renting a studio in the early seventies: "I went there and I went there and I went there and I didn't make any art. I began to try to make a dance, a painting, or something. I take a great deal of time to open everything up—the studio had cast-iron shutters—and a great deal of time to close everything up, and in between I can't think what I'm doing here. I was walking in circles, stopping, and trying to think of some dancing to do and putting my hands in my pockets and changing my focus and starting again. I do that for weeks and weeks and one day, I said, Maybe this is the dance. What is it you're doing? How many steps was that? Where do you look when you stop? I began to teach myself the thing I was doing that I thought was nothing because I didn't have any something. That became the piece I called *Oh, Yes.*"[10]

■

Douglas Dunn: "Early 70s—Only nothing can contain everything; only stillness embrace all movement; only simplicity all complexity and extremity."[11]

■

Nancy Stark Smith: "Where you are when you don't know where you are is one of the most precious spots offered by improvisation. It is a place from which more directions are possible than anywhere else. I call this place the Gap. The more I improvise, the more I'm convinced that it's through the medium of these gaps—this momentary suspension of reference point—

that comes the unexpected and much sought after 'original' material. It's 'original' because its origin is the current moment and because it comes from outside our usual frame of reference."[12]

∎

According to Robert Dunn, Paxton's dances were "the most anxiety-provoking" of all the choreographers at Judson. "They were wide open and unencompassable. . . . There was nothing very much to grasp onto. You just had to undergo them."[13]

∎

Marianne Preger-Simon, about dancing in Merce Cunningham's *Spring-weather and People* (1955): "[A]t one point in the dance, a group of four of us stood in one place and position for what seemed like fifteen minutes, though it was actually a much shorter time. We weren't doing nothing—we were standing still. It was not a time to relax and rest, but more like a bird stopping in midflight on the tip of a branch, before taking off again."[14]

∎

Douglas Dunn on Grand Union: "I recall a shtick several of us were trying: when 'nothing' was going on at rehearsal, you say, 'Stop: now repeat whatever you were doing during the last thirty seconds.' And then that memory of unpremeditated moves would become set as a bit."[15]

∎

This excerpt is from John Cage's "Lecture on Nothing," originally printed in 1959. It appears in his first collection, *Silence*, on pages divided into forty-eight units, each with forty-eight "measures." In the interests of economy, I am not replicating the original spacing here.

> I have nothing to say and I am saying it and that is poetry as I need it. . . . Slowly as the talk goes on, slowly, we have the feeling we are getting nowhere. That is a pleasure which will continue. If we are irritated, it is not a pleasure. Nothing is not a pleasure if one is irritated, but suddenly, it is a pleasure, and then more and more it is not irritating (and then more and more and slowly). Originally we were nowhere; and now, again, we are having the pleasure of being slowly nowhere. If anybody is sleepy, let him go to sleep.[16]

CHAPTER 23

GRAND UNION AS LABORATORY

Each Grand Union dancer entered into the improvisational fray with different instincts, and they all exited Grand Union with a different cache of tools. During those six years, they were also making their own work and thus became even stronger in their own diverging directions. It's hard to tell which playground influenced which. However, it's clear that Grand Union was a catalyst and instigator for continued work: Steve developed Contact Improvisation; Barbara started her Contemplative Dance Practice; Douglas had never choreographed until a GU "rehearsal" at which only one other person showed up; Trisha first expressed her wish for dancers to "line up" during Grand Union; Nancy brought her newfound improvisational talents to her work with musicians; and David got a clue about how to make a group dance, not to mention that his playwriting ability sprouted during those years. What they all shared in Grand Union and carried forth into their separate lives as choreographers was a strong sense of play.

The clearest, most nameable development emerging from Union labor was Contact Improvisation. As part of the 1972 Oberlin residency, Paxton's afternoon workshop yielded *Magnesium*. A short piece with risky tumbling, bumping, lifting, and rolling, it was infused with an egalitarian air, a democracy of roles. Steve was expanding what he and others were already doing in Grand Union: "I think one of the first Contact Improvisation moments that I noticed in Grand Union I had done with Barbara in certain duets, but they just felt like regular male/female duets. But with Doug, there was a long duet that we did in which we took each other's weight ... and I recognized that we were doing it by touch, not by how it looked or what kind of set-up might be expected."[1]

Steve felt compelled to explore this form further. He didn't want it to go the way of all improvisation—to disappear.[2] One of his ideas for Grand Union went directly into *Magnesium*:

> Something that I scored for the Grand Union led to Contact Improvisation. It was a solo on a mat that started off low, rolling and stretching thru the legs, and ended up high, with leaping rolls and catches.... Basically it was an investigation of the body in space where the feet didn't have to be on the ground. ... It was the place where I went through the basic perceptual stuff, peripheral vision, horizon change, the kind of stretching that makes rolling and falling easy ... having established a form in which the head doesn't have to be upright, what new way of seeing the world does that entail? The world just goes whirling around your eyes, and you have to find other sources of stability—momentum and sense of gravity are the major ones.[3]

He continued to develop his idea after Oberlin while teaching at Bennington, where it became more of a duet form. Once he named the form and debuted it in SoHo in June 1972, it spread like wildfire, attracting both dancers and nondancers. Nancy Stark Smith launched the journal *Contact Quarterly* to explore the ramifications of this growing phenomenon. Contact is now practiced on every continent except Antarctica, and annual festivals in cities from Freiburg to Buenos Aires attract hundreds of people.[4] Steve credits Grand Union with nurturing the movement language that went into Contact Improvisation: "The vision of Contact Improvisation was in part provoked by the constant flowing forms we encountered when Grand Union was cooking. Grand Union provided a constantly changing view of possibilities of form, performance, space, audience. A perception of flux."[5]

Although the Oberlin residency was a key part of the launching pad, Paxton also drew on previous influences like aikido, the Living Theatre, Forti's dance constructions (particularly the centrality of touch), the early choreography of Trisha Brown and Carolee Schneemann at Judson, working with Rainer on *CP-AD*, and his own past as a gymnast. Grand Union was a laboratory not only for the physical discoveries of Contact Improvisation, but also for how to talk about

GU at LoGiudice, 1972. Steve Paxton arching over Brown. Photo: Gordon Mumma.

it. Catterson's log of the 1971 loft performances notes: "Steve gave a lecture on falling down, curving down, and rolling—despite all of his elaborate descriptions he didn't demonstrate for the longest time. The suspense was hysterical!"[6]

Stark Smith enjoyed the predawn sessions at Oberlin so much that she told Steve she wanted to be included in the next iteration of *Magnesium*. Paxton readily accepted that the male-female barrier could be breached. When he invited students from Oberlin, Bennington, and University of Rochester to live and work together for ten days before the first performance at the John Weber Gallery, he was taking the communal aspect of Grand Union a step further. According to Stark Smith's memory, "We kind of lived in the midst of whatever it was that was beginning to take effect, because we spent so much of the day rolling around and being disoriented and touching each other and giving weight."[7]

Contact Improvisation wipes away assumptions about gender and other hierarchies. In a 2016 interview with Stark Smith, Steve talked about "aligning" one's own Small Dance with that of another person. The result, he said, is a duet of two "followers" rather than one leading the other. "In between the two people, a third thing arrives."[8] This faith that something will spring up out of what may look like passivity is inherent in Grand Union's ethos.

Being against hierarchies of all types, Steve is reluctant to be considered the "leader." When addressing the Contact Improvisation practitioners at an anniversary gathering in 2008, he said, "[M]y job was to make up a way to teach it. I had felt the form in my own body and I wanted to find a way to express it to you guys. And I think you had all felt it in your bodies. But anyway, I couldn't progress without collaboration. It's a mutual form."[9]

After ten years, Steve left the Contact Improvisation fold to work on his own. His abdication of the leadership role in some way parallels Rainer's stepping down as choreographer of CP-AD. As Nancy Stark Smith said, "He framed this work; he gave us tools, and then he stepped aside so that the individuals could really discover something."[10]

∎

From her work with Grand Union and other experiences, Barbara developed Contemplative Dance Practice, which she taught at Naropa University (formerly Naropa Institute) in Boulder for decades. The elements of Grand Union that contributed to Contemplative Dance Practice were these overlapping ideas: being in the moment, simplicity, sticking with one thing, and honoring the possibility of "group mind."

For Dilley, investing in the present was something she learned on the job, as it were, in Grand Union. "That combination of demand and fluidity in those Grand Union shows ... to not be strategizing about anything, not to figure out anything in the past or future ... [meant] you had to work with what was happening right in front of you."[11]

Dilley's line of inquiry was more about how dance fits into life than how it fits onto a stage. When she performed her *Wonder Dances* at the Walker Art Center in 1975, dancer/choreographer/critic Linda Shapiro wrote, "Because for her dancing is a process inseparable from the life process, her performance is more an intimate rite than a public display."[12] These intimate rites eventually involved meditation, and it was the intertwining of dance and meditation that formed the basis of Dilley's Contemplative Dance Practice. This includes the "little disciplines" of slow motion, stillness, repetition, and imitation. All are modes that naturally seeped into GU performances. Both Grand Union and her Contemplative Dance Practice formed an "open space for observation." The mystical side of her furnishes this as an aside: "The ancients find places on the land favorable for receiving messages from the unseen."[13]

One of her "intimate rites" was a solo I saw in 1971 titled *Dancing Before the Beloved (Dervish)*. Spinning was all she did, and flowers (on the crown of her head, waist, wrists, and ankles) were all she wore. Sitting on the floor in a circle around her, we waited for a single candle to be passed around so that we could each use it to light the candle placed in front of us. The performance was an opportunity to meditate on time passing, the continuity of one revolving body, and the nature of ritual.[14]

In her teaching, Barbara favored ideas of great simplicity. She named "five basic moves": standing, walking, turning, arm gestures, and crawling. She channeled these actions into "corridors" or "grids," structures that make the performer aware of space and the contagion of movement.[15] She introduced a form of Follow the Leader using peripheral vision. This was one of the ideas she tried out on Grand Union members—until it was determined that none of them wanted to do her Follow the Leader or Steve's Small Dance or anyone else's ideas. However, her Follow the Leader score evolved into Herding and Flocking, which she introduced in the Natural History of the American Dancer. These structures, she wrote, were "about locating collective mindbody and playing together."[16]

Sometimes being in the moment means resisting rather than going with an impulse. Dilley said that Grand Union "taught me both how to trust my impulses and also how to stick with material, which is the other end of the spectrum. Impulse is extremely seductive." She felt that Trisha, in particular, set an example for focusing intently on the activity at hand.[17]

The "group mind" that Dilley sensed in Grand Union is something she sought to replicate in the Natural History.[18] She also wanted to create an environment in her teaching that was conducive to group mind, "with insight and absurdity."[19] I duly note that during the group interview, both Douglas and David objected to the term "group mind," suspecting that it ignores people's individuality. (Steve had no objection to it; he has used the term himself.) But Barbara's definition— "a wild, deep play that coaxes the ensemble to cross over into that under-consciousness"—does allow for individuality.[20]

Barbara was a sensual dancer, and at the same time very spiritual. I think GU gave her the space to work toward bringing body and mind together, and that is one of the deep pleasures of watching the Grand Union videos.

■

Douglas hadn't choreographed before Grand Union and had no plans to go that route. But one day he showed up for a GU rehearsal and nothing happened—and then something happened: "Barbara and I arrived on time, and nobody else arrived. We were sitting there ... and wondering why people weren't arriving.... [F]inally I said ... 'Do you want to do something?' She said, 'OK, sure.' So I said, 'I'm gonna lie down on my front here with my arms and my legs out, and why don't you just sit on me. And then after a while see if you can change your position without touching the floor.'"[21]

His first concert, titled "One Thing Leads to Another" (1971), was a shared evening with his then romantic partner Sara Rudner at Laura Dean's loft in SoHo. They each made bits for both of them to perform. He gave Rudner, a dancer of divine lucidity who was in Twyla Tharp's early company, the task he had worked out with Barbara during that underpopulated rehearsal. She would sit on his back for two-and-a-half-minute segments. "She would set [the clock] and take a position and it would go bing! And she would reset it and take a new position. ... I was a dead man."[22]

Like Steve, Douglas enjoyed stillness both for its contrast with movement and as an activity in itself. Critic Marcia B. Siegel described a moment at La MaMa in 1975 when Dunn stood in one place, moving only his mouth and his eyebrows.[23] Douglas took stillness even further when he made the remarkable installation *101* (1974). He built an edifice of three hundred wooden beams that filled his SoHo loft, top to bottom, side to side. You could climb through it until you arrived at a lightbulb near the ceiling. Under that fixture lay Douglas,

Douglas Dunn
with Sara Rudner
in rehearsal for
"One Thing Leads
to Another," 1971.
This duet started in
a GU rehearsal with
Dilley. Photo: Robert
Alexander Papers,
Special Collections,
New York University.

strapped to horizontal beams, his hands and feet bound as though he were a sacrificial lamb. He was even more of a "dead man" than in his piece with Rudner. This "installation performance" was open to viewers four hours a day for seven weeks. Douglas was testing how far he could take stillness.[24] Part of his purpose was to rebound from all the movement-movement-movement he was immersed in with Merce Cunningham's company.

Douglas's ability to transform a performance space continued in Grand Union. At UCLA's Royce Hall in 1976, he felt the theater was so much larger than GU's usual intimate spaces that he decided he needed to do something to connect the stage with the audience. So he stretched a string from the proscenium to the balcony so the audience could feel a "symbolic connection."[25] And there was, as mentioned in chapter 6, that time he built a bridge to fill up the visual and aural space.

Another way to change the space is to disrupt the edges. At Seibu Theater in Tokyo, Douglas backed into the black traveler curtain that framed the central figure who was, at that moment, David. Douglas danced with the drapery, advancing and retreating, toward and away from David. He was playing with the physical as well as the metaphorical border between onstage and offstage.

Once Douglas caught the choreography bug, he kept experimenting. During the Grand Union years alone, he made or co-made about fourteen works. Although he is currently interested in making dances rather than improvising, he admits that "the tremendous openness about who I could be and what I could do"[26] in GU has given him a wellspring of fortitude.

■

Trisha was the most experienced choreographer in the group (other than Rainer) as well as the most experienced improviser (including Rainer). So in a way she had less need for a laboratory. She'd already had a lab, and it was called SoHo. She had explored task, gravity, resistance to gravity, and the body in the environment. But Grand Union was about interacting with other performers. In this realm, I would say, she investigated four aspects that she incorporated into later work: talking while dancing, "lining up" and recall, highly inventive partnering, and deploying large objects.

Talking while dancing is one of the reasons she agreed to join Grand

Union. She was curious about how she might implement words in her own way. In early Grand Union sessions, she made sure she practiced talking and also encouraged David in his talking. Regarding the first GU rehearsal Trisha came to, David wrote (again, referring to himself in the third person): "Trisha dances and talks about a house with many floors. David dances'n talks—and adds floors to her house—and her story—and adds laughing. His laughing morphs into crying'n he keeps talking. Trisha—having got interested in talking—gets more interested in talking and moving—and working with David."[27]

Trisha had already slipped a quiet, functional kind of talking into her late sixties pieces. In task dances like *Leaning Duets I and II* (1970 and 1971), a dancer might say to her partner, "I need you to give me more leeway here" or "Can you twist this way?" With "Sticks" (part of *Structured Pieces I*, 1973), which became a section of *Line Up* that I performed many times, we had to alert the others whenever the tip of our stick lost contact with the woman's stick adjacent to us. I might say, "Mona, I'm off," in which case we would all hold still while I managed to get the end of my stick to touch hers again, and then I would say "I'm on" so that we could resume the task. This kind of verbal keeping track accompanied the many instances of Trisha and Barbara's gymnastic grapplings in Grand Union.

But another kind of talking—telling stories, with David being the prime perpetrator—may have given Trisha the impetus she needed to embark on the solo that became *Accumulation + Talking + Water Motor*. She made this piece in stages, "upping the ante" with each new addition. In the final version, she spliced two different stories into two different solos: *Standing Accumulation* and *Water Motor* (1978). When she performed this piece, you could see she relished the physical and mental challenges, which have been nicely captured in Jonathan Demme's 1986 film, *Accumulation With Talking Plus Water Motor*.

Another Grand Union ploy that carried over to Trisha's work was carting people around as though they were objects. In one LoGiudice video, David and Trisha first confer, then lift and relocate three of the other dancers, one at a time. Whether it was Douglas or Barbara or Yvonne, the person stayed still or continued what she or he was doing. This kind of carrying the body as an object went into *Group Primary Accumulations* (1973). In this piece, four women on the ground accumulate thirty movements (as in 1; 1,2; 1,2,3; and so on) in unison and *keep* the movement going as two people start lifting and moving them to a different location. It's as though they are mechanical dolls that have been wound up and can't stop. In the early performances of *Group Primary*, the two movers were David and Douglas. It was a role they knew well.

When I was dancing with Trisha, we were immersed in the process of making *Line Up* for a year. At the time, I didn't know the main idea had antecedents in GU. In one LoGiudice video there's a scene in which David and Barbara are playing out their attraction/aggression toward each other with giddy volatility, and the others line up a few feet away and watch them. What followed was a rerun, a mode that GU members could hop into at any moment. David retold "what just happened" as Barbara stepped out of a line to help him. During the hubbub of that particular re-run, Barbara said, "Well, we were here. David says I was back here." Yvonne said, "I went like that," motioning David to come to where she was. David said to Trisha, "You took a step forward." Trisha said, "You took a tentative step forward. I took a large one. Steve, you took a little tiny baby step and I went far ahead of you." This was exactly the kind of exchange we had in Trisha Brown's company during the recalling phase of the building process of *Line Up* (1977)—discussing and dissecting what just happened, in detail. (See the interlude after this chapter for a more complete memory of *Line Up*.)

Steve told me recently that Trisha deliberately tested the idea during those early days of Grand Union: "She first articulated *Line Up* in a Grand Union rehearsal. We tried it out desultorily, but she tried it out later on her own company. That seemed to express the tension in the relation between GU and her proper choreography, to me. With the gift of her first company, she had a chance to herd those cats."[28]

I was one of those cats who was happily herded by Trisha in the years after she exited Grand Union.[29] Of course, what we did while "lining up" was not exactly being herded but engaging in a project of turning improvisation into choreography.

In their early gymnastic forays, Trisha and Barbara sometimes involved Nancy. Catterson reports that as early as 1971, the three teamed up to do handstands: "Their bodies became intertwined, limbs supporting others' limbs, a continual precarious balance with each delicately making shifts of the limbs."[30] It was this kind of thing—

sculptural shape-shifting, though with much greater inventiveness—that showed up in Brown's works during and after GU. This rich vein culminated in the "pitch and catch" section of *Newark (Niweweorce)* (1987), in which the dancers created interlocking, moving architecture, initiated from surprising points of connection.[31]

Two physical objects that have surfaced in Trisha's choreography also gained her attention in Grand Union: the foam mattress and the ladder. *Pamplona Stones* (1974), the spare, elegantly goofy duet she choreographed with Sylvia Palacios Whitman, made whimsical use of a very large piece of foam. At one point, the foam plank gets curved in such a way that it hides parts of the two women's bodies, creating the illusion that one *very* wide woman is sitting behind it, hugging the sides of the foam. This bespeaks Trisha's love of illusion as well as her wit and humor. Back in Grand Union's loft performances, Catterson noted that Barbara and Trisha used a "huge piece of foam rubber as a sitting cushion, a backpack, a slide, and a hammock with the two chairs."[32] Sounds to me like it could have been the seed for a section of *Pamplona Stones*.

Trisha loved climbing. In Grand Union she climbed on ladders, hung on two-by-fours, and walked atop a ballet barre. It's part of the same love of disorientation that gave us *Walking on the Wall* (1971). To elucidate only one of those examples: at La MaMa in 1975, a ladder was brought in by Barbara and Steve. Steve lay on his back, raised his legs in a not-quite shoulder stand, and balanced the bottom of the ladder on the soles of his feet. Trisha impulsively dove partly through the rungs of the ladder, thought better of it, then started climbing it, with Barbara and Douglas girding her. Steve lowered his pelvis to the floor, the better to give Trisha a foothold, and made suggestions from his position on his back. She climbed high enough to get her hands on the top rung, to much applause.

This love of climbing found its way into several of her later works, including *El Trilogy* (2000), with music by jazz composer Dave Douglas. In one section Diane Madden, who has been dancer, rehearsal director, and co-associate director of the company, improvised with an eight-foot ladder. "We had a little bit of a structure," Madden told me. "The first half or so was me wearing the ladder, and the second half was me climbing on it."[33] At times the ladder ended up wrapped around her neck, prompting Trisha to dub it "the ladder necklace." For

GU at La MaMa, 1975. Brown on ladder, Paxton on ground, Dunn and Dilley (mostly hidden). Photo: Babette Mangolte.

Madden, a contact improviser before beginning to dance with Trisha in 1980, a big part of the process was the dialogue that went along with the one-on-one rehearsals. Her account reveals Trisha's continuing interest in improvisation:

> When I was improvising, she kept asking me, "What are you doing? How are you making your choices?" It was a lot about the process—or the act—of listening … listening to my movement and those questions of Where am I and what can I do from this place? In dealing with an eight-foot ladder, whether you're wearing it or climbing on it, that's a key process: Where am I, where is the ladder, feeling it, and then from that place making a compositional choice. Also listening to the phrasing where there's a balance of action and stillness. And, because of how striking the ladder is visually, allowing for something to have time to be seen … allowing something to have a life. And then also listening to the sound of the ladder—it was a noisy thing— and also listening to the sound of the music.… The Dave Douglas band was improvising.[34]

Trisha felt the need to balance out the general mayhem of Grand Union with something supremely simple. Her *Accumulation* series achieved that. When I was on tour with Trisha, she once told me that while performing *Group Primary Accumulation*, "I'm thinking, This is all there is." Very different from the everything-at-once commotion of Grand Union. In fact, as she told Rainer: "[I]n counterbalance to the Grand Union and all of that extreme pain and pleasure that comes from letting it all hang out, I was doing my own work. The *Accumulations* were very carefully organized, each gesture, however absurd, meticulously studied."[35]

■

Nancy Lewis was more of a performer than a choreographer. She shone during a performance, whether it was set or improvised. Perhaps to emphasize that she had no ambitions to choreograph, she called her 1971 solo concert at The Cubiculo "Just Dancing." It included works by Rainer, Gordon, Paxton, Jack Moore, and Remy Charlip.[36] The solo by David Gordon, *Statue of Liberty*, was originally part of *Sleep Walking* at Oberlin. She also added her own improvisation with a pianist playing live. "Someone was playing the piano, kind of classical modern piano, and I just danced and ended up on a high note. My legs and arms went up and that was it."[37]

She earned a rave review from Don McDonagh in the *New York Times*: "Rich, unforced and admiring laughter was the background to Nancy Green's concert, Just Dancing." He called her rendition of Rainer's *Three Satie Spoons* (1961) a "strikingly good revival."[38] I saw it at The Cubiculo and I agree; she had the right irony, delicacy, and strength for that disciplined yet loony solo. Her solo concert at the Walker as part of the 1971 residency was positively reviewed by critic Linda Shapiro, who wrote that Lewis "projects a glamour which is both juicy and deadpan."[39]

In her interview with Sally Banes, Nancy was forthright about the problem of originality. She said that while working in the studio, she would catch herself bounding into the air as Steve would do or talking in a repetitive rhythm like David would do, and she would think, "Oh no, this is not original."[40] But that did not put a dent in her dancing, which she continued doing until the eighties.

∎

For David, the edict to improvise eventually freed him from the judgment of executing a particular phrase correctly. What began as a crutch in Grand Union performances, namely the sequence of Rainer's *Trio A*, could eventually be left behind while he put his own imagination into play. "When I was onstage dancing in *Trio A* ... I was extremely self-conscious. I was aware of being watched and possibly being graded in relation to the material and anybody else. In the Grand Union that all went away.... I became the person who it was possible to invent and do and respond to anything because there was no thing that was the perfect thing I should have been doing."[41]

Once he lost his inhibitions, David could further explore concepts that served him later: first, what he called "double reality"; second, assuming a character; third, a way to develop group work; and last, how to turn an abstract event into a story.

David first participated in an example of "double reality" (which also might be called "self-commentary") during a pre–*CP-AD* performance of Rainer's group at Pratt that contained a seed of Grand Union. This was not planned, but a happenstance that bubbled up from the loose structure. "At some point there was a discussion about the thing we were doing and whether we were doing it right, and it was an audible discussion. It had to do with the section in which everybody stood in a circle and somebody fell and you had to get caught. You wanted it to be a surprise but you didn't want to get hurt. What was the intention, and now we were talking about it, and people were laughing and listening to us talk about the thing we were doing. That, for me, was a changing point."[42] This kind of self-commentary showed up in many of David's later works.

The character element came with generous dollops of campiness. In the Walker Lobby performance of 1975, he was a smooth-talking emcee in a TV contestant show, and at La MaMa, also in 1975, he was an arrogant pasha auditioning dancers. The double reality popped up often in David's later work, for instance, in *Not Necessarily Recognizable Objectives (or Wordsworth Rides Again)* (1978), in which David and Valda have a very lifelike argument, and it's not until they switch roles—or you're close enough to see the script posted on the wall— that you realize this was totally planned.

In the sixties at Judson, David had made only solos and duets; he had no idea how to approach group work. During Grand Union's early loft performances, he initially refused to join the others in improvising. The breakthrough came after he visited Steve in the hospital and came away with the "I'm slipping" scene described in chapter 7. When two of the other dancers echoed his words and movement, he felt he had found a way forward: "Suddenly it's like the arrow in a sign [that] shows you a direction to go in. They were framing me in a way which amplified what I was doing, and the amplification came back to me to do something *about*."[43]

Another factor that edged David toward group choreography was that during that same period, Yvonne asked David to somehow keep her group of students together while she was in India. His admission years later: "The thing that was more horrible to me than making work was teaching."[44] So instead of giving a class, he worked on a piece for the students. One of them was Pat Catterson, who included this experience in the log about Grand Union she kept in order to show Rainer upon her return. About the first rehearsal with David, she wrote: "We did a sleeping thing leaning against the wall. Then standing up, nodding off, attempting gestures in our sleep such as scratching, grabbing, adjusting, rubbing our face, and so on. We did this for ninety minutes!"[45] This was the beginning of *Sleep Walking*, which was first done at a loft on 13th Street in February 1971 and then, in different versions, at later residencies.

At Oberlin he made *The Matter*, which passed through many versions in the ensuing years. It's a large group piece that incorporates many stillnesses. In the April 1972 version, the performers and audience filed in together to the Merce Cunningham studio in Westbeth Artists' Housing. Scattered among the clothed performers were a random few (including Valda) who were nude. The mix of professionals, students, and nondancers allowed, within David's structures, a certain amount of individual freedom.[46] It's ironic that *The Matter* was such a community piece, because David claims he never felt a desire for what he called the "communal, let's-all-work-together" ethic of either Judson or the Grand Union.[47]

By May 1972 David had developed his narrative abilities, gathering more voices than just his own, basically writing a theatrical scene on the spot. The way David describes this achievement is that he was translating the physical or conceptual explorations of his colleagues into a narrative: "I almost always framed with a gesture or sound or word something that turned the circumstance out of the spectacularly abstract way that Trisha and Steve could work and made it literal. It's all I could add; I couldn't add beautiful movement to what they did. I could add the circumstance in which it was happening."[48]

Applying this ability to his later works, he said, "I think ninety percent of the time in my entire career, that's what I do: I turn what seems like a physical movement relationship between two people into something *happening* between two people."

■

Yvonne left Grand Union—and dance—in 1972 to make films. Although she was entering a different medium, she brought her love of performers and performance with her. But film is an entirely different discipline, so there is not much I can say about GU being a laboratory for her future work. However, I have two examples. The first is from *In the College*, her work for Oberlin students. The final series of tableaux vivantes, based on the still shots of G. W. Pabst's 1929 film *Pandora's Box*, was something she also brought to the ending of *Lives of Performers*. The second example is only a hunch. One of the striking moments of her *Film About a Woman Who ...* (1974) is when the cam-

ISSUES AND ENDINGS

era zooms in on Yvonne's face, to which she has attached little pieces of paper with messages written on them. After seeing the video of the incident mentioned in chapter 16, when Trisha stuck a piece of paper to her forehead, I think it's possible that Yvonne got the idea from that moment. However, Yvonne was always looking for ways to incorporate written messages into performance and film. That was true in her earliest works at Judson, and it's true of her return to choreography in the last twenty years.

INTERLUDE

DANCING WITH TRISHA

I had seen Trisha Brown's work in a gallery space, and I loved the sense of mischief between the women performers. But the concert that has imprinted on my memory was at the Whitney Museum in 1971. Three of the pieces blew my mind: *Walking on the Wall*, so disorienting that it was practically hallucinatory; *Falling Duet I* with Barbara Dilley, as recklessly risk-taking as if they had been doing tricks on a high wire;[1] and *Skymap*, in which we, the audience, lay on our backs, looking up and following Trisha's words on tape while we beamed our imaginations up to the ceiling.

In a haphazard way, I let Trisha know I wanted to dance with her. Twice I ran into her on the street and expressed my interest. No response. Then, waiting in the checkout line at the grocery store—it was, no kidding, the Grand Union on LaGuardia Place—I found myself standing next to her. I was surprised that she knew my name. She asked me what I was doing these days. "I'm dancing with Sara Rudner and Kenneth King," I replied, "but I'm going to stop soon and just do my own work." Luckily, she ignored my answer and invited me to come to a rehearsal in her loft. That was November 1975. I found out later that one of the reasons she had asked me was that she knew I had studied with Elaine Summers, founder of "the great ball work," aka kinetic awareness, and an ally of Trisha's since the Judson days.

The beginning of my three years with Trisha overlapped with the end of her five years with Grand Union. When I came to the studio in November 1975, we first worked on making our own movement to fit into a highly complex accumulating and deaccumulating scheme. That was *Pyramid*. During the same period she was building the long "Solo Olos" phrase that would go into the larger work *Line Up* (1976).

When Trisha told us to "line up," I didn't know what she meant. But I quickly caught on. She meant: What does a line mean to you—and to your body? She meant she likes to see straight lines but she also likes messing them up. She meant she wanted to know what lines we could make between the walls and radiator and pipes and each other. Could it mean lining up our energy, could it mean being swept up into a big circular run? Could a perimeter be a line? She wanted to see a range of interpretations.

We created the main part of *Line Up* through a process of improvisation and recall. We would improvise on the instruction to "line up" for about ten seconds, then we'd go back and reconstruct what we thought we had just done. Trisha would step out and look at several segments strung together— which wasn't easy because she was in the piece and all our decisions were interdependent. Then she would keep the segment, or fiddle with it, or rip it up. We accumulated these bits over a year to make the fabric of an hour-long piece into which Trisha inserted a number of organized "line dances" she had made before.

For the final version of *Line Up*, we had set our improvisation in choreography, if not in stone. It was not easy for the audience to decipher any pattern in the main lining up sections. Those long sections appeared as chaos compared to the short, inserted line dances like "Sticks," "Spanish Dance," "Eights," and "Scallops." The line dances were easy on the eyes, creating a contrast with the less orderly parts that we made through improvisation. *New York Times* critic Anna Kisselgoff complained that "[a] middle section appears too long and does not make clear to the audience what the dancers' tasks are."[2] For us, it was about lines appearing and disappearing, relationships forming and dissolving. As with Grand Union, what one of us chose to do affected all of us.

In the making process, we had to be super conscious of each other. While improvising and recalling our actions, we were reconstructing memory, with the other women's bodies as our signposts. We had to realize, again and again, that the person next to us remembered something different in time, space, and gesture. The claim, "Wait, you were on this side of me and your shoulder was here," would be met with "No, my right shoulder was in line with Elizabeth's ear." Or, "I saw a gap from across the room and was making a line to bridge the gap." That process of going from thinking we remembered correctly to realizing we had it skewed was appealing to Trisha. She wanted to retain that rough-around-the-edges quality instead of polishing it to a sheen.

At one point, she built in a fleeting "surprise moment." We would pause, and then one of us would leap or flutter or spin or crumble, before we

Rehearsal for Trisha Brown's *Line Up* (1976), Trisha Brown studio. Standing, from left: Wendy Perron, Paxton (guest artist), Brown, Terry O'Reilly (guest artist). On floor, from left: Elizabeth Garren, Mona Sulzman, Judith Ragir. Photo: Babette Mangolte.

all moved on with the dance. Just anticipating that moment of guessing changes your mental makeup. Who will make the surprise move? Will I be the one? Can I delight or confound my peers with three, action-filled seconds?

Trisha took that unknowingness further. We tried to actually create a new segment in front of the audience. Like Yvonne in *CP-AD*, Trisha wanted to expose the making process—that was part of the art for her. I now see that attempt as a continuation of Grand Union's practice of revealing process.

While I was watching the Tokyo video from December 1975, the overlap between my starting to dance with Trisha and her last performance with Grand Union was brought home to me. Toward the end of the performance, Trisha stood up to perform "Solo Olos," the very movement phrase she was teaching us back in New York. The intricate sequence is danced forward and backward—hence the title.³ It was rare for anyone in Grand Union to perform a set work. In the early days, David Gordon ran through all his permutations of *Trio A*, and Yvonne slipped parts of her first solo, *Three Satie Spoons* (1961), into the mix at Oberlin when she was off to the side of the stage. But here was Trisha, performing this current transplant from her studio, center stage, as a soloist.

In the Tokyo video, after Trisha finishes "Solo Olos," the other dancers taunt each other to perform a solo while Trisha stretches out on the floor downstage to watch. Steve delivers a remarkable rendition of it, capturing the steady rhythm, the eccentric openings and closings, the brushing of the hand against the floor, the flat back while lowering the body to the ground. When Barbara gets up to do a solo, she doesn't try to emulate "Solo Olos." Instead, she lopes around the space, then zeroes in on a more rooted dance while Steve tells a story about Barbara's favorite birds. Expecting to be next in line to dance a solo, David feels put on the spot. He takes his feelings of insecurity—after all, he would be compared to Trisha, Steve, and Barbara—and transforms them into a grandiose act. He sings/wails a song of mock despair ("Do you know what it's *li-i-i-k-e*"), strutting and crouching like a rock star.

Watching this video of the Tokyo performance, I realized two things: first, that in a more direct way than I had thought, I was linked to the tail end of Grand Union, and second, that in some way Trisha had already left Grand Union.

CHAPTER 24

THE UNRAVELING, OR, AS THE TOP WOBBLES

After five or six years, the members of Grand Union were hanker-
ing to go out on their own. They were already giving their own concerts, sometimes shared with one another. Contact Improvisation was
taking off, so Steve was very much in demand. Douglas and David had
begun new careers as choreographers. Trisha was starting a new, more
professional company; Barbara was developing her Contemplative
Dance Practice at Naropa; Nancy was collaborating with musician
Richard Peck. What's more, the time for collectives seemed to be over.
The 112 Greene Street group had broken up and gone their own ways.[1]
On a practical level, the funding situation favored individual artists.

But something else was pulling Grand Union apart. The very things
we all loved about it were the things that shook it at its roots: the raw-
ness that made the audience feel anything could happen, the trust that
allowed both intimacy and confrontation, the democracy in which
everyone has their say. Anarchy doesn't last forever.

Paxton wrote the following analysis: "Originally nine choreographers and performers, it was an attempt to be a leaderless, democratic, spontaneously creative ensemble. As such it succeeded and then
failed. The initially stimulating freedoms became ambiguities after a
few years, and by the end in 1976 had fallen to suspicion, doubt, innu-
endos. Freedom attended by hope was a creative stimulus. Conversely,
lack of guidance attended by doubt was remarkably inhibiting."[2]

Possibly what was most inhibited was the potential for a harmo-
nious working out of problems. An example of the process turning
sour was the conflict over music. Part of Grand Union's MO was that
music would be chosen and played at random. It was taken for granted
that the members would go with the flow of whatever record or album

was thrown onto the record player. In the spirit of chance operations and found objects, they were cool with that—at first. But eventually the schism between tastes widened, with no means of compromise in sight. Barbara came to dislike the music that David or Steve or Douglas picked up at a local thrift shop or record store; she considered it pop or kitsch and preferred other music, possibly the music of Terry Riley. (Barbara doesn't remember the exact argument.) "She liked that music a lot and she wanted not to be dancing to this terrible *junk*," David said in our group interview. "She wanted to dance to good, better music, and that was the music she was interested in, which I *loathed*."[3]

Despite the differences in taste, Barbara still felt there was "some kind of mutual vision." However, she also felt there was "a lot of isolation in the group, and it was not easy to critique one another. We didn't know how to give it, and we didn't know how to take it. There was a lot of vulnerability and I think toward the end that came up a lot more."[4]

Originally the group valued that vulnerability; it felt brave to be exposed. Barbara described the state of openness that gave the group its frisson: "It sets the edges of your teeth against each other ever so slightly—you're putting everything out there, you're constantly opening up your receptors ... you're really wide open. It's not about comfort."[5]

Although the disregard for "comfort" was shared across the board, they still relied upon a copasetic vibe that wasn't always there. Douglas felt a certain ease when connecting with Steve or Barbara, but, he said, when he tried to get near David or Trisha, "they were like porcupines."[6]

That prickliness showed up in their after-performance talks too. Once, after a performance in which Nancy hurled a pillow across the room in what she thought of as "a streak of energy—like a shooting star," some of the others accused her of an aggressive act. She remembers sometimes being so harassed that she ended up crying at these postmortems.[7]

As we saw in chapter 17, Barbara was offended by Yvonne saying, in performance, "This is the nastiest concert I've ever been to." But that kind of thing started happening with regularity. "There were these sorts of highly visible neuroses suddenly popping out at times.... We never planned or intended or even discussed that experience, but it did happen.... We needed group therapy."[8]

Steve also felt that group therapy would have helped them deal with the conflicts that arose—and with keeping away from the ruts they would get into. He pointed out that because of the nature of on-going improvisation, "the actual pathways and interactions start to be more and more predictable."[9] Nancy, too, felt they "weren't making anything new" by 1976.[10] David didn't mention therapy, but he told Margaret Hupp Ramsay that avoidance made him irate.[11] Not surprisingly, without, as Steve put it, "guidance," the small things that were once merely annoying loomed as infuriating. At different times, both David and Barbara declared in performance, "I've had enough."

Barbara, who was so appalled when Yvonne badmouthed the group in public in 1972, later felt pretty free herself to trash the group in performance. At The Kitchen in 1974, she chastised David and Douglas for horning in on a jazzy solo of Nancy's: "You had to get in there, didn't you? There are fewer and fewer fine dances in this bullshit group."[12] When I asked Barbara about it, she said, "It was like we were a bunch of siblings. For me it was like watching my brothers gang up on my sister—that kind of feeling. They were really bullying her in a childlike guy kind of way. A lot of that Grand Union stuff was being able to act on some projection. So, whatever I was witnessing, I projected my story line on it and then I entered the action according to that projection."[13]

But it seems to me there was also a widening fault line that had to do with what constituted "material." Nancy was good at responding to others' overtures, but she didn't often initiate verbally. She was always up for spontaneous dancing without any conceptual base, whereas I think David felt that the dancing should have a conceptual motivation, thus earning the term "material." During the Missoula concert, he objected to her choice of "material." It was part of a bit he was doing of playing her teacher, but it was still a public critique.

Sometimes silence expressed disapproval as much as words. Douglas cites a performance at Barnard College in 1974 when Trisha stood on the periphery watching almost the whole time. She did not criticize them in public, but she later gave the group a critique in private.[14] Clearly the dancers were at different stages of their experience. Trisha, with years of maverick improvisation behind her, probably thought she was being helpful, while Douglas, young and adventurous, wanted to experiment in a judgment-free zone.

Nancy Stark Smith often traveled with Grand Union as part of the Paxton contingent. For years she was inspired by the more seasoned group:

> They went onto the stage with no plan, zero, and they just
> followed their interest. David would go into the costume
> room and find a wig, Douglas was stretching strings from the
> proscenium arch to the balcony.... Nancy, with her mandolin or
> whatever it was ... They all brought in something. This life, these
> relationships, would arise, and I would study how things arose
> and how they developed, when they were killed by something
> somebody did, or be resurrected, how they survived each other,
> how the material grew. I was just in awe of this, it was like
> magic.[15]

But Stark Smith, too, saw the downside that eventually eroded their goodwill: "I think the Grand Union were constantly obstructing one another. That was part of their modus as I observed it. It was not just agreeing and going along but going up against one another over and over and over again.[16]

The resentments mounted. The Tokyo festival, "Dance Today," in December 1975, included some of Trisha's dancers as well as Valda Setterfield, who was performing with David, and Simone Forti and a couple of her dancers. Two of Trisha's people, Elizabeth Garren and Judith Ragir, found themselves in a hot tub with a couple of the Grand Union performers. Elizabeth and Judith were taken aback by the casual negativity. "They were so freely talking and gossiping and real negative, making digs at other people," Elizabeth said later. "It was a revelation to me because they were my idols. They were having fun at other people's expense, as if we weren't there. That was a peek, like riding in the bus with rock stars and you see they have their asshole moments."[17]

■

During the later years, some critics felt that Grand Union's performances had gotten too comfortable. By 1974, writer Elizabeth Kendall felt Grand Union was succumbing to facile verbal routines and leaving the dance element behind. "I am a Grand Union fan. Flashes of 'meaning' have always come out of their performances. I used to feel that if I could just get to every performance, I would understand one whole process of living—at least among one group of people. I'm not so sure now, and the five members of Grand Union this time seem less fervent about meanings. What we glimpsed at the Kitchen on Monday May 27, was almost a situation comedy. It was very funny, but the comedy happened through talk."[18]

Kendall felt the group's strengths—"spontaneous shape, effortless balance, mysterious extra dimensions"—had faded away.[19] Amid all their ironic self-commentary, Kendall found a lack of "vigor or earnestness." She aired her disappointment in a stinging diatribe in *Ballet Review*, claiming, "The Grand Union are now playing pop versions, cartoons, of themselves."[20]

In a similar vein, a 1976 review in the *New York Times* written by Don McDonagh carried the headline "Grand Union's Skits Now More Formula Than Improvisation."[21]

However, other critics felt that the more they saw Grand Union, the more they got out of it. Robb Baker, who had written the in-depth feature in *Dance Magazine* in 1973, reviewed a spate of five performances in the New York area in 1974:

> [I]t seems the more they perform together in a single span of time, the better they get. Communication builds, connections come faster and faster, everything gets more and more cohesive. Improvisation—particularly when it walks the tightrope between pure movement improv and dialogue improv, daring all sorts of splicings of the two—is always a chancey [*sic*] business, and the more the individuals involved learn to trust each other and to sense developing patterns (of movement or thought), the more successful the end result is. So by the fifth performance (the second night at the Kitchen), things were so tight that it was like witnessing the whole dictation process (shorthand, transcription, and the typing of the final draft) without a break, telescoped in a single flash.
>
> Grand Union is performance about performing, talking about process, dancing about it. (Trisha Brown: "that was a terrific

ending." David Gordon: "what about a beginning? Do you have a beginning to follow that ending?")[22]

■

As wily as the dancers continued to be, the underlying resentments were becoming more perceptible. The occasional glimpses of hostility blossomed into whole scenes of thinly disguised fantasies. David was often annoyed at Nancy, yet it was Nancy who played into his scenarios more readily than anyone else. During the 1975 La MaMa performances, he enacted a death wish for Nancy that couldn't have been pleasant for her. While arranging sticks like a knapsack on her back, he announced, "A short tableau, the burning of [Saint] Joan. Very short, very final. When it's over, I want a big round of applause for the ashes." She played along, waving her arms and moaning, "Oh man it's getting to be hot." He swooshed his cape over her and pressed her down until she lay still on floor. He then sang a lament: "Oh Joan, oh Joan, burned to pieces. Just some ashes. Oh Joan, I believed in you. Oh Joan rise up. Oh Joan rise up and be birthed again. Oh get up, get up, get up." Nancy suddenly stood up with a squeal and a snarl: "I'm sick and tired of being ... [inaudible]." They stared each other down, until she said softly, "Not really." But he wasn't done. He attacked her from another angle: "Why do you talk to me like you're in a situation comedy? Why are you talking to me like 'My Little Margie?' Why don't you talk to me like you're Ethel Barrymore?" He sat down in a huff. Of course, one could say he was playing a character, but one could also notice that the character was verbally demeaning.

Granted some of this sharpness had always been par for the course. Douglas felt, however, that GU was still operating on a high plane. "I thought we were just getting better," he said about the last performances.[23] I would agree, as you can see from my interlude "People Improvisation," which is a review I wrote after the last La MaMa series in 1976.

That said, the very last performance on tour was a long, plodding session. As I mentioned, toward the end of this performance in Missoula, a heckler yelled "Bullshit." To my eyes and ears, watching the video, the problem was that the group got caught up in handling a video camera as a new toy onstage, plus there was no music until forty-three minutes in. Although David had funny moments and Nancy threw herself into a hilariously writhing dying solo, they all seemed fairly isolated. What I was happy to see, though, was that when attacked from the outside, they circled the wagons and supported each other. At the moment of the audience expletive, David didn't bat an eyelash (or rather eyelashes, since he had borrowed Valda's double-layer false eyelashes for the occasion) and sweetly asked, "What were you saying, Barbara?" She immediately replied, "I said 'bullshit.'" I think Steve appreciated her brilliant co-opting of the audience expletive, and a few minutes later, facing the audience, in whose midst Barbara had stationed herself, he gently wished her good night and extended that wish to the audience. Barbara started tidying up the stage, ending the evening on as ordinary a note as possible. Loud applause and, as mentioned, loud boos.

■

Here is the sequence of how the ending of GU happened. Trisha left the group after the December 1975 concert in Tokyo. She had always been wary that her own work might get swallowed up in this venture started by (if accidentally) her more visibly successful friend, Yvonne Rainer. The reason she gave when Banes posed the question was "to address full attention to my own choreography after many months of discomfort at not being able to edit or control the contents of a Grand Union concert."[24] For the Tokyo festival, she had brought three of her new dancers to perform as an adjunct troupe. (The fourth stayed home because she was too new and didn't know that repertoire. That was me.) Since she had been a pivotal influence for both David and Steve, and since both had become more invested in their work outside of Grand Union, they had lost interest in continuing with GU. David recalled that the conflicts of taste "resulted in a conversation with Steve … in which I said, 'I don't like this anymore, I'm not having a good time.' He said, 'We should stop it,' and I said, 'That's a good idea.' And he called everybody and said, 'We're gonna stop.' And we stopped."[25]

Barbara was probably also ready to call it quits. For personal reasons—"I was burning out on a kind of life style that was rootless"[26]—she felt drawn to a more stable life in Colorado.

■

My guess is that any group of wildly adventurous people would have hit an impasse sooner or later. It's remarkable that Grand Union kept the creative juices going for as long as it did. It's easy to see in the 1976 La MaMa video that without Trisha and Steve, the balance of personalities was off. And the pacing of the final performance, in Missoula, was deadly despite occasional inspired moments.

Decades later, Barbara's idea of what pulled them apart had evolved. Instead of feeling that the group became psychologically unhinged, she now feels the end was inevitable: "[I]t's like a cosmic pattern of some kind. The circumstances that brought us together were one thing, and then, we just kept going, like a toy top that keeps spinning and ... it wibbles and wobbles all over the place. As the momentum starts to subside, it wobbles a little from side to side and then it wobbles around in the space.[27]

Nancy's view was less philosophical: "Like any 250-watt bulb—it burned out."[28] As Richard Schechner, who has had plenty of experience with group dynamics, has observed, "The more you know about a person the harder it is to make new discoveries; the longer people work together the less sweeping are changes within individuals."[29]

One could call the six years of Grand Union simply a transitional period that allowed its members to further define themselves as artists. That is how it's been treated historically, partly because Grand Union left no choreographic traces. This band of anarchists was all process, no product. Only fleeting memories and a few old videos remain. But improvisation involves creative activity as much as choreography does. For each of these dance makers—and most of them are major figures in postmodern dance—this volatile period is a key to understanding their oeuvre.

Perhaps Grand Union was destined to be short-lived. Perhaps it had already done its job. It had refreshed the downtown dance world. It had shaken up ideas of space, of repertoire, of performance itself. It had dissolved the director/dancer hierarchy. It had hinted at crossing the gender divide. It had woven character play into abstraction. It had upped the ante of spontaneity. It had proven that a completely collaborative group could create unforgettable performance. And it was a springboard for the careers of six remarkable dance artists who helped create postmodern dance. Despite its instability—or because of it—Grand Union was a meteor flash across the heavens of dance history.

EPILOGUE AND

THREE LINGERING MOMENTS

Does Grand Union have a legacy? Is there a lineage that can be traced? Improvisation famously disappears after the moment of performance. One could point to the improvisation groups that sprouted up inspired by Grand Union: the Harry Martin Trio in Minneapolis, Tumbleweed in San Francisco (started by Theresa Dickinson), and three groups in New York City: the Natural History of the American Dancer, Central Notion Co., and Channel Z. Not to mention the myriad of Contact Improvisation networks and events. One could point to the growing number of college dance departments that offer some form of improvisation.[1] Or the many books on the subject.[2] But there is no way to know how much of this current burgeoning is due to Grand Union.

Perhaps the group's legacy lies in who the long-term GU dancers are and what they have continued to do. After all, part of the reason Grand Union was called "epic" by Deborah Jowitt[3] is the individual people involved. They were the bricks and mortar of postmodern dance. In that spirit, I provide here a quick update on each of the main players, including the traces of her or his work that continue to exist.

■

The expanse of David Gordon's career was revealed in the spring of 2017 when the Jerome Robbins Dance Division of the New York Public Library for the Performing Arts mounted his Archiveography exhibit, which has now morphed into a comprehensive—and entertaining—website at davidgordon.nyc. David has created intimate works as well as large productions all over the country. For his *United States* (1988) at Brooklyn Academy of Music, he collected stories, music, and poems from twenty-seven presenters in seventeen states. The Archiveography website recounts, by the decade, David's childhood memories, dances, scores, mishaps, happy coincidences, respect for Valda, and a few gems about Grand Union. It meshes his personal and professional lives, spinning his own form of narrative, just as he told his own stories within Grand Union. He sees the photography he studied in college, the store windows he designed, the proscenium stage, and his recent interest in creating graphics with blocks of words as all related to framing. In an email to me he acknowledged that commonality, saying, "The computer is my enda life rectangle."[4]

Trisha Brown's influence is recognized the world over. The promise of the Judson revolution has reached a choreographic peak with her works like *Opal Loop* (1980) and *Set and Reset* (1983). Major dance artists, like Bill T. Jones and Anne Teresa De Keersmaeker, admire her for inventing an entirely new dance vocabulary. She also developed new ways of organizing choreography, from the *Accumulation* series to her process of improvisation and recall that started with *Line Up* (1976) and *Water Motor* (1978). In addition, she broke conventions of stage performance, with the dance overflowing beyond the proscenium (*Glacial Decoy*, 1979) or the music emanating from outside the theater (*Foray Forêt*, 1990). She is beloved in Europe not only as a leading postmodernist but also as a director of innovative operas. Although she died in 2017, the Trisha Brown Dance Company is still in demand for giving workshops and for performances that often reimagine her early work in different spaces. Susan Rosenberg's book *Trisha Brown: Choreography as Visual Art* traces Trisha's connection to the art world, and an ArtPix DVD contains videos of her early work.[5] The Trisha Brown Dance Company Archive, with thousands of photographs, videos, scores, sets, and costumes, has recently been acquired by the Jerome Robbins Dance Division of the NY Public Library for the Performing Arts.

Douglas Dunn has choreographed nonstop since Grand Union. He continues to perform in his studio in SoHo (where he also teaches), on the streets, and in small dance festivals. His major works include *Gestures in Red* (1975), *Lazy Madge* (1976), *Pulcinella* (1980) for the Paris Opera Ballet, and *Stucco Moon* (1992). He appeared in Michael Blackwood's documentary *Making Dances: Seven Post-Modern Choreographers*, along with David Gordon and Trisha Brown. His long-term collaboration with visual artist Mimi Gross has yielded about fifteen vivid group works, including *Echo* (1980) and *Sky Eye* (1989). A book of his writings, *Dancer Out of Sight*, was published in 2012, and he has written for *Dance Magazine* and the art journal *Tether*. His website, www.douglasdunndance.com, includes a full chronology. As he said recently, "Now I want to make dances until I drop."[6]

After spending ten years as the reluctant father/hero of Contact Improvisation, Steve Paxton went in a new, more choreographic direction. The imagery of his 1982 solo *Bound* at The Kitchen seared itself into my memory. He developed a collaboration with percussionist David Moss that fed the impulsiveness of his movement. The peak of his solo improvisation practice came with *The Goldberg Variations* (1986–1992), which was a sublimely articulated response to Glenn Gould's rendition of Bach. Since then he has been developing his Material for the Spine—"to bring movement to consciousness"—in performance, video, and book form. His essays, interviews, and dialogues appear often in *Contact Quarterly*. The European organization ContreDanse has published a CD-ROM of his Material for the Spine and a slim compilation of his writings titled *Gravity* (2018). His long-term collaboration with fellow improviser Lisa Nelson yielded two spare, poetic evocations: *PA RT* (1983) with music by Robert Ashley, and *Night Stand* (2004). He now spends most of his time in his home in northern Vermont, surrounded by forest. As he said in a public talk at the Museum of Modern Art in 2018, "Every atom in the landscape in front of me that I look at every day is changing.... I feel like it's a living soup and I'm ... kind of dissolving into its space now."[7]

In 1974 Barbara Dilley, along with poet Larry Fagin and Mary Overlie, cofounded the Danspace Project, located at St. Mark's Church on the Lower East Side. Long a major force in the dance world, Danspace has welcomed Barbara back several times over the years. She also helped launch the movement program at the Buddhist-inspired Naropa University in Boulder and served as director of its dance program from 1974 to 1985. She devised scores for teaching improvisation and composition within her Contemplative Dance Practice, which mingles meditation and improvisation. She was so respected for her work there that was appointed president of Naropa, serving from 1985 to 1993. (Let's see ... how many women *or* dancers have become university presidents?) She continued making dances in projects like

Barbara Dilley reading from a book by Agnes Martin to Naropa students, Boulder, CO, 1975. Photo: Rachel Homer.

the Crystal Dance Company, the Mariposa Collective, Fearless Dancing Project, and the Naked Face Project. In 2009 she began gathering her memories and teaching strategies into a book titled *This Very Moment: teaching, thinking, dancing* (2015). In 2016 she retired, becoming professor emerita. The younger generation, she notes, has continued to adapt Contemplative Dance Practice's ability to connect mind and body to their own lives.[8] Toward the end of her book Barbara writes, "I am changing now and dancing is fading for me."[9] But her body consciousness is still a source of vitality. She is now exploring "how to be comfortably awake in my aging and not feel a victim of getting old."[10]

Nancy Lewis met musician Richard Peck while he was playing in Philip Glass's ensemble (as he continued to do for many years). They married in 1974 and performed together at venues like Dance Theater Workshop, Paula Cooper Gallery, and P.S. 1 in Queens (later annexed by the Museum of Modern Art). She had been invested in the col-

GU at NYC Dance Marathon, 14th Street Y, 1971. From left: Dilley, Gordon, Rainer, Brown. Visible in audience center, lying on the floor, Carolyn Brown; sitting behind her, James Klosty. Photo: Susan Horwitz, Jerome Robbins Dance Division, The New York Public Library for the Performing Arts.

lectivity of Grand Union and had no wish to start her own group or replicate the Grand Union experience in any way. After 9/11, she and Richard moved to Rhode Island, where she now does home health-care work.

In her twenty-five-year detour from dance (roughly 1973 to 1998), Yvonne Rainer directed seven experimental films, earning acclaim as an early feminist filmmaker. She returned to dance in 2000 at the invitation of Mikhail Baryshnikov in a pilot project for his Past-Forward production commemorating Judson Dance Theater.[11] Since then she has made about six full-length dance-and-text works and reconstructed the epic *Parts of Some Sextets* (1965), aka the Mattress Dance.[12] Her company, which performs at museums, colleges, and international festivals, sometimes reprises her early works like *Trio A* and *Three Seascapes*. Yvonne has published an autobiography (*Feel-*

ings Are Facts), many essays, and a book of poetry. Her classic book *Yvonne Rainer: Work, 1961–1973* was recently reissued by Primary Information. Jack Walsh's documentary film, *Feelings Are Facts: The Life of Yvonne Rainer*, has garnered awards on the film circuit. (Disclosure: I am one of the commentators.) She continues to write provocative essays and continues to be a subject (sometimes target) that scholars in dance, art, and performance have to contend with.

But these achievements I have cited are separate from Grand Union's legacy as a collective. It was a gathering of sublimely unruly spirits with no stated goal. But along the way, it invented a performance form that fused the freedom of childhood with an urban sensibility. It melded art and life in a way that captured the defiance, camaraderie, humor, and happenstance beauty of the time. And it sustained a trusting and democratic process for most of its six years.

I don't know if a leaderless improvisation group could exist today. The seventies was a time when individual creativity could flourish within a collaborative ecosystem. The fantasies, explorations, dares, and subversions that tumbled out of Grand Union coalesced into an experience that many of us were hungry for at that time. And that experience allowed for a wide range of reactions and emotions, including contagious moments of sheer joy.

■

I leave you with three memorable scenes that were not part of the narrative unfoldings.

LA MAMA 1975

Nancy stands, hands clasped behind her head, elbows outward, watching Steve and Douglas. They are lifting, hanging against, and dragging each other in a vigorous Contact Improvisation duet. Suddenly a narrow space opens up between them, and she simply steps into that space. Her left elbow is touching Steve's nose. Douglas offers Steve his hand to keep the contact. Steve holds his hand while his nose gently guides Nancy's elbow downward so her arms unfurl toward the ground; Steve and Douglas lower down, each of them circling their heads around one of her wrists, while she stays upright. Their heads hover in the nether regions of her torso. It's a sexual image but also an image of a mother and two children. She looks straight ahead, but every pore of her skin senses what is happening. She tilts her head slightly as the two men stay crouching on either side of her.

LA MAMA, A DIFFERENT PERFORMANCE, 1975

David has been walking around with his hands held up, palms facing inward. Because of the position, a character comes into focus: a surgeon about to operate. This is a surgeon with a difference: he uses his teeth as a scalpel. David kneels over Steve's prone body and, bares his belly, but we can't see what he's doing. He straightens up, and announces, "I made the incision." Keeping his sterile hands up in the air, he says, "Now I will giggle the colon." Nancy, always the ready accomplice, stuffs a tangled mass of wires under Steve's shirt. With his invisibly gloved hands, David carefully pulls the wires out, saying, "Here comes the disease." Steve covers his face with one arm, perhaps to keep from laughing. David then goes to "operate" on Barbara.

Meanwhile Trisha is rearranging the patients—with emergency-room haste. She puts Steve's arm on his chest, bends Barbara's knee, swats Steve's arm back to the floor, shoves Barbara's arm to one side. She pulls Nancy down, so Trisha now has three patients, but the way she's racing around, it seems like a whole hospital full of injured people. The audience is laughing continuously during her mad, zig-zagging dash. She's racing against time, while she manipulates their limbs again and again, to a ridiculous sound track of a hyper-fast waltz accented by the sound of a cuckoo. It's task dance on speed, a crazed nurse choreographing her patients—or a patient herself, fulfilling some mad compulsion.

LOGIUDICE GALLERY, MAY 1972

Barbara, wearing a red flowered skirt, stands on top of a chair, her back to her fellow dancers. She slowly gyrates her pelvis as though hula dancing. Sweetly provocative, it's a languid, lilting accompaniment to the Rolling Stones's "No Expectations." The song has a plaintive, sensuous quality, and the lyrics hint at indulging in the moment: "Take me to the station and put me on a train, I've got no expectations to pass through here again. Once I was a rich man, now I am so poor. But never in my sweet short life have I felt like this before." This is Barbara's meditative streak gone seductive.

Trisha and David decide on a plan. They pick up each dancer, one at a time, and transport that person to another spot. They have already done this with Yvonne and Douglas, and now they come for Barbara. Still standing on the chair, she is now arching way back—gorgeously precarious. They lift her together with the chair, and she keeps arching, a dangerously weeping willow. When they set her down, she resumes her hip swiveling with eyes closed.

APPENDIX A

CHRONOLOGY OF GRAND UNION
PERFORMANCES AND RESIDENCIES

Rutgers University, New Jersey — November 6, 1970
New York University, Loeb Student Center — mid-December 1970
Benefit for the Defense of the Black Panthers, NYU — January 14, 1971
Bob Fiore's loft, E. 13th Street, NYC — February 5, 6, 12, 13, 1971
Laura Dean's loft, 61 Crosby Street, NYC — April 1971
14th Street Y (Emanuel Midtown YM-YWHA), NYC — May 15, 1971
Prospect Park, Brooklyn — May 17, 1971
Walker Art Center, Minneapolis — May 24–31, 1971
San Francisco Art Institute — August 1971
Oberlin College, Ohio — January 3–22, 1972
112 Greene Street, NYC — February 6, 1972
State University of New York, Stony Brook — May 6, 1972
LoGiudice Gallery, NYC — May 28–31, 1972
Larry Richardson Dance Gallery, NYC — April 1–May 31, 1973
Buffalo State College — September 22–24, 1973
Contemporanea Festival, L'Attico Gallery Garage, Rome — January 6–9 & 14, 1974
Annenberg Center, University of Pennsylvania — February 9–10, 1974
San Diego State University — February 24–March 1, 1974
University of Iowa — March 7–8, 1974
Pratt Institute, Brooklyn — May 1, 1974
SUNY Stony Brook — May 4, 1974
Barnard College, Columbia University, NYC — May 8, 1974
The Kitchen, NYC — May 27–28, 1974
Lewiston State Art Park, Buffalo — July 25–August 1, 1974
Wolf Trap Farm Park, Virginia — August 22, 1974
La MaMa Annex, NYC — March 14–16, 1975
Walker Art Center, Minneapolis — October 4–9, 1975
MoMing Dance and Arts Center, Chicago — October 10–13, 1975
Seibu Theater, Dance Today Festival, Tokyo — December 12–17, 1975
La MaMa Annex, NYC — April 22–25, 1976
UC Santa Barbara — April 29–May 1, 1976
Royce Hall, UC Los Angeles — May 4, 1976
University of Montana, Missoula — May 8–10, 1076

APPENDIX B

PARTIAL PLAYLIST

This list is only possible with the miracle of Shazam. Before a friend down-loaded the Shazam app for me, I was searching for song titles via the lyrics that I managed to decipher from the videos. Only a fraction of GU's performances are covered because there are so few archival videos. Also, I learned that Shazam can't do its job when sounds like talking or laughing muddy the tunes, which was often the case. Sometimes I had no more information than the sounds I could hear myself from the video; for instance, that it was harpsichord music. Also missing are all the times the dancers launched into songs they knew or made up on the spot. The list is basically in chronological sequence, except that I've added an "Other" category for songs that were mentioned in interviews or reviews but couldn't be verified.

Oberlin, January 1972
"No Expectations," Rolling Stones
"Let the Good Times Roll," Harry Nilsson
"All I Ever Wanted," New Riders of the Purple Sage
"Without You," Harry Nilsson
"Coconut," Harry Nilsson

LoGiudice Series, May 28–31, 1972
"Coconut," Harry Nilsson
"Let the Good Times Roll," Harry Nilsson
"Jump into the Fire," Harry Nilsson
"Sonny's Jump," Sonny Terry and Brownie McGhee
"Stray Cat Blues," The Rolling Stones
"Salt of the Earth," The Rolling Stones
"Fig Leaf Rag," Scott Joplin
"Magnetic Rag," Scott Joplin
"Gimme Shelter," The Rolling Stones
"Country Honk," The Rolling Stones
"Let It Bleed," The Rolling Stones
"Live with Me," The Rolling Stones
"Göttingen," Barbara (Monique Andrée Serf)
"Sympathy for the Devil," The Rolling Stones
"No Expectations," The Rolling Stones
"Parachute Woman," The Rolling Stones

"Jigsaw Puzzle," The Rolling Stones
"Everybody Needs Somebody to Love," The Rolling Stones
"You Can't Catch Me," The Rolling Stones
"Heart of Stone," The Rolling Stones
"What a Shame," The Rolling Stones
"I Need You Baby (Mona)," The Rolling Stones
"Round & Round (It Won't Be Long)," Neil Young & Crazy Horse
"Down by the River," Neil Young
Unidentified harpsichord music
"In C," Terry Riley
"Where Do the Children Play," Cat Stevens
"Hard-Headed Woman," Cat Stevens
"Wild World," Cat Stevens
"Sad Lisa," Cat Stevens
"Gotta Get Up," Harry Nilsson
"Driving Along," Harry Nilsson
"Early in the Morning," Harry Nilsson

University of Iowa, March 1974
"Kecak: The Ramayana Monkey Chants," Indonesian music from the
    Nonesuch Explorer Series
"Cross Road Blues," Robert Johnson
"Terraplane Blues," Robert Johnson
"Surfin' USA," Beach Boys
"Something There Is About You," Bob Dylan
"He's Misstra Know-It-All," Stevie Wonder
"Love's Theme," The Love Unlimited Orchestra

La MaMa, March 1975
From the film *Pat Garrett and Billy the Kid*:
    "Main Title Theme (Billy)," Bob Dylan
    "Billy 1," Bob Dylan
    "Bunkhouse Theme," Bob Dylan
    "River Theme," Bob Dylan
    "La Passerella Di Otto E Mezzo," Nino Rota
Concerto Pour Flute in C Minor, Rv 441, Vivaldi, NY Philharmonic and
    Leonard Bernstein
Concerto Pour Piccolo in C Major, Rv 443, Vivaldi, NY Philharmonic and
    Leonard Bernstein
"Lukembi-Mbuti," Mbuti Pygmy Playing Lukenbi, Pygmies of the Ituri
    Rainforest
A waltz with bird whistles
"Turkey Chase," Bob Dylan
"Knockin' on Heaven's Door," Bob Dylan

African kalimba music
Medley of songs including "Go Down, Moses," "Swing Low, Sweet Chariot,"
    "Sometimes I Feel Like a Motherless Child," and "Look Away, Dixie Land,"
    in unknown instrumental versions

Walker Art Center, October 1975, Guthrie Theater
"It's Gonna Rain," Steve Reich (1965)

Walker Art Center, October 1975, Lobby
"Hang Up Your Hang Ups," Herbie Hancock
"Sun Touch," Herbie Hancock
"The Traitor," Herbie Hancock
Pomp and Circumstance, March No. 1 in D Major, Edward Elgar

La MaMa, April 1976
"Heaven," Tommy Tietjen
"Long Black Veil," The Band
"We Can Talk," The Band
"On a Night Like This," Bob Dylan
"Brown Sugar," The Rolling Stones
"Little Boy Blue," Rufus Feat, Chaka Khan

Missoula, May 1976
"125th Street Congress," Weather Report
"Put It Where You Want It," Average White Band

Other
"Gymnopédies," Satie, orchestrated by Debussy, Boston Philharmonic
"You've Got a Friend," Carole King
"Tiptoe Through the Tulips," Tiny Tim
"My Sweet Lord," George Harrison
"Lola," The Kinks
"You Angel You," Bob Dylan

ACKNOWLEDGMENTS

From the start of this project I've met with a bounty of goodwill. It seemed that whenever I mentioned Grand Union, little treasures appeared. Pat Catterson typed up the notes she had taken of the early GU performances in 1971. Thank you, Pat! Dancer/scholar Judith Brin Ingber dove into the archives of the *Minneapolis Tribune* to help with Walker Art Center research. Sculptor Barbara Kilpatrick offered me her long-treasured *Avalanche* from summer/fall 1973, which documented Grand Union's performance in Buffalo in an ingenious way.

At the Seattle Festival of Dance Improvisation, when I was complaining that the 1976 Missoula tape had gone missing, contact improviser Karen Nelson piped up and said, "Oh, I saw a video marked 'Missoula' at Steve Christiansen's house." Thus began a warm friendship with Steve Christiansen, who is legendary in the Contact Improvisation world for videotaping Paxton's *Magnesium* at Oberlin College in 1972. He had never been to Missoula and did not know how that video ended up in his hands, but we set to work on getting it digitized. It turns out that he had, at the bottom of a closet, another long forgotten video: the Oberlin performance of Grand Union that he had shot the same day as *Magnesium*.

I was on the phone with my old dance buddy Wendy Rogers, lamenting the lack of clues about the mysterious Lincoln Scott, when she said, "Hey, I went to high school with him!" She then launched a tireless search, leaving no stone unturned in trying to find him (hoping he was alive) as well tracking his dance life in the Bay Area before he headed to New York. In addition, Halifu Osumare researched the beginnings of the African American Studies Department at Berkeley High School for me.

While watching the Grand Union videotapes from LoGiudice Gallery, I spied, in the audience, a man with a camera who looked a lot like composer Gordon Mumma. My guess turned out to be right. Mimi Johnson, who was already an angel for donating the GU records of Artservices to the Jerome Robbins Dance Division of the New York Public Library for the Performing Arts, made it possible for me to meet him so that I could make my request. He dug into his archives and sent me all the original color slides of his shoot from 1972 — at no charge. Other photographers and institutions who have generously allowed me to use their photos pro bono are James Klosty, Tom Berthiaume, GregoryX, Theo Robinson, Bill Arnold, The Cunningham Trust, the Rauschenberg Foundation, and the Walker Art Center. Tom Brazil and

317

Lois Greenfield have done the extra labor of creating digital images from long-ago negatives.

Thanks to John Rockwell and Emily Macel Theys for reading early drafts and giving constructive suggestions. Thanks again to Emily for her crafty Internet search to find Becky Arnold, where mine had failed. Much gratitude to Joan Evans and Dianne McIntyre for articulating their experiences and for working with me on editing their interludes; to Miles Green (son of Nancy Lewis) for all the techno help, family lore, and identifying musical selections not found by the Shazam app; to Denise Luccioni for helping audiotape the group interview in 2017; and to Douglas Dunn Dancers archivist Sandra Gibson for swapping photos and information. Thanks to James Irsay for identifying Robert Johnson's "Cross Road Blues," and to students at Sarah Lawrence College for recognizing the Steve Reich music in the Walker Art Center clip. Thanks to Janet Wong, codirector of New York Live Arts, for digging up the audio file of the 2014 panel discussion with Dianne McIntyre; to curator Ana Janevski at the Museum of Modern Art for giving me access to the recording of Steve Paxton's talk there in 2018; to Jon Hendricks for providing the history surrounding The People's Flag Show; to the late Douglas Crimp for suggesting *Avalanche* staff photographer Gwen Thomas, who showed me fabulous contact sheets from Grand Union's Buffalo performance; to Elizabeth Fox for turning on the lightbulb of the Shazam app; to Jaime Kight for helping to transcribe one of the interviews; to Susan Manning for good advice on my title; and to Lori Brungard for assisting in verifying hundreds of endnotes—a diabolical task.

Thank you to archivist Jill Vuchetich for being such a good guide to the Walker Art Center archives; and to Elizabeth Garren and Bruce Drake for getting as excited as I did about those archives. Further, thanks to the Walker for commissioning my essay about GU for their online magazine, *Fourth Wall*, in 2018 and subsequently posting it on their permanent online Living Collections Catalog.

Thanks to the contingent of Trisha Brown, who has a special place in my heart: Adam Brown, Louisa (Weeza) Adams, Jared Bark, Sylvia Palacios Whitman, Richard Nonas, Trisha Brown Dance Company former associate director and dancer extraordinaire Diane Madden, executive director Barbara Dufty, and archivist Anne Boissonnault. And to my comrades from when I was dancing with Trisha in the seventies: Elizabeth Garren, Judith Ragir, and Mona Sultzman.

Other video finds: thanks to Lisa Nelson, who shot and, forty years later, digitized videos of Iowa and La MaMa; to Sophie Glidden-Lyon, archive project manager at La MaMa, for making additional La MaMa tapes available; and to Davidson Gigliotti for recommending Maurice Schechter, master converter of ancient-format reels. And of course, to Carlota Schoolman and her crew, who captured the vibe so beautifully in their shoot of the four GU performances at LoGiudice Gallery in 1972. What a treasure!

The Jerome Robbins Dance Division of the New York Public Library for the Performing Arts has been my go-to research base. Dance curator Linda Murray has been of invaluable assistance in negotiating difficult licensing situations for photography. Other staff members who have been helpful and knowledgeable include Tanisha Jones, Arlene Yu, Phil Karg, Daisy Pommer, Cassie Mey, Jennifer Eberhardt, and Tom Lisanti. Thanks to the staff of the Fales Collection at NYU's Bobst Library, starting with Charlotte Priddle, who helped with one ambiguous rights-holder situation, and Kelly Haydon and Allison Chomet. The Bennington College Crossett Library staff was helpful during the summer of 2017. Other resources include the Permanent Collection Documentation Office of the Whitney Museum; Paul Schlotthauer, librarian and archivist at Pratt Institute Library; Alison Hinderliter, the manuscripts and archives librarian at Newberry Library, and the staff of *Dance Magazine*.

Unending gratitude to the suspects themselves for their wondrous collaboration back then, and for their collaboration with me many decades later. In multiple visits, whether face to face, on the phone, or in emails, they have each given me their trust and responded to my questions with deeply thoughtful answers. They are, of course, Barbara Dilley, Douglas Dunn, David Gordon, Nancy Lewis, Steve Paxton, and Yvonne Rainer.

Thanks to Suzanna Tamminen, director of Wesleyan University Press, whose response to my idea was immediate and heartfelt. Within forty-five minutes of my emailed query in 2016, she wrote back, "You've made my day!" And to Sharon Langworthy, for her rigorous copy editing.

Thanks to Stephanie Skura for reintroducing me to the experience of improvisation as an over-the-hill dancer; to Tonya Lockyer and the Seattle Festival of Dance Improvisation for inviting me to present my research on Grand Union in 2018, and for responding with such curiosity and warmth. To Nick Perron-Siegel and Mary Wyatt, who helped with design ideas.

All the GU watchers I interviewed were generous with their time and memories. I've enjoyed extended email conversations with Pat Catterson, Nancy Stark Smith, Carlota Schoolman, Paul Langland, and Terry O'Reilly. For plain old friendly encouragement, I thank Stephan Koplowitz, Debra Wanner, and Vicky Shick.

An ocean of gratitude to my husband, Jim Siegel, who recognized the passion behind the project. I have felt his love, support, and challenge during each of the multiple drafts he has reviewed. His eye for clarity and organization rescued me many times. During our process together, he never said, "Oh no, not that chapter again!" Instead, he would say, "When will the next draft be ready for me to see?"

NOTES

Introduction

1. Sally Banes, *Terpsichore in Sneakers: Post-Modern Dance* (Middletown, CT: Wesleyan University Press, 1987), 226.

2. Barbara Dilley, *This Very Moment: teaching thinking dancing* (Boulder, CO: Naropa University Press, 2015), 114.

3. Group interview with author, July 26, 2017. The full quote is: "Grand Union, which was a miracle, for all the years of it until the end. I remember feeling embarrassed and preposterous and How could I be doing what I'm doing at this moment? And all of that worked splendidly and changed my life and changed everything that ever happened to me afterwards."

4. The tapes from the LoGuidice Gallery performances of 1972 are lodged in three places. I discovered them in this order: the Getty Research Institute in Los Angeles, the Fales Special Collection at New York University's Bobst Library, and the Jerome Robbins Dance Division of the New York Public Library for the Performing Arts. At the Library for the Performing Arts, it was not necessary to make an appointment, so I went to view the tapes often.

5. Sally Banes, "Choreographic Methods of the Judson Dance Theater," in *Moving History/Dancing Cultures: A Dance History Reader*, ed. Ann Dils and Ann Cooper Albright (Middletown, CT: Wesleyan University Press, 2001), 359; originally published in *Choreography: Principles and Practice*, ed. Janet Adshead (Surrey, UK: University of Surrey Press, 1987) and in Banes, *Writing Dancing in the Age of Postmodernism* (Middletown, CT: Wesleyan University Press, 1994), 211–26.

6. Sally Banes's project at the time was her dissertation, which was eventually published as *Democracy's Body: Judson Dance Theater, 1962–1964* (Durham, NC: Duke University Press, 1993). My project was the Bennington College Judson Project. I assigned Sally to write the essay "Earthly Bodies: Judson Dance Theater" for the BCJP's catalog in 1981 (pages 14–19). We shared resources, had many discussions about the material, and quoted from each other's interviews.

7. I have described this anxiety at greater length in Wendy Perron, *Through the Eyes of a Dancer: Selected Writings* (Middletown, CT: Wesleyan University Press, 2013), 8–10; previously published as "One Route from Ballet to Postmodern," in *Reinventing Dance in the 1960s: Everything Was Possible*, ed. Sally Banes (Madison: University of Wisconsin Press, 2003), 137–50.

8. Claire Barliant, "112 Greene Street," *Paris Review*, July 25, 2012, accessed January 8, 2018, www.theparisreview.org.

9. Skura's comment was part of a Q&A following my presentation about the Grand Union at the Seattle Festival of Dance Improvisation, Velocity Dance Center, in 2017.

10. As a dance faculty member at Bennington College, I conceived and co-directed the Bennington College Judson Project, which comprised artistic residencies at the college, a series of video interviews, a traveling exhibit of photographs and video, and two programs of reconstructions hosted by Danspace Project in New York City, ca. 1980–1983. Some of the videos, which are lodged at the Jerome Robbins Dance Division, NY Public Library for the Performing Arts, were included in the Museum of Modern Art's 2018–2019 exhibit *Judson Dance Theater: The Work Is Never Done.*

11. I co-curated the exhibition *Radical Bodies: Anna Halprin, Simone Forti and Yvonne Rainer, California and New York, 1955–72* in 2017.

12. Quoted in Calvin Tomkins, *The Bride and the Bachelors: Five Masters of the Avant-Garde* (New York: Viking Press, 1968), 18.

1. Anna Halprin, John Cage, and Judson Dance Theater

1. Wendy Perron, "Simone Forti: bodynatureartmovementbody," in *Radical Bodies: Anna Halprin, Simone Forti, and Yvonne Rainer in California and New York, 1955–1972*, exhibition catalog, ed. Ninotchka Bennahum, Wendy Perron, and Bruce Robertson (Art, Design and Architecture Museum, University of California, Santa Barbara in association with University of California Press, 2017).

2. Arch Lauterer was teaching stage design at the Bennington School of the Dance, including the summer of 1939, when it was hosted by Mills College in California. One of the performance spaces there was the Mills College Greek Theatre, which was a small, arena-style outdoor theater with steps for the audience to sit on. I think it's possible that this arrangement influenced his codesign of the Halprins' dance deck.

3. Ninotchka Bennahum, "Anna Halprin's Radical Body in Motion," in Bennahum, Perron, and Robertson, *Radical Bodies*, 63.

4. Janice Ross, *Anna Halprin: Experience as Dance* (Berkeley: University of California Press, 2007), 87.

5. Perron, "Simone Forti: bodynatureartmovementbody," 93.

6. John Rockwell, "A Collaborative Community: Ann Halprin and Her Composers," in Bennahum, Perron, and Robertson, *Radical Bodies*, 164.

7. Libby Worth with Helen Poynor, *Anna Halprin* (London: Routledge, Taylor & Francis Group, 2004), 23.

8. Perron, "Simone Forti: bodynatureartmovementbody," 93; and Laura Kuhn, ed., *The Selected Letters of John Cage* (Middletown, CT: Wesleyan University Press, 2016), 216.

9. Ross, *Anna Halprin*, 123.

10. Anna Halprin, quoted in Rockwell, "A Collaborative Community," 162, quoting from David W. Bernstein, ed., *San Francisco Tape Music Center, 1960s*

Counterculture and the Avant-Garde (Berkeley: University of California Press, 2008), 238.

11. Quoted in Rockwell, "A Collaborative Community," 167.

12. Kuhn, *Selected Letters of John Cage*, 265.

13. Richard Foreman (experimental theater director), interview with author, August 7, 2017.

14. Klaus Biesenbach and Christophe Cherix, eds., *Yoko Ono: One Woman Show, 1960–71* (New York: Museum of Modern Art, 2015), 106–9.

15. Quoted in Biesenbach and Cherix, *Yoko Ono*, 128.

16. Quoted in David Vaughan, *Merce Cunningham: Fifty Years* (New York: Aperture, 1997), 100.

17. Vaughan, *Merce Cunningham*, 101.

18. Mary Overlie, *Standing in Space: The Six Viewpoints Theory and Practice* (self-published, 2016), 90–91.

19. Deborah Jowitt, *Time and the Dancing Image* (New York: William Morrow, 1988), 314.

20. "I also found in the writings of Ananda K. Coomaraswamy that the responsibility of the artist is to imitate nature in her manner of operation. I became less disturbed and went back to work." "John Cage: An Autobiographical Statement," accessed June 19, 2018, http://www.johncage.org/autobiographical_statement.html.

21. Jill Johnston, "The New American Modern Dance," in *The New American Arts*, ed. Richard Kostelanetz (London: Collier-Macmillan, 1967),172.

22. Rockwell, "A Collaborative Community," 166.

23. *Feelings Are Facts: The Life of Yvonne Rainer* (2015), dir. Jack Walsh.

24. Other students that summer included June Ekman, Ruth Emerson, and Shirley Ririe.

25. Trisha Brown accepting an honorary degree at the Columbia College Chicago commencement in 2009: "Trisha Brown, '09 Columbia College Commencement," YouTube, posted January 6, 2011, accessed May 22, 2018, https://www.youtube.com/watch?time_continue=409&v=q1s3IMdimlg.

26. Told by, among others, Don McDonagh in *The Rise and Fall and Rise of Modern Dance* (New York: New American Library, 1970); Sally Banes in *Democracy's Body: Judson Dance Theater, 1962–1964* (Durham, NC: Duke University Press, 1993); Jowitt, *Time and the Dancing Image*; Banes in *Judson Dance Theater: 1962–65* (Bennington College Judson Project, 1981), exhibition catalog; Ramsay Burt in *Judson Dance Theater: Performative Traces* (London: Routledge, 2006); Perron in "What Was Judson Dance Theater and Did It Ever End," in Danspace *Platform 2012: Judson Now* (Danspace Project, 2012), exhibition catalog; Bennahum, Perron, and Robertson in *Radical Bodies*; and Ana Janevski and Thomas Lax, eds., in *Judson Dance Theater: The Work Is Never Done*, exhibition catalog (New York: Museum of Modern Art, 2018).

27. McDonagh, *Rise and Fall and Rise of Modern Dance*, 76.

28. The other two were Paulus Berensohn and Marni Mahaffey.

29. Using indeterminacy in composing is usually attributed to Cage, but Carolyn Brown contends that composers Earle Brown and Morton Feldman deployed this form before Cage. See Carolyn Brown, *Chance and Circumstance: Twenty Years with Cage and Cunningham* (New York: Knopf, 2007), 356.

30. Banes, "Choreographic Methods of the Judson Dance Theater," 352.

31. Banes, "Choreographic Methods of the Judson Dance Theater," 353.

32. David Gordon, untitled remembrance of Robert Dunn, *Movement Research Performance Journal* 14 (Spring 1997), 19.

33. Trisha Brown, conversation with author, 1970s.

34. "Simone Forti: Style Is a Corset," interview by Christophe Wavelet, *Writings on Dance*, nos. 18/19 (Winter 1999): 151.

35. In a 1983 letter to Bernstein, Cage writes: "Improvisation is not related to what the three of us are doing in our work" (Kuhn, *Selected Letters of John Cage*, 289). The two composers he is referring to are Earle Brown and Morton Feldman.

36. Trisha Brown, quoted in *Contemporary Dance: An Anthology of Lectures, Interviews and Essays with Many of the Most Important Contemporary American Choreographers, Scholars and Critics*, ed. Anne Livet (New York: Abbeville Press in association with The Fort Worth Art Museum, 1978), 45.

37. Yvonne Rainer, email to author, February 20, 2018.

38. For more on the history of the Y's place in modern dance, see Naomi M. Jackson, *Converging Movements: Modern Dance and Jewish Culture at the 92nd Street Y* (Hanover, NH: Wesleyan University Press/University Press of New England, 2000).

39. Jackson, *Converging Movements*, 88.

40. Yvonne Rainer has mentioned Jack Moore's presence several times. Moore had assisted Louis Horst in his composition classes at ADF. Later he was a faculty member at Bennington College, spanning the time from when I was a student there (1965–1969) to when I was a teacher (1978–1984).

41. Steve Paxton, group interview with author, July 26, 2017. Hoving was a prominent member of the José Limón Dance Company from 1949 to 1963 and a favorite teacher at American Dance Festival.

42. Banes, *Democracy's Body*, 77.

43. Walker, "Talking Dance: Yvonne Rainer and Sally Banes," *Fourth Wall* (blog), September 26, 2001, accessed March 5, 2016, https://walkerart.org /magazine/talking-dance-yvonne-rainer-and-sally-banes.

44. Susan Rosenberg, *Trisha Brown: Choreography as Visual Art* (Middletown, CT: Wesleyan University Press, 2017), 15.

45. Yvonne Rainer, *Feelings Are Facts: A Life* (Cambridge, MA: MIT Press, 2013), 174.

46. Ross, *Anna Halprin*, 49–69.

47. Kuhn, *Selected Letters of John Cage*, 5.

48. The prepared piano involves inserting objects like screws and bolts into

the strings inside a piano. Cage first used this method in an effort to make an African sound for a dance by Sylvilla Fort at the Cornish School. For more on his discovery, see *"How the Piano Came to Be Prepared,"* in John Cage, *Empty Words: Writings '73–'78* (Middletown, CT: Wesleyan University Press, 1979).

49. *Robert Rauschenberg: Among Friends* (exhibit at Museum of Modern Art, 2017); Brown, *Chance and Circumstance*, 20–21; and Mary Emma Harris, quoted in Joan Acocella, "Whose Pants: Rashaun Mitchell, Silas Riener and the Playful Legacy of Merce Cunningham," *New Yorker*, November 26, 2018, 80–82.

50. Brown, *Chance and Circumstance*, 362.

51. Barbara Dilley, *This Very Moment: teaching thinking dancing* (Boulder, CO: Naropa University Press, 2015), 82; and Brown, *Chance and Circumstance*, 439–40.

52. "Judson at 50: Steve Paxton," Interviews: Steve Paxton, *Artforum*, July 24, 2012, accessed October 2017, https://www.artforum.com/interviews/judson-at-50-steve-paxton-31419.

53. All of Paxton's quotes in this paragraph are from an interview with the author specifically for an article titled "Misha's New Passion" that appeared in *Dance Magazine*, November 2000.

54. Johnston, quoted in Banes, *Democracy's Body*, 88.

55. "Simone Forti: Style Is a Corset." After describing to Wavelet how she complied with Whitman's request, Forti laughed and said, "I was so in love.… You can see that, in respect of feminism, I still had a lot to learn" (151).

56. David Gordon, "1963—Random Breakfast," '60s Archiveography, accessed October 17, 2019, http://davidgordon.nyc/works/1963/random-breakfast.

57. David Gordon, "It's About Time," *The Drama Review* 19, no. 1 (March 1975): 45.

58. Gordon, quoted in Banes, *Democracy's Body*, 124.

59. Jill Johnston, "From Lovely Confusion to Naked Breakfast," *Village Voice*, July 18, 1963, posted on davidgordon.nyc.

60. Banes, "An Interview with David Gordon," *eddy*, Winter 1977, 20.

61. "Judson at 50: Steve Paxton."

62. Yvonne Rainer, email to author, February 20, 2018.

63. Yvonne Rainer, interview with author, Bennington College Judson Project, 1981.

64. Lynn Gumpert, introduction to *Inventing Downtown: Artist-Run Galleries in New York City, 1952–1965*, exhibition catalog, ed. Melissa Rachleff (New York: Grey Art Gallery, NYU in association with Delmonico Books, 2017), 22.

65. Thomas J. Lax, "Allow Me to Begin Again," in *Judson Dance Theater: The Work Is Never Done*, 22. Fred Herko was a ballet-trained dancer who was very involved in Judson from the first concert. Tragically, he jumped to his death in 1964.

Interlude: Simone Forti's Life in Communes

1. Howard Moody, *A Voice in the Village: A Journey of a Pastor and a People* (New York: Xlibris Corporation, 2009), 59.

2. Ellen Pearlman, *Nothing and Everything: The Influence of Buddhism on the American Avant-Garde, 1942–1962* (Berkeley, CA: Evolver Editions, 2012), 52–53.

3. Judith Stein, *Eye of the Sixties: Richard Bellamy and the Transformation of Modern Art* (New York: Farrar, Straus and Giroux, 2016), 107–8.

4. Quoted in "Simone Forti: Style Is a Corset," interview by Christophe Wavelet, *Writings on Dance*, nos. 18/19 (Winter 1999): 151.

5. *See-Saw* was first performed at the Reuben Gallery in 1960 and was not termed a "dance construction" until years later. It consists of two people, usually a woman and a man, playing out the balancing of a relationship on a seesaw. It is largely improvised. The first cast was Yvonne Rainer and Robert Morris. For more, see Simone Forti, *Handbook in Motion* (Northampton, MA: Contact Editions, 1998), 39. Also see Meredith Morse, "Between Two Continents: Simone Forti's *See-Saw*," in *Simone Forti: Thinking with the Body*, exhibition catalog, ed. Sabine Breitwieser (Salzburg: Museum der Moderne, in association with Hirmer, 2014), 37–44.

6. In *Huddle*, a group of people hunkers down in a football-style huddle. One at a time, each person extricates from the group and climbs up and over the mound formed by their upper backs. *Slant Board* is performed on a slanted surface with ropes attached. The task is to cross the space holding onto the ropes while feeling the pull of gravity. In *Herding* the performers herd the audience into a different area within the space. During the 1961 performance at Yoko Ono's loft, the audience was standing, as in a gallery, rather than seated as in a theater. For more detail on these dance constructions, see Forti, *Handbook in Motion*, 59, 56, and 67; and *Simone Forti: Thinking with the Body*, 80–126.

7. Simone Forti, quoted in "Simone Forti: Style Is a Corset," 151 and 153.

8. Forti, *Handbook in Motion*, 18.

9. Richard Foreman, interview with author, August 7, 2017.

10. Forti, *Handbook in Motion*, 18.

2. Only in SoHo

1. Laurie Anderson, "I'm Thinking Back," in *The Kitchen Turns Twenty: A Retrospective Anthology*, ed. Lee Morrissey (New York: Haleakala, 1992), 37.

2. Roslyn Bernstein and Shael Shapiro, *Illegal Living: 80 Wooster Street and the Evolution of SoHo* (Vilnius, Lithuania: Jonas Mekas Foundation, 2010), 49.

3. Bernstein and Shapiro, *Illegal Living*, 128.

4. Richard Kostelanetz, *SoHo: The Rise and Fall of an Artists' Colony* (New York: Routledge, 2003), 48–49.

5. Sally Banes, *Greenwich Village 1963: Avant-Garde Performance and the Effervescent Body* (Durham, NC: Duke University Press, 1993), 65.

6. Kostelanetz, *SoHo*, 52; and Philip Glass, *Words without Music: A Memoir* (New York: Liveright, 2015), 231–33.

7. Bernstein and Shapiro, *Illegal Living*, 78.

8. Bernstein and Shapiro, *Illegal Living*, 82, 98, 78.

9. Bernstein and Shapiro, *Illegal Living*, 77, 80.

10. Bernstein and Shapiro, *Illegal Living*, 50.

11. Glass, *Words without Music*, 97.

12. Bernstein and Shapiro, *Illegal Living*, 90.

13. Trisha Brown accepting an honorary degree at the Columbia College Chicago commencement in 2009: "Trisha Brown, '09 Columbia College Commencement," YouTube, posted January 6, 2011, accessed November 18, 2019, https://www.youtube.com/watch?v=q1s3IMdimlg&t=412s.

14. Bernstein and Shapiro, *Illegal Living*, 191.

15. Bernstein and Shapiro, *Illegal Living*, 120–21. It was here, at 80 Wooster, that he began to explore light and prisms, which became his mature work.

16. Trisha Brown with Susan Rosenberg, "Forever Young: Some Thoughts on My Early Work Today," in *Trisha Brown Dance Company: A Year-Long Series of Performances at Dia:Beacon*, exhibition catalog (Dia Art Foundation, [2009–2010]), unpaginated, https://www.diaart.org/media/_file/brochures/trisha-brown-dance-company-2.pdf.

17. Now available via ArtPix DVDs and on the Internet.

18. Richard Nonas, interview with author, April 3, 2018; Jared Bark, interview with author, June 20, 2018; and David Bradshaw, interview with author, August 21, 2018.

19. Trisha Brown, "How to Make a Modern Dance When the Sky's the Limit," in *Trisha Brown: Dance and Art in Dialogue 1961–2001*, exhibition catalog, ed. Hendel Teicher (Andover, MA: Addison Gallery of American Art, distributed by MIT Press, 2002), 289.

20. The LoGiudice Gallery was on Broome Street in SoHo, just downstairs from The Kitchen Center. It exhibited some of the major minimalists in the early seventies like Richard Serra, Mark Di Suvero, and Jo Baer and was the first in the United States to sponsor a wrapped building by Christo and Jeanne-Claude. However, it didn't last long. The owner, Joe LoGiudice, borrowed money he could not repay and fled to Mexico in 1973. Judith Stein, *Eye of the Sixties: Richard Bellamy and the Transformation of Modern Art* (New York: Farrar, Straus and Giroux, 2016).

21. Bernstein and Shapiro, *Illegal Living*, 99–101.

22. Hendel Teicher, ed., *Trisha Brown: Dance and Art in Dialogue*, 316.

23. Susan Rosenberg, *Trisha Brown: Choreography as Visual Art* (Middleton, CT: Wesleyan University Press, 2017), 133–34.

24. Wendy Perron, "Exporting SoHo," in *Through the Eyes of a Dancer: Selected Writings* (Middletown, CT: Wesleyan University Press, 2013), 32–36; originally published in *SoHo Weekly News*, December 30, 1976.

25. Bernstein and Shapiro, *Illegal Living*, 60.

26. Richard Foreman, interview with author, August 7, 2017.

27. Kostelanetz, *SoHo*, 52.

28. Kostelanetz, *SoHo*, 78; David Gordon, interview with author, May 21, 2018.

29. D. Dunn, email to author, October 23, 2017.

30. Bernstein and Shapiro, *Illegal Living*, 70.

31. Mary Overlie, *Standing in Space: The Six Viewpoints Theory and Practice* (self-published, 2016), 132–33; the performance pieces were titled *Glass Imagination I* (1976) and *Glass Imagination II* (1977).

32. Jessamyn Fiore, ed., *112 Greene Street: The Early Years (1970-1974)* (New York: David Zwirner in association with Radius Books, 2011), exhibition catalog, 19.

33. Bernstein and Shapiro, *Illegal Living*, 175.

34. For more on Matta-Clark, see Fiore, *112 Greene*; and Lydia Yee, ed., *Laurie Anderson, Trisha Brown, Gordon Matta-Clark: Pioneers of the Downtown Scene* (New York: Barbican, 2011), exhibition catalog.

35. Richard Goldstein, *Another Little Piece of My Heart: My Life of Rock and Revolution in the '60s* (New York: Bloomsbury, 2015), 123.

36. Fiore, *112 Greene Street*, 9.

37. Bill Beckley, interview with author, July 11, 2018.

38. Fiore, *112 Greene Street*, 21.

39. Fiore, *112 Greene Street*, 10.

40. Fiore, *112 Greene Street*, 21.

41. Judy Padow, interview with author, August 4, 2017.

42. Steve Paxton, email to author, August 24, 2017.

43. Douglas Dunn, interview with author, March 6, 2017.

44. Douglas Dunn, interview with author, January 15, 2019.

45. Fiore, *112 Greene Street*, 26.

46. Fiore, *112 Greene Street*, 19.

47. Claire Barliant, "112 Greene Street," *Paris Review*, July 25, 2012; and Roberta Smith, "Back in the Bronx: Gordon Matta-Clark, Rogue Sculptor," *New York Times*, January 12, 2018, C21.

48. Beckley, interview with author, July 11, 2018. The dumpster event is listed in Fiore, *112 Greene Street* as a "sculptural installation" as part of an open house on May 19–21, 1972.

49. Terry O'Reilly, email to author, January 14, 2019.

50. Fiore, *112 Greene Street*, 147.

51. Fiore, *112 Greene Street*, 159, 187.

52. Barliant, "112 Greene Street."

53. Fiore, *112 Greene Street*, 27.

54. Fiore, *112 Greene Street*, 33.

55. Fiore, *112 Greene Street*, 53.

56. Fiore, *112 Greene Street*, 107.

57. Beckley, interview with author, July 11, 2018. This performance/installa-

tion is listed as occurring on March 17–29, 1973, in the "Timeline," in Fiore, *112 Greene Street*, 184. I note that decades later, Elizabeth Streb, who maintained a friendship with Trisha Brown in the latter part of the older choreographer's life, also created a "flying machine."

58. Glass, *Words without Music*, 214.

59. Jared Bark, interview with author, June 20, 2018.

60. Ben Schaafsma, "Other Options: A Closer Look at FOOD," *Journal of Aesthetics and Protest*, no. 6, accessed November 6, 2018, http://www.joaap.org/6/lovetowe/schaafsma.html.

61. Barbara Dilley, *This Very Moment: teaching thinking dancing* (Boulder, CO: Naropa University Press, 2015), 126.

62. Nancy Lewis, interview with author, June 4, 2017.

63. Lori Waxman, "The Banquet Years: FOOD, A SoHo Restaurant," *Gastronomica: The Journal of Critical Food Studies* 8, no. 4 (Fall 2008): 28.

64. Waxman, "The Banquet Years."

65. Barliant, "112 Greene Street."

66. Goldstein, *Another Little Piece of My Heart*, 100–101.

67. For complete information on Clark Center, see clarkcenternyc.org, accessed August 9, 2018.

68. Danielle Goldman, *I Want to Be Ready: Improvised Dance as a Practice of Freedom* (Ann Arbor: University of Michigan Press, 2010), 103.

69. Sally Banes, "Spontaneous Combustion: Notes on Dance Improvisation from the Sixties to the Nineties," in *Taken by Surprise: A Dance Improvisation Reader*, ed. Ann Cooper Albright and David Gere (Middletown, CT: Wesleyan University Press, 2003), 82.

70. Gus Solomons, email to author, March 20, 2018.

71. Kostelanetz, *SoHo*, 149.

72. Woody and Steina Vasulka, a married couple who were early video artists, cofounded The Kitchen in the former kitchen of Mercer Arts Center at the Broadway Central Hotel in 1971. See Lee Morrissey, ed., *The Kitchen Turns Twenty: A Retrospective Anthology* (New York: Haleakala, 1992).

73. Kathy Duncan, "On Dance: Grand Union," *SoHo Weekly News*, June 13, 1974.

74. Glass, *Words without Music*, 227.

75. Waxman, "The Banquet Years," 27.

3. How *Continuous Project—Altered Daily* Broke Open and Made Space for a Grand Union

1. Yvonne Rainer, *Feelings Are Facts: A Life* (Cambridge, MA: MIT Press, 2006), 334.

2. The film of this work session, shot by Michael Fajans, is viewable, under the title *Continuous Project—Altered Daily*, at the Jerome Robbins Dance Division of the New York Public Library for the Performing Arts at Lincoln Center, *MGZIDVD 5-6123.

3. *Yvonne Rainer: Work 1961–73* (Halifax: The Press of the Nova Scotia College of Art and Design; New York: NYU Press, 1974), 126.

4. Marcia B. Siegel, *At the Vanishing Point: A Critic Looks at Dance* (New York: Saturday Review Press, 1972), 268–69.

5. Quoted in Jack Anderson, *The American Dance Festival* (Durham, NC: Duke University Press, 1987), 133.

6. Rainer, *Work: 1961–73*, 146.

7. I'm referring to her "disappearing" as the leader of Grand Union, then her suicide attempt in 1971, and finally her departure from the dance world when she began to make films in 1972–1973. She reentered the dance world in 2000, but in a 2017 collaborative performance with Forti and Paxton titled *Tea for Three* at Danspace Project, she preset a suitcase so she could make a staged getaway before the ending—or to prompt the ending—of the performance.

8. Barbara Dilley, *This Very Moment: teaching thinking dancing* (Boulder, CO: Naropa University Press, 2015), 96.

9. Rainer, *Work: 1961–73*, 148.

10. Rainer, *Work: 1961–73*, 149

11. Tresa Hall, "Yvonne Rainer," *University News* [University of Missouri, Kansas City], 7, no. 6, November 1969.

12. Margaret Hupp Ramsay, *The Grand Union (1970–1976): An Improvisational Performance Group* (New York: Peter Lang, 1991), 37.

13. Rainer, *Feelings Are Facts*, 317–18.

14. Annette Michelson, "Yvonne Rainer, Part One: The Dancer and the Dance," *Artforum* 12 (January 1974): 60.

15. Quoted in Jeffrey S. Weiss with Clare Davies, *Robert Morris: Object Sculpture, 1960–1965* (New Haven, CT: Yale University Press, in association with Castelli Gallery, 2013), exhibition catalog, 307.

16. Rainer talks about her "rage at the narcissism of traditional dancing" in "The Performer as Persona: An Interview with Yvonne Rainer," interview by Liza Béar and Willoughby Sharp, *Avalanche*, no. 5, Summer 1972, 50.

17. Rainer, *Feelings Are Facts*, 225–26.

18. Susan Sontag, "Happenings: An Art of Radical Juxtaposition," in *Against Interpretation and Other* Essays (New York: Dell, 1966), 265–76.

19. Yvonne Rainer, interview by Tim Griffin, *Index Magazine*, 2002, accessed February 10, 2017, http://www.indexmagazine.com/interviews/yvonne_rainer .shtml.

20. Rainer, *Work: 1961–73*, 134.

21. Peggy Phelan, "Yvonne Rainer: From Dance to Film," in *A Woman Who … Essays, Interviews, Scripts*, by Yvonne Rainer (Baltimore: Johns Hopkins University Press, 1999), 8.

22. My source here is a ten-minute video excerpt of *Continuous Project—Altered Daily* (1970) at the Whitney Museum archive.

23. The other readers, as listed in Rainer, *Work: 1961–73*, 128, were George Sugarman, Norma Fire, and Carrie Oyama.

24. Don McDonagh, "Films Are Backdrop for Robust Dances of Yvonne Rainer," *New York Times*, April 1, 1970, 38.

25. McDonagh, "Films Are Backdrop for Robust Dances of Yvonne Rainer."

26. Don McDonagh, "Rainer Troupe Seen in Rose Fractions," *New York Times*, February 6, 1969.

27. Nancy Mason, "Yvonne Rainer and Co. in Continuous Project—Altered Daily," *Dance Magazine*, June 1970, 74–75.

28. Robert S. Mattison, *Robert Rauschenberg: Breaking Boundaries* (New Haven, CT: Yale University Press, 2003), 176.

29. Janice Ross, *Anna Halprin: Experience as Dance* (Berkeley: University of California Press, 2007), 190.

30. Group interview with author, July 26, 2017.

31. Quoted in Ramsay, *Grand Union*, 37–38.

32. Rainer, *Work: 1961–73*, 109.

33. Catherine Kerr, interview with author, July 18, 2018.

34. Quoted in Jack Walsh's documentary film, *Feelings Are Facts: The Life of Yvonne Rainer* (2015).

35. Rainer, *Feelings Are Facts*, 322.

36. Asking dancers to create movement within a structure was part of the process for many choreographers, including Twyla Tharp, Trisha Brown, Bill T. Jones, and me.

37. Barbara Dilley, interview with author, January 11, 2017.

38. Sally Banes, "An Open Field: Yvonne Rainer as Dance Theorist," in *Yvonne Rainer: Radical Juxtapositions 1961–2002*, exhibition catalog (Philadelphia: Rosenwald-Wolf Gallery, University of the Arts, 2002), 24.

39. David Gordon, '70s Archiveography, accessed November 15, 2017, http:// davidgordon.nyc/script/70s-archiveography-part-1. For those too young to remember or not from that region, Grand Union was a supermarket chain primarily in the northeastern United States from roughly the 1950s to the 1980s. Because of the supermarket, they had to incorporate under a different name. So the legal entity became Rio Grande Union.

40. Nancy Lewis, email to author, December 31, 2017.

41. Douglas Dunn, email to author, December 29, 2017.

42. Carrie Lambert-Beatty, *Being Watched: Yvonne Rainer and the 1960s* (Cambridge, MA: MIT Press, 2008), 245.

43. Anna Kisselgoff, "Casual Nude Scene Dropped into Dance by Rainer Company," *New York Times*, December 16, 1970, accessed July 20, 2019, https://timesmachine.nytimes.com/timesmachine/1970/12/16/78822492.html ?pageNumber=51.

44. Deborah Jowitt, "Yvonne Say No Roses," *Village Voice*, January 14, 1971, 44.

45. Pat Catterson, interview with author, July 15, 2017.

46. Barbara Dilley, interview with author, January 11, 2017.

47. John Rockwell, "Disciplined Anarchists of Dance," *New York Times*, April 18, 1976, 50.

Interlude: The People's Flag Show

1. Jon Hendricks and Jean Toche, *The Guerrilla Art Action Group: 1969–1976: A Selection* (New York: Printed Matter © 1978).

2. Howard Moody, *A Voice in the Village: A Journey of a Pastor and a People* (New York: Xlibris Corporation, 2009), 256.

3. Moody, *Voice in the Village*, 259.

4. Moody, *Voice in the Village*.

5. Hendricks and Toche, *Guerrilla Art Action Group*.

6. Yvonne Rainer, *Yvonne Rainer: Work 1961–73* (Halifax: The Press of Nova Scotia College of Art and Design; New York: New York University Press, 1974), 172.

7. Becky Arnold, interview with author, July 23, 2018.

8. Grace Glueck, "A Strange Assortment of Flags Is Displayed at People's Flag Show," *New York Times*, November 10, 1970.

9. Paul Krassner, "The Trial of Abbie Hoffman's Shirt," *Huffington Post*, June 8, 2005, accessed January 13, 2018, https://www.huffingtonpost.com/paul-krassner/the-trial-of-abbie-hoffma_b_2334.html.

10. Glueck, "Strange Assortment of Flags."

11. Moody, *Voice in the Village*, 259–60.

12. Hendricks and Toche, *Guerrilla Art Action Group*.

13. Quoted in Michael Kiefer, "Tempest in a Toilet Bowl," *Phoenix New Times*, June 6, 1996, accessed January 13, 2018, http://www.phoenixnewtimes.com/arts/tempest-in-a-toilet-bowl-6423956.

14. For an account of the various versions of *Trio A*, see "A Dancer Writes: Yvonne Rainer's *Trio A* Now" and essays by Pat Catterson and Jens Richard Giersdorf, *Dance Research Journal* 41, no. 2 (Winter 2009).

4. A Shared Sensibility

1. Mimi Johnson, interview with author, September 30, 2017.

2. Deborah Jowitt, *Time and the Dancing Image* (New York: William Morrow, 1988), 303–37.

3. Steve Paxton, "Performance and Reconstruction of Judson," *Contact Quarterly* 7, no. 3/4 (Spring/Summer 1982): 58. This essay is based on a performance residency and reconstructions that I produced as part of the Bennington College Judson Project. Paxton would have observed Cage with musicians while he was a member of the Merce Cunningham Dance Company from 1961 to 1964.

4. Carolyn Brown, *Chance and Circumstance: Twenty Years with Cage and Cunningham* (New York: Knopf, 2007), 217.

5. Yvonne Rainer, *Yvonne Rainer: Work 1961–73* (Halifax: The Press of Nova Scotia College of Art and Design; New York: New York University Press, 1974), 111.

6. Group interview with author, July 26, 2017.

7. Quoted in David Vaughan, *Merce Cunningham: Fifty Years* (New York: Aperture, 1997), 100.

8. Barbara Dilley, *This Very Moment: teaching thinking dancing* (Boulder, CO: Naropa University Press, 2015), 114.

9. Carolyn Brown, *Chance and Circumstance*, 4.

10. Sally Sommer, phone interview with author, March 20, 2018.

11. Paxton, "Performance and Reconstruction of Judson," 57.

12. Brenda Dixon Gottschild, *Digging the Africanist Presence in American Performance: Dance and Other Contexts* (Westport, CT: Praeger, 1998), 16.

13. Gottschild, *Digging the Africanist Presence in American Performance*, 50.

14. Gottschild, *Digging the Africanist Presence in American Performance*, 51.

15. Gottschild, *Digging the Africanist Presence in American Performance*, 50–58.

16. Robyn Brentano, "Outside the Frame: Performance, Art, and Life," in *Outside the Frame: Performance and the Object: A Survey History of Performance Art in the USA Since 1950*, exhibition catalog (Cleveland: Cleveland Center for Contemporary Art, 1994), 38.

17. Yvonne Rainer, *Feelings Are Facts: A Life* (Cambridge, MA: MIT Press, 2006), 170.

18. Brown, *Chance and Circumstance*, 31.

19. Janet Mansfield Soares, *Louis Horst: Musician in a Dancer's World* (Durham, NC: Duke University Press, 1992), 208.

20. Robb Baker, "Grand Union: Taking a Chance on Dance," *Dance Magazine*, October 1973, 42.

21. American Dance Festival, "Trisha Brown," YouTube, posted October 30, 2008, accessed January 14, 2018, https://www.youtube.com/watch?v=Jmowfl Vkork.

22. Jack Anderson, *The American Dance Festival* (Durham, NC: Duke University Press, 1987), 117–18.

23. Interview with author, January 11, 2017.

24. Dilley, *This Very Moment*, 95.

25. Rainer, *Feelings Are Facts*, 343–44.

26. Quoted in Martha Eddy, *Mindful Movement: The Evolution of the Somatic Arts and Conscious Action* (Bristol, UK: Intellect, 2016), 58.

27. Sally Banes, *Greenwich Village 1963: Avant-Garde Performance and the Effervescent Body* (Durham, NC: Duke University Press, 1993), 235.

28. "Barbara Dilley ... in the Dancing Room: A Dialogue with Liza Béar," *Avalanche*, no. 12, Winter 1975, 35.

29. Steve Paxton, "The Grand Union: Improvisational Dance," *The Drama Review* 16, no. 3 (September 1972): 130.

1. Richard Nonas, email to author, March 31, 2018.

5. Barbara Dilley

1. Barbara Dilley, *This Very Moment: teaching thinking dancing* (Boulder, CO: Naropa University Press, 2015), 51.

2. Barbara Dilley, interviewed by Jean Nuchtern (Colonomos), April 26, 1976, Oral History Project transcript, Jerome Robbins Dance Division, New York Public Library for the Performing Arts, 18.

3. Dilley *This Very Moment*, 62.

4. Dilley, Oral History Project transcript, 18. Helen Tamiris, a notable modern dancer, was a charismatic performer as well as a choreographer of concert works and musicals. Her themes were usually related to social issues like unemployment, war, and racism, and she helped start the dance wing of the Federal Theater Project of the Works Progress Administration in the 1930s. From 1960 to 1964, she and her then husband, Daniel Nagrin, codirected the Tamiris-Nagrin Dance Company. Nagrin was also a major modern dance figure who, in the seventies, started his own improvisation group, the Workgroup.

5. Aileen Passloff was active in the pre-Judson group called Dance Associates, along with David Vaughan, Paul Taylor, Donya Feuer, and James Waring. It was her solo, titled *Tea at the Palaz of Hoon*, performed at the Living Theatre, probably in 1959, that inspired Rainer to want to choreograph.

6. Dilley, *This Very Moment*, 63.

7. All of the information about *Story* and *Field Dances* and the rest of this paragraph are from Vaughan, *Merce Cunningham: Fifty Years* (New York: Aperture, 1997), 129–31.

8. Barbara Dilley, interview with author, January 11, 2017.

9. Sally Banes, *Democracy's Body: Judson Dance Theater, 1962–1964* (Durham, NC: Duke University Press, 1993), 195.

10. Robb Baker, "Grand Union: Taking a Chance on Dance," *Dance Magazine*, October 1973, 44.

11. Dilley, *This Very Moment*, 65.

12. Banes, *Democracy's Body*, 92.

13. Banes, *Democracy's Body*, 168–69; and Jill Johnston, "Fall Colors," October 31, 1963, in *Marmalade Me*, new and expanded ed. (Hanover, NH: Wesleyan University Press, 1998), 95.

14. Barbara Dilley, interview with author, January 11, 2017.

15. Yvonne Rainer, interview with author, February 13, 2017.

16. Barbara Dilley, "Barbara Dilley ... in the Dancing Room," *Avalanche*, no. 12, Winter 1975, 34.

17. Dilley, Oral History Project transcript, 25.

18. Quoted in Banes, *Terpsichore in Sneakers: Post-Modern Dance* (Middletown, CT: Wesleyan University Press, 1987), 222.

19. Dilley, *This Very Moment*, 75.

20. Dilley, *This Very Moment*, 47.

21. Dilley, Oral History Project transcript, 29.

22. Dilley, Oral History Project transcript.

23. Dilley, Oral History Project transcript, 22.

24. Dilley, Oral History Project transcript, 28.

25. Quoted in Baker, "Grand Union: Taking a Chance on Dance," 46.

26. Email to author, February 23, 2018.

27. Dilley, *This Very Moment*, 65.

28. Quoted in Melinda Buckwalter, *Composing while Dancing: An Improviser's Companion* (Madison: University of Wisconsin Press, 2010), 15.

6. Douglas Dunn

1. Douglas Dunn, interview with author, March 6, 2017.

2. Dunn, interview with author, March 6, 2017.

3. Dunn, interview with author, March 6, 2017.

4. Douglas Dunn, *Dancer Out of Sight: Collected Writings of Douglas Dunn* (New York: Ink, Inc., 2012), 115.

5. Margaret Hupp Ramsay, *The Grand Union (1970–1976): An Improvisational Performance Group* (New York: Peter Lang, 1991), 91–92; Lewis Segal, "Improvisation by Grand Union," *Los Angeles Times*, May 4, 1976.

6. Dunn, *Dancer Out of Sight*, 42.

7. Dunn, interview with author, March 6, 2017.

8. Dunn, interview with author, March 6, 2017.

9. Dunn, interview with author, March 6, 2017.

10. Dunn, *Dancer Out of Sight*, 43; originally quoted in *Dance Ink* 1, no. 2 (December 1990): 25.

11. Dunn, interview with author, March 6, 2017.

12. Dunn, interview with author, March 6, 2017.

7. David Gordon

1. This citation and those in the rest of this paragraph can be found on David Gordon's website Archiveography, where his own account of his life and work is listed decade by decade (http://davidgordon.nyc/).

2. In his email of July 21, 2019, David enumerated these names as teachers; Ilya Bolotowsky, Ivan Chermayeff, Burgoyne Diller, Jimmy Ernst, Harry Holtzman, Ad Reinhardt, and Kurt Seligman.

3. Sally Banes, "An Interview with David Gordon," *eddy*, Winter 1977, 18.

4. This list draws from David Gordon's email to the author, July 27, 2017, as well as Gordon's untitled reminiscence from *Movement Research Performance Journal*, no. 14 (1997): 19.

5. Gordon, *Movement Research Performance Journal*, 19. The name Pete was Paul Taylor's childhood nickname.

6. David Gordon, email to author, August 3, 2017.

7. Deborah Jowitt, "Pull Together in These Distracted Times," in *Dance Beat:*

Selected Views and Reviews 1967–1976 (New York: Marcel Dekker, 1977), 133; originally published in *Village Voice*, March 31, 1975.

8. Joyce Morgenroth, *Speaking of Dance: Twelve Contemporary Choreographers on Their Craft* (New York: Routledge, 2004), 45.

9. Quoting from Arlene Croce, "Profiles: Making Work," *New Yorker*, November 29, 1982, accessed March 8, 2018, http://archives.newyorker.com/?i=1982-11-29#folio=050, 81.

10. David Gordon, interview with author, May 21, 2018.

11. David Gordon, email to author, July 21, 2019.

12. Quoted in Robb Baker, "Grand Union: Taking a Chance on Dance," *Dance Magazine*, October 1973, 42.

13. David Gordon, "It's About Time," *The Drama Review* 19, no. 1 (March 1975): 44.

14. David Gordon, interviewed by Gia Kourlas, June 4, 2012, Oral History Project transcript, Jerome Robbins Dance Division, New York Public Library for the Performing Arts, 30.

15. Quoted in Sally Banes, *Terpsichore in Sneakers: Post-Modern Dance* (Middletown, CT: Wesleyan University Press, 1987), 101, original review by Robert Morris, *Village Voice*, February 10, 1966, 15.

16. Banes, "An Interview with David Gordon," 22. I want to add that, since the concert in question was shared with Rainer and Paxton, the ethics of Rainer's lover writing the review are questionable.

17. Baker, "Grand Union: Taking a Chance on Dance," 44.

18. Banes, "Interview with David Gordon," 22.

19. Group interview with author, July 26, 2017.

20. Group interview with author, July 26, 2017.

21. David Gordon, email to author, July 21, 2019.

8. Steve Paxton

1. Steve Paxton, *Gravity* (Brussels: Contredanse Editions, 2018), 6.

2. This quote is from a public preperformance conversation between Paxton and Simone Forti at REDCAT, May 11, 2016, accessed December 14, 2018, https://openspace.sfmoma.org/2016/06/notes-from-simone-forti-and-steve-paxton-in-conversation/.

3. David Gordon, untitled reminiscence, *Movement Research Performance Journal*, no. 14 (1997), 19.

4. Steve Paxton, quoted in Wendy Perron, "Simone Forti: bodynatureartmovementbody," *Radical Bodies: Anna Halprin, Simone Forti, and Yvonne Rainer in California and New York, 1955–1972*, exhibition catalog, ed. Bennahum, Perron, and Robertson (Oakland: University of California Press, 2017), 107; originally from Paxton, email to author, August 27, 2015.

5. Steve Paxton, "Trance Script: Judson Project Interview," interview by Nancy Stark Smith, *Contact Quarterly* 14, no. 1 (Winter 1989): 20; originally interviewed for the Bennington College Judson Project around 1980.

6. As seen on the Rauschenberg Foundation website, accessed January 14, 2018, https://www.rauschenbergfoundation.org/art/archive/66v00400.

7. Quoted as part of an email exchange between Paxton and Ralph Lemon in March 2016, in Thomas Lax, ed., *Ralph Lemon*, Modern Dance Series (New York: MoMA, 2016), 53.

8. Steve Paxton, email to author, May 23, 2018.

9. Paxton, "Trance Script," 17–18.

10. Yvonne Rainer, *Feelings Are Facts: A Life* (Cambridge, MA: MIT Press, 2006), 241.

11. This episode is described by Deborah Jowitt, "Yvonne Say No Roses," *Village Voice*, January 14, 1971, 44.

12. Rainer, *Feelings Are Facts*, 241–42.

13. Quoted in Bennington College Judson Project, *Judson Dance Theater: 1962–1966*, exhibition catalog, ed. Wendy Perron (Bennington, VT: Bennington College, 1981), 50.

14. "Judson at 50: Steve Paxton," Interviews: Steve Paxton, *Artforum*, July 24, 2012, accessed October 2017, https://www.artforum.com/interviews/judson -at-50-steve-paxton-31419.

15. Steve Paxton, "The Grand Union: Improvisational Dance," *The Drama Review* 16, no. 3 (September 1972):130.

16. Quoted in Wendy Perron, "Trisha Brown on Tour," *Dancing Times* 86, no. 1028 (May 1996).

17. See Kay Larson, *Where the Heart Beats: John Cage, Zen Buddhism, and the Inner Life of Artists* (New York: Penguin Books, 2012), 79. Note: Larson talks about Cage being taken with the combination of Dada and Zen. She did not use the term Dada Zen, but I felt it was apt.

18. Yvonne Rainer, Robert Rauschenberg Oral History Project, Columbia Center for Oral History Research, Columbia University, accessed August 25, 2018, https://www.rauschenbergfoundation.org/artist/oral-history/yvonne -rainer, 55.

19. Group interview with author, July 26, 2017.

20. "Judson at 50: Yvonne Rainer," Interviews: Yvonne Rainer, *Artforum*, July 10, 2012, accessed April 2, 2018, https://www.artforum.com/interviews /judson-at-50-yvonne-rainer-31348.

9. Trisha Brown

1. Louisa Adams (Trisha Brown's sister), email to author, July 13, 2018.

2. Trisha Brown, "How to Make a Modern Dance When the Sky's the Limit," in *Trisha Brown: Dance and Art in Dialogue 1961–2001*, exhibition catalog, ed. Hendel Teicher (Andover, MA: Addison Gallery of American Art, distributed by MIT Press, 2002), 289.

3. Trisha Brown, quoted by Jared Bark, interview with author, June 20, 2018.

4. Trisha Brown, quoted in *Contemporary Dance: An Anthology of Lectures, Interviews and Essays with Many of the Most Important Contemporary Ameri-

can *Choreographers, Scholars and Critics,* ed. Anne Livet (New York: Abbeville Press in association with The Fort Worth Art Museum, 1978), 44.

5. As pictured in Hendel Teicher, *Trisha Brown: Dance and Art in Dialogue 1961-2001* (Andover, MA: Addison Gallery of American Art, MIT Press, 2002), 277–80.

6. Quoted in Livet, *Contemporary Dance,* 45.

7. Quoted in Livet, *Contemporary Dance,* 48.

8. Simone Forti, *Handbook in Motion* (Northampton, MA: Contact Editions, 1980), 31–32.

9. Yvonne Rainer, "Trisha Brown by Yvonne Rainer," *Bomb,* October 1, 1993, accessed December 27, 2017, https://bombmagazine.org/articles/trisha -brown/.

10. David Gordon, interview with author, November 12, 2018.

11. Group interview with author, July 26, 2017.

10. Nancy Lewis

1. Nancy Lewis, interview with author, June 16, 2017.

2. Nancy Lewis, email to author, June 18, 2017.

3. Jack Anderson, *The American Dance Festival* (Durham, NC: Duke University Press, 1987), 77.

4. Yvonne Rainer, interview with author, February 13, 2018. In an email on January 23, 2019, Nancy wrote, "Jack wanted me to act as though putting on lipstick, mentioning Marilyn Monroe looking in a mirror."

5. Miles Green, conversation with author, September 19, 2018.

6. This feat, in the La MaMa 1976 series, was reported to me by several people. When Robb Baker described it in his review in *Dance Magazine* (August 1976), he added, "thus effectively climaxing the evening" (21).

7. Marcia B. Siegel, "Did Anybody See My Monster Dress?," *SoHo Weekly News,* March 27, 1975, in *Watching the Dance Go By* (Boston: Houghton Mifflin, 1977), 322.

8. Deborah Jowitt, dance review, *Village Voice,* May 24, 1973.

9. Group interview with author, July 26, 2017.

10. Nancy Lewis, interview with author, June 16, 2017.

11. Nancy Mason, "Nancy Green in 'Just Dancing,'" *Dance Magazine,* February 1972, 82.

12. Nancy Lewis, email to author, June 28, 2017.

13. Linda Shapiro, "Dance: Nancy Lewis and Barbara Dilley: Solo," *Many Corners* (a weekly neighborhood newspaper for the West Bank area of Minneapolis), undated review, 19.

11. Yvonne Rainer

1. Yvonne Rainer, *Feelings Are Facts: A Life* (Cambridge, MA: MIT Press, 2006), 160.

2. Rainer, *Feelings Are Facts*, 203. Passloff's dance was performed at the Living Theatre.

3. Yvonne Rainer, interview with author, February 14, 2017.

4. Yvonne Rainer, *Yvonne Rainer: Work 1961–73* (Halifax: The Press of Nova Scotia College of Art and Design; New York: New York University Press, 1974), 13.

5. Yvonne Rainer, interview with author, Bennington College Judson Project, 1981. "What I got into was a look of indeterminacy, which was perhaps a look of a work made by some kind of a collage strategy, whereby there is a kind of provisional look of it: it doesn't have to be this way; it might be another way. I guess a lot of Judson work had that kind of look to it."

6. The "No Manifesto" first appeared as a postscript to Rainer's essay titled "Some Retrospective Notes on a Dance for 10 People and 12 Mattresses Called *Parts of Some Sextets*, performed at the Wadsworth Atheneum, Hartford, Connecticut, and Judson Memorial Church, New York, in March 1965," *Tulane Drama Review* 10, no. 2 (Winter 1965): 168–78. The original version, along with "A Manifesto Reconsidered" (2008), is available at http://www.lavrev.net /2013/12/yvonne-rainers-manifesto.html, accessed April 2, 2018.

7. Yvonne Rainer, untitled reminiscence, *Judson Dance Theater: 1962–1966*, exhibition catalog, ed. Wendy Perron (Bennington, VT: Bennington College Judson Project, 1981), 54.

8. Rainer's celebrated 1966 essay with the maximal title, "A Quasi Survey of Some 'Minimalist' Tendencies in the Quantitatively Minimal Dance Activity Midst the Plethora, or an Analysis of *Trio A*," first appeared in *Minimal Art: A Critical Anthology*, ed. Gregory Battcock (New York: Dutton, 1968), 263–73 and reappeared in Yvonne Rainer, *Yvonne Rainer: Work 1961–73* (Halifax: The Press of Nova Scotia College of Art and Design; New York: New York University Press, 1974), 63–69.

9. Yvonne Rainer, interview with author, February 14, 2017.

10. See Bruce Robertson, "Dance Is Hard to See: Yvonne Rainer and the Visual Arts," in *Radical Bodies: Anna Halprin, Simone Forti, and Yvonne Rainer in California and New York, 1955–1972*, exhibition catalog, ed. Ninotchka Bennahum, Wendy Perron, and Bruce Robertson (Oakland: University of California Press, 2017), 120–47. In a different kind of homage, Donald Judd named his daughter Rainer.

11. "Aimless repetition" and "without grace" are courtesy of Frances Herridge, "The Avant-Garde Is at It Again," *New York Post*, February 7, 1969; "excruciatingly boring" was Clive Barnes's phrase in *New York Times*, February 16, 1969; and "ghastly," "totally undistinguished," and "pitiable" buttressed his diatribe "Disaster: Dance: Village Disaster Concert of Old and New Works at Judson Church Unveils Just One Minor Talent," *New York Times*, January 11, 1966.

12. Yvonne Rainer, interview with author, February 13, 2018.

12. Lincoln Scott and Becky Arnold

1. Deborah Hay, email to author, June 21, 2018.

2. Barbara Dilley, email to author, February 23, 2018.

3. Four reactions from informal conversations. Jared Bark said, "I remember when he changed his name to Dong, we all rolled our eyes." Nita Little felt the name was chosen deliberately as an affront to society. David Bradshaw thought maybe he didn't realize that "dong" is a vulgar word for male genitalia. Steve Paxton thought perhaps Scott was rejecting his given name as a slave name. In any case, he changed it back to Lincoln Scott by the mid-seventies.

4. Theresa Dickinson had been dancing with Tharp in the summer of 1969, when both Tharp and Rainer were at American Dance Festival at Connecticut College. They were working on their respective commissions, Rainer on CP-AD and Tharp on *Medley*. All the dancers from both groups were living in the same dorm and easily socialized together. So when Grand Union came to the Bay Area two years later, it was natural to connect with the former Tharp dancer. Dickinson points out that there were many personal connections: Douglas Dunn's partner, Sara Rudner, was in Tharp's company; Dickinson married Lew Lloyd shortly after his divorce from Barbara Dilley. Theresa Dickinson, email to author, July 24, 2017.

5. Betsy Frederick, interview with author, September 9, 2017.

6. Conversations with Wendy Rogers on February 13, 2017, September 8, 2017, and December 19, 2018, and email, February 14, 2018. In addition, according to Halifu Osumare, Berkeley High School was one of the first American public secondary schools to have an African American Studies Department. See Osumare, *Dancing in Blackness* (Gainesville: University Press of Florida, 2018), 166.

7. Wendy Rogers, interview with author, February 13, 2017.

8. Ruth Beckford (1925–2019) is an underappreciated dance hero. As a teenager, she toured with Katherine Dunham, about whom she wrote a biography in 1979, and she was the first African American to dance with Anna Halprin. She created a modern dance program for the city of Oakland, California, through the Parks Department. She helped coordinate the Black Panthers' free breakfast program for children in 1969. Beckford has also acted in several movies. I spoke with her on the phone in August 2018, and she said she felt that she and Halprin were still "like sisters."

9. Wendy Rogers kindly sent me an image of the flyer.

10. Betsy Frederick, interview with author, February 5, 2018.

11. Steve Paxton, email to author, May 24, 2018.

12. David Bradshaw, interview with author, August 21, 2018.

13. In this film by Robert Frank, Lincoln Scott enters about thirty-five minutes into it. Available via Electronic Arts Intermix, it is posted at http://www.ubu.com/film/gmc_food.html, accessed October 1, 2018.

14. I gleaned this information from conversations with Yvonne Rainer and Steve Paxton.

15. Cynthia Hedstrom, interview with author, July 26, 2018.

16. Cynthia Hedstrom, interview with author, February 13, 2018.

17. Douglas Dunn, email to author, July 2, 2018.

18. Sally Sommer, interview with author, March 20, 2018.

19. Steve Paxton, email to author, May 24, 2018.

20. Quoted in Banes, *Terpsichore in Sneakers: Post-Modern Dance* (Middletown, CT: Wesleyan University Press, 1987), 226.

21. Simone Forti, interview with author, August 24, 2018.

22. David Bradshaw, email to author, August 25, 2018.

23. Forti, interview with author, August 24, 2018

24. Nita Little, interview with author, August 3, 2018.

25. Steve Paxton, email to author, May 24, 2018.

26. Yvonne Rainer, email to author, April 14, 2018.

27. Pat Catterson, email to author, March 14, 2018.

28. Becky Arnold, interview with author, July 23, 2018.

29. Catherine Kerr, interview with author, July 18, 2018.

30. Arnold, interview with author, July 23, 2018.

31. Arnold, interview with author, July 23, 2018.

Interlude: People Improvisation

1. Yvonne Rainer, "Some Thoughts on Improvisation," in *Yvonne Rainer: Work 1961–73* (Halifax: The Press of Nova Scotia College of Art and Design; New York: New York University Press, 1974), 299.

13. First Walker Art Center Residency, May 1971

1. Group interview with author, July 26, 2017.

2. Letter from Weil to New York Review Presentations, January 2, 1970, Walker Art Center Archives, "Performing Arts 1958 to 1980," Box 27 of 31.

3. "Suzanne Weil in Conversation with Philip Bither," Walker Art Center, June 13, 2001, accessed November 13, 2017, https://walkerart.org/magazine /suzanne-weil-in-conversation.

4. Documents in Walker Art Center Archive.

5. Irene Parsons, "The Nose Knows No Color, or: No Confrontation Is in Vain," June 9, 1971, 53, unidentified publication via Western Press Clipping Exchange, Walker Art Center Archive.

6. Scott Bartell, "Review," *Minnesota Daily*, June 3, 1971.

7. Peter Altman, "Spectators, Dance Troupe Collaborate," *Minneapolis Star*, May 28, 1971.

8. Elizabeth Garren, interview with author, September 14, 2017.

9. Judith Ragir, interview with author, April 20, 2017.

10. Linda Shapiro, "The Harry Martin Trio," *Minnesota Preview*, August 1974.

11. David Gordon interview with author, November 12, 2018.

12. Becky Arnold, interview with author, July 23, 2018.

13. Judith Brin Inger, interview with author, December 2, 2016; and email to author, January 22, 2018. Ingber, a longtime resident of Minneapolis, is a well-known dancer and dance scholar who edited the landmark book *Seeing Israeli and Jewish Dance* (Detroit: Wayne State University Press, 2011).

14. Nancy Lewis, email to author, July 6, 2018.

15. Mike Steele, "Grand Union Performs at Walker," *Minneapolis Tribune,* May 29, 1971.

16. Altman, "Spectators, Dance Troupe Collaborate."

17. Quoted in Sally Banes, *Terpsichore in Sneakers: Post-Modern Dance* (Middletown, CT: Wesleyan University Press, 1987), 227.

14. Oberlin College Residency, January 1972

1. Brenda Way, email to author, July 27, 2018.

2. Nancy Stark Smith, interview with author, October 2, 2017. She spoke of the revelatory impact of the Tharp residency, remembering this specific instruction regarding Rose Marie Wright: "Twyla said, 'Do what she's doing'— I didn't even notice she was doing anything; she was scratching her nose and fixing her hair and shifting her weight. But that was the thing we were supposed to be noticing and doing. So the field had already opened up for all kinds of movement to be included in a choreographer's palette."

3. Kimi Okada, interview with author, July 23, 2018.

4. Blau was an early director of Beckett plays who started the Actor's Workshop in San Francisco. Another connection is that when Blau taught at California Institute of the Arts, he hired Allen Kaprow to teach there in the late sixties and early seventies. Kaprow asked Simone Forti to substitute for him there, and CalArts is where she met and worked with Charlemagne Palestine.

5. Kimi Okada, email to author, August 17, 2018.

6. Nancy Lewis, email to author, November 4, 2018.

7. Video of Paxton's talk at Juniata College, c136 (thirty-sixth anniversary of Contact Improvisation), 2008, accessed August 5, 2008, https://www.youtube.com/watch?v=XrUeYbUmhQA.

8. Steve Paxton in *Caught Falling: The Confluence of Contact Improvisation, Nancy Stark Smith, and Other Moving Ideas,* ed. David Koteen and Nancy Stark Smith (Northampton: Contact Editions, 2008), xiv. In an email on January 28, 2019, Steve was more specific: "I think Doug Winter suggested grasping one's foot with the hand on the same side to induce a safe-feeling shoulder roll."

9. Doug Winter, interview with author, July 24, 2018.

10. Steve Christiansen, a student at Antioch at the time, had heard about Grand Union through his friend Michael Fajans. Both were early video buffs, and Fajans had filmed Yvonne Rainer's group in 1969 at Connecticut College, within a year of its becoming Grand Union. The *Magnesium* video is now included in *Contact Improvisation Archive: Collected Edition 1972–1983,* produced by Videoda (East Charleston, VT: Contact Editions, 2014), DVD.

11. Steve Paxton speaking at Juniata College, c136.

12. Barbara Dilley, email to author, August 13, 2018.

13. Yvonne Rainer, *Feelings Are Facts: A Life* (Cambridge, MA: MIT Press, 2006), 388.

14. Quoted in Rainer, *Feelings Are Facts*, 389.

15. Linda Shapiro became a choreographer and director of New Dance Ensemble, the repertory company based in Minneapolis. After NDE folded in the 1980s, she continued to write about dance.

16. Linda Shapiro, interview with author, September 16, 2017.

17. David Gordon, interviewed by Gia Kourlas, June 4, 2012, Oral History Project transcript, Jerome Robbins Dance Division, New York Public Library for the Performing Arts, 30.

18. Paul Langland, email to author, July 26, 2019.

19. *The Matter* has been performed many times in many versions, including at the Danspace Project in 2012 and the 2018 exhibit of *Judson Dance Theater: The Work Is Never Done* at the Museum of Modern Art.

20. Karen Smith, "David Gordon's *The Matter*," TDR 16, no. 3 (September 1972): 117–27; Gordon's statement describing *Sleep Walking*, accessed January 13, 2019, http://davidgordon.nyc/sites/default/files/program_pdf/DG%20 Artistic_f004_Sleepwalking%201971%2072%2073_i007_Duet%20version %20197y%20program_p.pdf.

21. David Gordon, interview with author, November 12, 2018.

22. David Gordon, '70s Archiveography, accessed April 9, 2018, http://david gordon.nyc/script/70s-archiveography-part-1.

23. This video was also shot by Steve Christiansen in 1972. In 2018, Christiansen unearthed his original Oberlin tapes, and together we arranged for them to be converted, "baked," and digitized by master converter Maurice Schechter.

24. Doug Winter, interview with author, July 24, 2018.

25. An article, cowritten for the Oberlin student newspaper, contained this statement: "Dong does not consider himself fully a dancer." It also mentioned that he was the only GU member who had not studied with Cunningham. I know the latter claim to be true but cannot vouch for the former. Quoted in Peter Klein (misspelled as Kelin) and Felicity Brock, "Ongoing Story of a Grand Union," unidentified Oberlin publication, apparently January 1972. Source is Artservices publicity packet.

26. All Brenda Way's quotes are from interview with author, July 24, 2018.

27. I realized the role of Steve's teaching at Bennington in spring 1972 via conversations on August 3, 2018, with Nita Little, who was a student there that semester.

Interlude: Nancy Stark Smith on the Small Dance

1. "Editor Note: Caught by Surprise," *Contact Quarterly* 22, nos. 2, 3 (1997): 3.

2. David Koteen and Nancy Stark Smith, *Caught Falling: The Confluence of Contact Improvisation, Nancy Stark Smith, and Other Moving Ideas* (Northampton, MA: Contact Editions, 2008), 28.

3. Nancy Stark Smith, interview with author, October 2, 2017.

4. Nancy Stark Smith, "A Subjective History of Contact Improvisation: Notes from the Editor of *Contact Quarterly 1972–1997*," in *Taken by Surprise: A Dance Improvisation Reader*, ed. Ann Cooper Albright and David Gere (Middletown, CT: Wesleyan University Press, 2003), 162–63; originally published in *Contact Quarterly* 10, no. 2 (Spring/Summer 1985).

15. The Dance Gallery Festival, Spring 1973

1. Steve Paxton, email to author, January 17, 2019.

2. This quote and the two in the next paragraph are all from Jowitt's weekly dance review in the *Village Voice*, May 24, 1973.

3. Nancy Lewis, email to author, January 19, 2019.

4. This episode was reconstructed by Nancy Lewis looking at the photo via email and responding to the author, August 26, 2019.

5. Lisa Nelson, interview with author, October 24, 2017.

6. Additional interviews, Disk Two: Bonus Material, *Feelings Are Facts: The Life of Yvonne Rainer*.

7. Simone Forti, interview with author, December 4, 2016.

8. Bob Telson, interview with author, January 27, 2019. Telson, a prolific songwriter, became known for composing the award-winning *Gospel at Colonus* (1983).

9. Quoted in Sally Banes, *Terpsichore in Sneakers: Post-Modern Dance* (Middletown, CT: Wesleyan University Press, 1987), 228.

10. Lewis, email to author, January 20, 2019.

11. Steve Paxton, email to author, January 18, 2019.

12. Don McDonagh, "Grand Union Offers Unstructured Dance Experience," *New York Times*, April 3, 1973, 49, accessed July 20, 2019, https://www.nytimes.com/1973/04/03/archives/grand-union-offers-unstructured-dance-experience.html.

13. Sally Sommer, quoted in Margaret Hupp Ramsay, *The Grand Union (1970–1976): An Improvisational Performance Group* (New York: Peter Lang, 1991), 8–9.

14. According to the final report written by Artservices, the dancers were each supposed to receive a minimum of $100 a week for the eight weeks, but because the unearned as well as the earned income fell short, the dancers each received only $100 for the entire run. NYSCA's grant of $3,000 was expected to be part of a total budget of $9,300, but none of the nineteen foundations approached came through. Also, to recoup their expenses, GU planned to take 25 percent of the box office of their guests, but some of the guests decided not to charge admission. That's not too surprising because GU itself had often performed for free.

IV. Narrative Unfoldings

1. Nancy Lewis, email to author, October 27, 2018.

2. Marianne Goldberg, review of *The Grand Union (1970–1976): An Improvisational Performance Group*, by Margaret Hupp Ramsay, *Dance Research Journal* 26, no. 2 (Fall 1994): 34–35.

Interlude: Dianne McIntyre and Sounds in Motion

1. This forum was a "Bill Chat" titled "When Did the Avant-Garde Become Black?," moderated by Bill T. Jones at New York Live Arts, March 24, 2014.

17. Third LoGiudice Video, May 1972

1. Yvonne Rainer, *Feelings Are Facts: A Life.* (Cambridge, MA: MIT Press, 2006), 336.

2. All three were longtime teachers at Mills College. Marian Van Tuyl founded the dance department in 1938 and continued there until 1970, touring with her own group for some of that period. Interestingly, she collaborated with both Louis Horst and John Cage. She made a piece with Horst in 1925 and wrote several articles about him thirty years later. In 1940, she was eager for Cage to establish his dreamed of but never materialized Center for Experimental Music at Mills. Eleanor Lauer had danced in Van Tuyl's company. Rebecca Fuller is now Emeritus Professor of Dance. All taught composition via Horst's methods. Trisha has called them "women of achievement." Susan Rosenberg, *Trisha Brown: Choreography as Visual Art* (Middleton, CT: Wesleyan University Press, 2017); Laura Kuhn, ed., *The Selected Letters of John Cage* (Middletown, CT: Wesleyan University Press, 2016); Janet Mansfield Soares, *Louis Horst: Musician in a Dancer's World* (Durham, NC: Duke University Press, 1992); Marian Van Tuyl, in *Dance On with Billie Mahoney*, prod. Bill Mahoney (Kansas City, MO: Dance on Video, 1986); and Betsy Frederick, email to author, November 1, 2019.

18. Fourth LoGiudice Video: From Darkness to Light

1. Novak had danced in Anna Halprin's *Parades and Changes* in 1965 and later came to Oberlin in 1972 to be one of two "narrators" in Rainer's *In the College*. For more on Rainer's suicide attempt, see *Feelings Are Facts: A Life* (Cambridge, MA: MIT Press, 2006), 374–78.

2. Rainer, *Feelings Are Facts*, 376.

3. Her journal from that trip appears in *Yvonne Rainer: Work 1961–73* (Halifax: The Press of Nova Scotia College of Art and Design; New York: New York University Press, 1974), 173–89, and in a slightly different form in *Feelings Are Facts*, 353–78.

4. Quoted in William Coco and A. J. Gunawardana, "Responses to India: An Interview with Yvonne Rainer," *The Drama Review* 15, no. 3 (Spring 1971): 140.

5. For a fuller discussion of Rainer's transition from dance to film, see *Feelings Are Facts*, 390–410; and Peggy Phelan, "Yvonne Rainer: From Dance to

Film," in *A Woman Who ... Essays, Interviews, Scripts*, by Yvonne Rainer (Baltimore: Johns Hopkins University Press, 1999), 3–17.

6. Douglas Dunn, interview with author, March 6, 2017.

7. David Gordon, interview with author, May 21, 2018.

8. Steve Paxton, email to author, August 26, 2017.

9. Barbara Dilley, interview with author, August 4, 2017.

10. Rainer, *Feelings Are Facts*, 376.

11. Nancy Lewis, interview with author, September 4, 2017.

12. Group interview with author, July 26, 2017.

19. Gender Play and Iowa City, March 1974

1. Yvonne Rainer, *Feelings Are Facts: A Life* (Cambridge, MA: MIT Press, 2006), 183.

2. Sally Banes, "An Interview with David Gordon," *eddy*, Winter 1977, 19.

3. David Gordon, interview with author, November 12, 2018.

4. Group interview with author, July 26, 2017.

5. Group interview with author, July 26, 2017.

6. Documentary film *If the Dancer Dances* (2018), directed by Maia Wechsler, written and produced by Lise Friedman and Wechsler, shown at Dance on Camera Festival, July 2018, available at https://ifthedancer.com/.

7. Doran George, "Untitled Grief: (This Is Not a Memorial for Diane Torr)," *Contact Quarterly* 43, no. 1 (Winter/Spring 2018): 16.

8. Quoted in "The First Burning Question," *Dance Magazine*, November 2013, 47.

9. Douglas Dunn, "Disappearances ... and a Portfolio," *Tether* 3 (2017): 93.

10. Referred to by Nancy Goldner, "Dance," *Nation*, April 12, 1975, 444.

11. Barbara Dilley, email to author, August 10, 2018.

12. Nancy Lewis, interview with author, June 19, 2018.

13. Grand Union Records, (S)*MGZMD 132–2, folder 45.

Interlude: The Judith Dunn/Bill Dixon Improvisation Group

1. David Gordon, email to the author, July 14, 2019.

2. David Gordon, untitled reminiscence, *Movement Research Performance Journal* 14 (Spring 1997): 19

3. For example, Robert Dunn deployed his 1959 piece *Doubles for 4* to accompany Judith's *Indexes* and her *Witnesses* at Judson in 1963. Four people set up a card table with chairs, sat down, and dealt cards that gave instructions for clapping patterns. When they completed the deals, they packed up and left whether or not her solo was finished. At the same time, Robert was in the audience with a transistor radio tuned to a Latino station. Sally Banes, *Democracy's Body: Judson Dance Theater, 1962–1964* (Durham, NC: Duke University Press, 1993), 184.

4. Judith Dunn, "We Don't Talk about It; We Engage in It," *eddy*, no. 4 (Sum-

mer, 1974): 13; originally published in the Bennington publication *Quadrille*, Fall 1973, 9–12.

5. Quoted in Susan Green, "How Modern Dance Took Root in Vermont," *Burlington Free Press*, March 5, 2012, accessed December 19, 2018, https://www .bennington.edu/news-and-features/how-modern-dance-took-root-vermont.

6. Susan Sgorbati, "The Emergent Improvisation Project: Embodying Complexity," *Contact Quarterly* 32, no. 1 (Winter/Spring 2007): 41–42.

7. Barbara Ensley, interview with author, October 21, 2017.

8. Quoted in Danielle Goldman, *I Want to Be Ready: Improvised Dance as a Practice of Freedom* (Ann Arbor: University of Michigan Press, 2010), 68.

9. Bill Dixon, "Collaboration: 1965–72, Judith Dunn—Dancer/Choreographer; Bill Dixon—Musician/Composer," *Contact Quarterly* 10, no. 2 (Spring/Summer 1985): 9.

10. Dixon, "Collaboration: 1965–72," 8.

11. Ensley, email to author, October 17, 2017.

12. Megan Bierman, email to author, January 20, 2019.

13. Cheryl Lilienstein, email to author, January 20, 2019.

20. Second Walker Residency, October 1975

1. Paxton's typed proposal for a video workshop at Minneapolis College of Art and Design: "Would like to make as long a 'loop' as possible with Grand Union format: Daytime T.V. If an hour loop can be arranged, would include soap opera, commercials, talk show and news, with on-the-spot reportage to be used for last performance," cited in "Steve Paxton and the Walker: A 50-Year History," walkerart.org.

2. This sequence can be viewed as a clip embedded in my online article, "How the Grand Union Found a Home Outside of SoHo at the Walker," at walkerart.org.

3. Allen Robertson, "Grand Union," *Minnesota Daily*, October 17, 1975, referenced in Margaret Hupp Ramsay, *The Grand Union (1970–1976): An Improvisational Performance Group* (New York: Peter Lang, 1991), 60.

21. Public/Private, Real/Not Real

1. Sally Banes, "Spontaneous Combustion: Notes on Dance Improvisation from the Sixties to the Nineties," in *Taken by Surprise: A Dance Improvisation Reader*, ed. Ann Cooper Albright and David Gere (Middletown, CT: Wesleyan University Press, 2003), 79.

2. Marcia Marks, review of "James Waring and Dance Company," *Dance Magazine*, March 1963, 59.

3. Robertson, "Grand Union."

4. Richard Lorber, "The Problem with Grand Union," *Dance Scope* 7, no. 2 (Spring/Summer 1973): 30.

5. Nancy Goldner, "Dance," *Nation*, April 12, 1975, 445.

6. Robert Morris, "Re Grand Union" (Artservices publicity materials, Box 132, Folder 16, Jerome Robbins Dance Division, NY Public Library for the Performing Arts).

7. Susan Foster, *Reading Dancing: Bodies and Subjects in Contemporary American Dance* (Berkeley: University of California Press, 1986), 195.

8. Marcia B. Siegel, "Did Anybody See My Monster Dress?," *SoHo Weekly News*, March 27, 1975, in *Watching the Dance Go By* (Boston: Houghton Mifflin, 1977), 321–23.

9. Jack Anderson, "Dance View: The Move to Dance Drama," *New York Times*, February 14, 1982, accessed November 3, 2018, www.nytimes.com/1982/02/14 /arts/dance-view-the-move-to-dance-drama.html.

10. In October 1974, Grand Union members were frustrated by what they felt was obtuse press coverage. They invited critics and friends to a discussion. This meeting included GU members Brown, Dilley, Dunn, Gordon, and Lewis, and critics Robb Baker, Kathy Duncan, Deborah Jowitt, John Howell, and Marcia B. Siegel. Friends included Carolyn Brown, James Klosty, and Sara Rudner. The transcript was edited by Douglas Dunn and Robert Pierce and finally published in April 1976 as "The Grand Union, Critics and Friends," *SoHo Weekly News*, April 29, 1976.

11. Nancy Lewis, interview with author, November 1, 2018.

12. Group interview with author, July 26, 2017.

13. Sally Sommer, interview with author, March 20, 2018.

14. Group interview with author, July 26, 2017.

15. Group interview with author, July 26, 2017.

16. Group interview with author, July 26, 2017.

17. Quoted in Banes, "Spontaneous Combustion," 78–79; originally spoken in "Beyond the Mainstream," *Dance in America*, directed by Merrill Brockway, aired in 1980 on PBS, WNET, New York.

18. Kathy Duncan, "On Dance: Grand Union," *SoHo Weekly News*, June 13, 1974.

19. Richard Foreman, interview with author, August 7, 2017.

20. "Ballet: Brides and Turtles in Dance Program: Avant-Garde Throng Turns Out for Show by Rauschenberg," *New York Times*, May 13, 1965, C33.

21. Her comment, made in a passing conversation, was quoted in "Thank You for Being a Friend," a dialogue between Bruce Hainley and David Velasco at *Artforum*, posted November 25, 2016, accessed January 29, 2019, https://www .artforum.com/performance/bruce-hainley-and-david-velasco-talk-about-tea -for-three-2016-64991.

22. Goldner, "Dance," 445.

23. David Gordon, Archiveography, davidgordon.nyc.

24. Douglas Dunn, interview with author, March 6, 2018.

25. "Barbara Dilley . . . in the Dancing Room: A Dialogue with Liza Béar," *Avalanche*, no. 12, Winter 1975, 35.

26. Barbara Dilley, interview with author, January 11, 2017.

27. Sam Wasson, *Improv Nation: How We Made a Great American Art* (Boston: Houghton Mifflin Harcourt, 2017), 4.

28. Dilley, interview with author, January 11, 2017.

29. Robb Baker, "New Dance," *Dance Magazine*, August 1974, 70–72. The article was written in all lowercase letters, adopting the kind of eccentric capitalization and punctuation that Jill Johnston made popular. I have converted it to conventional punctuation.

Interlude: Leaderless? Really?

1. Mimi Johnson, interview with author, September 30, 2017.

2. Hoover, quoted in Margaret Hupp Ramsay, *The Grand Union (1970–1976): An Improvisational Performance Group* (New York: Peter Lang, 1991), 106.

3. Paxton, "The Grand Union: Improvisational Dance," *The Drama Review* 16, no. 3 (September 1972): 130.

4. Elizabeth Kendall, "The Grand Union: Our Gang," *Ballet Review* 5, no. 4 (1975–1976): 52–53.

5. Marcia B. Siegel, "Did Anybody See My Monster Dress?," *SoHo Weekly News*, March 27, 1975, in *Watching the Dance Go By* (Boston: Houghton Mifflin, 1977), 321.

6. Quoted in Ramsay, *Grand Union*, 88.

7. Juliette Crump, interview with author, January 23, 2018.

8. Judy Padow, interview with author, August 4, 2017.

9. Carol Goodden, interview with author, November 9, 2018.

10. Johnson, interview with author, September 30, 2017.

11. Theresa Dickinson, email to author, July 24, 2017.

12. Group interview with author, July 26, 2017.

13. Douglas Dunn, interview with author, March 6, 2017.

14. Alix Kates Shulman, ed., *Red Emma Speaks: An Emma Goldman Reader* (New York: Schocken Books, 1983), 60. I recommend this book for a more thorough understanding of the tenets of anarchism as laid out by Goldman.

15. Rainer, *Feelings Are Facts: A Life* (Cambridge, MA: MIT Press, 2006), 66.

16. Rainer, *Feelings Are Facts*, 108.

17. Sally Banes, *Greenwich Village 1963: Avant-Garde Performance and the Effervescent Body* (Durham, NC: Duke University Press, 1993), 31.

18. Handwritten statement found in Grand Union Records, *MGZMD 132, Box 1, at the Jerome Robbins Dance Collection, NY Public Library for the Performing Arts.

19. Jill Johnston, "Which Way the Avant-Garde?," in *Marmalade Me*, new and expanded ed. (Hanover, NH: Wesleyan University Press, 1998), 117; originally published in *New York Times*, August 11, 1968.

20. Deborah Jowitt, "Pull Together in These Distracted Times," *Village Voice*, March 31, 1975, in *Dance Beat: Selected Views and Reviews 1967–1976* (New York: Marcel Dekker, 1977), 132.

21. In response to Christian Felber's paper, "Contact vs. Capitalism" (presented at the Contact Festival in Freiburg, 2014), Paxton quotes Kropotkin's *Mutual Aid: A Factor of Evolution* (1902): "The animal species, in which individual struggle has been reduced to its narrowest limits, and the practice of mutual aid has attained the greatest development, are invariably the most numerous, the most prosperous, and the most open to further progress." *CQ Unbound*, 2015, accessed November 25, 2019, https://contactquarterly.com/cq /unbound/view/contact-vs-capitalism#$.

22. Statement found in Artservices materials, Jerome Robbins Dance Division, NY Public Library for the Performing Arts, MGZMD 132.

22. Getting into the Act

1. Richard Nonas, interview with author, April 3, 2018.

2. Mary Overlie, interview with author, August 17, 2017.

3. Terry O'Reilly, email to author, June 19, 2019.

4. Jared Bark, interview with author, June 20, 2018.

5. John Rockwell, "Disciplined Anarchists of Dance," *New York Times*, April 18, 1976, 50.

6. Carrie Lambert-Beatty, *Being Watched: Yvonne Rainer and the 1960s* (Cambridge, MA: MIT Press, 2008), 222–23.

7. Deborah Jowitt, "Yvonne Say No Roses," *Village Voice*, January 14, 1971, 44.

8. The rest of this paragraph is drawn from Catterson's notes, unpublished, which she gave me excerpts of.

9. Risa Jaroslow, interview with author, October 10, 2017.

10. Robb Baker, "New Dance," *Dance Magazine*, August 1974, 70–72.

11. Baker, "New Dance," 70–72. Two notes for the reader here. First, again, Baker adopted a Jill Johnston–style noncapitalization and nonpunctuation mode. Perhaps he thought it matched the "anarchy" of Grand Union. For the sake of readability, I have applied conventional punctuation to the original text. Second, just a reminder that in the seventies, the race of audience members was usually given no more than a mention in reviews. If Baker were writing today, no doubt he would have elaborated on the racial situation a bit more.

12. Michael Kirby, edited transcript of a lecture, in Anne Livet, ed., *Contemporary Dance: An Anthology of Lectures, Interviews and Essays with Many of the Most Important Contemporary American Choreographers, Scholars and Critics* (New York: Abbeville Press in association with The Fort Worth Art Museum, 1978), 167.

13. Scott Bartell, "Eccylema," *Minnesota Daily*, June 3, 1971.

14. Allen Robertson, "Grand Union," *Minnesota Daily*, October 17, 1975.

15. Quoted in Ramsay, *Grand Union*, 128.

16. Juliette Crump assured me that the dance students appreciated it.

17. Quoted in Ramsay, *Grand Union*, 128.

18. Quoted in Sally Banes, *Terpsichore in Sneakers: Post-Modern Dance* (Middletown, CT: Wesleyan University Press, 1987), 238. I followed up with a phone conversation on November 1, 2018.

19. Robb Baker, "Mary Hartman, Mary Hartman," *Dance Magazine*, August 1976, 20.

20. Elizabeth Kendall, "The Grand Union: Our Gang," *Ballet Review* 5, no. 4 (1975–1976): 45; email to author, July 5, 2018.

21. Deborah Jowitt, "Pull Together in These Distracted Times," *Village Voice*, March 31, 1965, in *Dance Beat: Selected Views and Reviews 1967–1976* (New York: Marcel Dekker, 1977), 132.

22. Nancy Goldner, "Dance," *Nation*, April 12, 1975, 445.

23. Arthur Sainer, "The Core Is the Mystery of Life," *Village Voice*, May 3, 1976, 116.

24. The quotes are from the October 1974 meeting that was edited and published as "The Grand Union, Critics and Friends," *SoHo Weekly News*, April 29, 1976. However, the quote by Robb Baker does not appear in that group interview, but in a less edited transcript found in the clippings file of the Jerome Robbins Dance Division.

25. Deborah Jowitt, "The Spring Dance Storm Is Here!," *Village Voice*, May 17, 1976.

26. Barbara Dilley, interviewed by Jean Nuchtern (Colonomos), April 26, 1976, Oral History Project transcript, Jerome Robbins Dance Division, New York Public Library for the Performing Arts, 23–24.

27. Jowitt, "Pull Together in These Distracted Times," 132–33.

28. Quoted in Robb Baker, "Grand Union: Taking a Chance on Dance," *Dance Magazine*, October 1973, 46.

Interlude: Musings on Nothingness

1. Allen Robertson, "Grand Union," *Minnesota Daily*, October 17, 1975.

2. Clive Barnes, "Village Disaster: Concert of Old and New Works at Judson Church Unveils Just One Minor Talent," *New York Times*, January 11, 1966.

3. Paul Taylor, *Private Domain: An Autobiography* (San Francisco: North Point Press, 1988), 80.

4. Doris Hering, "Seven New Dances by Paul Taylor," *Dance Magazine*, December 1957, 83–84.

5. Mary Overlie, *Standing in Space: The Six Viewpoints Theory and Practice* (self published, 2016), 31.

6. Untitled diary excerpts, *Movement Research Performance Journal* 14: "The Legacy of Robert Ellis Dunn (1928–1996)," originally published as "Judson Days," *Contact Quarterly* 14, no. 1 (Winter 1989): 9–10.

7. Charles Mingus, quoted in Gene Santoro, *Myself When I Am Real: The Life and Music of Charles Mingus* (New York: Oxford University Press, 2000), 271.

8. Oliver Sacks, *The River of Consciousness* (Toronto: Vintage Canada, 2017),

quoted in "The Three Essential Elements of Creativity," Brain Pickings, ed. Maria Popova, accessed January 17, 2018, www.brainpickings.org.

9. Carrie Lambert-Beatty, *Being Watched: Yvonne Rainer and the 1960s* (Cambridge, MA: MIT Press, 2008), 45.

10. David Gordon, interview with author, November 12, 2018.

11. Douglas Dunn, *Dancer Out of Sight, Collected Writings of Douglas Dunn* (drawings by Mimi Gross; designed and produced by Ink, Inc., 2012), 42.

12. Nancy Stark Smith, "Taking No for an Answer," *Contact Quarterly* 12, no. 2 (Spring/Summer 1987): 3.

13. Don McDonagh, *The Rise and Fall and Rise of Modern Dance* (New York: New American Library, 1970), 83.

14. Marianne Preger-Simon, *Dancing with Merce Cunningham* (Gainesville: University Press of Florida, 2019), 100.

15. Douglas Dunn, email to author, May 16, 2018.

16. John Cage, "Lecture on Nothing," in *Silence* (Middletown, CT: Wesleyan University Press, 1973), 109, 119–20.

23. Grand Union as Laboratory

1. Group interview with author, July 26, 2017.

2. "Judson at 50: Steve Paxton," Interviews: Steve Paxton, *Artforum*, July 24, 2012, accessed October 2017, https://www.artforum.com/interviews/judson-at-50-steve-paxton-31419.

3. Steve Paxton, "A Dialogue with Liza Béar: Steve Paxton: Like the Famous Tree …," *Avalanche*, no. 11, Summer 1975, 24.

4. Nancy Stark Smith, interview with author, October 2, 2017. I add here that I was delighted to watch a workshop given by Beijing CI in the summer of 2019. I learned that Beijing CI has more than five hundred WeChat followers.

5. Sally Banes, *Terpsichore in Sneakers: Post-Modern Dance* (Middletown, CT: Wesleyan University Press, 1987), 229.

6. Catterson unpublished notes.

7. Quoted in Cynthia Novak, *Sharing the Dance: Contact Improvisation and American Culture* (Madison: University of Wisconsin Press, 1990), 64.

8. "The Politics of Mutuality: A Conversation with Steve Paxton at the Kitchen Table," *Contact Quarterly* 43, no. 1 (Winter/Spring 2018): 36–38.

9. "The Politics of Mutuality."

10. Nancy Stark Smith, interview with author, October 2, 2017.

11. Barbara Dilley, interview with author, May 16, 2018.

12. Linda Shapiro, "Dance: Nancy Lewis and Barbara Dilley: Solo," *Many Corners* [weekly neighborhood newspaper for West Bank area of Minneapolis], undated review, 19.

13. Barbara Dilley, *This Very Moment: teaching thinking dancing* (Boulder, CO: Naropa University Press, 2015), 55–56 and 137.

14. Dilley, *This Very Moment*, 105; Wendy Perron, *Through the Eyes of a*

Dancer: Selected Writings (Middletown, CT: Wesleyan University Press, 2013), 19–20.

15. Dilley, *This Very Moment*, 58–60.

16. Dilley, *This Very Moment*, 108.

17. Barbara Dilley, interview with author, May 16, 2018.

18. Dilley, *This Very Moment*, 127.

19. Dilley, *This Very Moment*, 114.

20. Dilley, *This Very Moment*, 114.

21. Group interview with author, July 26, 2017.

22. Douglas Dunn, interview with author, March 6, 2017.

23. Marcia B. Siegel, "Did Anybody See My Monster Dress?" *SoHo Weekly News*, March 27, 1975, in *Watching the Dance Go By* (Boston: Houghton Mifflin, 1977), 322.

24. Douglas Dunn's experience with the audience members trickling in, including me, is recorded in "Disappearances ... and a Portfolio," *Tether* 3 (2017): 80–83. I had been rehearsing with Sara Rudner in the loft she shared with Douglas until his construction of *101* made it undanceable, so I was naturally curious to see what kind of performance had blocked our rehearsal space.

25. Douglas Dunn, interview with author, January 15, 2019.

26. Dunn, interview with author, March 6, 2017.

27. David Gordon, '70s Archiveography, accessed May 10, 2018, http://davidgordon.nyc/script/70s-archiveography-part-1.

28. Steve Paxton, email to author August 7, 2017.

29. Although some people call the mid-seventies group Trisha's "first company," the official start date of the Trisha Brown Company (later the Trisha Brown Dance Company) is 1970. At that time the company members were mostly her friends—including Suzanne Harris, Carol Goodden, and Sylvia Palacios Whitman—who were visual artists who could move well. The exception was Carmen Beuchat, who had been a professional dancer in Chile. Around 1974, Trisha decided to assemble a more professional company, and I was the first dancer she hired who had already danced professionally in New York. Sometimes people refer to that group (my group) as her first company.

30. Catterson unpublished notes.

31. This final section of *Newark (Niweweorce)* was so iconic that it was intentionally appropriated, practically verbatim, by choreographer Beth Gill in her *New Work for the Desert* (2014).

32. Catterson unpublished notes.

33. Diane Madden, interview with author, May 14, 2018.

34. Madden, interview with author, May 14, 2018.

35. Quoted in Susan Rosenberg, *Trisha Brown: Choreography as Visual Art* (Middletown, CT: Wesleyan University Press, 2017), 109; Yvonne Rainer, "Engineering Calamity with Trisha Brown," *Writings on Dance*, nos. 18/19 (Winter 1999); originally published in the *Village Voice*, September 17, 1985.

36. Nancy Mason, "Nancy Green in 'Just Dancing,'" *Dance Magazine*, February 1972.

37. Nancy Lewis, interview with author, June 16, 2017.

38. Don McDonagh, "Admiring Laughter for Nancy Green in Dance Program," *New York Times*, December 16, 1971.

39. Linda Shapiro, "Dance: Nancy Lewis and Barbara Dilley: Solo," *Many Corners* (a weekly neighborhood newspaper for the West Bank area of Minneapolis), undated review.

40. Quoted in Banes, *Terpsichore in Sneakers*, 228–29.

41. Group interview with author, July 26, 2017.

42. David Gordon, interview with author, May 21, 2018.

43. Gordon, interview with author, May 21, 2018.

44. David Gordon, interview with author, August 7, 2000, for article on Past-Forward.

45. Catterson unpublished notes.

46. Karen Smith, "David Gordon's *The Matter*," TDR 16, no. 3 (September 1972): 117–27.

47. Gordon, interview with author, August 7, 2000.

48. Gordon, interview with author, May 21, 2018.

Interlude: Dancing with Trisha

1. This improvised duet was one of the most kinetically harrowing dances I've seen. The trust between Trisha and Barbara was exhilarating to behold. Deborah Jowitt called the duet "gorgeously fearless" in her review, "Country Dance," *Village Voice*, April 8, 1971; reprinted in Deborah Jowitt, *Dance Beat: Selected Views and Reviews 1967–1976* (New York: Marcel Dekker, 1977), 116–18; adapted for *Contact Quarterly* 43, no. 1 (Winter/Spring 2018): 10.

2. Anna Kisselgoff, "Review/Dance; For 20 Years, Distinctly Trisha Brown," *New York Times*, March 9, 1991.

3. We later built spinoff sections called "Branch" and Spill," the latter made with our own movement according to Trisha's written instructions. We learned to reverse or go into one of these adjunct sections on a dime, following the calls of another dancer serving as a kind of square dance caller.

24. The Unraveling, or, As the Top Wobbles

1. Richard Nonas, quoted in Jessamyn Fiore, ed., *112 Greene Street: The Early Years (1970–1974)* (New York: David Zwirner in association with Radius Books, 2011), exhibition catalog, 63–65.

2. Steve Paxton, "Two Book Reviews," *Contact Quarterly* 19, no. 1 (Winter/Spring 1994): 10. This passage was part of his review of Margaret Hupp Ramsay's book *The Grand Union* (1970–1976).

3. Group interview with author, July 26, 2017.

4. Quoted in Margaret Hupp Ramsay, *The Grand Union (1970–1976): An Improvisational Performance Group* (New York: Peter Lang, 1991), 71.

5. "Barbara Dilley ... in the Dancing Room: A Dialogue with Liza Béar," *Avalanche*, no. 12, Winter 1975, 35.

6. Douglas Dunn, interview with author, March 6, 2017.

7. Nancy Lewis, interview with author, June 16, 2017.

8. Barbara Dilley, interview with author, May 16, 2018.

9. Quoted in Ramsay, *Grand Union*, 69.

10. Nancy Lewis, interview with author, June 19, 2018.

11. Ramsay, *Grand Union*, 70–71.

12. Quoted in Ramsay, *Grand Union*, 67; originally quoted in Robb Baker, "New Dance," *Dance Magazine*, August 1974.

13. Barbara Dilley, interview with author, September 18, 2018.

14. Douglas Dunn, interview with author, March 6, 2017.

15. Nancy Stark Smith, interview with author, October 2, 2017.

16. Stark Smith, interview with author, October 2, 2017.

17. Elizabeth Garren, interview with author, September 14, 2017.

18. Elizabeth Kendall, "Performers and Personae," *Dance Magazine*, August 1974.

19. Elizabeth Kendall, "The Grand Union: Our Gang," *Ballet Review* 5, no. 4 (1975–1976): 54.

20. Kendall, "The Grand Union: Our Gang," 45 and 50.

21. Don McDonagh, "Grand Union's Skits Now More Formula Than Improvisation," *New York Times*, April 25, 1976.

22. Robb Baker, "New Dance," *Dance Magazine*, August 1974.

23. Douglas Dunn, interview with author, March 6, 2017.

24. Sally Banes, *Terpsichore in Sneakers: Post-Modern Dance* (Middletown, CT: Wesleyan University Press, 1987), 230–31.

25. Group interview with author, July 26, 2017.

26. Barbara Dilley, interview with author, May 16, 2018.

27. Barbara Dilley, interview with author, January 11, 2017.

28. Quoted in Banes, *Terpsichore in Sneakers*, 234.

29. Richard Schechner, *Environmental Theater: An Expanded New Edition including Six Axioms for Environmental Theater* (Montclair: Applause Theatre & Cinema Books, 1973, 1994), 283.

Epilogue and Three Lingering Moments

1. A few of the colleges and universities that offer improvisation are Bennington, Middlebury, Oberlin, Sarah Lawrence, Bates College, Franklin & Marshall College, The Five College Dance Department, Ohio State University, Denison University, Texas Christian University, The University of Utah, University of Michigan, NYU Tisch School of the Arts, Juilliard, and UCLA.

2. Examples include *Composing while Dancing*, by Melinda Buckwalter; *Taken by Surprise*, edited by Ann Cooper Albright and David Gere; *Dance Improvisations*, by Joyce Morgenroth; *Dance Improvisations: Warm-Ups, Games and Choreographic Tasks*, by Justine Reeve; *The Moment of Movement: Dance*

Improvisation, by Caroline McCluskey; *Sharing the Dance*, by Cynthia Novack; *Dances That Describe Themselves*, by Susan Foster; and *The Oxford Handbook of Improvisation in Dance*, edited by Vita L. Midgelow. The venerable journal *Contact Quarterly*, which is accessible digitally, carries many articles on improvisation.

3. Deborah Jowitt, "Tea for Three? Take a Seat," *DanceBeat* (blog), October 28, 2017, accessed March 1, 2019, http://www.artsjournal.com/dancebeat/2017/10/tea-for-three-take-a-seat/.

4. David Gordon, email to author July 21, 2019.

5. "Trisha Brown: Early Works 1966–1979," *ArtPix Notebooks*, 2005, DVD (available at artpix.org).

6. Douglas Dunn, interview with author, March 6, 2017.

7. Steve Paxton, "Post-Performance Artist Conversation: Steve Paxton and David Velasco," December 13, 2018 (part of *Judson Dance Theater: The Work Is Never Done*, September 16, 2018–February 3, 2019, The Museum of Modern Art).

8. "Barbara Dilley: On Contemplative Dance @ SILO," Dance-Tech TV, posted January 11, 2015, accessed December 14, 2018, http://dance-tech.tv/videos/barbara-dilley-on-contemplative-dance-silo/.

9. Barbara Dilley, *This Very Moment: teaching thinking dancing* (Boulder, CO: Naropa University Press, 2015), 194.

10. Barbara Dilley, interview with author, September 18, 2018.

11. The PastForward project of Baryshnikov's White Oak Dance Project involved Gordon, Brown, Paxton, and Forti as well as Deborah Hay and Lucinda Childs.

12. This reconstruction was the brainchild of Emily Coates, who had danced in Yvonne's work since 1999. Like all of Rainer's major works since 2006, it was produced by Performa, the organization founded and directed by RoseLee Goldberg that is devoted to works of performance art.

SELECTED BIBLIOGRAPHY

Anderson, Jack. *The American Dance Festival*. Durham, NC: Duke University Press, 1987.

Baker, Robb. "Grand Union: Taking a Chance on Dance." *Dance Magazine*, October 1973.

Banes, Sally. *Democracy's Body: Judson Dance Theater, 1962–1964*. Durham, NC: Duke University Press, 1993.

———. *Greenwich Village 1963: Avant-Garde Performance and the Effervescent Body*. Durham, NC: Duke University Press, 1993.

———. "An Interview with David Gordon." *eddy*, Winter 1977, 17–25.

———, ed. *Reinventing Dance in the 1960s: Everything Was Possible*. Foreword by Mikhail Baryshnikov. Madison: University of Wisconsin Press, 2003.

———. *Terpsichore in Sneakers: Post-Modern Dance*. Middletown, CT: Wesleyan University Press, 1987.

Béar, Liza. "Barbara Dilley ... in The Dancing Room." *Avalanche*, no. 12, Winter 1975.

Bennahum, Ninotchka, Wendy Perron, and Bruce Robertson, eds. *Radical Bodies: Anna Halprin, Simone Forti, and Yvonne Rainer in California and New York, 1955–1972*. Art, Design and Architecture Museum, University of California, Santa Barbara in association with University of California Press, 2017. Exhibition catalog.

Bernstein, Roslyn, and Shael Shapiro. *Illegal Living: 80 Wooster Street and the Evolution of SoHo*. New York: Jonas Mekas Foundation, 2010.

Cage, John. *Silence: Lectures and Writings by John Cage*. Middletown, CT: Wesleyan University Press, 1973.

———. *The Selected Letters of John Cage*. Edited by Laura Kuhn. Middletown, CT: Wesleyan University Press, 2016.

Cooper Albright, Ann, ed. *Taken by Surprise: A Dance Imrpovisation Reader*. Middletown, CT: Wesleyan University Press, 2003.

Dilley, Barbara. *This Very Moment: teaching thinking dancing*. Boulder, CO: Naropa University Press, 2015.

Dixon Gottschild, Brenda. *Digging the Africanist Presence in American Performance*. Westport, CT: Praeger, 1996.

Dunn, Douglas. *Dancer Out of Sight: Collected Writings of Douglas Dunn*. Drawings by Mimi Gross. New York: Ink, Inc., 2012.

Fiore, Jessamyn, ed. *112 Greene Street: The Early Years (1970–1974)*. New York: David Zwirner in association with Radius Books, 2011. Exhibition catalog.

Forti, Simone. *Handbook in Motion*. Northampton, MA: Contact Editions, 1980.

Foster, Susan. *Reading Dancing: Bodies and Subjects in Contemporary American Dance*. Berkeley: University of California Press, 1986.

Goldman, Danielle. *I Want to Be Ready: Improvised Dance as a Practice of Freedom*. Ann Arbor: University of Michigan Press, 2010.

Gordon, David. '70s Archiveography. Accessed November 15, 2017. http://davidgordon.nyc/script/70s-archiveography-part-1.

Hendricks, Jon, and Jean Toche. *Guerrilla Art Action Group, 1969–1976: A Selection*. New York: Printed Matter, 1978.

Johnston, Jill. *Marmalade Me*. New and expanded ed. Middletown, CT: Wesleyan University Press, 1998.

———. "The New American Modern Dance." In *The New American Arts*, edited by Richard Kostelanetz, 162–93. New York: Collier Books, Horizon Press, 1965.

Jowitt, Deborah. "Chapter 8: Everyday Bodies." In *Time and the Dancing Image*, 303–37. New York: William Morrow, 1988.

———. *Dance Beat: Selected Views and Reviews 1967–1976*. New York: Marcel Dekker, 1977.

Koteen, David, and Nancy Stark Smith. *Caught Falling: The Confluence of Contact Improvisation, Nancy Stark Smith, and Other Moving Ideas*. Northampton, MA: Contact Editions, 2008.

McDonagh, Don. *The Rise and Fall and Rise of Modern Dance*. New York: New American Library, 1970.

Moody, Howard. *A Voice in the Village: A Journey of a Pastor and a People*. New York: Xlibris Corporation, 2009.

Novack, Cynthia J. *Sharing the Dance: Contact Improvisation and American Culture*. Madison: University of Wisconsin Press, 1990.

Overlie, Mary. *Standing in Space: The Six Viewpoints Theory and Practice*. Self-published, 2016.

Paxton, Steve. "Performance and the Reconstruction of Judson." *Contact Quarterly* 7, no. 3/4 (1982): 57.

Perron, Wendy, ed. "A Celebration of Robert Ellis Dunn." Special issue, *Movement Research Performance Journal* 14 (Fall 1997).

Rainer, Yvonne. *Feelings Are Facts: A Life*. Cambridge, MA: MIT Press, 2006.

———. *Yvonne Rainer: Work 1961–73*. Halifax: The Press of Nova Scotia College of Art and Design; New York: New York University Press, 1974.

Ramsay, Margaret Hupp. *The Grand Union (1970–1976): An Improvisational Performance Group*. New York: Peter Lang, 1991.

Rosenberg, Susan. *Trisha Brown: Choreography as Visual Art*. Middletown, CT: Wesleyan University Press, 2017.

Ross, Janice. *Anna Halprin: Experience as Dance*. Berkeley: University of California Press, 2007.

Stein, Judith E. *Eye of the Sixties: Richard Bellamy and the Transformation of Modern Art*. New York: Farrar, Straus and Giroux, 2016.

Teicher, Hendel. *Trisha Brown: Dance and Art in Dialogue 1961–2001*. Andover, MA: Addison Gallery of American Art, MIT Press, 2002.

Vaughan, David. *Merce Cunningham: Fifty Years*. New York: Aperture, 1997.

Walsh, Jack, dir. *Feelings Are Facts: The Life of Yvonne Rainer*, 2015. Digital film, 82 mins. Film and bonus material available at www.feelingsarefacts .com; sold by Canyon Cinema, http://canyoncinema.com/catalog/film /?i=5168.

INDEX

Note: Page numbers in italics refer to illustrations and captions.

Craske, Margaret, 79
critics and reviewers, 12, 22–23, 35,
  52, 110, 132, 135–36, 291; on *CP-AD*,
  49–50; dance, 56–57, 244, 249; GU
  and, 104, 111, 117, 243, 264, 268,
  270, 348n10. *See also* reviews
Crosby, Bing, 92
Crump, Juliette, 254
Crystal Dance Company, 305
Cubiculo, The, 112, 173, 176, 285, 286
Cummings, Blondell, 43
Cunningham, Merce, 14, 54, 57, *68*,
  70, 126, 130, 174, 178, 203, 222, 253;
  GU members and, 67, 69, 71–72, 79,
  96–97, 109–10, 182, 198, 343n25;
  studio of, 16, 143; style and technique of, 15, 140; works of, 20,
  67–68, *80*, 80, 272. *See also* Merce
  Cunningham Dance Company;
  Merce Cunningham Studio

Dadaism, Dadaists, 14, 15, 22, 46, 69,
  75, 102
Dalva, Nancy, 249
DanceAfrica, 42
Dance Brigade (Wallflower Order
  Dance Collective), 203
Dance Constructions (Forti), 25, 27,
  149
Dance Magazine, 56–57, 72, 269–70,
  304; Baker in, 262–63, 265, 298
Dance Observer, 269
Dancer Out of Sight (Douglas Dunn,
  2012), 159–60, 304
Dancers' Workshop (Halprin), 122
Dance Theater Workshop, 305
Dance West, 119
Daniel Nagrin's Workgroup, 153
Danspace Project, 43, 238, 304,
  322n10, 330n7
Dara, Olu, 173
Davis, Bill, 81
Davis, Chuck, 42
Davis, R. G., 253

Day 1 (Judith Dunn and Bill Dixon,
  1971), *221*, 221–25, *222*
deadpan, 67, 70, 99, 105, 112, 131, 159,
  166, 286
Dean, Laura, 43, 86, 278
De Keersmaeker, Anne Teresa, 303
Demme, John, 281
democracy and democratic ideals, 81,
  88, 253; GU and, 249, 253–54, 294
Deren, Maya, 113
Dewey, John, 12
Dickinson, Theresa, 118, 254–55, 302,
  340n4
Dietrich, Marlene, 249
Dilley, Barbara Lloyd, 1, 3, 8, 35, 40,
  44, 61, 62, 64, 79–83, 94, 110, 120,
  121, *124*, 127, 156, 165, 179, 200, *203*,
  205, 237, 244, 251–52, 262, 264,
  267–68, 278, 281, 291, 295, 300,
  340n4; audience and, 70, 266–67;
  Central Notion Co. and, 235, *236*;
  Contemplative Dance Practice
  of, 273, 276–78, 294; *CP-AD* and,
  50–51, 55, 57, 81; dancing of, 6,
  79, 268, 354n1 (1st); early life and
  career of, 43, 67, 69, 79, 82, 152,
  153, 304–5; Evans on, 235–36, 238,
  239; Gordon and, 93, 246, 251; GU
  and, 72–73, 225, 301; GU members
  and, 2, 86, 101–2, 107, 110, 118, 119,
  254, 278; in GU's Black Panther Defense Committee benefit, *100*; in
  GU's Dance Gallery festival performances, *154*, *155*, 156, *157*; in GU's
  Iowa City performances, *205*, 205–
  8, 210–19, *214*, *218*, 245; in GU's La
  MaMa Annex performances, 248,
  255–56, *265*, *284*, 307–8; in GU's
  LoGiudice Gallery performances,
  165–67, 169–72, 179–80, 182–85,
  184, *185*, 192, *193*, 195–96, *195*,
  196, *250*, 282, 308–9; in GU's NYC
  Dance Marathon performance,
  306; in GU's Oberlin College per-

Reid, Albert, *80*

Remick, Lee, 249

Reuben Gallery, 25

reviews, 35, 135, 350n11; by Baker, 298–99; in *Ballet Review*, 298; in *Dance Magazine*, 56–57; of Gordon's *Walks and Digressions*, 93; of GU performances, 43, 61, 125–28, 135–36, 244–45, 265; of GU's Dance Gallery festival performances, 152–53, 157–58; of GU's Walker Art Center performances, 228, 244, 263, 268; of Judson Dance Company concerts, 24; of Lewis's performances, 112; in *The Nation*, 265; in *New York Times*, 268–69, 298; by Perron, 125–28; of Ragir's improvisational group, 133; of Rainer's works, 49–50, 56; of Ramsay's *The Grand Union (1970–1976)*, 161–62; of Waring concert, 243

Rexroth, Kenneth, 113, 256

Riley, Terry, 116, 295

Ringgold, Faith, 63–65

Rinpoche, Chögyam Trungpa, 82

Ririe, Shirley, 323n24

risk, 94, 140, 243, 248

ritual, 12, 277

"River Deep, Mountain High" (Ike and Tina Turner), 49

Roberts, Louise, 176

Robertson, Allen, 244, 263, 268

Rockwell, John, 12, 15, 62, 261

Rodgers, Rod, 42

Rogers, Helen Priest, 79

Rogers, Wendy, 119, 122

Rolling Stones, "No Expectations," 308

Ross, Charles, 13, 23, 29, 30, 54, 57

Ross, Janice, 12

Rouson, John, 46

Rudner, Sara, 73, 278, *279*, 280, 340n4, 348n10; Perron and, 290, 353n24

Ruskin, Mickey, 120

Rutgers University, GU's performances at, 61, 137

Sacks, Oliver, 270

Sainer, Arthur, 265

St. Denis, Ruth, 142

St. John, Jill, 112

St. Mark's Church, 304

St. Vincent's Hospital, 93, 189, 190, 192

San Francisco Art Institute, GU's performances at, 118, 161, 192, 254

San Francisco Bay Area, 12, 113, 119, 148, 302, 340n4

San Francisco Mime Troupe, 24, 253

Sanjo, Mariko, 42

Saret, Alan, 28

Sartre, Jean-Paul, 270

Satie, Erik, 17, 114

Saul, Peter, 124

Schechner, Richard, 301

Schlichter, Joseph, 29–30

Schmidt, Gregory, 237

Schneemann, Carolee, 274

Schoolman, Carlota, 165

School of American Ballet, 139

Schubert, Franz, 143

Schumann, Peter, 253

Schwitters, Kurt, 90

Scott, Lincoln (Dong), 118–22, *121*, 144; changes name, 340n3; early life and career of, 119; in *FOOD*, 120, 340n8; GU and, *36*, 60, 121, 248; in GU's NYC Dance Marathon performances, *163*; in GU's Oberlin College performances, 140, 144–46, *145*, *147*, 148, 343n25; in GU's Walker Art Center performances, *134*, 135, *135*; in *Trio A with Flags*, 64, *66*

Scott, Marion, 18

Seattle Festival of Dance Improvisation, 71

INDEX

ABOUT THE AUTHOR

WENDY PERRON, author of *Through the Eyes of a Dancer: Selected Writings*, had a thirty-year career as a dancer/choreographer. She danced with the Trisha Brown Company in the 1970s and choreographed more than forty works for her own group. She has been on the faculty at Bennington, NYU Tisch School of the Arts, The Juilliard School, and Princeton and has lectured on contemporary dance across the country, in Russia, and in China. As associate director of Jacob's Pillow Dance Festival in the early 1990s, she initiated the International Improvisation Workshop. The former longtime editor in chief of *Dance Magazine*, Wendy has also written for the *New York Times*, the *Village Voice, Contact Quarterly*, vanityfair.com, and publications in Europe and China. She has taught dance journalism at several dance centers and has co-curated exhibits on the intersection of dance and art. In 2011 she was the first dance artist to be inducted into the New York Foundation for the Arts' Hall of Fame.